"It's happening in front of our eyes: the middle class is under relentless assault. Author Wayne Allyn Root identifies villains and puts forth solutions for you, your family, the GOP, and America."

—**STEVE FORBES**, editor in chief of *Forbes* magazine and chairman of Forbes Media

"What makes Wayne Allyn Root's critique of our economy especially important is that he goes beyond the usual conservative cast of villains and explains how the Federal Reserve Board and its Wall Street cronies fleece and undermine the middle class, during their working years and in retirement. *The Murder of the Middle Class* is a great read primarily because it does more than round up the usual suspects."

—**DICK MORRIS**, former presidential advisor, political consultant, media commentator, and *New York Times* bestselling author

"Wayne Allyn Root is America's new Paul Revere, warning us that a new enemy is coming to destroy us—our own government! If we don't heed his message, we will be losing our status as the world's superpower."

—**MARK SKOUSEN**, economist, author of *The Making of Modern Economics*, editor of *Forecasts & Strategies*, and producer of the FreedomFest conference

"Wayne Allyn Root lays everything on the line in this book. Liberals wouldn't dare put their own family members on welfare but they are destroying millions of lives with their condescending federal programs. And it's not just the poor but the middle class, as well. Many who haven't managed to work their way into the upper class have been sucked into the vortex of government dependency. To salvage the middle class we must first salvage its dignity by cutting the apron-strings of Uncle Sam, and Wayne shows us how."

—**PHIL VALENTINE**, nationally syndicated radio talk show host

"Wayne Root takes apart the charade that defines the Obama presidency. Though Obama publically wages war on the rich, it's the middle class that suffers the collateral damage. Taxes, mandates, and regulation undermine real wages, disproportionally lowering the living standards of America's rapidly disappearing middle class. Wayne leads the counter-attack with this fabulous book! Every middle class American should listen to him."

—**PETER SCHIFF**, CEO of Euro Pacific Capital, host of *The Peter Schiff Radio Show*, and author of *The Real Crash, America's Coming Bankruptcy: How to Save Yourself and Your Country*.

"Wayne Root's book about *The Murder of the Middle Class* will hopefully be a wake-up call for Americans who believe that, as Thomas Paine observed, 'The duty of a patriot is to protect his country from its government.'"

—**MARC FABER**, founder of Marc Faber Limited, Hong Kong; editor, *The Gloom, Boom & Doom Report*; and financial commentator on CNBC and Bloomberg

"The greatness of America is embodied in the ability of its citizens to rise to any level of success upon which they set their hearts and work ethic. I do not believe in a class system in America, but rather income levels that can be transited by rugged American individualism and economic liberty. However, there is an assault against middle-income America—depressed wages, fiscal and economic policies that constrain, not empower. My fellow conservative warrior Wayne Allyn Root highlights this problem and offers solutions as to how we can restore the growth, opportunity, and promise that has enabled the American Dream for all. The empty liberal progressive socialist promises since the Great Society have only advanced a welfare nanny state. Wayne provides a road map to restoring American economic exceptionalism for our middle-income citizens."

—**ALLEN B. WEST**, lieutenant colonel (US Army, Retired), member of the 112th U.S. Congress, author of *Guardian of the Republic*

"As a former prosecutor, I can say the book title *The Murder of the Middle Class* could not be more accurate. What is happening to the middle class is not some random event like a tornado or earthquake that is totally unpredictable. This is a slow and deliberate strangulation of the middle class. It is premeditated and purposeful. America's middle class is being wiped out and unless we start listening to people like Wayne Allyn Root, we will lose America's greatest asset forever … and with it America."

—**JUDSON PHILLIPS**, founder, Tea Party Nation

"Wayne Allyn Root is a man who dares to be different, a free thinker who spawns more ideas in a single day than most people do in a lifetime. Wayne is a man on a mission to save what may not be salvageable: America's middle class. When Wayne speaks you're silly if you don't listen—*intently*."

—**CHET COPPOCK**, Chicago's #1 sports personality, radio voice of Notre Dame football and the Chicago Black Hawks

"Wayne Allyn Root has been a conservative warrior since age three, when he campaigned in his father's arms for Barry Goldwater. Today he's an international business speaker and branding expert. His goal is to save the GOP by teaching conservatives how to brand, market, promote, communicate, and sell a message. GOP, are you listening? Read Wayne's book."

—**RICHARD VIGUERIE**, chairman, ConservativeHQ.com, and conservative fundraising pioneer known as the "funding father of conservative strategy"

"Author Wayne Allyn Root, the quintessential Ronald Reagan American success story, seized the opportunity provided by our 'shining city on a hill.' Wayne wants to keep that path to a brighter future available for everyone. The Tea Party movement erupted on the political scene after being disgusted with politicians of both political parties for growing government and squeezing out the middle class. Wayne has the ideas to lead us out of the wilderness."

—**SAL RUSSO**, co-founder of Tea Party Express

"The Tea Party movement was born out of the idea that working Americans were getting the short end of the stick. Back in 2010 the Tea Parties pulled off the biggest landslide victory in modern political history because of the anger and outrage over a rigged system that favors big government, big business, and big media. Wayne Allyn Root's book lays out the case for continuing this Tea Party revolution and how to fight for the principles that will right the course of the nation."

—**JENNY BETH MARTIN**, president and co-founder of Tea Party Patriots and author of *Tea Party Patriots: The Second American Revolution*

"Author Wayne Allyn Root uncovers in detail the shocking plan to execute *The Murder of the Middle Class*. He proves what's really happening in Washington, names the co-conspirators, and lays out the case for indictment. He then challenges the GOP to attack boldly, abandon big business, and save the middle class. If Republicans don't listen to Wayne Allyn Root's advice, they are either ignorant, delusional, naïve, or corrupt."

—**ROBERT RINGER**, *New York Times* #1 bestselling author of *Winning through Intimidation* and *Looking Out for #1*

"I sensed we were in trouble, but I didn't realize how much until I read Wayne Allyn Root's book, *The Murder of the Middle Class*. Unlike other doom and gloom books, this one clearly explains in detail what is happening and presents an action plan to help protect you, while also giving you the tools you need to help reverse this disaster. This book should be required reading for every middle class American."

—**JOSEPH SUGARMAN**, chairman of BluBlocker Sunglasses Corporation and bestselling author of eight books, including *Triggers*

"Either by design or incompetence, the middle class—America's unique invention—has been systematically decapitated by leftist politicians and policies over the last fifty years. At the center of this tragedy is Barack Hussein Obama. The murder of the middle class is accelerating. Author Wayne Root tells you what happened, why, identifies the perpetrators, then provides the game plan to save the day."

—**BILL CUNNINGHAM**, host, *The Bill Cunningham Show*

"What's happened to the middle class? Wayne Allyn Root offers his view in the new book, *The Murder of the Middle Class*. It's an indictment of both major parties and all the people who think that you can keep piling burdens on the already overburdened. Wayne cuts through bull like battery acid, citing chapter and verse of the problem of those who're putting the squeeze on all of us in the middle—and provides some answers."

—**JIM BOHANNON**, nationally syndicated radio talk host

"Wayne Root has given us a practical road map to save the most important segment of our nation—the middle class. If we lose the middle class, we lose what makes America great. We cannot and should not allow this to happen. Wayne's plan will work! America's politicians should listen to the sage advice offered in *The Murder of the Middle Class*."

—**CRAIG SMITH**, founder and chairman of Swiss America, author, and regular guest on Fox News

"I built a vitamin company started in my basement into the number one online vitamin retailer in the world, took it public on NASDAQ, earned the *Inc.* 500 Hall of Fame and created over one thousand American jobs. Today because of regulations, taxes, healthcare and legal bills, it's three times more expensive and a hundred times harder than when I started. The government is murdering the economy, jobs, and the great American middle class. Wayne Allyn Root is right on the money! Read this book to defend and save yourself."

—**WAYNE GORSEK**, founder and chairman of DrVita.com

"We all need to read *The Murder of the Middle Class* whether we agree or not, because we all know something is going terribly wrong in America."

—**JIM ROGERS**, Wall Street legend and bestselling author of *Street Smarts: Adventures on the Road and in the Markets*

"*The Murder of the Middle Class* is intriguing and important."

—**MICHAEL MEDVED**, nationally syndicated talk radio host

THE
MURDER
OF THE MIDDLE CLASS

STARRING . . .

The Obama Crime Family, Assorted Communists,
Lawyers, Unions, Government Employees, IRS, NSA,
Big Business, Illegal Immigrants, the Fed,
George Soros, Warren Buffett, and Environmental Nazis

A DETAILED PLAYBOOK PLAYBOOK WITH SOLUTIONS TO SAVE:

- AMERICA,
- CAPITALISM,
- THE MIDDLE CLASS,
- THE GOP, AND . . .
- YOU!

THE MURDER

OF THE MIDDLE CLASS

HOW TO SAVE YOURSELF AND YOUR FAMILY
FROM THE CRIMINAL CONSPIRACY OF THE CENTURY

WAYNE ALLYN ROOT

REGNERY PUBLISHING

A Salem Communications Company

Library of Congress Control Number 2014941194

ISBN: 978-1-62157-221-3

Published in the United States by
Regnery Publishing
A Salem Communications Company
300 New Jersey Ave NW
Washington, DC 20001
www.Regnery.com

Distributed to the trade by
Perseus Distribution
250 West 57th Street
New York, NY 10107

Manufactured in the United States of America

10 9 8 7 6 5 4 3 2 1

Books are available in quantity for promotional or premium use. For information on discounts and terms, please visit our website: www.Regnery.com.

*This book is dedicated to the epitome
of the great American middle class:*

*My father David Root, small businessman
and owner of a two-man butcher store,*

and

*My grandfather Simon Reis, immigrant, small businessman,
and owner of a four-man butcher store*

Contents

They have plundered the world, stripping naked the land in their hunger…they are driven by greed, if their enemy be rich; by ambition, if poor…. They ravage, they slaughter, they seize by false pretenses, and all of this they hail as the construction of empire. And when in their wake nothing remains but a desert, they call that peace.

—Tacitus, Roman senator and historian[1]

Introduction

This book isn't about an ordinary murder. It's about the murder of ambition, work ethic, rugged individualism, self-reliance, personal responsibility, opportunity, and hope—the very qualities that made America the greatest nation ever known and produced the greatest and richest middle class in world history.

It's a murder of the spirit, a slow agonizing death—like being in a coma for thirty years, while your own family members stop recognizing you, while everyone you know gives up hope, gets on with their lives, moves away, or dies off.

The murder of the middle class is happening in America at this very minute—and it goes on relentlessly, day after day, hour after hour, squeezing the life out of the hard-working, ambitious, responsible, family-loving Americans who used to make our country great.

Don't think the great American middle class will ever die?

Look at history. History repeats, and those who don't study it are destined to fail.

Another group of free and independent Americans were once reduced to dependence and misery.

We're not the first Americans who had their independence stolen. The Native American tribes were a proud, brave, self-reliant people. They led a wonderful life—until they were conquered by the United States military. While there were undoubtedly atrocities on both sides, America's goal was not genocide, to wipe the Indians off the face of the earth.

What we did to the Native Americans may have been worse. We marched them onto reservations. We gave them thousands of acres of land. How generous. We promised to take care of them. We took away their weapons—because they'd never need to hunt again. We gave them free land, free food, free medicine, free schooling, and free money in the form of welfare checks. They'd never have to provide for themselves ever again. If it sounds like paradise, it was not.

It was a deal with the devil.

The proud, resourceful warriors turned into alcohol-addicted welfare recipients, desperate and dependent on government for their very survival. These great fighters forgot how to fight. These great hunters forgot how to hunt. They just sat and drank themselves to death to forget the nightmare their lives had become. They sat and drank while waiting for the rotten food, the crummy clothes, and the crappy welfare checks to arrive.

With the U.S. government "taking care of them," the Indians forgot how to thrive. Except for a rare few (no matter how bad the situation, there are always those amazing rare few who rise above the miserable conditions in which they are born), they lost all ambition, all hope, and all opportunity to change their station in life. Getting drunk was their only way to escape the misery of their horrible lives. The result has been generations living in abject poverty and misery, dying of alcoholism, suicide, and liver disease and their children suffering from fetal alcohol syndrome.

This national tragedy that befell Native Americans wasn't temporary or short term. And it isn't over. Over a hundred years later, the repercussions still reverberate among American Indians.

According to the Indian Health Services, the rate of alcoholism today among Native Americans is SIX TIMES the U.S. average.[1] One in ten Indian deaths is alcohol related. Fetal alcohol spectrum disorder among some Native American tribes is SEVEN TIMES the national average.[2]

Suicide is an epidemic among Native American teens, more than TRIPLE the rate of other young Americans. At some Indian reservations, teen suicide is nine to nineteen times higher among Native Americans than among other youth.[3]

At Pine Ridge Indian Reservation in Nebraska, over 50 percent of the forty thousand residents live below the poverty line and unemployment is over 80 percent. Alcohol is banned on the reservation, yet almost 5 million cans of beer were consumed by the residents in one year alone (2010). Twenty-five percent of the children suffer from fetal alcohol disorders.[4]

This past March the *Washington Post* described the toxic problems still experienced by Native Americans: poverty, unemployment, domestic violence, sexual assault, alcoholism, drug addiction—and, at the base of it all, "crushing hopelessness." The *Post* quoted Tulalip Tribal Court Judge Theresa Pouley saying that Indian children's "experience with post-traumatic stress disorder rivals the rates of returning veterans from Afghanistan."[5]

Alcoholism is the familiar scourge, but these days drugs are at the top of the list of problems for Native Americans. According to the congressional testimony of William P. Ragsdale, director of the Bureau of Indian Affairs, methamphetamine use "is destroying lives in Indian country."[6]

But why are Native Americans in such crisis? Why do they suffer from "crushing hopelessness"? Why do they live in such abject poverty? Why are there no jobs for them? Why is life on the reservation so horrible that it causes post-traumatic stress disorder? Isn't the federal government "taking care of them"?

Yes, and that's the problem. *The government.* The same government that provides everything for you takes everything away from you—your hope, self-respect, ability to take care of yourself, work ethic, and ambition. The United States government destroyed a proud people by taking away their spirit. We "provided for them," thereby taking away their ability to provide for themselves.

Wikipedia blames the problems of "Alcohol and Native Americans" on "low self-esteem."[7] But what causes low self-esteem? No job, no dreams, no opportunity to change the future—just sitting around waiting for a government check. Your self-esteem would be low too...if your life wasn't in your hands...if you had no potential to improve your quality of life...if the government gave you just enough to survive, to live in misery, but never enough to improve, or to start a business, or to hope to ever move up in the world.

We're not talking about mass murder like Hitler or Stalin or Pol Pot committed. We're talking about a different kind of murder, one far more insidious, because it's a slow-motion death. Dependency leads to violence, alcoholism, and drug abuse just to numb the pain of having no opportunities, no future. It's more like torture than simple murder. It goes beyond murdering one individual and spreads down to each succeeding generation.

Government robs you of opportunities and drains the meaning from your life. It's a slow-motion train wreck. And it's not just happening on Indian reservations anymore. It's coming straight for the American middle class. The same government that "provided for the every need" of Native Americans now wants to provide for your every need from cradle to grave.

They offer you free money (welfare), free food (food stamps), pay for not working (unemployment and disability), free medical care (Obamacare), free housing (housing allowances), free meals at school for your children, free phones (Obamaphones), even free contraception. But there is a cost for "free." The cost is your soul, your spirit, your ambition, your achievement, your life.

Government is a vampire that sucks your very blood. Government destroys your life by making you dependent, until you forget how to actually take care of yourself. Government is a drug dealer, and it'll get you hooked—only on welfare checks, not heroin.

You'll be helpless, hopeless, clueless, desperate, despondent, and dependent—just like the American Indian. "They'll take care of you" sounds wonderful. But it leads to the death of your spirit and soul.

That's what is happening right now to the American middle class—the greatest, most prosperous, energetic, independent, creative group of people, and the happiest, that the world has ever seen. The middle class in the United States was the dynamic engine of the world's economy. Our middle class was the city on the hill, the hope of the world's "huddled masses yearning to breathe free."

But now the American middle class is the victim of an insidious plot. That's the murder plot I lay out in detail in this book. If you want to stay independent—and not let go of the American Dream—you need to wake up to the FACTS. You need to understand how the middle class is being murdered...who is doing the dirty deed...by what devious means and methods they're getting it done...and when, where, and why the plot was hatched.

And then you need the weapons to fight back.

So read on...

PART ONE

The Murder of the Middle Class

CHAPTER 1

The Evidence for the Crime

The private sector is doing fine.
—**Barack Obama**

DID YOU KNOW?

- Sixty percent of jobs lost since the recession began were middle class jobs, compared to only 22 percent of new jobs created
- Almost 2 million Americans have disappeared from the workforce every year Barack Obama has been president
- America's second largest employer is a temp agency
- The number of people who say they're middle class has fallen by 17 percent since Obama was elected

The American middle class is dying—and not from natural causes. There's nothing natural or inevitable about the destruction of the middle class that's happening in America today. But before we delve into the plot, and who's responsible, let's review the FACTS and little-known statistics that demonstrate the crime beyond a reasonable doubt. The fact is, the middle class in America is disappearing at a rate that will make your head spin.

The number of Americans who call themselves middle class was 53 percent in 2008. In 2014 it stands at 44 percent. That's a drop of 17 percent in *only five years*—the five years since Obama was elected president.[1]

For the first time in history our middle class isn't #1 in the world. Canada's middle class is now number one.[2] And the entire rest of the world is catching up fast. Soon we'll be #10, then #20. How low can we go?

China is set to pass America as the world's #1 economy. THIS YEAR (2014).[3] What an embarrassment. The USA has had the unchallenged #1 economy in the world since 1872 (when we passed the UK). One hundred and forty years of world dominance... up in smoke.

The same thing is happening to entrepreneurs and small business. For the first time in history businesses in America are being destroyed faster than they are starting.[4] Amazing.

There are now 70 percent more Americans collecting government checks than working full time in the private sector (148 million "takers" vs. 86 million "makers"). This isn't a conservative opinion. It's a fact provided by the U.S. Census Bureau.[5]

The Mysterious Disappearance of Middle Class Jobs

There are 1,148,000 *fewer* Americans working today than seven years ago, even though the population has grown by over 16 million.[6] The number of working-age Americans without a job has increased by nearly 10 million in Obama's first five years as president. That means each and every year of Obama's presidency, almost 2 million more Americans disappear from the workforce.[7] Only 31 percent of Americans now work full time.[8] The number of working-age Americans who are not working is now in the range of 100 million.[9]

Since 2000, the number of working-age Americans who do not have a job has increased by 27 million.[10]

The Civilian Labor Force Participation Rate is the lowest in thirty-five years.[11]

Seventy percent of the working-age Americans no longer working are under age fifty-five. There are 4.2 million of these "missing workers" under age fifty-five.[12]

The average full-time male employee now earns less (adjusted for inflation) than forty years ago.[13]

What kind of jobs have been lost? Sixty percent of the jobs lost during the recession were middle class jobs. But only 22 percent of the new jobs added are middle class jobs with decent wages.[15]

In America today, one out of every ten jobs is filled by a temp agency.[16]

America's second largest employer is a temp agency.[17]

Forty percent of U.S. workers now make less than $20,000 per year.[18]

Men Not at Work

For men, the workforce participation rate is *the lowest in recorded history.*[14]

In this Obama economy, 40 percent of American workers now earn less than the *1968* minimum wage.[19]

And that's for people still lucky enough to be working at all. The average duration of unemployment is now three times higher than in 2000.[20]

Since Obama has been in office, the average length of unemployment has increased from nineteen weeks to thirty-seven weeks. That's the highest since record keeping began in 1948.[21]

The number of Americans unemployed for twenty-seven weeks or longer continues to grow. In February we added another 203,000. This grim category of long-term unemployed now numbers 3.8 million.[22]

Research shows that only 11 percent of the long-term unemployed had found steady work again one year later. That means if you're out of work for twenty-seven months or longer, your odds of finding a job even one year from now are about one in ten.[23]

According to economist John Williams of ShadowStats.com, if you factor in all the short- and long-term discouraged workers, and all those who are underemployed, the real unemployment rate is over 20 percent—higher than most years during the Great Depression.[24]

Just How Bad Is the Private Sector Economy under President Obama?

- McDonald's recently hired 62,000 job applicants and turned down 938,000. That means in this Obama economy, the odds of getting a minimum wage job at McDonald's (6.2 percent acceptance rate) are tougher than getting accepted at Harvard (6.9 percent acceptance rate).[25]
- In this Obama economy, 23,000 people applied for 800 job openings at two new Walmart stores in Washington, D.C. That means the odds of getting a low-paying job at Walmart (3.5 percent acceptance rate) are tougher than of getting accepted at Harvard (5.9 percent acceptance rate).[26]
- In this Obama economy, 1,600 people applied for 36 low-paying jobs at a Maryland ice cream plant. That's a 2 percent acceptance rate, meaning it's easier to get into Harvard than to get a job scooping ice cream.[27]
- In this Obama economy, 22,000 people applied for 300 flight attendant jobs at Delta Air Lines. That acceptance rate of 1.3 percent means the odds of getting a low-paying flight attendant job at Delta Air Lines are about five times tougher than the odds of getting accepted at Harvard.[28]
- In this Obama economy, the mobile car wash company Cherry is accepting only 1 percent of job applicants. So once again the odds of getting a minimum wage job washing cars are tougher than getting accepted at Harvard.[29]
- California recently accepted 900 job applicants out of 120,000 for $45,000-per-year prison guard jobs. That 1 percent acceptance rate means the odds of getting a prison guard job in California are far worse than the odds of getting accepted at Harvard.[30]
- In this Obama economy, 4,000 people applied for 250 jobs at a California Target store. AOLJobs.com reported that the 6.25 percent acceptance rate means the odds of getting a low-paying job at Target are tougher than of getting accepted at Harvard or Yale.[31]

If you gathered all the unemployed people in America in one place, they would constitute the sixty-eighth largest country in the world.[32]

Back in 1980, less than 30 percent of all jobs in the United States were low-income jobs. Today, more than 40 percent of all jobs in the United States are low-income jobs.[33]

The number of lower-wage workers with a four-year college degree DOUBLED between 1979 and 2011.[34]

Fifty-three percent of all college graduates in America under age twenty-five are either unemployed or underemployed.[35]

A new study shows that *forty-one of fifty states* have lost private sector jobs under Obama.[36]

And the employment situation just keeps getting worse. While the Fed spent over $1 trillion (of new debt) to pump up the economy in 2013, FEWER jobs were created in 2013 than in 2012.[37]

About 60 percent of the jobs created since the recession supposedly ended in 2009 pay $13.83 per hour or less.[38]

Will the jobs picture get better? A new report from *OOQ* (*Occupation Outlook Quarterly*) predicts that of the ten fastest-growing job categories for the next decade, nine will pay (on average) less than $35,000 per year.[39] This is America's future. If you're one of the "lucky few" who has a job, you'll need food stamps and housing allowances just to survive on your low salary.

The Sudden Suspicious Prosperity of the Welfare State

More Americans now receive entitlements than work full time.[40]

In the first five fiscal years of the Obama presidency, the U.S. spent a staggering $3.7 trillion on welfare programs. That's five times more than the budgets for NASA, the Department of Education, and the Department of Transportation *combined*.[41]

The number of Americans living in poverty increased by almost 7 million in Obama's first term.[42]

The 46 million Americans living in poverty is a population twice as big as the entire population of Syria.[43]

Poverty in Obama's America is not an inner-city problem. Today there are 16 million Americans living in poverty... *in the suburbs*.[44]

There are now more poor Americans living in the suburbs than in the city.[45]

The number of Americans living in poverty in the suburbs has risen by more than 60 percent since 2000.[46]

Fifteen percent of the American population is now on food stamps.[47]

The number of Americans getting food stamps is now bigger than the population of the entire Northeast United States—including New York City, Boston, and Philadelphia.[48]

The food stamp rolls in America are larger than the population of Spain.[49]

The number of Americans on disability is now bigger than the population of Greece. In fact, the rolls are growing so fast that you might call people going on disability one of the fastest-growing sectors of our "economy."[50]

In 1965 one out of every fifty Americans was on Medicaid. Today, approximately one of every six Americans is on Medicaid.[51]

An incredible 82,457,000 Americans live in households receiving Medicaid benefits.[52]

Experts predict that Obamacare will add 21 million more Americans to the Medicaid roles, in the greatest expansion of the welfare state in history.[53]

Over 100 million Americans are getting some form of welfare. (Almost one out of every three Americans.) That does not include Social Security or Medicare.[54] More Americans are receiving welfare than working full-time year-round jobs.[55] As of late 2013, 49.2 percent of American households were receiving checks from the government. Now that Obamacare is the law of the land, that number is sure to increase dramatically.[56]

Almost half of all students in public school now come from low-income families. In seven states it's 50 percent or higher.[57]

About 57 percent of all children in the United States are living in poverty or defined as low-income.[58] For the first time in history over 1 million public school students are HOMELESS.[59] Twenty percent of all Americans had difficulty buying the food their family needed in the past year.[60]

"Food and nutrition assistance" to struggling Americans now takes up 72 percent of the budget of the U.S. Department of Agriculture.[61]

The Vanishing of Middle Class Wealth and Security

Close to 50 percent of Americans don't even have $500 in savings.[62]

The net worth of the average American family is down a whopping 40 percent.[63] The typical American family earns less today than in 2008[64]— more than $4,000 less, in inflation-adjusted figures.[65] Most who have 401(k) retirement accounts are getting into debt faster than they are saving for retirement.[66]

As of January 2014, more Americans had had their health insurance cancelled than had enrolled in Obamacare.[67]

Only 14 percent of workers believe they can ever retire comfortably.[68]

Meanwhile the typical American family has seen its real income (adjusted for inflation) fall for five years in a row under Obama.[69] Real disposable income started off 2014 by suffering the worst drop in forty years.[70]

Median household income (even using flawed government CPI adjustment models) is 7.3 percent below where it was in 2000. That means the average American family has gone backward fourteen years.[71]

Retail sales are now down 6.9 percent below the June 2005 peak. Household income is down 7.3 percent below the levels of 2000. So how is the typical American family surviving? During this same fourteen-year period, credit card, auto, and student loan debt are up by more than double—from $1.5 trillion to $3.1 trillion. At the same time food stamp use is up by 175 percent (30 million more Americans on food stamps).[72]

The rate of homeownership has fallen for eight years in a row.[73]

Under Obama, the middle class is paying the highest electricity bills in history.[74]

Fifty-six percent of Americans have "subprime" credit.[75]

Just 33 percent of Americans think their children will have a better quality of life than they did.[76]

Over 70 percent of middle class Americans believe they either can never afford to retire, or won't be able to retire until at least age eighty or older.[77]

Thirty-seven percent of Americans now expect to work until the day they die.[78]

Nearly two out of three now say America "no longer offers everyone an equal chance to get ahead."[79]

A typical family on welfare, food stamps, and various other entitlements under Obama is better off than the typical working family with two children.[80]

The Disturbing Demise of Small Business

Small business in particular is suffering. The percentage of self-employed Americans is the lowest in history.[81]

New business startups are at the lowest level in history.[82]

That's a shame, because starting your own business used to be the path to financial independence.

President Obama poses as a champion of small business, but in reality he has created a *hostile work environment* for anyone thinking about starting a company or hiring employees.[83] According to Susan Dudley of the George Washington University Regulatory Center, "By the administration's own estimates, the rules it issued in FY2012 alone imposed more costs on the economy than all the rules issued during the entire first terms of Presidents Bush and Clinton, combined."[84]

Then in 2013, the cost of new government regulations that went into effect in that one year cost $112 billion. That's $447 million for every day that the government was open for business.[85]

A Hostile Work Environment

Facts about startups under Obama are damning. According to economist Tim Kane, the statistics about new companies under recent presidents tell a story of dramatic decline under Obama. Jobs at startups per capita (1,000)[86]:

George H. W. Bush: **11.3**
Bill Clinton: **11.2**
George W. Bush: **10.8**
Barack Obama: **7.8**

That's a 28 percent drop during Obama's presidency.

In the World Economic Forum's rank of "Global Competitiveness," the U.S. has fallen four years in a row under Obama.[87] And the U.S. has fallen in the rankings of the "Economic Freedom Index" for five straight years under Obama, for the first time in history.[88]

A recent poll from the National Association of Manufacturers and National Federation of Independent Businesses tells the tale. Fifty-five percent of all small business owners would NOT start a business today, if when they started their business they had known what they now know about this economy.[89]

A majority of small business owners believe the economy is in a worse position for them to succeed than the year when Obama took office.[90]

Two-thirds believe this economy makes it hard for them to hire workers, for which they blame government. Sixty-nine percent say Obama's regulatory policies have hurt small businesses and manufacturers.[91]

Fifty-four percent say countries like China and India are more supportive of small business than the United States under Obama. Could that opinion have something to do with the fact that IRS audits of small business owners were up dramatically from 2009 to 2011?[92]

The Dangerous Downgrading of Middle America's Standard of Living

But at least we still have decent healthcare and education, right? WRONG.

The middle class in America used to be able to count on a good education system and the best medical care in the world. But now that Obamacare is the law of the land, one recent poll reported 83 percent of doctors are thinking of retiring[93]—just when Obamacare is supposed to be adding millions of new patients.[94]

Millions of Americans lost their health insurance in late 2013, but the worst has passed, right? Actually no. An independent analysis of Obamacare predicts that 50 to 100 million employees of both small and big business could lose their health insurance by the fall of 2014.[95]

The higher taxes and higher health insurance bills caused by Obamacare don't matter to the super-rich. A few hundred dollars per month in increases are meaningless chump change to them. But middle class Americans can't afford to lose an extra $300 or $500 per month. That's the difference between paying the rent or not.

Keep in mind the super-wealthy get a big bonus. They own shares in the health insurance and big pharmaceutical companies benefiting from Obamacare. They may lose $500 per month in higher premiums and taxes, but with Obamacare forcing all Americans to purchase the insurance companies' products, they can look forward to making thousands of dollars per month in the appreciation on their stocks.

And the poor don't care about this extra $500 per month either because they're not paying it. Few object to a "free lunch." So who pays the bill? It falls directly on small businesses and the middle class. Who is this money redistributed to? Obama's biggest donors and voters: the rich and the poor. *Coincidence?*

This is *The Murder of the Middle Class*.

For their higher premiums and deductibles and extra taxes, the middle class will get a lower quality of care, longer waits, and the loss of the best doctors from their insurance plans. Think I'm wrong? Then how do you explain seventy-two-day waits to see a doctor in Boston? Massachusetts has its own state-run version of Obamacare. This is the future of healthcare for a country that just added 30 million patients with no new doctors.[96]

The rich will be fine. They won't wait—they'll simply pay cash for concierge doctors. The poor don't mind waiting—it's better than having no healthcare. But the middle class just had their quality of healthcare ruined. It's a tsunami of bad outcomes for one group.

Meanwhile, the public education system the middle class used to be able to depend on is wrecked under Obama and his good friends in the teachers unions. The rich don't care; they already send their children to pricey private schools. How will we turn the economic collapse around if our workers are uneducated? An international survey shows that U.S. adults rank twenty-first in math skills among twenty-three advanced economies.[97]

They say the future belongs to the young. Will our children save us? Not likely. In 2013, U.S. high school student verbal SAT scores were the lowest in history.[98]

The Unexampled Flourishing of the Super-Rich

Meanwhile, Warren Buffett, George Soros, and Jeffrey Immelt are doing just fine. The mega-wealthy, the big Obama donors, the giant corporations, and the big unions are prospering like never before.

"The Middle Class Is Steadily Eroding," reports the *New York Times*. "Just Ask the Business World." While restaurants and appliance makers that used to cater to people with middle class incomes are losing their customer base, companies that provide luxuries to the rich are booming.[99] In real estate, "Ultraluxury Apartment Sales Drive Records in Manhattan."[100]

"No wonder Neiman-Marcus and Wal-Mart are doing well while J.C. Penney and Sears are nearing collapse," says the *Wall Street Journal*. J.C. Penney and Sears are in danger of going broke because their business model is serving the formerly flourishing American middle class. But that's not where the money is, anymore. It's in serving the super-rich, like Neiman-Marcus, or else in drastic discounting, like Walmart. A Pew Research study shows a whopping 16 percent drop in adults living in middle-income households.[101]

"The rich keep getting richer—and the gap between the super rich and poor has widened even more under President Barack Obama," according to a Breitbart report.[102]

From 2007 to 2012 sales at Walmart were up a grand total of about 1 percent annually. At Whole Foods—representing wealthy America (its customers have double the average income of Walmart shoppers)—sales in the same five years were up about 10 percent per year (from $6.5 billion to $10.5 billion). That's a 10-to-1 difference in growth of sales!

If we use general merchandise as a barometer, let's compare middle America vs. upscale America again. Walmart, Target, Sears, J.C. Penney, Kohl's and Macy's sales from 2007 to 2012 were down by 3 percent. On the other hand, upscale retailers like Tiffany's, Saks, Ralph Lauren, and Nordstrom were up by 30 percent during the same period! That's a dramatic difference: down 3 percent vs. up 30 percent.[103]

The more regulations there are, the bigger government gets, the higher taxes go, the better for the ultra-rich, the connected, and the Fortune 500.

Their armies of lobbyists and lawyers guarantee them special tax credits, exemptions, and write-offs. They'll find ways around the draconian new financial laws, healthcare mandates, environmental regulations, and labor laws.

As a matter of fact, big business gets an added benefit as these taxes, rules, and regulations destroy small business competitors. Without competition, they can just pass the bill on to middle class consumers. You'll drown under the weight, but they'll swim just fine.

The middle class don't have lobbyists, connected lawyers, or big contributions to give. The little people are regulated, mandated, intimidated, and taxed to death. You can't compete, can't start a new business, and can't expand your current business—if you can even keep the doors open despite the mounting, suffocating regulations. It's impossible for you to pursue the American Dream. You're hopelessly trapped, working for crappy wages for some big business (big political donors to the Democrats who write the regulations!) for the rest of your life. You run in place like a gerbil on a treadmill. Lose that dead-end job, and you're on welfare.

The hard-working businessmen and women, the good-wage-earners, and the professionals at the heart of the American economy are losing their place in society. The class that made the United States the most prosperous country in world history is dying.

This is... *The Murder of the Middle Class.*

I could go on for another twenty pages, but I think you've gotten the message, loud and clear. Most of you have heard or read none of these statistics in the mainstream media. Why? Why are the government and the mainstream media afraid to tell you the truth about how bad things really are?

Now that you know the facts, how confident are you feeling about your middle class future? Your children's future? Your job security? Your healthcare? The future of America?

The cold hard truth is that we are experiencing unimaginable economic wreckage, crisis, and collapse.

After reading pages of remarkable facts, do you have any doubt the middle class is being targeted, savaged, destroyed, annihilated, starved, strangled, wiped out, and murdered?

None of this is a coincidence. This is a cold, calculated plan to collapse the U.S. economy under the weight of debt and entitlements, bankrupt small business owners, destroy capitalism...and murder the middle class.

CHAPTER 2

The Crime Scene

The inherent vice of capitalism is the unequal sharing
of blessings. The inherent virtue of Socialism
is the equal sharing of miseries.
—Winston Churchill, who also pointed out that
"Socialism is a philosophy of failure"

DID YOU KNOW?

- 3.4 million (mostly middle class) Californians left the former "Golden State" between 1990 and 2010
- The average time it takes the police to respond to an emergency call in Detroit is 58 minutes
- The odds of getting a job at Ikea in Spain are worse than the acceptance rate at Harvard

Where is the middle class dying? That's easy to answer. Wherever the Democrats are in charge. Politicians on the left always complain about "inequality" and say they want "social justice," but wherever and whenever they get into power, the rich get richer, the poor get poorer, and the middle class starts to disappear. Even Ezra Klein at the left-wing Vox website admits that the data show, "Inequality is highest in Democratic districts."[1]

What turned Detroit, which used to be the beautiful "Paris of the West," into a hellhole? Remember when California was the Golden State? Now it's the "home of the greatest number of American billionaires and poor people, land of the highest taxes and about the worst schools and roads in the nation."[2] What rusted the rust belt? What blight is destroying American cities and whole states? That's another easy question. *The exact same Democrat-socialist politics that are now being inflicted on the entire United States.*

It's just as true outside the United States, too, except that in Europe the socialist parties use more truth in advertising—they go ahead and call themselves Socialists or Social Democrats. The labels are more honest, but the policies are just the same, and so are the results. Wherever they're in power, the middle class mysteriously vanishes.

The Death of Detroit

In *The Ultimate Obama Survival Guide*, I laid out in detail how completely dysfunctional, depressed, and insolvent Detroit was after fifty years of Democrat control of the city government there.[3]

Here's an update since I wrote that book: Detroit is now officially bankrupt. On July 18, 2013, Detroit became the largest U.S. city to ever file for bankruptcy, with almost $20 billion in debt.[4]

The true irony is that a half century after we dropped atomic bombs on Hiroshima and Nagasaki, those Japanese cities are rebuilt, thriving, and gleaming, while our own Detroit looks like a city destroyed by an atomic bomb. Go figure. Detroit is a violent abandoned war zone inside America. Detroit was a great American city, but today it's America's very own Kabul, Baghdad, or Benghazi.

Who is to blame for the death of Detroit? The Democrats, who have been in charge in Motown for more than half a century. Democrats won Detroit's city hall in 1962. They quickly instituted big taxes, big spending, big entitlements, and big unions—all the hallmarks of big government. The rest is history. It was all downhill from there.

Detroit has been under 100 percent Democrat Party rule for a half century. You don't often see a Republican on the streets of Detroit. Even if there were an actual Republican on the streets of Detroit, the odds are high he'd be dead by the time police got there to attempt a rescue! Think I'm kidding or exaggerating? The Detroit police have thrown in the towel. The Detroit Police Officers Association actually issued a warning, "Enter Detroit at your own risk."

One-Party City

The last Republican to be elected mayor of Detroit was Louis Miriani, who was defeated by a Democrat in 1962.

Average response time for police is fifty-eight minutes.[5] That's just enough time to be raped, beaten, tortured, and murdered...with enough time left over for the killers to ransack and loot your home.

That fifty-eight-minute wait is only if the police come at all. The 911 system is a mess.[6]

If you are lucky enough to survive a vicious assault by Detroit's thugs, good luck finding an ambulance. Paramedics recently admitted that half of Detroit's city-owned ambulances are broken.[7]

There is no going back. A bankruptcy judge approved the filing in December 2013. Detroit is over $18 billion in debt (that's the number quoted by the bankruptcy court).[8] The city has $11 billion in government employee retirement obligations and thirty thousand retired government employees.[9] Who is going to pay all those over-generous public employee pensions—the cushy retirement funds that skyrocket out of control wherever Democrats happen to be in office?

Meanwhile, 53.6 percent of all children in Detroit are living in poverty. And the statistics in other Democrat-run cities are almost as bad: 39.6 percent of children in Memphis are poor, 40.1 percent of children in Atlanta, 48 percent in Cincinnati, and 52.6 percent of children in Cleveland.[10]

The Blue Blight

But the murder of the middle class isn't just happening in formerly great American cities. Whole "blue" states lead the nation in taxes, spending, regulations, and coddling union workers at the taxpayers' expense.

(These are states that may occasionally elect a Republican governor, but the best any Republican can hope for is to put the growth of the ever-expanding welfare state on hold for a while.)

And SURPRISE! Those states are where you see the middle class—and the American Dream—disappearing faster than anywhere else in America. The telltale signs: High unemployment. Economic stagnation. And moving vans taking people out of those states in search of a better life.

California, which was once the "Golden State," "synonymous with opportunity…a beacon to the middle class, a place where it was believed that you could author the future on your own terms," is now also in the top ten for income inequality. Over the two decades leading up to 2010, 3.4 million Californians left the state—a bigger percentage of the population than moved out of any other state. Who left? The "everyday citizens who've found themselves priced out of what was once called the California dream." California has become a "Land of Inequality" dominated by "the super-rich and the super-poor."[13]

Moving On Out

United Van Lines reports that the "blue" Northeast is once again "the most prominent region on the high-outbound traffic list." New Jersey, New York, Connecticut, and Massachusetts are all in the top ten.[11] With the middle class leaving, no wonder two of those same "blue" states in the Northeast—New York and Connecticut—lead the nation in income inequality.[12]

Decline and Fall

Democrats complain about inequality, but it always seems to get worse whenever their policies are in effect. Look at the state of the economy in European countries where "Social Democrat" or "Socialist" governments have been in power. They've put the same policies in effect as our Democrats have imposed on Detroit, California, and the other "blue" parts of America—and that President Obama is now imposing on the entire United States.

If you're not convinced by the disappearance of the middle class from the "blue" parts of America, you need look no further than the European Union (EU). To be kind to Obama, the economic model of most EU countries looks a lot like what many people think is Obama's goal for America. Personally, I believe Obama's goal is much more of a Marxist Communist one. But, giving him the benefit of the doubt, let's look at the EU and ask, "Is this what we want for America?"

The Eurozone unemployment rate is a ridiculously high 12.1 percent. That's *reported* unemployment, after government has massaged the figures.[14]

Auto sales in the EU were the lowest in recorded history in 2013.[15]

The Drowning Man

Spain's unemployment is currently a mind-boggling 26.7 percent, with youth unemployment of 57.7 percent.[16] Twenty thousand people applied online within forty-eight hours for four hundred low-wage jobs at an Ikea store in Spain recently.[17] Bad loans in Spain just rose to the highest level in history.[18]

In *The Ultimate Obama Survival Guide* I wrote about "EuroVegas," the Spanish resort being planned by Sheldon Adelson, the American billionaire chairman of Las Vegas Sands. Adelson wanted to invest $30 billion to build one of the largest resorts in world history outside Madrid, including twelve hotels, six casinos, a convention center, three golf courses, theaters, shopping malls, bars, and restaurants—and to create an estimated 260,000 jobs.[19]

Wonderful news for Spain, right? Spain is the largest economic basket case in the EU, with unemployment approaching 30 percent.

Update: Well guess what? Since I last wrote about EuroVegas, it was announced the entire project is now cancelled.[20]

Why? Sheldon Adelson was outraged at the treatment he received from the Spanish government. They turned down many of his requests, including a waiver on their anti-smoking law and a guarantee that taxes would not be changed after he made his $30 billion investment. Spain said "no"...so Sheldon said "no dice" to wasting $30 billion of his money on such ungrateful, delusional, economically ignorant people. Goodbye, Spanish economy.

One of the Spanish Socialists' complaints was that EuroVegas would create low-level jobs. At least they would have been jobs! It's not smart to turn down 260,000 jobs when your country has a youth unemployment rate of almost 60 percent. This is something that I naively assumed any sane person would agree with until I read the head of the CBO's testimony in front of Congress touting, as a major benefit of Obamacare, that Americans could now choose not to work rather than having to accept low-paying jobs.

The EuroVegas story sums up what we are facing in America. This is it in a nutshell, folks. If it's up to the socialists in power, none of us will have a job. Not if anyone wants to smoke. Heaven forbid. Not if there's gambling involved. Not if anyone has to "lower themselves" to accept low wages; better no jobs than low wages. Not if a barrel of oil is used. Not if a tree is damaged. Not if a snake or mouse is harmed. (Excuse me, the oil, snake, and mouse are all reasons to not have jobs in America, I don't know about Spain.) None of it is worth the tradeoff for 260,000 jobs and $30 billion pumped into a dying economy. What Spain just did is like a dying man crawling in the desert turning down an offer of water because it may have come from a pool where a snail darter lived.

The Basket Case

The Spanish middle class is disappearing at a rapid rate. The death of the middle class may be far advanced in Spain. But the other countries in the EU aren't far behind. Citigroup predicts unemployment of 32 percent in Greece by 2015.[21] More Greeks are now unemployed than working. The Greek youth unemployment rate hit 62 percent in 2013.[22] The odds of getting a minimum wage job in Greece are worse than the acceptance rates at Harvard.[23]

It should come as no surprise that Greece is run by a Socialist government. However, give the Greeks credit. At least they tell the truth in naming their political parties. That's more than we can say for Obama's party in America.

"Okay," you say, "so liberal, socialist policies have put a couple of small EU countries in desperate shape." The fact is the EU's bigger countries are in even more trouble.

When You're in a Hole, Stop Digging

France is the fifth largest economy in the world. In 2013 the French Labor Minister let it slip that France is "totally bankrupt."[24] Unemployment in France is up nine quarters in a row and recently hit a sixteen-year high.[25] Unemployment has risen thirty of the last thirty-two months in France. It is up 2.5 percent in just the past five months.[26] France has endured thirty consecutive years of unemployment over 7 percent. Yes, I said THIRTY STRAIGHT YEARS of the kind of unemployment we call a "crisis" in America.[27]

Witnessing the disasters escalating in the rest of Europe, the brilliant French decided to double down. They elected a Socialist government. In response to economic decline caused by too much spending and taxing, the French voted for MORE spending and taxing. Who do they think they are—**Obama's America?**

The Socialist president of France, François Hollande, sounds like an Obama clone—the same campaign promises, the same delusional thinking, the same disastrous tax-and-spend policies. Hollande promised to save France's collapsing economy with fantasy, bread, and circuses. He promised to *increase* spending, dramatically increase taxes on the wealthy (who are all busy fleeing the country), hire sixty thousand new teachers with big pensions... and here's where the French rely on comedy to hide tragedy... roll back the age of retirement from sixty-two to sixty.[28] That's right, Socialists believe when a country is teetering on the verge of bankruptcy, the solution is to hire more government employees and allow everyone to stop working and collect a government pension at a *younger* age.

Does this lunacy and insanity sound familiar? It's the Obama agenda *squared*.

What is the response to France's 75 percent income tax rates, a separate wealth tax, a 70 percent payroll taxes on employers, huge VAT taxes on every purchase, and laws that make it virtually impossible ever to fire an employee? Wealthy business owners are fleeing France in record numbers.[29]

Where are they going? Ironically to the UK, which just ended their experiment with taxing and demonizing the rich. England's top income tax rate is 45 percent versus 75 percent in France. There is no additional wealth tax. Capital gains are a relatively low 28 percent. Or the French are escaping to Switzerland, which has no estate tax. Or to Belgium, which has no capital gains tax.[30]

It's time to write off France. If you offered me stock in France's future for five cents on the dollar, I'd still sell short.

Axis of Dysfunction

Just 9 percent of the French think their children will be better off than they are. In Italy only 14 percent think their children will be better off.[31]

Italy is the ninth largest economy in the world. Poverty in Italy just reached the highest level ever recorded.[32]

The president of Italy is warning of widespread violent insurrection in the streets in 2014.[33]

Even Germany, the EU's supposed economic powerhouse, is in severe trouble, with record poverty. A new financial study of Germany's economy reports "entire cities and regions have been plunged into ever deeper economic and social crisis." Ulrich Schneider, executive director of the Joint Welfare Association, added, "All the positive trends of recent years have come to a standstill or have reversed...."[34]

The fact is that big government, big unions, big spending, big taxes, and big debt ruin entire cities (like Detroit), states (like California) countries (Spain, Greece, Italy, France), and even continents (Europe).

Nightmare in Venezuela

It's as if the European socialists and our Democrats missed the collapse of the Soviet bloc—and the history of Cuba for the past fifty years. What's happening in Venezuela right now doesn't seem to make any impression on them, either. Socialist governments that set out to stamp out all inequality always end up creating worse inequality. Government cronies get rich, and almost everyone else gets poorer. And the middle class gets out—if they can.

Thanks to a government that insists on "social justice" and "equality," Venezuelans are dealing with shortages of toilet paper and food. The government is blaming citizens for hoarding to cope with the shortages—which the government itself created.[35] And as *USA Today* reports, middle class Venezuelans are fleeing to Miami.[36]

Escape Routes: Closed

The Murder of the Middle Class is plain to see—from San Francisco to New York, from Greece to France.

Now for the *really* bad news. The crime scene is coming to *where you live*.

Until recently, if you wanted to escape high taxes and welfare benefits, out-of-control regulations, bloated public employee pensions, and a poisonous business climate, you could just move from California to Nevada, or leave Massachusetts for New Hampshire. Millions of middle class Americans voted with their feet. They brought even more prosperity to newly adopted states like low-tax, low-government-spending, low-regulation Texas.[37]

But simply fleeing the murder of the middle class is not an option anymore. The same policies that have ruined California and Detroit are now being imposed on all Americans by President Obama, with the help of his willing accomplices in Congress, the federal bureaucracy, the public employees' unions, and the media—with the same awful results.

But you've already seen the FACTS about the destruction of the middle class in chapter one of this book. There can be no denying that the middle class is suffering an untimely demise. In the next chapter, I'll explain exactly why that matters.

CHAPTER 3

The Victim

The most perfect political community is one in which the
middle class is in control, and outnumbers both of the other classes.
—Aristotle

DID YOU KNOW?

- The top 40 percent of income-earners in America pay 106 percent of the taxes
- That's possible because so many low-income Americans pay negative income tax!
- The United States has been known for its large, prosperous middle class since the time of the American Revolution

So who cares? Maybe the middle class *is* dying. But what's the big deal about the middle class, anyway—will we even miss it when it's gone?

The rich get richer, the poor get poorer. That's been going on for all of history. It's just the way of the world—right?

Not in America, it isn't!

The middle class made our country great.

During the American Revolution, Benjamin Franklin pointed out that America was different from the old European despotisms: Americans weren't divided into the idle rich and the miserable poor. On the other side

27

of the Atlantic, in Europe, it was mostly just haves and have-nots. But here it was different. America was populated by independent farmers, industrious craftsmen, and educated professionals who made up a strong, prosperous middle class. Even the day laborers who worked on the farms were paid better than their counterparts in the Old World, and they had opportunities that Europeans couldn't dream of. They could save and invest in themselves, get out on their own and make something of themselves, and become their own bosses. Americans knew that their success depended on their own ambition and hard work.

The Middle Class Made America the Greatest Nation

From that start, the American middle class went on to become the world's economic powerhouse. And they created a nation that was the envy of the world. Because of the middle class, America had a great standard of living, economic opportunities for everyone (including immigrants from all over the world)... and FREEDOM. The middle class worked hard. They were thrifty. They valued education and family life. The American middle class was where you found the virtues that the Founders knew were absolutely necessary to preserve liberty.

There is little argument that America became the greatest nation in world history. The most powerful. The most wealthy. The country offering the most freedom. And the country that had the strongest middle class in world history.

The American middle class built an economy so great that people the world over risked their lives to escape their countries to come to ours. An economy so great the world gave it a name: "the American Dream." An economy so great that people the world over believed America's streets were "paved with gold."

America's individual and economic freedoms, equality of opportunity, and reliance on capitalism created economic growth never before experienced anywhere in world history. Our extraordinary economy lifted more people out of poverty than ever before and supported the strongest middle class ever.

Not everyone in America got rich, but the American middle class lived a quality of life richer than most of "the rich" in other countries. We started more small businesses (by far) than any other country in the world. We led the world in venture capital. We had the most successful and prosperous stock market in the world. We managed to create more millionaires and billionaires than the rest of the world. We managed to win two world wars. And, if we didn't invent it, we provided the capital and economic engine to bring pretty much everything the world cares about to the market.

What Made America the Greatest Nation in World History?

But why did America become the engine of the world economy? What produced this kind of once-in-world-history magic? Is it the air? The water? The dirt? Luck? What is responsible for this miracle?

The U.S. economy has been built around creating equality... *of opportunity.* That is the cornerstone of our economy. Freedom—individual and economic—is at the core of our Constitution. And that freedom ensures equality of opportunity for all citizens.

Equality of outcome, the central tenet of socialism and communism, was *never* on the minds of our Founding Fathers. Yet somehow, without following the Communist Manifesto, we managed to build the greatest nation and the greatest economy in world history.

That's because in America the prosperity of the middle class was earned. It was real. It wasn't a utopian dream. It wasn't a fantasy about the government making everyone perfectly equal by declaring "social justice" (or reading inspiring words off a teleprompter).

Without any guarantee of equality of outcome, millions of immigrants like my grandfather Simon Reis came to America without a dime to their name but with loads of ambition, dreams of greatness, and unmatched work ethic. My grandfather turned a four-man butcher store into his American Dream. That couldn't happen in any other country in the world.

Then along came Barack Obama, obsessed with America being a country of inequality. He burst on the scene with one goal in mind—to change everything and start anew. He spoke about it in every speech. He bristled with anger. His entire agenda and every policy were intended to change the system—to create "social justice," "equality," and "fairness." He said his agenda was "fundamentally transforming the United States of America."[1]

The result? The transformation is well under way.

With equality of outcome as his focus, Obama is making America just like all the other mediocre countries of the world.

We may actually owe a debt of gratitude to Obama. He has proven once and for all what made America great. It isn't the air. It isn't the water. It isn't the dirt.

If those things made us great, why aren't Mexico and Canada great? They share our borders. Why isn't Cuba great? It's right off our Florida coast. Why didn't those countries dominate the world? Why did America?

And it sure isn't a focus on social justice, equality, and fairness of outcome. Countries that have made those principles the centerpiece of their economy have fallen by the wayside. They created only poverty and "shared misery." Except, of course, for the elite political class and super-rich in those countries (who murdered their own middle class and exploited the poor). That's how socialism always creates inequality much worse than the inequality it sets out to get rid of.

Why didn't the old Soviet Union dominate the world like we did? Why can't North Korea compete with South Korea? Compete? North Koreans are literally starving to death.

Why isn't Europe a powerhouse like America? Why are Greece, Italy, Spain, Portugal, and France all economic basket cases? Those countries all cared far more about equality than we ever did. They tax the rich at far higher rates. Yet they all have sky-high unemployment, massive numbers of citizens on the dole, a struggling middle class, and economies on the verge of Armageddon.

Thank you Mr. Obama. You have once and for all proven what made America great. Not just great, but **THE greatest nation in world history**.

Our Constitution never guaranteed equal happiness or wealth. It only guarantees that everyone will have equal opportunity to _pursue_ happiness.

Opportunity creates mobility and economic growth. Opportunity creates jobs by the millions. Opportunity created the "American Dream" and those famous streets "paved with gold." And opportunity created the greatest middle class in history. Opportunity creates economic growth, which is the only way to reduce poverty and catapult millions into the middle class.

And what creates opportunity? **Economic freedom**—limited government, fewer regulations, and low taxes. That's the magic bullet. Economic freedom is the primary thing that separates America from every other country in world history. Our Constitution gives more freedom and power to the individual. It puts the people ahead of the government. Historically, America made it easy to start a business, people were celebrated for their success, and they were incentivized to take risks because in America you got to keep more of your own money. Your money belonged to you, not the government. That was it. That was the difference.

America was the king of economic freedom. Well, the new "2014 Economic Freedom Index" is out. The facts are in. Under Obama, the unthinkable has happened—the United States has dropped out of the top ten for the first time in history. We have moved down the list all five years under the OCF (Obama Crime Family). Obama in five short years has killed the goose that laid the golden egg.[2]

Taxes are too high. Regulations are smothering and strangling small business. Jobs are being killed. The middle class is being murdered. The American Dream is on life support. America is in decline.

And here's the fact that should make you sick. Canada is ahead of America for economic freedom. Who will pass us next? Mexico?

There is no debate about the importance of economic freedom. Just look at who is at the bottom of the list: North Korea, Cuba, Zimbabwe, Somalia, Venezuela, Angola, Syria, Iraq, Iran, Afghanistan. Heard enough? It's pretty clear from that list that economic freedom is important, and that a lack of economic freedom ruins people's lives. Or do you volunteer to live in North Korea, Iran, or Zimbabwe?

Nations in the top quartile of economic freedom had an average per capita GDP of over $36,000 compared with under $5,000 for nations in the bottom quartile. Economic freedom literally adds years to your life. Life expectancy is 79.2 years in that same top quartile versus 60.2 years in the bottom.[3]

Because of Obama, we now know exactly what made America great. We know exactly what created the greatest middle class in world history. We also know exactly what can quickly kill the American Dream. And if we are able to save it now, we know to never again take it for granted.

It was always our economic freedom that made America great. Obama is taking that away at an alarming rate.

If we want our greatness back, we have to embrace economic freedom, low taxes, far fewer regulations, and more opportunity. Those are the things that created the American Dream. Those are the things that can save the American Dream. Those are the only things that can save the middle class.

Let me repeat again. This book is dedicated to showing you in detail how this all happened. Step by step. The murder of the middle class did not happen by mistake. It wasn't done out of ignorance. This is a purposeful plan. It has been in the planning stages for decades. And it's not the work of one man. You are about to meet the perpetrators. But first, let's take a closer look at the victim of the crime—the formerly great American middle class.

An America without the Middle Class?

Under Obama, suddenly the unstoppable American economy is stopped cold in its tracks. Our GDP is in quicksand. The great American jobs juggernaut is in reverse. We have chronic unemployment, the lowest workforce participation rate in thirty-five years, and massive deficit and debt.

You've now read the FACTS at the start of this book. We have millions unemployed, millions more under-employed. Forty-seven million are on food stamps—more than the population of Spain. More Americans are receiving entitlements than working in the private sector. We now have the lowest number of business start-ups in three decades. Twice as many Americans are living in poverty as the population of Syria. Thousands lined up for menial jobs, with less chance of getting a fast food restaurant job than getting into Harvard.

Under Obama, America is no longer the America of the American Dream. Suddenly we aren't the greatest. Suddenly the middle class is threatened with extinction. Suddenly we are rather ordinary. Suddenly we've lost our mojo. Suddenly we are like the famous musician, Prince ... we are "the country formerly known as America."

Without the great American middle class, this country is not going to be the same America we know and love. If the murder of the middle class succeeds, we will end up living in a country divided between the rich elites (Obama and his accomplices) and the poor (dependent on government for everything). As we'll see again and again in this book, the middle class is being reduced to a state of dependency. That's how tyrants stay in power. That's precisely why Cubans drive donkey carts and 1958 Oldsmobiles, while Venezuelans suffer toilet paper shortages, and the desperate masses in those countries don't have the wherewithal to rise up against the dictators who rule them. They've gotten too used to depending on the government—and the elites who run it. The Russians cried when Stalin died.

Why I Am an S.O.B.

I was born into the great American middle class. I am an S.O.B.—son of a butcher. I'm also the grandson of a butcher. My father and grandfather were special people. They represented the greatness of America: the salt-of-the-earth work ethic, faith in God, hunger, ambition, morality, patriotism, and love of family. They both believed with all their hearts in American exceptionalism. That faith and rock-solid belief paid off for them and for our whole family—as it has for millions of previous generations of Americans.

Both my father and my grandfather (my mother's father) started with nothing, and as butchers, both worked for minimum wage for years until finally saving up enough money to open their own butcher stores. In the greatest nation ever created and blessed by God, my father and grandfather achieved the American Dream, albeit in different ways. Their stories demonstrate that America offers great opportunity—but no guarantee of success. That difference is at the root of America's greatness.

My grandfather, Simon Reis, came to America from Germany with only the shirt on his back and the coins in his pocket. Yet he became a successful small business owner. His four-man butcher store was a success for thirty years. My grandfather taught me much of what I know about business. He also taught me to appreciate and celebrate small business owners: the economic engine of America's great economy and the heroes of the workplace. They are the financial risk-takers and job creators. I call them "Financial First Responders."

Middle Class Values, Middle Class Success

Grandpa Reis taught me that government doesn't "help" or "save" business owners. Government only gets in the way. Government, he taught me, is your silent partner—just like the mafia. They want a big chunk of your money for taking none of the risk and doing none of the work. Just like the mafia, they extort you with threats and intimidation. But the mafia wants 10 percent in return for protection. Government expects 50 percent and offers no protection. So actually the mafia offers a much better deal!

My grandfather also taught me that the only jobs government creates are the ones that cost taxpayers money (with bloated salaries, obscene

In America, You're Anybody's Equal

My grandfather was quite a character, the kind that made America great. No, he never became rich like the Kennedy family. But Joseph Kennedy was his customer, and my grandfather was proud of it. A middle class butcher, first-generation immigrant, and small businessman sold meat to Joe Kennedy, a billionaire business mogul. My grandfather said, "That's what makes America great." In America, the rich may have more money, but at bottom they're not that different—not a special class of superior human beings above the rest of us.

pensions, unaffordable benefits, guaranteed job security no matter how incompetent you are, and early retirement).

My father David Root had a very different path in life. He too started in poverty. He was born in Brownsville, Brooklyn, and his father died young, in the "poor ward" of a Brooklyn hospital—leaving a wife with no job, no income, and seven young children. Somehow they survived without ever taking a dime in welfare. The Root family asked for and accepted nothing from government. All seven young children got jobs (some shining shoes) and supported their widowed mother. Those lessons in self-reliance and work ethic led all seven children to live solid, productive, happy middle class lives.

My father worked for lousy wages for over twenty years until he saved enough money to start his own butcher store. Unfortunately, he chose a poor location and had much fiercer competition than my grandfather when a supermarket with much cheaper prices for meat moved right next door to my dad's butcher shop. For twenty-five years he struggled to make a living with his little two-man butcher store. He may never have gotten rich, but he was rich in spirit. He loved owning his own business and being his own boss. That was his dream—never again to have to take orders from anyone. On his deathbed he told me that outside of his family, starting his own business was the greatest thing he ever did. He also told me it could only happen in America.

The American Dream

Even though it never made him rich, that small business allowed my father to pay for his two children to attend Columbia University. Can you imagine? A middle class blue-collar butcher was able to send both his kids to an Ivy League college. That fulfilled his American Dream. David Root hit the lottery—even if he himself never got rich. He was the proudest father in the world.

My sister went on to graduate from Columbia Law School and became an attorney for a prestigious Park Avenue law firm. I became a self-made entrepreneur, vice presidential nominee, national media personality, political commentator, bestselling author, and business speaker. And now my daughter Dakota has graduated from Harvard University with honors.

As Don King would say, "Only in America."

My immigrant grandfather and first-generation-American father owed their success to a country that allowed the middle class to thrive. The whole Root family owes our success and mobility to those two small butcher stores—and to the two middle class butchers to whom America gave the freedom and opportunity to pursue their dreams.

My father and grandfather were no Kennedys or Rockefellers. But they earned enough by owning their own small businesses to live wonderful middle class lives. They owned their homes. They bought new cars every four years. We ate out once a week. We went on vacation once, sometimes twice a year. And my father and grandfather knew that their children would do better than they had. They proved the American Dream isn't easy or quick. But it works—if you don't waste your time being negative and bitter, complaining and protesting, envying and resenting the rich and behaving like the downtrodden and dependent poor. We weren't rich, but we lived a rich life.

That is the life that is dying in America today. *The Murder of the Middle Class.*

The Productive Class

It was the middle class that made America great, not the rich elites, academics, politicians, or bureaucrats. Small business was the economic engine of the greatest economy in world history. Capitalism, social mobility, and the economic and individual freedoms guaranteed by the U.S. Constitution have lifted more people out of poverty than all other political systems in world history combined. Those things are the very foundation of the American Dream.

Today they are being MURDERED.

The middle class is quite simply the productive class. The core of the middle class is men and women who own, operate, and work in small business. They are not rich. They will never be Donald Trump or Warren Buffett or Bill Gates. But they earn a decent living. They enjoy a quality lifestyle. They spend the money that makes the economy go and grow. They spend the money to create most of the jobs. They spend the money that pays most of the taxes. Those taxes fund government and build the roads, highways, bridges, airports, hospitals, and colleges. In other words, we DID "build that."

This group isn't the super-wealthy "1 percent." But they include the top 10 percent, who pay over 70 percent of the taxes in America.

And the top 20 percent, who pay 92.9 percent of the taxes.[4]

And the middle class certainly includes the top 40 percent, who pay 106 percent of the taxes. Yes, the correct figure is 106 percent (because so many at the bottom now pay negative taxes—they file returns, but they get money they never earned "returned" back to them).[5]

Good luck, America, getting along without this productive class.

Yes, Mr. Obama, we did build that. We in the middle class built America with our blood, sweat and tears, ambition, sacrifice, and courage.

Until now, the middle class had one great hope driving us to risk and sacrifice—the knowledge that our children could have more opportunity and a better life than we have. In America, that's at the very core of every middle class family's life and aspirations. If you work for it, put your nose to the grindstone and fight for it, your life will be the better for it, and your kids will benefit.

Until now.

The Decline of the Middle Class

What are the words that defined the American middle class until now? Fighters. Strivers. Patriots. Lovers of God, family, and the American Dream. Upward mobility. Those willing to sacrifice for faith, freedom, and country.

Look at words that define the middle class in this Obama Depression: Decline. Despair. Misery. Malaise. Denigrated. Conned. Fleeced. Plundered. Struggling. Failing. Drowning. Chumps.

And soon, if the political class, big business, and media elites have their way, the word that will best describe us will be...

Serfs.

We'll be hopeless, helpless, desperate, dependent members of the poor huddled masses. This is where things are headed. This book will lay out the case: This is no mistake or coincidence of fate. This is a purposeful plan. In fact, it's a criminal conspiracy.

Two Classmates

How do I know? Because I was Barack Obama's classmate at Columbia University, where we were taught the exact plan that's being executed today. In this book I will lay out that plan in detail. It's quite a story.

We were two polar opposite classmates. One classmate, a blue collar son of a butcher, loved America, celebrated capitalism, and felt a debt of gratitude for the opportunity and mobility given to his family. The other classmate also came from humble beginnings, yet he hated America, despised capitalism, and resented how America treated him and his family.

I was a proud member of the middle class. He wanted revenge on the middle class. I wanted to thank America and embrace capitalism. He wanted to curse America and bring down the capitalist system. We were two classmates with strong opinions and outsized ambitions, polar opposites in every way.

Obama's goals? To create "social justice" and equality (i.e., shared misery) and to ensure equal outcomes by spreading the wealth around (i.e., communism: "from each according to his ability, to each according to his need.").

I outline below how we were taught the plan to accomplish these goals at Columbia University—to destroy good-paying jobs, starve small business, make the middle class dependent on government, and overwhelm the system with debt.

This book exposes how the president of the United States is implementing that plan today. This book lays out the indictment of Barack Obama. Because no man—even a president—is too big to jail.

But Obama isn't in it alone. To complete an "inside job" this big requires a lot of help. One man can't destroy America from within. It takes a criminal conspiracy.

My classmates at Columbia University were almost all children of privilege and power: spoiled brats, members of the lucky sperm club, guilt-ridden about their wealth, power, and luck of birth.

Never having lived a middle class life, never having had a middle class butcher dad and homemaker mom who sacrificed so much for them, these arrogant spoiled brats despised the middle class for their ambition, work ethic, love of country, faith in God, and what my spoiled classmates saw as a naïve belief in the American Dream. My very presence at Columbia angered and enraged these wealthy prep school brats. I was the example that proved their liberalism, progressivism, socialism, and communism a lie. I proved that America was fair.

My storybook life—from the son of a first-generation American just getting by on the meager profits from a blue collar business, to a successful student at an Ivy League university—proved that anyone could make it in America. My presence at Columbia proved that no one needed government to equalize things—all anyone needed was a belief in the American Dream, a great family, a great attitude, and a willingness to work and risk. My very presence proved it does not take a village or a government to raise a child; it takes two great parents who believe in God, country, and capitalism.

Aristocrats and Serfs

The goal of Obama and his socialist-fascist-elitist political class cabal is a two-class society: a small privileged class of the super-rich and connected; combined with a desperate, dependent poor class.

By the way, this is how most societies have functioned throughout history. Think aristocracy and serfs. Think *Downton Abbey*. Think *Braveheart*. And guess what? Both classes are dependent upon big government. The rich can always be counted on to support big government in order to curry favor (corporate welfare, government contracts, bailouts, and stimulus). The poor are always dependent on government for survival.

What's missing from this picture is an independent middle class that doesn't need or want government's help. That's trouble. The middle class gets in the way of big government's plans to control the masses. That's why the middle class must be eliminated. Hence *The Murder of the Middle*

Class by killing upward mobility, the American Dream, and the capitalist economy that fosters independence and rewards ambition and personal responsibility.

America is the beacon, the shining light on the hill. America is the proof for millions of "serfs" trapped under the rule of tyrants the world over that freedom exists, that the individual can triumph. America gives hope to the wretched masses of the whole world, that one day they can be free.

But not anymore—not if America's very ideals are stamped out by *The Murder of the Middle Class*.

What has been done to the middle class in the past five years is unimaginable and mind-numbing. But you need to face the truth before you can act on it. Then you'll need to put a plan in place to protect yourself and save our nation. The great news is this book will present that plan and give you options.

But first, it's time to face the facts. The middle class is being murdered in America... and our own president's fingerprints are all over the crime scene.

CHAPTER 4

The Chief Suspect

Pick the target, freeze it, personalize it and polarize it.
—from Saul Alinsky's **Rules for Radicals**

DID YOU KNOW?

- The point of the IRS scandal was to put the Tea Party out of play and steal the 2012 election for President Obama
- The November 2012 jobs report was inflated to win the election for the Democrats
- The Obama administration uses selective investigation and prosecution to punish its critics—including movie makers, bond rating agencies...and me

Who is killing the middle class in America?

Let's review some key pieces of evidence.

We've seen that in the last five years, the number of unemployed working-age Americans has grown by almost 10 million.[1]

Also, remember that the percentage of Americans who self-identified as middle class in 2008 was 53 percent, while in 2014 it's only 44 percent.[2]

What happened in 2008?

I seem to recall a certain presidential election.

What is different about America in the last five years?

41

Barack Obama.

The president would be any intelligent detective's No. 1 suspect in *The Murder of the Middle Class.*

A Conspiracy against the Middle Class

Let me be clear. Obama alone could never kill off the middle class. This criminal conspiracy has many participants and moving parts. It includes big business, big unions, big bureaucracy, lawyers, central bankers at the Federal Reserve, billionaires like George Soros and Warren Buffett, the United Nations, Ivy League intellectuals, the media elite, an entrenched political class including establishment RINO Republicans, and various anarchists, communists, and terrorists intent on the destruction of America.

But it's hard to doubt that Obama is the ringleader. He is "the chosen one" to carry out the conspiracy, to lead, to lie, and to accelerate the destruction and the collapse.

When the police are investigating a murder, they look at the criminal records of the suspects. A jury may not be told about previous convictions, but homicide detectives know every detail of their suspects' criminal pasts. They also know that career criminals are more likely than the average man on the street to be the person they need to talk to.

So it only makes sense to look at Barack Obama's record. When it comes to political crimes, Barack Obama is the ultimate career criminal.

After all, Chicago is Obama's hometown. His politics and policies are Chicago's politics and policies. Obama runs America "the Chicago way." Chicago has been run for decades by 100 percent Democrats. Moody's Investor Services just downgraded Chicago's debt to right above junk bond status. In other words, Chicago is on the verge of bankruptcy and insolvency.[3]

But Chicago is not just another "blue" city blighted by the Democrats who have been running it into the ground for decades. It's ground zero for shameless, aggressively corrupt, Alinskyite Democrat politics.

Obama's hero was Saul Alinsky—a radical Marxist intent on destroying capitalism. The president even quotes Alinsky in his speeches.[4]

Alinsky wrote a book called *Rules For Radicals*, dedicated to Lucifer, the Devil. That's a fact. Go to your local library and check the book out. On the very first page you'll find the dedication.

Rules for Radicals is a book political science students like Obama and me studied at Columbia University. Alinsky's advice was to hide your intentions. Call your opponent a radical even though you are the true radical. Scream that the other guy is ruining America, while you are the one plotting its destruction. Claim again and again that you are saving the middle class, while you are busy wiping them out. Deny, deny, deny. Lie, lie, lie. Obama learned well from Alinsky.

The brand of politics Obama learned from Alinsky and his Chicago mentors has no respect for the rule of law. Alinskyites, like most socialists, believe the end justifies the means. They're thugs who set out to grab power by any means they can, legal or not. So it should come as no surprise that Barack Obama has committed countless serious and not-so-subtle crimes against the American people. How lawless is the Obama administration? Many of the dirty deeds and scandals of Obama & Co. are public knowledge. Let's start with the most astonishing crime.

How Obama Stole the 2012 Election

Saul Alinsky taught Obama to identify a target and destroy it. In the 2012 election, the Tea Party was that target.

The 2010 elections were a HUGE embarrassment to President Obama. The power, energy, and passion of the Tea Party won the GOP an amazing sixty-three House seats, six Senate seats, six governorships, and seven hundred seats in state legislatures. It was a historic landslide. Obama's entire agenda was threatened.

Yet the mainstream media wants us to believe that only two years later, in 2012, that Tea Party energy and passion were gone... *overnight*. Perhaps the Tea Party changed back to fans of Obama and the Democratic Party? What a fairy tale.

The 2012 presidential election was stolen by Obama, the Democratic Party, the IRS, and government employee unions.

The real story is that Obama's IRS delayed, distracted, hounded, harassed, intimidated, and persecuted Tea Party groups. Without IRS attacks and interference, Tea Parties would have had the same influence and momentum as in 2010, when their energy and passion led to a shocking landslide defeat for Obama and his allies.

There is no need to debate the question any longer. We now have emails from IRS officials stating that the Tea Parties had to be stopped if Democrats wanted to win the election.[5] We have emails confirming that IRS officials were acting as political partisans inspired by President Obama to stymie Tea Party groups and win the 2012 election for their side.[6]

Because of this Tea Party targeting by the IRS, the intimidation factor kicked in. (Who's not intimidated by the IRS?) Donors were scared to death, and donations dried up. The plan worked to perfection.[7]

This was no mistake or coincidence. Congressman Dave Camp confirmed that 100 percent of the groups targeted for audits were conservative groups.[8]

Instead of massive Tea Party rallies and record-setting fundraising for conservative candidates, Tea Party groups were distracted, hounded, harassed, and intimidated by the IRS. They were busy being asked about the names of their members, the names of their speakers, the content of their Facebook posts, and even the content of their prayers.[9]

Even individual board members of Tea Party groups were targeted for attack. The IRS made a point of stating in their massive request forms that all information obtained could be made public. Why? To intimidate Tea Party members by threatening to slander and demonize them and destroy their careers.[10]

Criticize Obama and George Soros, and Get Audited

Professor Anne Hendershott, the prominent Catholic sociologist, spoke out against President Obama's policies and exposed George Soros's funding of liberal Catholic organizations. She got a frightening phone call from the IRS demanding that she appear at the IRS "alone and in person" for an audit.[11]

But this IRS scandal didn't stop at targeting the Tea Parties. It extended to virtually any effective critic of the president. Dr. Benjamin Carson, who dared to lecture Obama at the National Prayer Breakfast in Washington, D.C., was targeted by the IRS.[12] GOP Senate candidate Christine O'Donnell was targeted and smeared by the IRS.[13]

Obama is shameless. Even after the IRS scandal broke, the administration is still harassing the president's critics. Conservative author and filmmaker Dinesh D'Souza was selectively indicted and his movie producer partner Gerald Molen was targeted by the IRS after releasing the hit documentary about Obama entitled *2016: Obama's America*.[14] (*2016* was the second-highest-grossing political documentary since 1982, just behind *Fahrenheit 9/11*.[15] It's unthinkable that George W. Bush would have sicced the IRS on Michael Moore. But then Bush, for all his faults, was no Alinskyite.)

Conservative filmmaker Joel Gilbert, who produced *Dreams from My Real Father*, was apparently harassed by the IRS, too.[16]

Sarah Palin's father was targeted six times by the IRS.[17] Christian ministers like Franklin Graham were targeted by the IRS.[18] Big GOP donors like Idaho billionaire Frank VanderSloot were targeted by the IRS.[19]

Are you starting to sense a pattern here? Any decent prosecutor could put someone away for life for this kind of widespread conspiracy.

Does anyone not in the Kool-Aid-drinking mainstream media believe it was a coincidence that Obama met with IRS union boss Colleen Kelley at the White House the day before the targeting of Tea Parties by the IRS began?[21]

Start a Tea Party Group, and Watch the Federal Investigators Get in Line to Harass You

Catherine Engelbrecht is a wife, PTA mother, and small businesswoman. After she founded a Tea Party group in 2010, her businesses and family were subjected to more than fifteen attacks by the IRS and other federal agencies. Before getting involved with the Tea Party, Engelbrecht had never been contacted by a government agency in her life.[20]

Was it a coincidence that IRS Commissioner Douglas Shulman visited the White House at least 157 times during Obama's first term?[22]

Was it a coincidence that IRS official Sarah Hall Ingram made 155 visits to the White House, and shared confidential taxpayer information with officials there?[23]

These IRS officials made more White House visits than any other members of the Obama administration. Attorney General Eric Holder was only there 62 times. Secretary of State Hillary Clinton only visited 43 times. Homeland Security Chief Janet Napolitano was only there 34 times. So the IRS was more important than national defense, terrorism, and criminal justice? The IRS is obviously Obama's BFF (Best Friend Forever).[24]

If this wasn't a widespread criminal scandal, then why did IRS official Lois Lerner take the Fifth Amendment?[25] Why did top IRS officials hire the best Washington, D.C., law firms that money can buy?[26]

It's now proven that top IRS officials and lawyers were aware of this scandal since 2011.[27] Why did no one stop it? The answer is obvious. My bet: they were busy directing and overseeing it!

Have Obama or the IRS learned their lesson? Nope. Long after the scandal went public, the IRS was at it again—asking for the names of Hollywood stars who belonged to "Friends of Abe," the organization for Hollywood conservatives. Why did the IRS want those names? To audit all of them.[28]

Long after the scandal went public, the IRS was intimidating a stage-4 cancer victim after he appeared on Fox News to criticize Obamacare. In another incredible coincidence, cancer patient Bill Elliott got his audit letter the same day as C. Steven Tucker, the insurance agent who was helping him with his coverage, got a letter from the IRS.[29]

Do you remember Nixon's Articles of Impeachment? President Nixon resigned before he could be impeached and removed from the presidency for charges that had been voted by the House Judiciary Committee. Article No. 2 was the crime of using the IRS to punish his political opponents and silence free speech.[30] Don't look now, but we've got another Nixon in the White House. The difference is that Barack Obama's IRS scandal makes Richard Nixon look like a minor league rookie.

Don't take my word that IRS employees were openly rooting and working for Obama. Ask the government watchdog agency OSC (Office of the Special Counsel). It turns out that one IRS employee at the "IRS help line" greeted callers with a chant to reelect Obama. She faces severe discipline.

Another IRS employee is being disciplined by OSC for telling a taxpayer that she supports Democrats because "Republicans [are] already trying to cap my pension...."

The OSC received complaints about IRS employees at the Dallas IRS office wearing pro-Obama political stickers and clothing and even downloading pro-Obama screensavers on their work computers.[31]

I wonder how many IRS employees supported Obama's reelection at all costs but never wore Obama hats, T-shirts, or had Obama screensavers on their computers?

Was the fix in? Lois Lerner, the IRS official at the center of this conspiracy, spoke out loud about hoping to get a job with the Obama campaign group "Organizing for Action" after she retired from the IRS.[32]

Now it turns out that this same IRS official shared confidential taxpayer information of a conservative non-profit with a Democrat Congressman Elijah Cummings. That group, "True the Vote," was intimidated and persecuted to extraordinary levels.[33]

Are you starting to understand this was an Obama White House–Democratic Party–government employee conspiracy to hijack the election?

This Time, It's Personal

This story is personal to me, because I was one of the victims of Obama's criminal use of the IRS to target his enemies. I spent three years (2011–2013) under attack by the IRS. Clearly my nonstop criticism of Obama in the mainstream media caught his attention. I told my story of IRS targeting and intimidation at Fox News (and many other conservative media) in the spring of 2013.[34]

The IRS attack on me was so over-zealous and out of bounds that I was forced to hire one of the nation's top tax law firms. My legal team took the case to tax court, where we won a complete victory.

FIVE DAYS LATER, the IRS announced a new tax audit of me. I'm not a billionaire or a wheeling, dealing hedge fund CEO. I'm just a small businessman—but someone in government thought I needed to be intimidated, punished, and silenced.

Multiple legal and tax experts confirmed they had never heard of an American taxpayer being attacked by the IRS in such a manner only five days after winning in tax court. They agreed this could only happen if I was on Obama's "Enemies List."

The attack was chilling, intimidating, and very expensive. It was meant to bleed me dry and teach me a lesson—if you dare to criticize Obama, get ready to lose everything.

Unlike any other IRS target, I was Obama's classmate at Columbia University. I have not hesitated to express my theories about Obama's scandals. My commentary and theories were widely covered by conservative media like Rush Limbaugh, Sean Hannity, Glenn Beck, Mike Huckabee, Bill Cunningham, and even Geraldo.

I'll leave it for you to decide, but is it possible that my criticisms of the president hit too close to home and Obama or his top aides (see Valerie Jarrett or David Axelrod) ordered the IRS to make my life miserable?

Regardless of how you feel about my criticisms of the president... even if you disagree with me... even if you hate me... even if you think my criticisms were out of bounds... even if you think Obama was justified... the fact is, if Obama (or his top aides) gave the orders, a crime was committed. Nixon's Articles of Impeachment make that clear.

The Cover-Up

What the biased mainstream media refuse to do is connect the dots. None have the courage to state that the fix was in. It's so obvious that the Obama White House directed this conspiracy to hijack the election. Government employees went along with it because Obama is "their man." It's the same reason government employee unions campaign and contribute millions of dollars to Democratic candidates across the country.

Then when his IRS intimidation was exposed to the public and Congress demanded investigations, Obama made sure "the fix was in." He appointed a lead investigator who has donated almost $7,000 to Obama's two presidential campaigns and the DNC (Democratic National Committee). Can you imagine if a Republican president appointed a Republican donor to investigate his biggest scandal? Don't make me laugh.[35]

This wasn't just any crime, folks. Obama has gotten away with the greatest and most daring act of fraud in world history. They *stole the presidential election*.

That brings up a serious question: IS THIS PRESIDENT TOO BIG TO JAIL?

Faking Government Statistics

IRS intimidation and persecution wasn't the only fraud perpetrated by Obama to ensure his reelection. Obama's loyal government employees also made another crucial contribution—they faked jobs reports. In September of 2012, just before the election, we heard miraculous unemployment reports that made it sound like the economy was turning around. Hundreds of thousands of jobs were supposedly created in one month—873,000 new jobs, to be exact.[36] Happy days were here again. "Bravo, Obama," said the adoring mainstream media.

But I smelled a rat. I warned in the media that the books were cooked. I predicted this would turn out to be pure fraud, and voters were being scammed. I accused Obama and his henchmen in the government bureaucracy of fixing the election.[37] Democrats and the mainstream media (I know, I repeat myself) called those charges preposterous. They said it was impossible to fake jobs reports.

Guess who was right? Whistleblowers have come forward to report that government employees faked the jobs reports.[38] I guess they wanted the man who protects their bloated salaries, obscene pensions, and corrupt unions to be reelected. Apparently they would stop at nothing to keep the gravy train rolling, so they made up reports about job increases out of thin air. Why were government employees so desperate to reelect Obama that they were willing to commit crimes? Obama is their meal ticket.

The entire election was pure fraud, based on fantasy. Americans walked into the voting booths hearing fresh news that indicated the economy was improving and jobs were dramatically increasing. Overnight jobs numbers had gone from "doom and gloom" to the great breakthrough. Jobs were being created by the hundreds of thousands…in one month! Can you imagine how bright the future could be under Obama? That was the narrative as voters walked into the voting booths. But it was 100 percent fake. The numbers were made up out of thin air, and voters made their final decisions based on pure fraud.

Plus, this fraud endangered our entire economy. The Federal Reserve bases billion-dollar decisions on interest rate hikes and quantitative easing (QE) on jobs reports. If those reports contain job increases that don't actually exist, the Fed is moving in the wrong direction. Statistics were faked that falsely elected a president and could cause billions of dollars in damage to the U.S. economy for years to come.

I ask again: IS THIS PRESIDENT TOO BIG TO JAIL?

Obamacare Fraud

And that's not the end of Obama's election fraud. Before the election, Obama knew tens of millions of Americans would lose their health insurance. Yet he knowingly committed fraud by lying to the American people about it. Not once, but repeatedly. He didn't just tell intentional lies to pass Obamacare, he kept telling those same lies to deceive American voters and get reelected.

Did Obama commit intentional fraud? Without a doubt. His own administration's internal estimates (for three years) were that MOST Americans covered by employer plans would lose their insurance. That number is 156 million Americans affected. How do we know that? The number appears in the *Federal Register* for June 17, 2010.[39]

Those same White House internal projections showed that up to 80 percent of small businesses and their employees were doomed to lose their insurance. All of this was known while he kept lying to us, "If you like your health care plan, you can keep your health care plan." Obama's reelection was based on this fraud.

Who would have voted for Obama if they knew most of us were about to lose our insurance, doctor, hospital, medical choices, or our jobs—or perhaps a combination of all of the above?

Who would have reelected Obama if we knew that our insurance premiums would increase more in the few months after Obamacare took effect than in the eight previous years COMBINED?[40]

Who would have elected Obama if they knew his plan would cause premiums to rise 56 percent? And then double *again* in the year after that?[41]

Would voters have reelected him if they knew that cancer patients would lose their insurance? Or that children with cancer would lose their doctor? Or that patients with MS would lose the prescription drug that has kept them alive and functioning?

But wait (as late-night infomercial pitchmen like to say), "There's more."

When the citizens went to the "state of the art" Obamacare website for help, to try to save themselves, they found it defective. It turns out the website was built so poorly, the personal information of consumers can be easily stolen. And it's not just online scam artists we're worried about. The "Obama navigators" themselves might do the stealing—after all, it turns out many of them have criminal records.[42]

How about the company Obama hired to build the defective website? Obama gave a contract for hundreds of millions of dollars to a foreign firm with less than stellar credentials. Why? Does Obama believe no American firm was qualified to build a website? Worse, it was a NO-BID contract to a firm headed by one of Michelle Obama's friends from the Princeton Black Alumni Association. Why "no-bid?" Where did all that money go? Don't you wonder how many of those millions of taxpayer dollars are committed to Democrat causes, or are now sitting in a Swiss bank account?[43]

Then to fix the defective website, Obama hired another firm that files its taxes in a foreign country and employs primarily foreign workers.[44] Can you even imagine if a Republican president did this, what the media headlines would say?

Can you imagine if any of this happened at a private company? Can you hear the outrage and accusations coming from consumer protection advocates over the lies told and sold to consumers? Can you imagine the shareholder lawsuits over spending hundreds of millions on a defective website, all given to a friend of the CEO's wife? If the Obamas were in business instead of politics, they would be indicted.

Once again: IS THIS PRESIDENT TOO BIG TO JAIL?

Remember the TV infomercial pitchman Kevin Trudeau? His TV advertisements ran day and night on cable TV channels. The government claimed that his product (a weight-loss book) was a fraud. Kevin Trudeau was convicted and sentenced to ten years in prison in February 2014.[45]

Ten years in prison for selling a diet book. I have no doubt Trudeau is a crook. It's not the first time he's spent time in jail. But compared to Obama, he is a minor league pickpocket.

Trudeau scammed about a million people out of $30 each for a book. Obama's scam cost millions of Americans their health insurance. Obama's scam raised prices dramatically on the whole country. With rates up 56 percent in a matter of months and set to double again this year or next, Obama's lies, fraud, and misrepresentation may have cost consumers hundreds of billions over the next decade.

Trudeau's lies and misrepresentations didn't cost a single person their health or their life. Obama's scam has cost cancer patients their insurance policies, doctors, and lifesaving drugs. I'm certain we'll soon hear about sick Americans who died from the stoppage of treatment. I'm certain the stress alone will kill already sick patients. I'm certain we'll hear about overwhelmed patients who committed suicide over the loss of coverage.

Trudeau's lies didn't cost a single American his or her job. Even the Congressional Budget Office reports that Obama's scam will cost 2.3 million jobs over the next decade.[46] But that figure doesn't include the full-time jobs lost over the past four years since Obamacare was passed. It doesn't include people reduced to surviving on part-time work, plus food stamps, because of Obama's fraud.

Trudeau's scam didn't cost a Las Vegas man $407,000 in medical bills. Obamacare did.[47] How many more are out there who lost coverage, then got a big medical bill?

So who is the real fraud here? If Kevin Trudeau deserves ten years in prison (and I'm sure he does), shouldn't Obama receive a life sentence for the lives he has ruined, the financial losses in the billions, the no-bid contracts to a friend of his wife, the millions of dollars of taxpayer money lost building a defective website, and the destruction of the entire U.S. health-care system?

So: IS THIS PRESIDENT TOO BIG TO JAIL?

Lawless Tyranny

But Obama's crimes go beyond fraud. We've had dishonest and devious presidents before. What America has never had before—at least not since George III—is a ruler who presumes to rule us without any respect for the Constitution, the rule of law, and our representatives in Congress.

If our representatives in Congress won't pass Obama's laws, he simply goes over their heads with dubiously legal regulations and executive orders. "Cap and Trade" legislation on greenhouse gasses failed in Congress. So Obama just told his EPA (Environmental Protection Agency) that they could make companies pay for their emissions anyway.[48] The House of Representatives wouldn't pass Obamacare until pro-life members of Congress were guaranteed it wouldn't include abortion. After it passed, Obama's HHS (Department of Health and Human Services) went ahead and wrote abortion pills into the regulations—and required Catholic nuns to pay for them![49] When the president's signature "achievement," the Rube Goldberg machine known as Obamacare, showed signs of collapsing from its own absurdities, Obama didn't bother asking Congress to amend it. He just unilaterally changed the law with "waivers" for which he has no legal authority.[50]

The lawlessness of this administration has gotten so outrageous that constitutional scholars are sounding the alarm. During a February hearing before Congress, law professor Jonathan Turley warned that Obama has accelerated the rate at which the president makes the other branches of government irrelevant, to a pace that is almost unimaginable. Because of Obama's actions, Turley said, America is at "a constitutional tipping point."[51]

Turley sounded like he was referring to a dictator. "My view [is] that the president has in fact, exceeded his authority in a way that is creating a destabilizing influence in a three branch system," Turley testified in front of Congress. And ". . . the rate at which executive power has been concentrated in our system is accelerating. And frankly, I am very alarmed by the implications of that aggregation of power." The scariest part of all? Turley is a liberal Democrat who voted for Obama.[52]

They say a fish rots from the head down. Obama's disregard for rules has trickled down to other levels of government. Harry Reid, Obama's henchman in the Senate, dispensed with a century of tradition to allow Obama's appointees to be approved by a simple majority vote—the so-called "nuclear option." Why? To confirm appointees and lifetime federal judges with such radical Marxist backgrounds that they could never be approved without rigging the system. The main reason for this power grab? To stack the U.S. Court of Appeals for the District of Columbia, widely considered the second most powerful court in the land. That court will now rule the way Obama needs them to rule in order to protect Obamacare and Obama's unconstitutional executive orders.[53]

Obama's tyrannical ways even extend to the military. Obama has fired more commanding generals in the past year, along with hundreds of junior officers on track to become generals, than any president in history. It's a scene right out of *The Godfather* when Al Pacino offs every opponent standing in the way of his absolute power.[54]

Why do we put up with a chief executive who acts like a cross between a mafia don and George III? IS THIS PRESIDENT TOO BIG TO JAIL?

Intimidation and Extortion

Why don't most Americans know about these blatant abuses of power? Because the media knows its place—to cover up Obama's crimes. In the few instances when the media gets curious and stops cheerleading for the president for long enough to notice anything fishy, Obama and Attorney General Eric Holder intimidate them. They use the NSA to spy on the press.

See the Associated Press scandal. Obama spied on AP reporters, as well as a Fox News reporter. Even the Kool-Aid-drinking *friends* of Obama are treated like enemies in this paranoid police state. The message is, "Don't stray off the reservation."

But just to make sure the media gets the message, the Obama administration proposed a much bigger plan to intimidate the entire media. In early 2014 an FCC (Federal Communications Commission) plan was leaked to the public. The FCC planned to put government monitors and "researchers" into newsrooms to "question" reporters, editors, producers, and even station owners about how they decide which stories to run and how they decide which stories should be headlines. One FCC commissioner warned that if newsrooms failed to comply with the questions, they could lose their FCC license to broadcast. No mafia-style intimidation there, huh? Luckily Fox News made this story a headline and the FCC backed down. Cockroaches always run from the light.[55] But the fact the Obama administration even tried to put their goons into newsrooms to intimidate the media says it all.

Then there's the intimidation of the ratings agencies. Standard & Poor's downgraded America's debt under Obama. So guess what happened next to Standard & Poor's? *The Department of Justice hit them with a $5 billion lawsuit for "fraud."*[56] Egan-Jones also dared to downgrade America's debt—twice. Can you guess what soon followed? *The Securities and Exchange Commission charged Egan-Jones with "material misrepresentation."*[57]

In early 2014 Obama indicted both the former Republican governor of Virginia and movie producer Dinesh D'Souza, both outspoken critics of the Obama administration.[58]

Were these investigations and indictments a coincidence? No more than if a business owner stopped paying kickbacks to the mafia and his business suddenly wound up fire-bombed. These were messages. Messages you can't ignore—like a dead fish at your front door.

All of the fraud this president has committed is child's play compared to the pure extortion and blackmail his administration has engaged in— and they're gearing up for worse. Soon, just the way he has used the IRS to snoop into his enemies' financial history, he'll be able to use Obamacare to snoop into your medical records. Obamacare regulations demand that your doctor ask about your sexual history. That information will now be in the hands of government (a.k.a. Big Brother).[59]

Almost all of us have secrets we don't want publicly exposed, because exposing them could cost you your career, reputation, or worst of all, your spouse and family.

Are we willing to live with the fact that our government keeps dissenters and critics in line with blackmail and selective criminal prosecutions? I ask again: IS THIS PRESIDENT TOO BIG TO JAIL?

Using the IRS to steal an election is bad. Faking jobs reports is bad. Committing fraud to pass your healthcare plan is really bad. Intimidation and extortion are very bad. But they are just part of a long list of crimes committed by this administration. All in the name of staying in office, so they can get away with the crime of the century, *The Murder of the Middle Class*.

Any one of these scandals would have forced a Republican president out of office long ago. *Obama owns all of them.*

Has there ever been an American leader involved in this many lies, frauds, scandals, violations of the Constitution, and cover-ups? There's enough crime here for a century of presidents. Bernie Madoff would blush at what Obama has pulled off. Forget impeachment, it's time for criminal prosecution.

One last time, I ask: IS THIS PRESIDENT TOO BIG TO JAIL?

CHAPTER 5

The Accomplices

In order to become the master, the politician poses as the servant.
—**Charles de Gaulle**

DID YOU KNOW?

- The average government employee makes twice as much as the average private sector employee
- Since 2000, federal government employee compensation has grown by 36.9 percent versus 8.8 percent for private sector employees
- Almost 10,000 Illinois government employees collect pensions of over $100,000 per year

Obama is the ringleader of the plot to murder the middle class. He's responsible for the purposeful plan to destroy your spirit, to kill your options, to break you from personal responsibility and individuality, to addict you to government dependency. But Obama is just one man. He has plenty of help. So in this chapter I'm going to "out" the co-conspirators of the greatest conspiracy in history...

The Murder of the Middle Class.

Can you guess who is the deadliest organized crime family in our country's history? If you guessed the Gambinos, you're wrong. It's the

OCF—the Obama Crime Family. The Obama gang is killing jobs, strangling business, intimidating opponents, making the energy industry "sleep with the fishes," and wiping out the middle class.

Don Obama and his cronies are very much like the Gambino Crime Family—except the Gambinos were *nicer*. You see, the mafia almost never goes after "civilians." They only intimidate, extort, and kill other mobsters or "associates" active in the insular criminal world. If only Obama was that discriminating.

All in the Family

Obama and his Crime Family *always* target civilians—i.e., the middle class actually working for a living, and small businesses trying to make a living by producing goods and services other people are willing to pay for. Who's in the OCF? Government employees, of course. The mainstream media. The environmental Nazis. But I repeat myself. OCF members work for government. Then they leave the government and step right into cushy positions in the media, or with big law firms. Or they lobby the government for more environmental regulations—then get a job working for the EPA enforcing those same regulations. It's all one big happy incestuous family.

As a matter of fact, as of the writing of this book, over twenty members of the same mainstream media who have protected Obama and covered up for his many scandals have gone to work for the Obama administration.[1]

But it gets worse. Many key members of the mainstream media are related by blood or marriage to key members of the Obama administration. These people work for the biggest billion-dollar media conglomerates (CBS, ABC, CNN).[2] They keep their love of big government "all in the family."

We've seen that the president is perfectly willing to use the IRS to intimidate critics, silence free speech, and steal an election. Violating the Constitution means nothing to Don Obama and his partners in crime—in the federal bureaucracy, in the Democratic Party, in the media. Lying and committing fraud against the people mean nothing to the OCF. Whether Congress approves of new laws proposed by Obama means nothing—he just enforces his agenda through executive orders, bypassing the people's elected representatives. Ruining the economy and rigging the system against small business and the middle class mean nothing to the president and his willing accomplices.

Government Employees: The Privileged Class

How did America become broke and insolvent? How did we build up an unimaginable $17 trillion in debt, and somewhere between $100 trillion and $200 trillion in unfunded liabilities? How did we allow the American Dream to become a nightmare? Obama's most powerful accomplices in this destruction of America and the middle class taxpayer are the members of the new privileged class: government employees.

On his farewell tour after twelve years as mayor of New York City, Michael Bloomberg alluded to "the Labor-Electoral Complex." This describes the cozy relationship between politicians and government employee unions.[3] The public employees' unions get the politicians elected; the politicians stay in office by giving away the store (i.e., all the taxpayers' money, in the form of bloated salaries, bloated benefits, and ridiculously bloated pensions) to the union members.

The reign of Mayor Bloomberg is the perfect example of this cancer that is burdening the taxpayers, bankrupting the country, and killing the middle class. When Bloomberg took office in 2001, New York City spent $1.5 billion per year on government employee pensions. Today the city spends a mind-boggling, incomprehensible $8.2 billion—almost a 500 percent increase (while inflation rose only 35 percent).[4]

Government employee salaries, benefits, and pensions are eating up federal, state, and local budgets across America. There is no way to pay these bills. Soon the jig will be up. Thirty-eight local governments have filed for bankruptcy since 2010.[5]

Government employees are the true 1 percent. America has far too many of them (21 million), they're paid far too much, and their union demands are straining taxpayers to the breaking point. They have become a privileged class that is sucking the blood out of the American middle class.

How would you like to retire with $6 million? $8 million? $10 million? All you have to do is become a government employee to hit the jackpot.

You don't believe me? Do the math. I recently talked with a retired New York City toll taker. His salary averaged about $70,000 per year over twenty years. But in his last few years he worked loads of overtime and added in accumulated sick days to get his salary in those final years up to $150,000. His pension is based on his final years' salary. This is a common pension-padding ploy. He bragged that he will now get a taxpayer-funded pension of $120,000 a year for the rest of his life. He's only fifty years old. The average fifty-year-old male has a life expectancy of almost eighty. With automatic cost-of-living increases, that's $5 million over the next thirty years—*for not working.* For a toll taker. And, of course, we're also paying his medical bills.

No country, no budget, no taxpayers anywhere in the world can afford this. Ask Greece.

Multiply this times 21 million government employees (on the federal, state, and local level) and you now get a sense of what is bankrupting America.

Over 77,000 federal government employees earn more than the governor of their state.[6] It was reported by *USA Today* that the *average* federal civil servant compensation is $123,049 per year. That's more than double what private sector workers earn (average of $61,051). An exhaustive, detailed study by the Cato Institute recently proved that average federal employees earn TWICE as much as private sector workers in similar jobs. Since 2000, federal government employee compensation has grown by 36.9 percent versus 8.8 percent for private sector employees.[7]

In Clark County (Las Vegas) the average firefighter compensation was $199,678 per year.[8] When he retires at age forty-five or fifty, we owe his pension based on that obscene salary. But here's the clincher—when he finally dies, the taxpayer has to continue paying the pension to his *spouse.* Add up the damage to the economy. It is catastrophic. Talk about a 1 percenter—a single firefighter could retire and be paid $8 to $10 million for not working for the rest of his life. This is madness.

The *Las Vegas Review Journal* reported that more than a third of the Las Vegas teachers union's entire $4.1 million annual budget went to pay just nine union leaders.[9] The executive director received $632,546, while the CEO of the union-created Teachers Health Trust was paid $546,133.

And this doesn't even scratch the surface of how much is spent by the unions to bribe Democrat politicians to keep the gravy train rolling. All of this money comes from teachers' union dues which, of course, come straight out of taxpayers' pockets as higher teacher salaries.

So next time you hear educators scream that we must spend more money on education, because "it's for the kids," you'll know the truth. It's for the unions. It's always been for the unions. Bernie Madoff has nothing on the government employee union scam.

Illinois teachers are retiring on $399,652 annual pensions.[10] Yet Chicago teachers go on strike because "they aren't paid enough." Of course, they say there isn't enough money to educate the children. Well it's no wonder there's no money left for the kids, if teachers are retiring on $400,000-per-year pensions.

But that's just an aberration, right? WRONG. Almost ten thousand Illinois government employees collect pensions of over $100,000 per year. The number getting six-figure pensions just increased 47 percent in one year! One retired teacher will collect $11,868,155 in pension payouts over a normal lifetime. Yes, I said $11 million.[11]

Do you know many middle class people in the private sector retiring with $5 to $10 million in the bank? They are few and far between. But that's exactly what a private sector employee would need in the bank on the day of his or her retirement to match the $100,000-per-year pensions, plus healthcare benefits, plus the cost of living increases that government employees get, paid out over thirty to fifty years.

Lawyers

More bad news: far too many of those government employees are lawyers—starting with President Obama himself. The worst news is that Obama is a lawyer. This fact explains a lot. Lawyers think they know everything about everything. In particular, lawyers think they know *everything* about business.

The only thing worse than knowing nothing about a subject, is not knowing anything about a subject and *thinking* you know everything. As a small business owner, I can tell you from firsthand experience that lawyers repeatedly destroy business deals. Why? Because they don't know anything about business. They are only trained in law school about how to destroy a business, how to steal money from productive people, how to stop people from doing business, and how to kill jobs. Then they come out into the real world to practice law. They think they are "experts." But they don't know what they don't know. So they spend the rest of their careers damaging business and killing jobs with their ignorance and dangerous arrogance.

But once they are elected to office, that's when the *real* destruction of jobs begins. Put these same lawyers in charge of making economic policies and the damage is multiplied and magnified. Lawyers run and ruin economies all over the world.

Since most politicians and legislators are lawyers (a huge conflict of interest that should be banned), laws governing business are written so that lawyers are required in almost every aspect of business. That's how they justify their fat fees. They write the laws that make themselves necessary.

For a lawyer-politician there is always a far better choice than admitting they don't know the answer. Obama's economic stimulus plan was a great example. It was rushed through without debate, even though almost a trillion dollars was involved. It was passed even though none of our Congressmen or women had time to read it. It was based on "shovel-ready jobs" even though there were no shovel-ready jobs. It was all based on fraud. How do I know? Because Obama joked about it later, admitting there never were any shovel-ready jobs.[12]

The stimulus was even passed despite negative predictions from the Congressional Budget Office (CBO). The CBO reported that whatever slight uptick in jobs and economic activity it produced in the first year or two would be negated over the long term. The CBO predicted that the debt created by the stimulus package would decrease Gross Domestic Product (GDP)—that is, *damage* the U.S. economy—over the next decade. The CBO said the economy would be better off if we did nothing.[13]

But no lawyer or politician could possibly do nothing. The lawyers-turned-politicians have one credo: we're better off doing something, to prove we are in charge, even if it's bad for the economy. That's how they prove their value to us. They are always there to do SOMETHING, if only to show us that we "little people" couldn't live without them.

Obama is a lawyer. His wife Michelle is a lawyer. Hillary Clinton is a lawyer. Almost every key member of Obama's staff and cabinet is a lawyer. Recognize a pattern? They all believe in the power of government to change and control our lives. They all believe only government can fix our economy. They all believe they know what is best for you, your family, and your business. Even though this same government can't even run the U.S. Postal Service without losing billions of dollars per year.[14] Even though they've lost $40 billion (and counting) on running Amtrak.[15] Even though they've lost $20 trillion (and counting) on the war on poverty, yet the result is…a record number of Americans now living in poverty.[16] Even though, as we have seen, their management of the country itself has led to $17 trillion (and counting) in debt and well over $100 trillion in debt plus unfunded liabilities.

Here are two statistics you need to know that explain everything happening in America today:

Problem #1: America has the most lawyers of any country in the world. That is a recipe for economic disaster.[17]

Problem #2: The average state in America has 39 lawyers per 10,000 residents. But Washington, D.C., has 803 lawyers per 10,000 residents. That's ten times higher than even the states with the most lawyers (New York and California).[18]

That, folks, explains EVERYTHING. That explains why the economy is failing. Why there are no jobs. Why the American Dream is disappearing. Why the middle class is being murdered. Why your life gets worse every day. Why your children's future looks bleak…

Because the lawyers are in control.

The Fed

Government employees in general are bankrupting the country. But the ones at the Federal Reserve are Obama's top-level enforcers in *The Murder of the Middle Class*. Suffice it to say the reason the Fed prints

$1 trillion per year in fake money, out of thin air, to artificially pump up the stock market, isn't to help you. This massive Ponzi scheme inflates the income, bonuses, and stock ownership of the richest men and women in America, who just happen to be the biggest political donors.

As if on cue, just as I was in the middle of writing this book, it was announced that Ben Bernanke left the Fed with a debt of $4.1 trillion.[19] Where do you think that $4.1 trillion went? Into the pockets of bankers, Wall Street CEOs, the CEOs of publicly traded companies, and the heads of union pension funds. It made Warren Buffett billions richer just in the past year. But it's just a bill for the middle class. It's debt. You and your children owe it back. It was a transfer of wealth from you and your off-spring to the wealthiest people in America.

I'm sure you've heard the term QE (short for quantitative easing). Quantitative easing is nothing more than the Fed printing trillions of dollars of fake money out of thin air, thereby burying our children and grand-children under mountains of debt. Actually, these days, they don't even have to use a printing press. Just a few keystrokes on a computer get the job done.

The Fed's $3.2 trillion QE[20] is a massive Ponzi scheme for bankrupting the middle class. The Wall Street banks and hedge fund fat cats are like the early investors in Ponzi's scheme, who got rich and walked away safe with their profits. The middle class are like the investors further down Ponzi's pyramid, who were ruined. The bankers rake in the profits; the middle class goes broke.[21]

The Fed created artificially low interest rates—actually a rate of zero—all in the name of "stimulus." How did that work out? There are still no jobs and we have experienced the slowest post-recession economic growth in history. Who benefited? Just banks and Wall Street firms like Goldman Sachs and JP Morgan.

Check your student loan. Is the interest rate zero? Check your credit card debt. Is the interest rate zero? They took the Fed's free money by the trillions and they took their loans at zero interest rates...and gave the middle class nothing—except obscene interest rates on our credit card and student loans.

How about the loan the banks gave you to start your business? Oh I forgot, the banks won't give loans to small businesses. Did they help you

A Historical Root Quotation Everyone Should Study

"Little by little business is enlarged with easy money. With the exhaustless reservoir of the Government of the United States furnishing easy money, the sales increase, the businesses enlarge, more new enterprises are started, the spirit of optimism pervades the community. Bankers are not free from it. They are human. The members of the Federal reserve board will not be free from it. They are human.... Everyone is making money. Everyone is growing rich. It goes up and up...until finally some one whose judgment was bad, some one whose capacity for business was small, breaks; and as he falls he hits the next brick in the row, and then another, and then another, and down comes the whole structure. That, sir, is no dream. That is the history of every movement of inflation since the world's business began, and it is the history of many a period in our own country. That is what happened to a greater or less degree before the panic of 1837, of 1857, of 1873, of 1893, and of 1907....[W]hen credit exceeds the legitimate demands of the country the currency becomes suspected and gold leaves the country."[22]*

—A Politician Named Root

This quotation from a politician named Root describes "to a T" the economic crisis of 2008 that started us on this downhill spiral: the bailout, the bankers' mistakes, the stock market collapse, the credit freeze, and the reaction of the Federal Reserve. But these aren't my words. And they weren't spoken about the government banking crisis and bailout of 2008. Yes, they are the words of a politician named Root. Just not this Root. Those words were spoken in 1913 by Elihu Root, U.S. senator from the state of New York.

with your underwater mortgage? I didn't think so. Remember, it was the middle class taxpayer who loaned the banks the trillions from our taxes and our future debt obligations. Now they won't loan to us, even though we saved them. When we bailed them out, their credit was a shambles.

Now they won't loan to us because our credit isn't perfect. How's that deal working out for the middle class?

Is it extreme or "radical" to suggest eliminating the Fed? My namesake Elihu Root had the same exact advice back in 1913 when arguing against the formation of a central bank. If only we had listened to a politician named Root back then.

But wait, isn't the Fed necessary to prop up the value of the dollar, create jobs, keep inflation at bay, and save the economy? How has that worked out? There are no jobs, the economy stinks, the dollar has lost 98 percent of its value since the Fed was created, and the worst period of inflation in the history of America has been the last hundred years, with the Fed in charge. The Fed is murdering the middle class.

Of course, I know the stock market is up. Is that a great feat? In Venezuela the stock market is hitting all-time highs too, but the people are starving in the streets. Anyone can print fake money, drop it on Wall Street and make stocks go up. That's no magic act. The Fed is using debt—pawning your children's future—to make Wall Street bankers and CEOs richer, while your kids owe the money back. That's called "robbing Peter to pay Paul." It's generational theft.

In 2005 the genius Fed chief "Helicopter Ben" Bernanke said not to worry about housing prices because they'd never before declined nationally.[23] He predicted that we'd continue to enjoy "full employment."[24] He defended derivatives as "perfectly safe," posing no danger to stock markets.[25]

In early 2008, Bernanke didn't even know we were in a recession. He was quoted as saying, *"The Federal Reserve is not currently forecasting a recession."*[26] In July of that year he said Fannie Mae and Freddie Mac were in "no danger of failing."[27]

How scary is that?

Bernanke was badly wrong about every single important topic in the economy—from recession, to housing, to subprime mortgages, to Fannie Mae and Freddie Mac.[28]

As a reward for his world-class incompetence, Obama nominated Bernanke for another term. Clearly a case of the blind leading the deaf and dumb…*mostly dumb*. These are the geniuses in charge of the U.S. economy.

Heckuva Job, Fed!

- Our dollar has lost about 98 percent of its value since the Fed was founded.[29]
- Our national debt is five thousand times larger than when the Federal Reserve was founded in 1913.[30]
- The greatest period of economic growth in the history of America (between the end of the Civil War and 1913) came when there was no Federal Reserve and no income tax.[31]
- The United States had no net inflation until the Fed was created in 1913. Since then we've had constant periods of inflation. The worst inflation has come since the Gold Standard was abandoned in 1971.[32]

Except who says they care about the U.S. economy? Main Street is where the middle class lives and works, and who cares about the middle class? Obama and his Fed have other fish to fry. The Fed's strategy is simple: flood the economy with "easy money" by artificially lowering interest rates and printing more money. That gives the Wall Street bankers and hedge funds Ponzi-scheme opportunities to get even richer. It also creates an artificial, temporary economic boom to help politicians get elected (or in Obama's case, reelected).

Politicians desperately need to find a way to pay for all their giveaways, handouts, goodies, corporate welfare, bailouts, stimulus packages, and entitlements that they use to buy votes. The middle class is the patsy. We are left holding the bag. The debt they ring up will have to be paid for generations to come by middle class taxpayers and their children. Everyone wins but the middle class.

The Fed is like a drug dealer who wants his customers to become addicted—to debt. The worse the debt gets, the more money our government needs to borrow—from the Fed. The Federal Reserve is like a legal LOAN SHARK who keeps us endlessly in debt and dependent on...*the Fed*.[33]

Amazingly, the Fed has only three official mandates: protect the value of the dollar, keep inflation in check, and create full employment. How's that going?

Listen to the words of Thomas Jefferson, the Founding Father who authored our Declaration of Independence: *"I believe that banking institutions are more dangerous to our liberties than standing armies. If the American people ever allow private banks to control the issue of their currency, first by inflation, then by deflation, the banks and corporations that will grow up around the banks, will deprive the people of all property until their children wake-up homeless on the continent their fathers conquered."*

To put it bluntly, we must find a way to eliminate the Fed before the Fed eliminates the middle class.

The Mainstream Media

So have you heard all these facts about government employee pensions and the Fed on your regular TV news shows? Read them in the newspaper? I didn't think so. There is no bigger Obama co-conspirator than the mainstream media. How does a man this dangerous get elected president of the United States, let alone, reelected? The answer: THE MEDIA.

At Columbia University I had a front row seat on the future media elite. When I read *Columbia College Today* magazine, I can see exactly where all my classmates work today. So what are the professions that most of my Columbia classmates chose? Media and government. There you have it. There's the conspiracy. They went to college together. They think alike. They work together today. And what is it they think about all day? Hatred for America, capitalism, and the Republican Party. I saw it every day on display at Columbia. The most radical and dangerous of my classmates are now in the media. I had a front row seat. I am a witness. Today they run the biggest shows on television and radio and the biggest newspapers—places where you get your news every day.

What I learned from my front row seat at Columbia is that leftist-progressive-Marxists like my classmates believe they are morally superior to the rest of us. It is their mission to save the world from prejudice, patriotism, racism, greed, intolerance, and inequality. The success America has achieved is a sign of everything these radical leftists despise. Worse, it is proof that everything they believe is pathetically wrong. So they need to erase our success (and our history).

Anyone not on board with their agenda is labeled ignorant, racist, intolerant, greedy, closed-minded, or dangerous. That person must be slashed, burned, slandered, and destroyed. See Ted Cruz, Mitt Romney, Sarah Palin, George W. Bush, Dick Cheney, Ronald Reagan, Newt Gingrich, Barry Goldwater, and an endless list of conservative leaders.

According to the media, conservatives never espouse tax cuts out of sound economic principles. We just want to throw welfare mothers, children, and the elderly into the streets. We don't want to empower job creators, we just support "the rich." In the eyes of the biased leftist media, conservatives are always acting out of ignorance, greed, and their favorite word—*racism*. Any other viewpoint than the leftist, pro-Obama view is "radical," "extreme," "racist," and "out of the mainstream."

The incident that sums it all up best was my classmates giving a celebratory standing ovation for the assassination attempt on Ronald Reagan. Suffice it to say these people went on to populate the highest echelons of American media. If you cheer for the death of a great man for "the crime" of being a Republican and capitalist, it's not a stretch to assume you'll have a hard time giving a fair and unbiased interview to Republicans in the future. This extreme hatred and bias against conservatives is on display every day, in virtually every media outlet.

The sad fact is the media has given up on the quaint idea of unbiased reporting. They don't even try to hide their love and adoration for Obama and his socialist policies. They've literally run a 24/7/365 public relations campaign on his behalf. It's so obvious, so over-the-top, that it's ridiculous, embarrassing, and scandalous.

In reality, the left is out of the mainstream. Look at "climate change." Obama and the Obama cheerleaders in the media talk about this issue all the time. Democratic senators conducted an all-night vigil in early 2014 to focus attention on "climate change." Twenty-seven times they used the word "denier" to refer to anyone who dares to question their dubious claims that man-made warming is a danger to the planet. And yet "climate change" is near the very bottom of issues the public is actually concerned about—well below the economy, and jobs. The media has no interest in reporting the news, their goal is clearly to *make* the news—whether you like it or not.[34]

It's also interesting to note the media has rarely mentioned the Climategate scandal. Thousands of emails proving a conspiracy were released. Did you hear about this on the evening news?[35]

Cases of media bias to aid the leftist big government conspiracy to murder the middle class abound. The same mainstream media that downplayed or covered up the Obama IRS scandal played up the Chris Christie "Bridgegate" scandal. The "big three" television networks ran stories about a Republican governor's traffic jam seventeen times more often *in twenty-four hours* than they covered Obama's IRS criminal persecution of political opponents in *six months*.[36]

Research proves that the mainstream media gave overwhelming ten-to-one coverage of Mitt Romney's inflammatory "47 percent" video versus a video of Obama admitting he believed in income redistribution (i.e., socialism).[37]

New research shows that newscasts on domestic policy issues on Spanish-language TV networks skewed left 45 percent of the time last year, skewed neutral 49 percent, and skewed right 6 percent. Is that reporting the news, or influencing the news?[38]

Then there's the outright deception by the media to help leftist causes. NBC news literally altered a recording to try to make George Zimmerman look guilty of murder.[39]

And a CBS *60 Minutes* editor altered the sound on a video to make a $100,000 electric car (Tesla) seem sexier and more appealing. Anything to help the leftist cause of green energy.[40]

Environmental Nazis and Climate Change Crazies

I don't use the word "Nazi" carelessly. I'm Jewish by birth. Many of my ancestors were murdered by the Nazis. I understand how strong a word it is. Yet what else would you call radical environmental wackos who think much of America's energy resources should be held hostage by sage grouse and prairie chickens?[41] These unhinged extremists are wrecking our economy and crippling our children's future over chickens. Hard to believe? It's 100 percent true. I kid you not.

The *Wall Street Journal* recently pointed out that almost half the land west of the Mississippi belongs to the federal government.[42] If they were to make that land off limits to oil drilling, fracking, farming, ranching, mining, and development, they would destroy the energy industry, kill millions of middle class jobs, and cause the U.S. economy to grind to a halt. Well don't look now, but it's happening.

Under pressure from "green activists" (a.k.a. Environmental Nazis) the Department of the Interior is attempting to use the ESA (Endangered Species Act) to put 50 million to 100 million acres of federal and private land either off limits or under the most extreme and invasive land-use rules in history.

Pushing this insanely dangerous policy are radical environmental organizations like "WildEarth Guardians" and the "Center for Biological Diversity." The stated goal of this organization: ending fossil-fuel production in the U.S.

Do you understand the implications of their goal? First, America would literally go bankrupt. Second, we'd be hostage to oil purchases from Muslim countries that hate us (and use our money to fund terrorism against us). Third, the middle class would be destroyed by a combination of much higher taxes, much higher energy prices, much higher food prices, and a loss of countless middle class jobs.

These ESA (Endangered Species Act) rules make EPA rules look downright moderate.

Keep in mind the sage grouse is found in eleven Western states. The prairie chicken sits atop the biggest oil fields in Texas. Let me restate the amount of land affected: 50 to 100 million acres. Say goodbye to energy production in America. Say hello to $1,000-per-month electric bills, $9-per-gallon gas, and 100 percent higher food prices (to pay for higher energy and transportation costs). Say hello to the unemployment line for anyone in the farming, ranching, mining, and energy business.

What do you call the farmers whose lives will be ruined by this policy? *Middle Class.* What do you call the ranchers? *Middle class.* What do you call the miners? *Middle class.* What do you call land owners who will have their rights taken away? *Middle class.* What do you call the workers at the oil and natural gas companies who will lose their jobs? *Middle class.* And what do you call millions of consumers who will pay dramatically higher energy bills? *Middle class.* Or perhaps more accurately "formerly middle class."

Because of Environmental Nazis we desperately need an **EHPA—** *Endangered Humans Protection Act.*

The kissing cousins of Environmental Nazis are the Climate Change Crazies. I call them crazies because they're out of touch with the facts.

For instance, it's a fact there has been no global warming in the past fifteen years.[43] It's a fact that sea ice in Antarctica is the thickest in recorded history.[44]

It's a fact that 2013 was one of the coldest years in the U.S. since 1895.[45] A new study of weather patterns in Iceland reports that "global warming" is no threat to our existence—it actually *reduces* extreme weather.[46]

But besides those facts, we can also look at history. History repeats. Well, throughout history "climate change" has always been around. One thousand years ago there was a long period of milder weather that brought Genghis Khan to power and then allowed him to conquer far-away lands. Was that "global warming?" Was it caused by man? It's interesting to note that man had no cars or factories one thousand years ago.[47]

The fact is man-made emissions are just a small part of the picture. There are fifteen hundred active volcanoes in the world,[48] not to mention large wildfires each summer in the Western United States that consume millions of acres. Both volcanoes and wildfires spew tons of pollution into the air.

Solar flares are a big factor in any level of global warming. Periods of increased solar activity correspond historically to long-term periods of warmer temperatures on earth, while periods of decreased solar flares correspond to long-term periods of cooler temperatures on earth. All of these factors are out of the control of mankind.

Plus, no matter how much damage we do to our own U.S. energy industry in order to reduce our own fossil fuel use, China, India, and other emerging economies will continue to spew enough pollution into the air to more than make up for our efforts. Which means anything we do is for naught, all the job losses for nothing, all the increased costs of fuel and electricity accomplish nothing.

If we listen to the Climate Change Crazies we'll be wrecking the entire U.S. economy for nothing. While that's happening, our biggest rivals (China, Russia, and emerging third world economies like India and Brazil) will throw caution to the wind and blow by us economically. The world will be more polluted than today, but America will no longer be the world's leading economic power.

If you thought Obamacare was bad for business and jobs, wait till you see what the Environmental Nazis are up to. They just put a homeowner in jail for collecting rainwater... *on his own property*.[49] Obama's EPA is trying to ban most wood-burning stoves.[50] The EPA's new proposed power plant regulations would destroy the entire coal industry.[51]

What else has the EPA made illegal? Well who knows? First you'll have to hire a lawyer just to read the nine hundred new regulations approved within ninety days of Obama's reelection.[52]

And now there's undeniable proof the folks at the EPA really are crazy. A large number of these onerous EPA regulations were created and implemented by John Beale, the highest-paid employee at the EPA, until he was forced to resign after he stole $900,000 from the government and lied to agency officials about a fantasy life as a CIA agent that never existed.[53]

This con man played a lead role in shaping EPA policies, Clean Air Act regulations, and the National Ambient Air Quality Standards. He pioneered the EPA's use of "secret science" to write regulations that cost private industry untold amounts of money, killed middle class jobs, and forced the closure of coal plants. He became the highest-paid employee of the EPA despite having no scientific or policy credentials. This is your government at work, ruining the U.S. economy—led by conmen, frauds, thieves, incompetents, and power-hungry tyrants with no credentials, given the power to rule over our lives. And some of them are in fact crazy!

Understanding that all of radical "climate change," "green energy," and environmental wacko policy is destroying the U.S. economy, murdering the middle class, and weakening America's standing as THE world's superpower, is it possible this is the goal of the "Climate Change Crazies"? That perhaps they aren't so crazy after all? Maybe they know exactly what they are doing?

What a brilliant cover! Instead of admitting you're a communist and America-hater, or your goal is to collapse capitalism, you simply scream from the highest rooftops that you care about clean air, clean water, and the health of little children. Who can argue with that?

Meanwhile you methodically use executive orders and EPA regulations to destroy the coal industry, ban oil drilling, slow fracking, handcuff other forms of fossil fuel exploration, deny permits for oil and natural gas plants, block storage of nuclear waste, and call anyone who disagrees with you a "climate change denier."

Oh, and one more trick. You bribe scientists with government grants that feed their families, pay the rent on their laboratories, and in some cases make them filthy rich. Then those scientists have a huge conflict of interest. Suddenly they agree that climate change is real, proven, and a scientific fact. Suddenly they are willing to create "proof" of global warming that just doesn't exist. Now you have the "science" on your side.

But let's just assume that man-made "global warming" or "climate change" is real. Even if that was true, the "cure" is far worse than the disease. Green energy is the equivalent of using chemotherapy to cure a common cold. The cure will kill you!

The Spaniards re-configured their entire economy to become the green energy capital of Europe.[54] The result is economic tragedy and disaster on an unimaginable scale. How else would you describe 27.7 percent unemployment, 57.7 percent youth unemployment,[55] and the loss of much of the entire country's pension funds[56] to try to stave off complete economic collapse?

Spain is drowning in green energy debt. The *Wall Street Journal* reported in early 2014 that green energy now makes up 25 percent of electricity generation in Spain. That has left a $41 billion hole in their budget—that's the difference between what it costs to produce and what utilities can charge for power. So in addition to dramatically higher electric bills, Spanish taxpayers have to pay for $41 billion in losses too.[57]

The EU is giving up on "renewable energy" targets because the "green energy" policies are wrecking the European economy.[58]

Why is green energy such a financial disaster? A study was done in Spain that proves for every job created by the green energy industry, 2.2 jobs are lost in the traditional economy.[59] Each green megawatt of energy destroys more than five jobs...each solar-powered megawatt destroys nine jobs...and each wind-powered megawatt destroys four jobs.[60]

This scenario is coming to America, as a result of Obama's obsession with green energy. There was the more than $90 billion for green energy loans, subsidies, and tax credits in the 2009 stimulus. Everyone has heard about the half billion dollars lost on one company, Solyndra, run by Obama donors. But there are fifty-two other "green" companies either bankrupt, headed for bankruptcy court, or in need of bailouts. Billions of middle class taxpayer dollars were squandered.[61]

The Department of Energy recently admitted that as much as 80 percent of the money for some green energy programs went to foreign firms employing non-American workers.[62]

Who pays? The poor don't care about fuel prices or electricity costs. Government pays many of their bills, subsidizes their housing, and often pays for their home heating oil. The super-rich don't care if electricity prices double or triple. If you have millions of dollars in assets, a $300 monthly electricity increase doesn't affect your life. But middle class Americans are being wiped out by the effects of this green energy debacle. Think of someone making $50,000 per year having to pay dramatically higher gas bills...electric bills...grocery bills...and health insurance premiums, all at once? Don't imagine, it's happening right now. It is no mistake or coincidence. Green energy is designed (along with everything else in the Obama agenda) to plunder and bankrupt the average American.

George Soros and the Open Society Foundations

Many billionaires are in the thick of the conspiracy to "murder the middle class." But most of these billionaires have no special agenda against

America, capitalism, or the middle class. They are just "crony capitalists" looking to multiply their wealth and expand their empires. (See Warren Buffett in the next chapter.)

But Hungarian-born billionaire George Soros is a far different breed. Soros has a political agenda: Marxism, socialism, progressivism. Call it any name you'd like—it's pure evil. And he isn't shy about putting his money where his mouth is. Name the problem in the world, and Soros is usually in the thick of it, funding the problem. Name the progressive organization, and Soros is funding it. Name the progressive politician, and Soros is right there behind him.

This is a man who has collapsed countries, regions, currencies, and banks (the Bank of England to be precise)[63] with his financial knowledge and manipulation. But his greatest talent is funding organizations central to destroying America, capitalism, and the middle class. Soros invests in every terrible politician, cause, and organization in this country through his OSF (Open Society Foundations).

Soros and OSF have been identified in the media as funding leftist-progressive-socialist fronts such as ACORN, Center for American Progress, MoveOn.org, Air America Radio Network, Media Matters, America Votes, American Institute for Social Justice, The Ella Baker Center for Human Rights, American Friends Service Committee, Association of Community Organizations for Reform Now, and hundreds of others.[64]

I did a little research about the groups Soros funds. Let me give you just a taste of what these groups stand for: "fairness"; "equality"; "social justice"; redistribution of wealth; massive social change; changing voting laws so ex-felons, parolees, and even present inmates can vote; funding community organizers; open borders and amnesty for illegal aliens; more spending by government; more welfare and entitlements; government-run single-payer healthcare; unilateral disarmament for America; "transforming of poor communities"; getting out the leftist message through sophisticated media techniques; accusing America and Israel of civil and human rights violations; defending radical Muslims; gun control; accusing America of causing human suffering across the globe; and of course stopping voter ID and getting out the progressive vote. One of the organizations funded by Soros and the OSF calls for a "revolutionary program to overthrow the capitalist system and rebuild the entire society on socialist principles." At least they're honest.[65]

Just re-reading this list of goals, I need a shower . . . for about a month . . . with industrial grade soap, a wire bristle brush, and scalding hot water. And an anti-nausea pill too.

By the way, it's no coincidence these groups helped elect and reelect Barack Obama. Obama owes Soros his life. Soros's OSF-funded groups are the foot soldiers for Don Obama. They're the chief enforcers for the Obama Crime Family.

But Obama's also getting a lot of help from some unexpected allies. Turn to the next chapter to see who else is an accomplice in *The Murder of the Middle Class.*

CHAPTER 6

The Unindicted Co-Conspirators

Et tu, Brute? ("You, too, Brutus?")

**—Julius Caesar, on realizing that even his friend Brutus
was in on the conspiracy to stab him to death**

DID YOU KNOW?

- According to Democratic pollster Pat Caddell, the GOP establishment wanted the Obama administration to harass Tea Party groups
- Chief Justice Roberts started writing a majority opinion declaring Obamacare unconstitutional—then changed his mind and voted to uphold the law
- GE, whose CEO is Obama crony Jeffrey Immelt, paid zero net income taxes from 2008 to 2011

You *expect* government employees, unions, lawyers, environmental Nazis, George Soros, and the rest of Barack Obama's political allies and minions to have it in for the middle class. But the plot to wreck the U.S. economy and reduce us all to welfare-dependent clients of Obama and his cronies is more insidious than that. The murder of the middle class wouldn't be succeeding if Obama hadn't first succeeded in co-opting some unlikely allies.

RINO Republicans

Obama is destroying America, but why is the GOP helping him?

Look around. Obama and his socialist cabal are destroying this country, step by step, minute by minute. It's a bloodbath out here.

Yet the GOP establishment, led by RINOs (Republicans in Name Only), is complacent and complicit. Why are they standing by as Obama destroys America? Are they stupid? Are they lazy? Are they cowards? Are they so dense they have no idea what's going on right in front of them? Are they in on it? Are they good actors just making believe they oppose Obama, but in reality they are on the same team? Are they suffering from Stockholm Syndrome? Or is Obama blackmailing them?

Stockholm Syndrome is a psychological phenomenon in which hostages exhibit irrational empathy, sympathy, and positive feelings toward their captors, sometimes to the point of defending them or apologizing to them. They are in a state of denial about who the bad guy is, and eventually take the side of the criminals who control their lives. Today's GOP establishment appears to suffer from this mental disorder.

Obama and the mainstream media call conservatives and patriots who believe in the exact same limited government principles as our Founding Fathers names like "radicals," "extremists," "terrorists," "extortionists," "legislative arsonists," "unhinged," and "racists."[1] We are compared to the KKK.

And the GOP establishment not only doesn't defend their own base (their most loyal supporters). They go along with Obama to belittle the few courageous conservative heroes trying to save America from disaster. According to Democratic pollster Pat Caddell, the GOP establishment in D.C. *wanted* the IRS to harass, persecute, and intimidate the Tea Parties. He believes the objective of the establishment GOP was to get the boots of principled conservatives off the neck of the RINOs.[2]

Are they suffering from STOCKHOLM SYNDROME?

Obama is rapidly turning America into a Big Brother Nanny State with nasty government bureaucrats controlling every aspect of our lives. He uses all the three-letter organizations to attack his political opposition: IRS, NSA, DOJ, FBI, SEC, EPA. Yet the GOP appears docile and apologizes for any attempt to resist.

Are they taking TOO MUCH PROZAC?

Then there's the corruption: The IRS scandal. The $600 million wasted on the defective Obamacare website. The contracts to build it awarded to foreign firms. The NO-BID contract awarded to friends of the president's wife. For less than this, Bill Clinton was impeached. For less than this, Richard Nixon was hounded out of office.

Obama purges the ranks of the military of anyone who disagrees with his policies.[3] These are the men responsible for keeping our children safe at night. Something is wrong. Certainly questions need to be asked and investigations opened.

Are they ASLEEP AT THE WHEEL?

The country is going under. All appears lost. And the GOP fumbles, retreats, and apologizes. It's tragic, but it's now clear to see: One party is filled with frauds, crooks, and Marxists out to bankrupt the U.S. economy, wreck capitalism, and destroy America. And the other party (the GOP) is filled with weak-willed cowards who are either scared of their own shadow, in cahoots with Obama, or suffering from Stockholm Syndrome.

What is causing the total lack of willingness by mainstream Republican leadership to stand up for the Constitution, the American middle class, and preservation of the American Dream? Is it the intoxication of political power? Are they just desperate to preserve their position as part of the ruling political class?

The only other explanation for their dereliction of duty is that Obama has pictures of these RINOs in compromising positions. Don't laugh. The Obama Crime Family plays at that level.

Given the cowardice and silence from establishment Republican politicians, do you doubt Obama and his goons are blackmailing them? If you don't believe that could be happening, you are naïve.

It sounds like a paranoid conspiracy theory. But then just a couple of years ago, who was crazy enough to believe that the president would use the IRS to persecute his political enemies, or the NSA to spy on millions of Americans' private emails and phone calls—until those charges were both proven to be true?

How else can you explain John Boehner calling Obama bad names and swearing to support smaller government, lower taxes, less spending, and reduce the debt...then turning around days later and agreeing to a deal to raise spending and taxes and increase the national debt?[4]

How else can you explain a true blue conservative patriot like Chief Justice John Roberts standing firm in opposition to Obamacare, writing the majority Supreme Court opinion striking it down, killing it...then suddenly reversing course to join the other side and writing a new majority opinion supporting and approving Obamacare?[5]

How else can you explain General "We Never Leave Anyone Behind" Petraeus (then head of the CIA), standing silently by while his CIA operatives were murdered and left behind in Benghazi? Obama refused to send help, yet Petraeus never said a word. Was he being blackmailed over an affair? Well, we now know that the general was having an affair with his biographer. How do we know that? Someone read his private emails.[6] So nothing I'm saying is all that far-fetched, now is it?

Obama obviously has ways of controlling people. That is the very essence of "Chicago Thug Politics." It isn't his wonderful speeches on a teleprompter that make conservatives abandon everything they believe in.

My belief is that Obama has "the goods" on the opposition. The president and his goons find their weakness, then hold the information over their heads like a sword. They've uncovered transgressions, corruption, insider trading, tax cheating, or photos of the political opposition in bed with the wrong person.

Or, it could simply be an outright bribe. Just like the mafia, it's an offer that's "too good to refuse." Vote our way and we'll give you a million-dollar lobbying job, or law firm partnership. Vote against us and we'll leak your embarrassing secrets and ruin your career and marriage. There is no other commonsense explanation for Republican leaders assisting Obama in his murder of the middle class.

Obama's BFF: Big Business

But establishment Republicans aren't the only traitors to the conservative cause. Big business has also joined in the plot to murder the middle class.

President Obama is a unique breed of socialist. He is a hybrid Socialist-Marxist-Fascist who understands he needs "cover" to destroy America. And what better "cover" than getting famous billionaires and credible high-profile CEOs from corporate America to support him and convince middle America to go along with the con? That's how Obama became BFFs (Best Friends Forever) with big business.

In *The Ultimate Obama Survival Guide* I laid out how the ground has shifted in America. Big business, Wall Street, the banks, and most of corporate America, which used to side with small business to support capitalism and conservatism, were seduced over to Obama's side by huge financial bribes.

Big business is all about greed. They'd sell out their mother to gain an extra billion dollars of profits on their quarterly reports to shareholders.

Obama's rants against the super-rich are just window dressing. It's all a "head fake" to cover the real plan. It's propaganda he uses to sell this con game to the masses. Obama's destructive agenda is not aimed at big business or the super-rich, it is aimed squarely at *you*: entrepreneurs, small business owners, and the middle class.

Instead of standing tough for capitalism, Wall Street was bribed by government bailouts and "stimulus" money. Small business and the middle class got the shaft (i.e., the debt and the responsibility to pay the bill). Now the New York bankers are enjoying a wonderful recovery. Wall Street is doing fine. Meanwhile, Main Street is stuck in the Obama Great Depression.[7] Small business is dying. But that's all part of the plan, supported by big business. This is how you kill the competition. *The Murder of the Middle Class.*

Next came Obamacare. Instead of teaming up with small business to resist socialized medicine, the way they did with Hillarycare in the nineties, big business teamed up with Obama to rob and murder the middle class.

The two thousand pages of Obamacare were drafted by a former health insurance lobbyist who subsequently went to work for the pharmaceutical industry.[8] Not only did a big business lobbyist help write the Obamacare bill, but after it passed more than thirty Obama administration big shots involved in overseeing the creation of the bill set up shop on K Street in

Washington, D.C., as lobbyists for medical, health insurance, and big pharmaceutical companies.[9]

With Obamacare, Big Pharma and big healthcare companies get billions in new revenue. And the middle class pays the bill. We're on the hook for the government subsidies.[10] And we're forced to buy the new Obamacare-compliant policies with inflated premiums and lousy benefits.[11] But that's all fine with big business—government is handing them the profits at our expense.

Then in the December 2012 fiscal cliff negotiations, Obama bribed big business with loads of corporate welfare, and they went along when he cut the throats of small businesses.

Big business was happy to accept higher individual income taxes, because most small business owners pay their taxes as individuals. The corporate titans at the Business Roundtable and the RATE Coalition (which includes AT&T, Ford, Lockheed Martin, and Home Depot) were all for big tax hikes on individuals—i.e., their small business competitors. At the same time, they tried to get a corporate income tax cut for themselves.[12] The $625 billion tax increase passed. Big business didn't get their corporate tax cut... *this time*. But boy did they get huge bribes—a $40 billion payoff in the form of crony capitalism handouts.[13] Billions in profits from the murder of the middle class.

Profiting from Poverty

All the wars in the history of America combined have cost about $7 trillion. The so-called "war on poverty" has cost $20 trillion and counting.[14] Despite all this spending to fight poverty, under Obama's watch we've seen the biggest increase of Americans living in poverty since the 1960s.[15]

Who paid for this gigantic, wasteful, failed war on poverty? The middle class. You know, the same group that pays for free healthcare for the poor...for free college education for the poor...for food stamps...for $15,000-per-pupil public school for illegal immigrants.

While the middle class is paying, who is benefiting? Big business. Where do the poor huddled masses spend their welfare checks, food stamps, housing allowances, and disability (for "bad backs" and "mental stress")? The money is spent at Walmart, McDonald's, and national supermarket chains. It supports Kraft Foods, Pepsico, Miller Beer, Coca-Cola, General Mills...the list goes on and on.

You don't have to take just my word for it. Walmart publicly admitted this past January that its profits are based on government checks. Walmart announced that cuts in the federal food stamp program hurt its fourth quarter profits. That means that middle class taxpayers are subsidizing Walmart (and every other big business) through the war on poverty. Poor people get checks from government, then spend it at Walmart. But those checks come from you. The national debt increases so Walmart can have bigger profits. Eventually all that debt is owed back by middle class taxpayers. But the top executives and shareholders at Walmart will be long retired with $50 million golden parachutes.[16]

And the "war on poverty" money is just the tip of the iceberg. The favors big business gets from government add up to really big money. Whether it's bailouts, stimulus, green energy, or government contracts, it all helps big companies like Goldman Sachs, Bank of America, Tyson Foods, and GE. It never helps the small butcher or baker on the corner of your street. Yet who pays the bill? Middle class consumers and small business.

The Murder of the Middle Class.

Tag-Teaming the Middle Class: The Online Sales Tax

As soon as any politician mentions "fairness," reach for your wallet. You're about to be robbed. Big government and big business are relying on you to be dumb. They want you to pay 5 percent more for every product you buy online...and like it because, it's "fair." Surely, we're not that dumb, are we?

There is no better example of the convergence of big business and big government as a wrestling tag team to fight the middle class into submission than the sudden push for the online sales taxes. Suddenly, everyone in D.C. is on the same greedy team. The cynically named "Marketplace Fairness Act" subjecting Americans to these taxes has already passed the

Senate. Yes, it's Obama and the Democrats pushing it. But look who is going along without a fight. Establishment RINO Republicans (a.k.a. Hoover Republicans) have signed on as cheerleaders. The lies they tell sound just like Obama-speak: they want to "level the playing field."[17]

Read the tea leaves. Big business is behind it. Why would big business want online sales taxes? Won't it cost them money? Won't oversight and accounting be an intensive and expensive pain?

Yes, but those costs are outweighed by the benefits of destroying their competition. This isn't about "fairness" or "leveling the playing field." Exactly the opposite. It's about putting small online businesses out of business. It's about making every online mom and pop business or small retail store with any idea of setting up a website to sell their goods, stop dead in their tracks. Big business doesn't want the competition.[18] With their deep pockets and layers of bureaucracy, big business is perfectly set up to collect the sales tax and distribute it to the government. But small businesses can't possibly afford to hire enough staff to oversee the distribution of sales taxes to not only fifty state tax agencies, but perhaps as many as nine thousand different sales tax jurisdictions within those states.[19]

But it's not just paying taxes to thousands of jurisdictions. The law being proposed opens the door to businesses being audited at any time by any one of the fifty states, or those nine thousand jurisdictions. Not a single small business in America could afford the legal and accounting bills. Right now, if you own a business in California, the only state audit risk out there is from California. But if online sales taxes are approved nationally, your small California business could be audited by California, New York, Michigan, and Illinois—all in the same quarter. Because of this massive compliance burden, small business will be forced out of business.

And that's precisely the point. That's why the big boys want the new tax. It makes big business the dominant player for online sales. Amazon, Walmart, and Target are the kings, while the rest of us are shut out of the game. That could be why just eight big businesses alone spent an average of $2.6 million on lobbying for an online sales tax in 2012,[20] and more than a hundred are on record supporting it.[21]

It's all about the billionaires pushing the little guys out of the way. And with small business out of the way, the billionaires will not only collect the

5 percent extra sales tax from the consumer, but they'll be able to add on another 5...or 10...or 20 percent of profit because they'll have less competition. Talk about the murder of the middle class!

No wonder big business loves the idea of this new tax. But why does government want a new online sales tax? Well that's easy. It's a gigantic money grab. All fifty states are desperate for the new revenues they'll get from taxing everything you buy online from a book...to music...to food...to a toothbrush. Governments across the USA never have enough money to spend. Here's a fresh new source. So all they had to do was get together with big business, to get the big business lobbyists to conspire with the state government lobbyists, to buy the votes they need in Congress. And, to make sure the voters don't throw the bums who vote for it out, next the lying politicians will try to convince the dumbed-down "sheeple" of America this is "fair" and good for them.

Folks, there is nothing "fair" about a new 5 percent tax on everything you buy online. You just agreed to $500 or $1,000 (if you have a big family like me) added to your online shopping bills. That's $1,000 per year in new taxes being stolen from your bank account. I say "stolen" because you get nothing in return for it. Just like that...it's *gone.*

If I buy a $1,000 product online from a company in Atlanta and pay $50 sales tax, what does that do for me? I don't live in Atlanta. I just got ripped off for nothing. Pure theft. Highway robbery. And because I don't vote in Atlanta, they can vote to raise the sales tax at any time and I have no say. This is the ultimate example of "taxation without representation."

By the way, what did my purchase cost the city of Atlanta or state of Georgia government? Absolutely nothing. My online purchases don't cost any state one cent. I don't drive on your roads. I don't fly from your airports. My kids don't go to your schools. I don't use your hospitals. I don't even walk on your sidewalks.

The big company that collected the tax lost nothing. They just passed it on to the consumer, and now their small business competition is out of the way. Again it is the middle class consumer who pays the bill. If my online sales tax bill is $1,000 per year, at the end of forty productive working years, I've just had an extra $40,000 stolen from me. Money I never paid before. Money that might help keep my business open in the Obama

Great Depression we are living through right now. Money that could help pay for my children's college education, or keep me out of poverty in my retirement.

So if you think an online sales tax is "fair"...*think again*. It's nothing but theft. It's just a new way for government to murder the middle class and leave us desperate and dependent on government (because we have no money left). And it's another way to tilt the playing field in favor of the companies that make the biggest donations to politicians (of both parties).

Immigration and the Chamber of Commerce

Immigration "reform" has nothing to do with "fairness." It's about handing big business a huge supply of cheap labor. It's about keeping wages down for American middle class workers. America has no jobs. Almost 100 million working age Americans are not working. So the one thing we don't need is more job seekers. Yet the goal of our politicians is to add 12 million new workers, all of whom are willing to work for the lowest wages possible. Does this make any sense?

Listen to the words of Tom Donohue, the CEO of the U.S. Chamber of Commerce (representing big business). Donohue addressed the shortage of qualified employees for high-tech and high-wage jobs in an op-ed earlier this year. Donohue said, "Immigrants can help bridge a growing skills gap in science, technology, engineering and math—the so-called STEM fields that are vital to a modern, competitive economy."

Then Donohue addressed the issue of unskilled labor. "Immigration can also address labor shortages in lesser-skilled fields where there are insufficient numbers of either qualified or willing U.S. workers to fill positions. Many studies have concluded that the greatest percentage of job growth in the United States through 2020 is expected in low- and moderate-skilled jobs that cannot be automated or outsourced. Services like home health and nursing home care, landscaping and hospitality cannot be provided without capable staff ready to do the work."[22]

So what the CEO of big business is saying is that a) Americans are unqualified for jobs that require a high degree of intelligence and education. And b) Americans don't want low-skilled jobs.

Well, there are simple answers to both problems. First it's clear our public school system is broken beyond repair. The result is that middle class children are having their futures ruined. Who runs the public schools? Teachers unions. So the answer is to break the teachers union monopoly that has ruined our children's future. Tie teacher pay to performance, fire under-performing teachers, and give parents more freedom and school choice.

Second, why don't we take the almost 100 million working-age Americans who aren't working; who are almost all on welfare, food stamps, disability, unemployment, and other entitlements; force them off government checks; spend the money to retrain them; and place them in all these jobs that big business claims cannot be filled by Americans? If anyone (no matter how uneducated) can fill low-skill positions like home healthcare, nursing care, landscaping, and hospitality, then demand that millions of Americans get off welfare and take those jobs? That's a simple solution that rebuilds the middle class, reduces the debt (by removing people from the welfare rolls), and eliminates the need for immigrants to fill all these jobs.

But the politicians and the CEOs of big business want to keep wages low, and the best way to accomplish that is to add 12 million illegal immigrants to the workforce. According to Harvard economist George Borjas, our immigration policies have reduced American wages by $402 billion a year, while increasing profits for employers by $437 billion a year.[23]

Obama and the Obama Crime Family benefit, too, as sadly the immigrants don't understand that it's the politicians who are rigging the system to keep them poor, helpless, and dependent. That's how they buy votes. They addict the new immigrants to low-wage jobs so they will require government checks just to pay the bills and the rent.

But neither the politicians nor big business pays the true cost of immigration. Already billions of dollars are spent on illegal immigrants on education, healthcare, prison, and entitlement programs. It is estimated that just fraudulent tax credits for illegal immigrants cost taxpayers $4 billion per year.[24]

Obama and his Marxist cabal don't want immigrants to get educated, improve their lot in life, or start businesses. That would free them from the big government plantation. If they succeeded in America, they might join the middle class. They might even vote Republican! That possibility threatens their modern day Tammany Hall.

But big business and RINO Republicans like things the way they are, too. Big business wants these illegal immigrants uneducated, unskilled, and dependent on low-wage jobs from big corporations. That keeps wages low for American middle class workers, too.

Both political parties are fighting for dependency. They want the people dependent on either big government, or big business. Either way the people lose.

Billionaires like Warren Buffett

No, Warren Buffett is not a Marxist like Obama. Buffett has nothing against capitalism. He just wants to own everything, control everything, and possess all the power. Buffett has no political agenda. His favorite politician is…Warren Buffett. His favorite political party is…Warren Buffett. His favorite cause is…Warren Buffett. He's just another ego-maniacal billionaire who thinks what's his is his…and what's yours is his.

But make no mistake. He is one of the leading co-conspirators in **The Murder of the Middle Class**. For some in this conspiracy, it's about social-izing the economy. For others (like Buffett) it's just about rigging the economy to benefit himself.

Buffett fights for higher taxes on "the rich." Funny how he already has his $50 billion. Higher income taxes won't touch his assets. He gave President Obama a great line for the State of the Union address, complaining that our tax system is so unfair his secretary pays more in taxes than he does.[25] Buffett could choose to voluntarily pay more taxes if it bothers him. Instead, Buffett converts all of his income to capital gains to *avoid* taxes.

Worse yet, his company, Berkshire Hathaway, has fought the government over $1 billion in past due taxes for a decade. He wants the rest of us to pay higher taxes, but he has stalled a billion dollar tax bill since 2002.[26]

Guess who else is avoiding taxes? According to Citizens for Tax Justice, more than two dozen Fortune 500 companies including GE, Pepco, and Duke Energy paid zero income taxes from 2008 to 2011.[27] If gigantic con-glomerates like GE—whose CEO just happens to be Obama crony Jeffrey

Fighting for the Little Guy? No, the Big Guy Is Fighting for Himself

Warren Buffett lobbies for higher inheritance taxes, arguing that rich people like him aren't paying their fair share. Isn't that noble of him?

No, it's in his self-interest.

As Timothy P. Carney has pointed out, Buffett's Berkshire Hathaway actually profits from high death taxes. When the owners of small businesses die and their families can't afford to pay the inheritance taxes without selling off the business, Berkshire Hathaway—whose business is acquiring other businesses—can scoop those small businesses up at fire sale prices.[28]

Immelt—and billionaires like Buffett pay no taxes, guess who gets stiffed for the bill? That's right, the middle class and small business. Obama is determined to raise your taxes to make up for the billions not paid by billionaires. But then isn't that what best friends are for?

Small business owners and middle class taxpayers can't afford tax lawyers, fancy tax shelters, or legal estate trusts. The middle class is always stuck holding the bag for "tax increases on the rich."

Obama crony Jeffrey Immelt's GE also lobbied for the infamous incandescent light bulb ban. I guess GE really cares about the environment, right? Not according to the *Washington Examiner*. No, GE's profit margins on light bulbs were too low, and the bulbs were so simple to manufacture that GE was vulnerable to competition from small business start-ups. But now that regular incandescent bulbs are outlawed, we're forced to buy much more expensive "environmentally friendly" bulbs—which GE manufactures in China, having closed the Virginia plant where they used to manufacture traditional incandescents.[29]

The little people are regulated, mandated, intimidated, and taxed to death. Obama's plan is to make it so you can't compete, can't start new businesses, and can't expand your current business. His plan is to make it impossible for you to pursue the American Dream, leaving you hopelessly trapped working for crappy wages for his big business donors for the rest of your life. Remember, they want you running in place like a gerbil on a treadmill.

And his billionaire big business cronies are helping him implement that plan.

Buffett supported Obamacare. How convenient. It was recently announced that Buffett's newest corporate acquisition, Heinz, would make a 57 percent cut in retiree healthcare benefits.[31] Hypocrite Warren Buffett doesn't want higher taxes so he can pay more. He doesn't want Obamacare so that millions of poor people can get free healthcare. Buffett wants higher income taxes and healthcare taxes so none of us can ever catch up or compete with him.

Don't lose sight of the fact that that Buffett also pushed for government and the Fed to sprinkle $85 billion per month into the economy (with the confusing name QE). That just gave Buffett the best year of his life, while the middle class drowned under debt and declining incomes. Buffett's wealth went up a mind-boggling $12.7 billion in 2013. That's $37 million per day.[32]

> ## Fighting for the Little Guy? No, the Big Guy Is Still Fighting for Himself
>
> Warren Buffett fought against the Keystone Pipeline that would have brought cheap oil to America, and created thousands of jobs. Obama's continued rejection of the pipeline means that only railroads can ship the oil. Guess who owns the major railroad in America? Warren Buffett. Oh yeah, he's looking out for the little guy.[30]

To make the value of Buffett's stocks go up, the Fed destroyed your children's future. The fake money printed to benefit Wall Street and billionaires like Buffett is debt that middle class taxpayers and our children will have to repay, with interest. We're suffering, while the Wall Street bankers and Buffetts of the world are raking in the profits—from *The Murder of the Middle Class*.[33]

CHAPTER 7

The Motive

They speak like Marx, rule like Stalin and live
like Rockefellers while the people suffer!
—**Protest sign in Venezuela, February 2014**

DID YOU KNOW?
- In 2013 VA hospitals banned Christmas carols and Christmas cards containing "Merry Christmas" and "God Bless You"
- Obama's administration is allowing asylum seekers with "loose" ties to terrorist organizations into the U.S.
- Obama has promised $7 billion of American taxpayers' money to upgrade the electricity system in Africa

We've seen how Obama and his cronies in both parties are murdering the middle class. But what's the motive for the crime? Big business cooperates out of greed, but what's the thinking behind the plot itself? What can Obama and his political allies possibly hope to achieve by destroying the American middle class—the freest, happiest, most prosperous class of people the world has ever known?

As we go in search of a motive for the crime, the first thing to understand is that Barack Obama's whole way of thinking is completely out of step with middle class America. After all, when Obama got a paying job in

93

a private sector business after college, he considered it "working for the enemy."[1]

The evidence is that the president still considers the private sector and everything else associated with middle class America "the enemy." Just look at his administration's assaults on America's Judeo-Christian values.

Values Out of Step with America

A recent global study reports that the most persecuted, oppressed, and intimidated religious group in the world today is Christians.[2] Yet our president never says a word about persecution of Christians. He mentions discrimination and prejudice toward Muslims, but not one word about Christians being killed at the hands of Muslims.

In Egypt seventy churches were burned and many Christians killed by the Muslim Brotherhood in 2013, yet Obama said nothing. As a matter of fact, Obama's White House spokesman made a joke about the killing of Christians in Egypt.[3]

Unimaginable in America... until Obama came along.

While the murder of Christians does not cross any "red line," Obama was mortified when radical Muslims murdered other radical Muslims in Syria. That passed Obama's "red line."[4]

Unimaginable in America... until Obama came along.

Are you aware that during the 2013 Christmas season, VA hospitals banned carolers from singing Christmas songs; banned gifts if the wrapping paper contained the words "Merry Christmas"; and refused to accept delivery of handmade Christmas cards from local school children because the cards included the phrases "Merry Christmas" or "God Bless you"?[5]

Unimaginable in America... until Obama came along.

Are you aware that the budget deal for 2014 cut military retiree pensions? Nancy Pelosi said the "cupboard is bare." Yet in that budget was $300 million to pay the mortgages of Muslims in the Middle East. The money goes to the Overseas Private Investment Corporation in partnership with the Palestinian Authority.[6]

Unimaginable in America... until Obama came along.

Are you aware that Christian prayers have been banned at some military funerals?[7] Are you aware Christian military chaplains have been harassed and banned from praying in Jesus's name or reciting passages from the Bible?[8]

Are you aware the Obama administration has forbidden religious ministers from participating in prayer services on federal property?[9] Christian minister Franklin Graham believes the military's effort to ban him and other Christian leaders from the National Day of Prayer observance at the Pentagon "is nothing short of an effort to stamp out Christianity from the military."[10] Are you aware that at a routine meeting held at a Mississippi military base with 158th Infantry Brigade leaders, an "equal opportunity officer" said the Army may not use the word "Christmas"?[11]

Unimaginable in America…until Obama came along.

Are you aware that cadets at the Air Force Academy have had Bible verses they wrote on their own personal dorm room whiteboards forcibly erased? Military lawyers claim the first amendment of the U.S. Constitution (guaranteeing free speech) does not include the right of religious expression.[12]

Unimaginable in America…until Obama came along.

While Obama desperately wants amnesty for 12 million illegal immigrants (a.k.a. "future Democratic voters"), his Justice Department desperately and aggressively fought to deport an asylum-seeking Christian home-schooling family (with six children) from Germany. If sent back to Germany, they would have had their children taken away from them, or faced an unaffordable fine for the "crime" of home-schooling. Yet the Obama administration still pushed the courts to deport them. At the last minute the outcry from Christians across this country was so overwhelming that Obama backed off and let the family stay. Obviously he felt he had much bigger fish to fry than to risk a rebellion over one family. But the intent was clear: Christian home-schooling families are not welcome in America, while Obama rolls out the welcome mat for illegal aliens who vote Democrat.[13]

Unimaginable in America…until Obama came along.

Are you aware that in January of this year the Obama administration relaxed asylum standards for foreigners with "minor" ties to terrorist or insurgent groups? As long as you didn't personally kill an American or set off a roadside bomb, but merely supported a group that did, or attended their meetings, or worked indirectly for them, Obama welcomes you to America with open arms. A U.S. senator called this "deeply alarming."[14] As Dennis Miller observed on Monday Night Football, "There is no such thing as a minor groin injury." Well there is no such thing as a "minor" terrorist either.

Unimaginable in America... until Obama came along.

In February of this year the Obama administration allowed a radical Muslim cleric entrance into the USA for a seventeen-city hate tour at U.S. mosques. This cleric is on record as calling for the death penalty for gays... suicide bombings against Israel... and "holy war against Westerners and Jews." You can't make this stuff up.[15]

Unimaginable in America... until Obama came along.

Obama also tried to appoint a radical lawyer who volunteered to defend cop killers to head the Civil Rights Division of the Justice Department. The cop killer this radical lawyer wanted so badly to defend had murdered a wounded policeman in cold blood with a point-blank shot to his head. The nomination was so offensive that even the Democratic-controlled Senate refused to approve the president's choice (only because Democrat senators were worried about the elections coming up).[16]

Unimaginable in America... until Obama came along.

Then there are Obama's spending priorities. Under Obama our nation is so broke we no longer have the money for White House tours... or to train Top Gun Navy fighter pilots... or to keep illegal immigrant felons behind bars... or to keep pools open for military children to swim in the hot summer... or to fund flyovers by military jets at military academy graduations... or to pay for fireworks displays for children to enjoy at military bases. All of those things were cut in order to pay for spending cuts in the 2013 "budget sequestration."

Yet somehow we found $100 million for our president and his family to take a trip to Africa where he pledged $7 billion of our taxpayer money to increase access to electricity... *for Africans.* Our electricity bills are the highest in history, straining middle class budgets to the breaking point.

Yet Obama wants to give $7 billion of your money to foreigners to lower their electric bills.[17]

Unimaginable in America... until Obama came along.

None of this crisis, chaos, corruption, or anti-Christian policy should come as a surprise. Remember Obama's Democratic delegates booed God *three times* at the 2012 presidential convention. (If you don't remember, that's because mainstream media simply forgot to show that scene to you.)[18] Then a few weeks later, at a Democratic campaign event in Iowa, a Democrat activist actually opened a meeting with prayer—thanking God for the "blessing" of abortion.[19]

Unimaginable in America... until Obama came along.

Yes, my fellow Americans, America is being destroyed from within. Who needs terrorists? Obama's plan is so much more efficient.

The Mystery at Columbia

But it's still a mystery where President Obama's strangely anti-American values came from in the first place—and what exactly he hopes to accomplish by murdering the American middle class, which he obviously hates and resents so deeply. Fortunately, I'm in a unique position to explore those questions because of my time as a classmate of Barack Obama's at Columbia University.

After all, my classmates at Columbia didn't just hate capitalism. They were also atheists who openly despised Judeo-Christian values. As I will explain in more detail later, we spent our days learning, discussing, and debating a plan to destroy America from within—that's the "fundamental change" of America that Obama talked about during the 2008 campaign.

The murder of the middle class here in America started over thirty years ago at Columbia University. Nothing happens by mistake, or coincidence, or out of the blue. Obama was groomed to be the ringleader to lead this criminal conspiracy. It all started at Columbia.

To understand the present and predict the future, you must first understand the past. I believe Columbia holds the key to everything happening to America today. Columbia may not have been the only place Obama learned to hate America, (after all, he did attend Harvard Law School...and he also lived for a time in Indonesia, where he studied at a predominantly Muslim public school), but Columbia is certainly where he learned to *deceive* America.

Columbia is where Obama learned how to commit fraud and lie to get his way. Columbia is where Obama learned a plan to carry out his dream of destroying America from within. Columbia holds the key to everything. Once you understand Obama at Columbia, you'll soon understand everything that has happened to America in the past five years...and everything on the way in the remaining years of Obama's presidency.

The Ghost of Columbia University

The Obama story starts with the very question of his attendance at Columbia. Where was he? Why does virtually no one from Columbia remember the future president of the United States? Was Obama "the Ghost of Columbia"?

You might ask, "What do Obama's college days have to do with his presidency today? The answer is *everything*. By college, a person's personality, attitude, and behavior are usually fairly well set. That's why Obama's Columbia days tell us so much about his behavior as president today.

What do I know about Obama at Columbia? *Nothing*. I never met him. As I've reported countless times, I was a political science major and pre-law at Columbia from 1979 to 1983. Even though I thought I knew everyone in the political science department, neither I nor any of my friends at Columbia ever met or saw Obama there.

For five years now (since 2007 when it became clear Barack Obama was running for president), I've been quoted in the media as saying that neither I nor anyone I've ever known or met from Columbia can remember meeting or even seeing our college classmate Barack Obama. Don't you think the media should be asking questions? Isn't this a very strange story?

Obama and I shared the same major—political science. We were both pre-law. It was a small class, about 700 students. The political science department was even smaller (maybe 150 students) and was a close-knit group. I thought I knew almost everyone in this department. (They sure

A Professor's Testimony

I tracked down Professor Henry Graff at his home in Westchester County, New York. Graff is one of the most legendary and honored professors in the history of Columbia University. He was THE American History professor at Columbia for forty-six years. And he was ironically also THE presidential historian at Columbia. He is more emphatic than yours truly that there are no Obama footprints at Columbia.

I was put on Professor Graff's trail by another Columbia classmate skeptical about Obama's story. He told me that Professor Graff had been the speaker for the Class of '53 on the same weekend as my thirtieth reunion. My friend was watching Graff answer questions from the crowd when he was asked about Obama at Columbia. Graff said, "I have my doubts he ever went here." The crowd was stunned.

I did some digging and located Graff's home phone number. Now retired, he was delighted to hear from me. He agreed to go on the record about Obama. I was in several of Graff's classes, and Professor Graff remembered me, unlike Obama, and was thrilled to hear from a former student. He sounded great—like he hasn't lost any of his trademark sharpness in the thirty years since we last met.

I was honored to learn that this legendary historian has been following my political career for many years. But he had no such cheery things to say about the president. Graff said, *"I taught at Columbia for forty-six years. I taught every significant American politician that ever studied at Columbia. I know them all. I'm proud of them all. Between American History and Diplomatic History, one way or another, they all had to come through my classes. Not Obama. I never had a student with that name in any of my classes. I never met him, never saw him, never heard of him."*

Even more important, Professor Graff knew the other history and political science professors. *"None of the other Columbia professors knew him either,"* said Graff.

Graff concluded our interview by saying, *"I'm very upset by the whole story. I am angry when I hear Obama called 'the first president of the United States from Columbia University.' I don't consider him a Columbia student. I have no idea what he did on the Columbia campus. No one knows him."*

But there is a caveat. Graff knows Obama was accepted at Columbia. And he knows he graduated. Obama's name was on the Class of '83 graduation list. Like me, Graff just never saw Obama in between.

all knew me—I was known far and wide as THE one and only conservative at Columbia.)

But Obama left no memories, made no lasting impression on his classmates. Think about this for a minute. Our classmate is the president of the United States. Shouldn't someone remember him? Shouldn't someone at least *claim* to have hung out with him?

I know of only two possible sightings. In five years of my questioning Obama in the media, exactly two classmates have contacted me. One says he *thinks* he saw Obama once in a bar across the way from Columbia blowing smoke rings in the air. Another called to say he *thinks* he saw Obama in the cafeteria at Barnard (our sister school for women only). Perfect—two possible Obama sightings in thirty years . . . one in a bar, the other at a women's cafeteria. That's the future president.

Barack Obama is AWOL most of the time as president. So I'm sure he was simply AWOL most of the time at Columbia too. Nothing ever changes.

The problem is, Obama defenders and the media (I know, is there a difference?) interpreted what I said wrongly. I never said Obama didn't attend Columbia. I said he was never in class. I said that while it was strange that only one or two students, one professor, and one foreign exchange student (who was his roommate off campus) claim to have ever seen him at Columbia, they prove he most probably attended the university. I'm sure he wouldn't be the first college student to rarely, if ever, attend classes. I said he was like "the Ghost of Columbia."

What that means is simple. Barack Obama is exactly the same today as he was as a student at Columbia thirty years ago: arrogant and egotistical. He's either too lazy or thinks he's too smart to have to actually do the work expected of him. Nothing has changed in thirty years.

I'm sure he was rarely ever in class at Columbia because he had more important things to do. Besides, he already knew everything. Obama has always believed Obama is brilliant and better than the rest of us. What more could Columbia teach him?

It's the same today. He rarely attends important meetings. This past February he skipped two national security meetings focused on Russia's intervention in Crimea and potential invasion of Ukraine, a crisis that could have led to World War III. Yet our president chose not to attend. Do you think this is conservative propaganda or exaggeration? Hardly. Obama's absence from national security meetings was reported by many national media, including Reuters.

Why did Obama skip the first meeting? He chose to attend a White House Film Festival. Just like his days at Columbia University, Obama had more important things to do.[20]

Even if Obama isn't impressed by Russia invading Ukraine, certainly he finds America's jobs crisis important, right? *Wrong.* Obama could find no time to meet about the sky-high unemployment in America either. Even the leftist Huffington Post reported in July of 2012 that Obama had not convened a meeting of his own Jobs Council in six months.[21]

Politico updated the report in January of 2013—Obama never bothered to convene one meeting of his own Jobs Council in a full year, even with unemployment and under-employment at crisis levels.[22] Even more remarkable, within two weeks of that story, Obama closed down his Jobs Council—with 12 million Americans still counted officially as unemployed.[23] With over 92 million working-age Americans not working, and men suffering the lowest workforce participation rate since record keeping began, Obama thought it unimportant to even have a Jobs Council?

So what was so important in Obama's life? Golf and fundraisers. PolitiFact.com, the non-partisan fact checker, confirmed our president golfed ten times and attended 106 fundraisers during just the original six-month period when he could find no time or interest to attend even one meeting of his own Jobs Council.[24]

And, where was Obama the night of the Benghazi attack? Both Defense Secretary Leon Panetta and Joint Chiefs of Staff Chairman Martin Dempsey testified they only spoke with Obama once that night.[25] Four brave Americans died while Obama was paying little or no attention. What could be more important than a U.S. embassy under attack with American lives at stake? What could be so important that Obama never checked in to ask a question or discuss a rescue attempt from 5:30 p.m. Eastern time until the next morning (when everyone was dead)?[26]

Just like in his college days, Obama believes he's too gifted to do the actual work of president. He's just too busy to have to worry about unemployed Americans. He's just too important to have to bother to check in every night. He obviously thinks he's more important than four American heroes under savage attack thousands of miles away. He's just not too concerned about "the little people."

History will show that George W. Bush, the man the leftist media portrayed as "arrogant," "elitist," and "out of touch," played twenty-nine rounds of golf as president, until quitting in August of 2003 out of respect for the troops in harm's way.[27]

Meanwhile the media portrays Barack Obama as a "man of the people"—and he has played 163 rounds of golf and counting, while America is at war ... while Russia threatens WWIII ... while the economy is in shambles ... while millions have given up hope of ever working again ... while record numbers of Americans are living in poverty ... while black unemployment is double that of white ... while food stamps, welfare, disability, and all entitlements soar to record levels.[28]

Nothing much has changed since Columbia University. Not Obama's personality, not his attitude, not his behavior. We have a president who thinks of himself as too smart ... too gifted ... too important ... too busy ... to give a damn about his job, or the economy, or the American people.

Or perhaps he does give a damn. Perhaps he knows exactly what he's doing.

Where Was Obama?

I do believe Obama went to Columbia. Obama was just never in class with the rest of us because he was (and still is) arrogant. Obama has always "skated by" with his intelligence and ability to B.S. And I'm betting Obama was too busy smoking pot, attending communist meetings, and hanging out with terrorists like Bill Ayers, plotting the downfall of America and capitalism. Don't laugh, *__it's working__!*

While that is just an educated guess, it turns out Obama's own autobiography, *Dreams from My Father*, backs me up. In it he admitted often attending socialist meetings at Cooper Union in downtown Manhattan while attending Columbia. With Obama, even your wildest guesses are often proven true.[29]

Oh and don't forget the image of Obama in a bar on Amsterdam Avenue (across from Columbia) smoking a cigarette, drinking a beer, and blowing smoke rings in the air. I'm sure he spent quite a lot of time drinking at bars, pontificating on his own brilliance, while blowing smoke rings. That sounds exactly like our president.

Foreign Student?

But there is more to the Columbia story than the fact that no one ever saw Obama or remembers him. How did Obama ever get accepted into Columbia in the first place? Why are his college records sealed? What has he got to hide?

Obama has never had a problem ripping open the sealed records of his political opponents. Every step of his career Obama has beaten his opponents by either having sealed documents just happen to be publicly exposed by anonymous sources, or by questioning their records (see Harry Reid calling Mitt Romney a tax cheat).[30] But not Obama. His records are always unavailable and have never been leaked. Obama always seems to have powerful forces on his side.

So, why doesn't he release his college records? My educated guess as to why Obama won't release his academic records is because they will show he's a fraud. My theory is that his "birther" critics have it backward. Obama isn't a foreigner portraying himself as an American. He's an American who misrepresented himself as a foreigner to gain entrance to Columbia University (and probably Occidental and Harvard Law too). That would make him a fraud.

Is my educated guess hitting too close to the truth? In the spring of 2013, MSNBC television host Rachel Maddow spent fifteen minutes on her national television show attacking me and calling me a "birther."[31] I scratched my head. First, because the Obama-loving, Kool-Aid-drinking mainstream media must think I'm pretty important. Otherwise why spend fifteen minutes of valuable national television airtime attacking Wayne Root? If I was unimportant, you'd ignore me, right?

But Rachel Maddow wasn't alone. Little ole Wayne Root was attacked viciously by *The Daily Show*, *Mother Jones* magazine, and CNN's Piers

Morgan—all at the same time.[32] And don't forget the IRS attacks. It's clear that Obama's defenders thought my stories were dangerous to Obama. Someone thought I was getting too close to the truth and had to be discredited.

Second, why would Rachel Maddow feel the need to lie and slander me? I'm not a "birther." A "birther" believes Obama is a foreigner, not legally qualified to be president. I have never believed that. I've never once in thousands of media interviews ever discussed his place of birth.

I've always believed Obama is 100 percent American, as American as P. T. Barnum. And I'm guessing that he lies and exaggerates like P. T. Barnum too. While Obama is not a foreigner, I believe he is very likely a fraud. A fraud who got into Columbia University by lying and misrepresenting himself as a foreign student. How else could he have gotten in? You see, it's almost impossible to transfer into any Ivy League college. For example, I had a close friend who works at Columbia check with the admissions department. Last year only three students were accepted for transfer into Columbia. Three in the entire country. I'm betting they were all A students at the top of their classes at Harvard or Yale. Not slackers and pot smokers who rarely attended class at Occidental.

Obama had zero chance of being accepted at Columbia, unless he cheated—unless he committed fraud by concocting a story about being an Indonesian foreign student, with an exotic background. Columbia loves "diversity." Columbia loves to brag about accepting poverty-stricken students from far-away exotic places like Indonesia. Obama had attended school in Indonesia during his childhood and had the records (and I'm betting the passport and citizenship papers) to prove it. I'm guessing Obama jumped to the front of the line by committing fraud. That's why his college records are sealed.

It's also important to note that Obama admitted never spending any time with Columbia classmates who didn't fit his radical image. He only wanted to befriend foreigners and fellow communists. Obama wrote in his autobiography *Dreams from My Father*, "*To avoid being mistaken for a sellout, I chose my friends carefully. The more politically active black students. The foreign students. The Chicanos. The Marxist professors and structural feminists and punk-rock performance poets.*"

It doesn't take a psychology degree to figure out Obama's fragile, ego-centric mindset. He spent his youth living a fantasy, wanting desperately to be foreign-born and exotic, instead of just a normal American kid from a struggling single-parent household. As a black teen with no dad, Obama undoubtedly faced racism and tough times. With help from mentors (like Frank Marshall Davis, a Communist, and Bill Ayers, a terrorist) he learned to despise America, his country of birth. As a dreamer and loner, maybe he started to believe his own story of exotic birth and then used that fantasy (a.k.a. fraud) to gain admittance to college. Columbia probably asked very few questions. They were thrilled to have an Indonesian student to brag about. They got what they wanted: "diversity."

In too deep, Obama would have had no way out. Ironically, if my educated guess is correct, Obama himself is the world's biggest birther. *He* is the one who created the foreign-born storyline.

Since selling this fraudulent story had succeeded beyond his wildest imagination, Obama would have been emboldened. So he used it again to sell a book as a young man in his twenties. I'm not guessing here. It's a fact that his book agent described Obama to publishers as "Born in Kenya and raised in Indonesia and Hawaii." There is physical proof of these exact words. Bleeding-heart liberal Manhattan book publishers bought it hook, line, and sinker. Today Obama calls that a "mistake" issued by his book agent. But where did the agent get that story from? I've written nine books. Trust me, I know the drill. Agents and publishers get the author's bio directly from the author. They don't say a thing about your background without verifying every word.[33]

I would love for Mr. Obama to release his college records and prove me wrong. But of course he won't...*he can't.* Because at the top of his college admissions transcript would be the two words that would destroy his presidency and legacy: "Foreign Student."

No, I'm not a "birther." I believe Obama is 100 percent American born. My educated guess is that "the murder of the middle class" is being led by an American who started his Ivy League college career by committing fraud. Once again, nothing has changed. As president, Obama commits fraud on a regular basis.

The Motive for the Crime

So how does this story of fraud at Columbia explain Barack Obama's motive for murdering the middle class?

Is he doing it just for the perks—the posh trips, the enormous motorcade, the adulation of the crowds? After all, Barack Obama has ridden the story of his exotic parentage and upbringing to fame and fortune already: an Ivy League education, a bestselling autobiography, the presidency of the United States. He's used to cashing in on his story.

But I don't believe Obama just wants to enjoy the perks of the office and the profits from looting the middle class. The murder of the middle class is not just about a lazy president, it's also about an arrogant one, a man who likes to think well of himself. While Barack Obama *wasn't* attending class at Columbia, what *was* he learning?

He was learning to preen himself on a leftist world view completely at odds with the middle class America we know and love. At Columbia—possibly more in the bars and the late-night bull sessions than even in the classes—Barack Obama was picking up an attitude about America and a plan for transforming it from a prosperous middle class nation into something very, very different. I'll lay out the plot in the next chapter.

CHAPTER 8

Where the Plot Was Hatched

*By crisis, we mean a publicly visible disruption in
some institutional sphere. Crisis can occur spontaneously
(e.g., riots) or as the intended result of tactics....*
—**Richard Cloward and Frances Fox Piven**[1]

DID YOU KNOW?

- A Duke professor recently explained that white people's claims that we live in a "post-racial" society are more proof of white racism
- The Cloward-Piven plan was the idea of a leftist Columbia professor and his wife in in the 1960s
- The Cloward-Piven strategy was to collapse the welfare state by overwhelming it with claims beyond what the government could afford to pay, in order to bring about socialism

Barack Obama may not have attended class very regularly at Columbia, but I guarantee you he talked politics and philosophy all day long with the minority, foreign, and Marxist pals that he graced with his presence. (Remember I got my information about who his friends were directly from Obama's autobiography.) Obama certainly absorbed the flavor of political thinking at Columbia at the time. This is a remarkable story that you need to hear.

Do you remember when Geraldo opened Al Capone's vault live on national TV? Well I'm about to solve the mystery of Obama. I'm about to break "the Obama code." I'm about to tell you everything about the way Obama and the people around him really think. I'm about to rip the lid off the true Obama plan to destroy our country. Because I was there when the plan was hatched.

I debated the students at Columbia for four years. I came to understand their radical thinking and political strategy. I knew I was in trouble when the first political science class I attended at Columbia was "Communism 101" taught by Professor Trotsky in the Fidel Castro Building, at the corner of Marx and Lenin. I'm only half kidding. My experiences at Columbia were not far off from that description.

Everyone needs to hear my story because what Obama and I learned at Columbia explains EXACTLY what Obama is doing to America today.

The economy in deep decline; the disappearance of jobs; the annihilation of the middle class; the demonization of business owners; the destruction of small business with onerous regulations and taxes; the overwhelming debt and spending of out-of-control government; the millions of Americans losing their health insurance; and the unimaginable increase in welfare dependency and now free healthcare. It's all easily explained when you hear what Obama and I learned at Columbia.

America's decline under Obama isn't due to mistake, ignorance, or the incompetence of a community organizer. It's a purposeful, brilliant plan hatched at Columbia University to destroy capitalism, American exceptionalism, Judeo-Christian values, and the American Dream.

Did you see the recent news story about the white Duke professor who said white people are still racist, no matter what they say or do? The very fact that they claim America is a "post-racial" society is just more evidence of a "suave but deadly" ideology.[2] You probably thought, He's a sick, mentally ill man. To the contrary—this is exactly what is taught every day at the elite Ivy League universities in America.

This is exactly what most of the so-called intellectuals at colleges like Columbia, Harvard, Yale, Princeton, Duke, and Penn espouse all day long. This is exactly what Obama and I were learning back in 1981 at Columbia. All of us majored in "white guilt."

Nothing has changed in the past thirty years—except that the crazy leftist ideas have trickled down from the Ivy League to Duke—and to the White House. More students than ever are still being brainwashed by radicals, Marxists, communists, and America-haters trying to foment revolution, hatred, and class warfare—and one of those students is now president of the United States.

What Obama learned at Columbia matters. What Obama talked about back then matters. What Obama's college experience was like matters. It all offers us insights into the man he is today, into his beliefs and mindset. The answers will shock and frighten you.

My classmates hated America. They spoke nonstop about "unfairness," "inequality," and lack of "social justice." Recognize those words? They are central to every Obama speech and policy. They are central to Obamacare. They are central to Obama's desire for high taxes and income redistribution.

My classmates were proud to openly call themselves socialists, communists, and Marxists. Some even proudly used the word "Bolshevik." They talked all day long about how the "white power structure" had to be dismantled. They hated the rich and despised CEOs and business owners—especially white ones. This is especially interesting since almost all my Columbia classmates were spoiled-brat white kids from the best prep schools in America, where their brainwashing (and massive white guilt) must have started early.

They hated capitalism and believed it had to be destroyed so America's wealth could be redistributed to create "fairness and equality." This is the same nonsense spouted by Obama and his Marxist cabal today (although it's couched in much subtler words).

At Columbia we studied *The Communist Manifesto*, Saul Alinsky's *Rules for Radicals*, and the Cloward and Piven plan to transform America. After class and at lunch or dinner political science students constantly discussed and debated these ideas.

Notice the way Obama sneers at Republican leaders of Congress, as if he's morally superior? He spends more time talking to the leaders of Iran, Venezuela, and North Korea than he does to the Republican leaders of Congress.

That attitude was born at Columbia, too. In *The Ultimate Obama Survival Guide* I explained how in 1981 when a student burst through the doors of our political science class and screamed, "The president has been shot. They've assassinated Reagan," my classmates yelled, hugged, high-fived, and jumped up and down cheering what they mistakenly thought was the death of a Republican president. Today most of my classmates are either in government with Obama or controlling the mainstream media. They talk about "moderation and compromise," but I always remember how thirty years ago they cheered for the death of a Republican president.

But there's more. We were taught a simple but brilliant plan. My classmates discussed it 24/7. It was their "American Dream." It was called "Cloward-Piven," after Columbia professor Richard Cloward and his wife Frances Fox Piven. The Cloward-Piven plan aimed to bring down American capitalism by overwhelming the welfare system with massive spending, entitlements, and debt. Once the overwhelmed welfare state breaks the capitalist system, we'll have to implement socialism.

This is the *exact plan* Obama has been implementing. The center-piece is Obamacare. It will cause the economy to collapse, wipe out the

Do These Sayings Ring a Bell?

"I think when you spread the wealth around, it's good for everybody."

"If you've got a business, you didn't build that."

Taxing the rich is "about fairness."

All those ideas were pounded into us by our Columbia professors and my guilt-ridden classmates. By the way, these people so concerned about "fairness" almost all hailed from Scarsdale, Great Neck, Greenwich, and Manhattan (some of the richest places in America).

middle class, and bring Americans to their knees begging government to save them.

Obamacare isn't about healthcare. It's about bankrupting the middle class and addicting it to government dependency. It's about redistributing wealth from the middle class and small business to Obama's supporters. Its goal is to wipe out the last vestiges of middle class America and create a two-class society. Obama learned well; it's working to perfection.

So that explains the plan. But how do you implement it? We were taught that at Columbia too. A key component of the implementation involved fooling the voters by calling yourself "moderate" and a "uniter," even though you are a radical Marxist. We were taught to never admit what you really believe in. We were taught you should demonize your opponents, calling them words like evil, greedy, extreme, radical, and even "terrorist." Look in the mirror and call your opponents the very things you are. Obama learned well.

The plan taught us you should hide your true intentions (in other words—lie, misrepresent, commit fraud) because "the ends justify the means." That's what Obama does every day as president. Obamacare isn't about income redistribution; it's about "saving the uninsured." Government regulations aren't meant to wipe out small businesses; they're to "protect us from global warming." Amnesty for illegal immigrants isn't about creating 12 million new Democratic voters; it's about "fairness." High taxes aren't about starving Obama's political opposition; they're to "create equality." Obscene government spending is never about creating more debt to overwhelm the system; it's always about helping widows and orphans. Higher teacher salaries to reward terrible performance aren't to enrich teachers unions so they can funnel hundreds of millions to Democrat politicians; they're "for the kids." Bailing out GM wasn't to save bloated auto union pensions; it was to "save jobs."

Every now and then the mask slips, and Obama blurts out some element of the Cloward-Piven plot that is his real agenda: "So, if somebody wants to build a coal plant, they can—it's just that it will bankrupt them."[3] "I think when you spread the wealth around, it's good for everybody."[4]

But most of the time he remembers to lie to cover up the Marxist agenda of destroying the middle class, redistributing wealth, and putting big government in control of our every move. Why the lies? We were taught at Columbia that "It's for the greater good" and "We know what's best for the masses." Obama learned well.

That's why every Obama speech starts and ends with "I'm here to save the middle class," while his actions are annihilating them.

At Columbia we also learned never to let a crisis go to waste. And, if there isn't a crisis, **create one.** That was the original Cloward-Piven idea. Overwhelm the welfare system with demands. First the government spends more and more, and then an emergency is declared—and you can usher in socialism. You can see Barack Obama doing the same thing today: we must act now, the Democrats and their media allies argue; we must raise taxes before the debt destroys us. Those same Democrats have driven up that debt, but at that point politicians, even Republicans, panic and see little choice but to support tax increases—which of course was the goal all along.

It's a vicious cycle. The more spending, the higher the debt...the worse the economy, the more people become frightened...the more they depend on government...the more they demand government intervention to "save" them...the more government checks they need to survive...the more necessary it becomes to increase spending...the easier it is to argue we must raise taxes to pay for all the spending and raise the debt ceiling. Rinse. Spin. Begin the cycle again. Until the whole house of cards collapses.

This is how dependence is created.

So you see, the root (excuse the pun) of every Obama policy, everything Obama does, and everything happening to the U.S. economy, all started at Columbia. The entire Obama agenda to overwhelm the system, wipe out the middle class, bankrupt small business, and destroy capitalism, was hatched at Columbia. Obama may not have attended class, but he learned well. He should have received the Karl Marx Award for "Student Most Likely to Destroy America."

So that's why Columbia matters. It gave us the ringleader of the conspiracy to murder the middle class. You must know your enemy before you can defeat him. Columbia University is a window into Obama's soul.

What Obama learned at Columbia—hatred for conservatives, hatred for America, a desire to "bring down the capitalist system," as my classmates used to say, and the specific detailed plan to do it—obviously has great importance and relevance today. Obama learned well. As a grown man he is carrying that plan out right in front of our eyes.

Cloward and Piven's stated purpose was to bring on a crisis that the capitalist system could not survive intact, in order to usher in socialism.

Look around you. What do you see?

You've read the FACTS about America under President Obama: *Massive unemployment. Crushing debt. Exploding welfare rolls.* The crisis is here! Can you doubt that we're on the very verge of the societal transformation that Cloward and Piven were planning for—and that Obama learned the tactics for at Columbia? In the next chapter, we'll see exactly how Obama and his allies are creating the crisis—*to **murder the middle class.***

CHAPTER 9

The Murder Weapons

You never want a serious crisis to go to waste. And what I mean by that is an opportunity to do things that you think you could not do before.
—**Rahm Emanuel**[1]

DID YOU KNOW?

- The cost of new regulations in Obama's first term alone was $70 billion
- Since Obamacare took effect, health insurance premiums went up more than in the previous eight years combined
- In February of 2014 the CBO announced that an additional 2.3 million jobs will be eliminated over the next decade as a result of Obamacare

The Cloward-Piven plan that Obama is following to bring down the capitalist system and murder the middle class depends on fomenting a crisis that will undermine America. But Obama and his cronies aren't satisfied with ginning up just one crisis. They're attacking the middle class—and American prosperity—on all fronts. Their murder weapons are many and various, and they're using them all. *The Murder of the Middle Class* is like Colonel Mustard in the library with the lead pipe...and the dagger.... and the rope...and the candlestick, the wrench, and the revolver, too. In this chapter we'll run down the list of weapons Obama and his allies are using to destroy the middle class, starting with the unprecedented levels of debt that this administration is racking up.

Drowning Us with Debt

When I wrote *The Ultimate Obama Survival* Guide, Obama was already the biggest spender in world history.[2] And he just keeps racking up more and more debt. Obama is on track to add $12 trillion to the national debt—a staggering three times as much as Bush in his eight years as president.[3]

The "marketable debt" of the U.S. government has increased by 106 percent under Obama, increasing from $5.749 trillion at the end of January 2009 to $11.825 trillion at the end of January 2014, according to the U.S. Treasury.[4]

Obama has managed to accumulate more marketable debt in his first five years in office than all the other presidents who preceded him *COMBINED.*[5]

But the true national debt is not $17 trillion, as the media incorrectly reports to make us feel better. According to USdebtclock.org the true national debt is really much larger because of over $129 trillion in unfunded liabilities.[6] That adds up to over $400,000 for every man, woman, and child in America.

If the U.S. debt was stacked in dollar bills, it would stretch 1.1 million miles into space, five times the distance from the moon to the earth.[7]

Under Obama even the official national debt now exceeds the entire annual output of the U.S. economy (about $16 trillion).[8] When Obama was elected president the dangerous debt-to-GDP ratio was under 70 percent. Today it is over 100 percent.[9]

Obama is not only the first president in history to produce four consecutive years of deficits over $1 trillion,[10] but his deficits add up to more than was produced by all other presidents in history COMBINED. George Bush is not known for getting federal spending under control, but the national debt increased more in the first three years and two months of Obama's presidency than in the entire eight years of Bush's presidency.[11]

As I pointed out in *The Ultimate Obama Survival Guide*, the national debt jumped $328 billion in one day under Obama, more than the entire budget deficit for the year 2007 under President George W. Bush.[12] Because of all of this debt, the U.S. credit rating has been downgraded for the first time in history.[13] Expect many more downgrades to come.

But it's not just the government that is spending more money than it takes in. Obama's policies are driving private citizens in America and the world deeper and deeper into debt. Total public and private debt as a share of GDP in advanced economies across the globe is 30 percent higher now than before the Lehman Brothers financial crisis in 2008—the year Obama was elected president.[14]

And here's the really scary thing. Interest rates are being kept artificially low. Today they are the lowest rates in history.

Any increase in interest rates in the future will eat up the entire budget and send the U.S. economy into a death spiral—not to mention bankrupting

Historical Interest Rates

Terence P. Jeffrey of CNS reports,

- "In January 2001, when President George W. Bush took office, the Treasury was paying an average interest rate of 6.620 percent on its marketable debt."
- "In January 2009, when Obama took office, the Treasury was paying an average interest rate of 3.116 percent on its marketable debt."
- "In January 2014, according to the Treasury, the U.S. paid an average interest rate of only 1.998 percent on its marketable debt."[15]

Do a little basic math, and you can see that the average interest rate on the U.S. government's marketable debt is now less than a third of the interest rate we were paying in 2001, when our marketable debt was only about 25 percent of what we owe now. If interest rates were to rise up from the historically low rates they are at now, our economy would be destroyed and our children's future would be doomed.

the middle class. We're already struggling to keep up with the payments on our home equity lines of credit, our student loans, and our credit card debt. If interest rates go up from their historically low rates, we'll lose our houses, default on our student loans, and hope to discharge our credit card debts in bankruptcy court. *The Murder of the Middle Class.*

The Student Loan Quicksand Trap

Education used to be the way Americans worked their way into the middle class. Generations of poor Americans—from the early colonists to the pioneers who won the West to the immigrants who came through Ellis Island—took advantage of the wonderful educational opportunities available in America to learn everything they could and make something of themselves. They learned to read and figure in one-room schoolhouses on the prairie, or they were taught by nuns in crowded Catholic schools in Brooklyn. Americans scrimped and saved to send their children to college. They knew that education would allow their children to do better in life than they had—to achieve the American Dream.

But now, government is turning that dream into a nightmare. Education has become a weapon for murdering the middle class—turning Americans into poor dependents of the government.

Student loans are a trillion-dollar disaster sucking at the middle class like quicksand. You think student loans are a "service" by government to help you? How naïve. The coming student loan disaster will make the famous sub-prime loan scandal look small by comparison. And who will be left holding the bag? The middle class, of course.

Why does a college education cost so much? There is a one-word answer: "government." Because plentiful loans are available to anyone who asks, colleges can afford to jack up tuition and fees and pay professors and administrators $250,000 to $500,000 per year. (See U.S. Senator Elizabeth Warren who was making over $400,000 per year to teach at Harvard Law School,[16] after claiming she was an American Indian.) Those gigantic salaries are for teaching a few hours a week. Don't forget these people also get six-figure pensions when they retire.

But that's still not the biggest rip-off of this big business called "higher education." That honor belongs to the student—loan-inflated, unaffordable tuition that is beggaring the middle class.

As usual, the rich don't care. They can pay the over-priced tuition, and they don't have to take out student loans at high interest rates. Their parents pay the bill. The poorest students don't care either. They get scholarships and Pell grants based on "need," and they pay the lowest interest rates on their loans. So, again as usual, it's the middle class that gets the shaft.

Don't forget Obama also forgives all student debt for government employees after a certain amount of time on the job.[17] Drop out of the independent middle class, crawl into the government bureaucracy, and problem solved!

But there is no forgiveness for middle class kids who work in the private sector. Why are only government employees forgiven this debt? You know why. Politicians, ALL of them, are bought and paid for by public employee unions.

The rich can afford the bill. The poor don't get a bill. Government employee union members get special favors. But guess who pays "full freight"? The children of the middle class. Middle class parents make too much to be given any break in the price of tuition, yet too little to afford gigantic bills for a college degree that no longer guarantees a job.

A slow motion disaster is coming our way. Middle class parents and students are being crushed by the burden of paying off these student loans, with interest. And get this—you can't discharge student loan debt even in a bankruptcy. This government debt will crush you, and you can never make it go away.

And student loan debt is growing.

A recent study by Fidelity® reports that 70 percent of the college class of 2013 graduated with college-related debt, averaging $35,200.[18]

Fifty percent of the students in the study were shocked by the debt they had accumulated. Just under 40 percent would have made different choices if they had understood the amount of debt they'd have upon graduation.

According to the Federal Reserve Bank of New York, the total amount of student debt has increased by 275 percent since 2003.[19]

As I was writing this book, the overall total of student loan debt hit $1.08 trillion (with a T), the highest level in history.[20] That's the second highest form of debt in America (behind only mortgages). Not surprisingly, delinquent loans also hit the highest level in history at 11.8 percent.[21]

Student loan debt is on pace to be double credit card debt in two to three years. The middle class is being crushed by the weight of this burden. And when the house of cards collapses, guess who will get the bailout bill? Generations of middle class children and grandchildren.

No one seems to make the connection. The middle class is being ripped off with grossly over-priced tuition to pay for grossly over-paid educators, who then kick back the money in campaign contributions to the Democrats. Guess whose employees made the list of the top ten Obama contributors (by employees of any institution) in 2012? Columbia, Stanford, Harvard, and the University of California.[22]

Then, in order to keep this con game going, government passes laws that make you a slave to this debt for life. If students were allowed to discharge these loans in bankruptcy, they would (by the millions). Then government would be forced to get out of the student loan business. College educators who vote virtually 100 percent Democrat would either lose their jobs or have their bloated salaries and obscene pensions cut in half.

But the government and the colleges are going to be just fine—with all the rules rigged in their favor. It's the middle class that's going to have the crisis.

To add insult to injury, these are the same $250,000-per-year professors who are brainwashing your kids to love Obama, hate capitalism, and trust government like obedient little serfs. It's a vicious cycle.

The education system is big business. My alma mater, Columbia University, just announced on January 30 that its "Columbia Campaign" fundraising ended with $6.1 billion raised—one of the largest fundraisers in history.[23]

Why does a business that can privately raise over $6 billion require government help? The answer, of course, is that it doesn't. But just like other big businesses their lobbyists fight (and bribe) to carve out laws, regulations, corporate welfare, and government schemes that favor them—and fleece you. It's *The Murder of the Middle Class.*

Strangulation by Regulation

Under Obama and his co-conspirators, America has become "Regulation Nation."

Back in 2010 I was quoted in *Time* magazine: "It's time to call Obama what he is: The Great Jobs Killer. With his massive spending and tax hikes—rewarding big government and big unions, while punishing taxpayers and business owners—Obama has killed jobs, he has killed motivation to create new jobs, he has killed the motivation to invest in new businesses, or expand old ones. With all this killing, Obama should be given the top spot on the FBI's Most Wanted List."[24] *I told you so.*

But as bad as the taxing and spending are, Obama has an even more insidious and effective weapon for killing the economy and murdering the middle class: *Strangulation by Regulation.*

The Institute for Justice found that back in the fifties only one of every twenty workers needed a license; today, it's close to one out of three. And those licensing requirements make no sense. Becoming an EMT requires an average of only 33 days of training, while to be a cosmetologist you need 372 days.[25] That's not about safety; it's about putting up barriers to people who are just trying to make a living.

Those licensing requirements are at the state and local level, and then federal regulation gets piled on top of them. The cost of new federal government regulations for just the year 2012 was $23.5 billion. That's for 2,605 new regulations, according to the GAO (Government Accountability Office). That's more regulations in one year than in the entire first *terms* of Clinton and Bush COMBINED.[26]

In Obama's first term, the cost of new regulations was $70 billion.[27] That's just the cost of *new* regulations, separate from what businesses already faced.

As bad as taxes are, regulations are the number one killer of middle class jobs. No matter how high taxes are, you can always make more money. But you can't do anything to mitigate regulations. And you can't gain more time in the day. The cost of these regulations is millions of hours for American business—that's time you can never get back. If you're a small business owner, it seems like half of your life is wasted filling out forms and complying with ever-increasing regulations. That's time you could have been active in your business producing products and services to make your customers' lives better, creating jobs, making money—or simply playing with your kids.

Those same regulations cost so much that small business owners either are discouraged from ever starting a business, or can't expand the business, or must lay off employees, or are forced out of business. In all four cases, jobs are killed. There is no positive job creation from regulations. Even the federal government's own Small Business Administration estimated in 2010 that regulations were costing small business $1.75 trillion.[28]

Regulations are insidious stealth weapons. They allow the Obama Crime Family to destroy the economy and murder the middle class without admitting what they're up to. They can't say publicly that they want to kill jobs, drive small business out of business, and destroy the great American middle class. But they can say that they want to create a new "green jobs" economy, or that they want to extend coverage to uninsured Americans. Then, once the regulations are in place *Surprise!* nobody can afford to build a coal-fueled power plant, and electricity bills skyrocket. Or millions of Americans have their suddenly "substandard" healthcare plans (that they were perfectly happy with) cancelled.

Big business has no problem with regulations. In fact they're happy about regulations because regulations drive their small business competitors out of business.[29] Read Timothy P. Carney's *The Big Ripoff* for numerous examples of big businesses that have welcomed and even lobbied for new regulations on their own industry.[30] Big businesses have armies of employees and lawyers to deal with new regulations. Or they move jobs offshore. So all that's left inside America to save middle class jobs is small business. Small business makes up 99.7 percent of employer firms and 63 percent of new private sector jobs.[31] Small business is our last hope. Yet small business is being strangled by regulations. Small businesses are left defenseless. They don't have armies of lawyers, accountants, lobbyists, and compliance officers to face the onslaught of big government regulations. It's a losing scenario. Few small businesses can survive strangulation by regulation.

Meanwhile, regulations inflate the price of everything we buy, and put the middle class lifestyle increasingly out of reach. Food, utilities, clothing, housing, transportation—you name it, it's more expensive because of government regulations. (Just imagine how cheap gas could be if the president would approve the Keystone Pipeline—and allow drilling on federal lands that are shut off to exploration for oil and natural gas.)[32] Regulation makes prices go up partly because of the costs businesses have to pay just to comply with the regulations. And it's partly because the regulations are a barrier to small business competitors; the regulations leave the big companies in control of the market, so they can charge us higher prices. That's exactly what happened when incandescent light bulbs were regulated out of existence. No wonder GE, whose CEO is Obama crony Jeffrey Immelt, lobbied for the ban on the traditional light bulbs that used to cost about seventy-five cents apiece. Now GE and a handful of other big businesses have a captive market for "green" light bulbs. The cheapest of those costs about eight times the price of an incandescent bulb. (You're supposed to save money because the new bulbs use less energy and last longer. But the reality doesn't always live up to those promises.)[33]

A 2008 study commissioned by the Small Business Administration estimated the annual compliance price for all federal regulations at $1.7 trillion that year. How can anyone keep up with all these regulations? How can any non-lawyer avoid violating some obscure law among tens of thousands? That's the point. Small business is being put out of business. And now, under Obama, hundreds of more *new* regulations are strangling small business and the middle class.[34] But the mother lode of new regulations is the president's healthcare "reform."

The Ticking Time Bomb: Obamacare

Quit calling Obamacare a failure. It's already a raving, rollicking success, and it's on the verge of succeeding even more brilliantly. You see, Obamacare was never meant to help America, or heal the sick, or lower healthcare costs. It was meant to be a ticking time bomb that would go off—conveniently, after Obama was reelected—and destroy the American middle class.

The RINOs and GOP establishment are either naïve, dumb, or complicit—or perhaps being blackmailed. In any case, they just don't get it.

Obamacare isn't a failure. The GOP establishment needs to stop calling Obamacare a "trainwreck." That means it's a mistake or accident. That means it's a gigantic flop. And it's NOT. Obamacare is a brilliant and purposeful attempt to damage the U.S. economy, kill jobs, bring down capitalism, and murder the middle class. Its goal is to bring us to our knees, so that we capitulate and agree to accept big government. And it's working.

The GOP is so stupid or corrupt that they either can't or won't see it. The only mistake with Obamacare is that the website didn't work. But that was just a bump in the road. Obamacare is back on track and working just the way it was intended to. This is a planned, purposeful attack. The telltale sign: the devastating effect the new Obamacare taxes are having on the economy.[35] The death of full-time jobs.[36] The gargantuan amount it will add to the debt.[37] The dramatic increase in health insurance rates—the highest in years.[38] The dramatic increase in deductibles.[39] The large number of doctors now thinking of retiring—bringing on a healthcare crisis of unimaginable proportions.[40]

Even one of Obama's biggest supporters—UNITE HERE, a healthcare workers' union that was the first union to endorse Obama for president—is pointing out that ". . . the ACA [Affordable Care Act] threatens the middle class with higher premiums, loss of hours, and a shift to part-time work and less comprehensive coverage."[41] Fox News said the union report "concludes that the law will transfer a billion dollars in wealth to insurance companies, uneven the playing field in the market, force employers to cut back on hours and result in pay decreases."[42] The union's report is entitled "The Irony of ObamaCare: Making Inequality Worse."[43] Thank you, union friends of Obama. I couldn't have said it better myself.

Even Obama's own internal White House studies reported from the beginning that 40 to 67 percent of those in the individual insurance market would lose their health coverage.[44] So obviously that was the plan.

Obamacare is succeeding on all counts. Remember, Obama's goal was never to heal the sick or save healthcare, it was to destroy capitalism by overwhelming the system with spending, entitlements, taxes, regulations, and debt. Boy has he succeeded. Here, in detail, is what Obamacare was created to do:

#1) Obamacare is intended to bring about the Marxist dream—redistribution of wealth. The middle class is being robbed so the money can be redistributed to the poor, who vote Democrat. If you're middle class, your rates (and taxes) are much higher. Why? Because in addition to your own healthcare costs you now have to pay for 40 million others who are getting subsidies and free Medicaid. You are stuck paying for everyone. *Brilliant.* According to the CEO of the prestigious Cleveland Clinic, 75 percent of Americans who enrolled in Obamacare now have higher premiums.[45]

#2) Obamacare is intended to wipe out the middle class and make us all dependent on government. Even Obama's own IRS predicts that health insurance for a typical American family will be $20,000 per year by 2016. How can middle class Americans possibly hope to spend $20,000 on health insurance and have anything left for food, housing, and basic transportation—let alone to send their kids to college, or ever go on a vacation? But if you drop out of the middle class, you can get a subsidy on the Obamacare exchanges. If you go on welfare, you can get free Medicaid. This is how you make middle class people dependent on government. That's how you get them addicted to government checks. *Brilliant.*

Even more insidious, Obamacare creates a glass ceiling for the middle class. One of my readers sent a note pointing out that the Obamacare subsidy on his state healthcare exchange cuts off right at $62,000 per year for a family with two adults. That means if a husband makes $31,000 per year and a wife makes $31,000 per year, and one of them is offered a $1,000 raise (bringing their combined income to $63,000) they would have to turn the raise down. Because a $1,000 raise would cost them their $10,000 Obamacare subsidy, therefore reducing their take-home pay by $9,000. How about a $20,000 raise? Well you'd gain $20,000, but you'd lose $10,000 in Obamacare subsidies, plus have to pay federal income taxes, state income taxes, and Social Security taxes on the extra $20,000. If you live in a high-tax state like New York or California, you could have next to nothing left out of a $20,000 increase in income. Obama has created a law that locks people into low wages and government dependency. *Brilliant.*

#3) As a bonus, Obamacare rules are intended to kill full-time, decent-paying middle class jobs. Obamacare ensures that the only jobs created from this time on are part-time or temp jobs.[46] Why? To make double certain the middle class is trapped with no way out. To make sure no one has the $20,000 per year to pay for health insurance, thereby guaranteeing they become wards of the state. *Brilliant.*

#4) Obamacare creates shared misery—a horrible healthcare system for all of us. Shared misery... that's how socialism works. Rather than some people, who work hard to afford it, having great healthcare, while others don't, socialized medicine destroys the healthcare system for everyone. Now we all share in the misery of a system with poor care and long waits. Of course, the mega-wealthy can always buy the best. Just be assured that Obamacare guarantees quality healthcare will be priced out of the range of the middle class. *Brilliant.*

#5) Obamacare is intended to bankrupt small business and starve the GOP of donations. Do you know a small business owner? I know hundreds of them. Their rates are being dramatically increased by Obamacare. Guess who writes the checks to Republican candidates and conservative causes? Small business. Even if a small business owner manages to survive, he or she will no longer be able to write a big check to the GOP. Money is the mother's milk of politics. Without donations, a political party ceases to exist. *Brilliant.*

#6) Obamacare is intended to make big business even richer and more dominant. Government is demanding that we buy health insurance from billion-dollar insurance companies. They've handed health insurance companies 30 to 40 million new customers and in many cases government is paying the bill. Where does government get the money? From middle class taxpayers. Even the Congressional Budget Office (CBO) projects that over $1 trillion will be redistributed from taxpayers to insurance companies.[47]

But wait, it gets worse. Obamacare has a built-in BAILOUT for insurers, just to make sure any losses from giving away healthcare for "free" to the poorest and sickest citizens are fully covered. A bailout is already in place. Who pays for the bailout? Middle class taxpayers. Billions of dollars are being redistributed from the middle class to billion-dollar multinational corporations.[48] *Brilliant.*

Guess who gets even richer than health insurance companies? Pharmaceutical companies. Government is now buying drugs for 30 to 40 million new patients. But that isn't all. Obama bribed Big Pharma with even more goodies. They received assurances from Obama that the government would bar lower-cost Canadian drugs from entering this country, thereby costing middle class consumers tens of billions, perhaps hundreds of billions in higher drug costs.[49]

Who gets the bill for more expensive prescription drugs? Middle class consumers. Who gets filthy rich through the power of government? Big business, big insurance, Big Pharma, and Obama's biggest donors. This is how you create a two-class society. *Brilliant.*

But there's an even bigger bonus built into Obamacare for big business. Obamacare encourages big companies to drop health insurance, so employees can find "better" policies on the Obamacare Health Exchanges. What a great bribe to big business. Billion-dollar companies are now off the hook for health insurance for lower-paid, unskilled employees, most of whom will get government subsidies. And the bill? It gets handed to middle class taxpayers.

Do you question this is actually happening? Big companies like Target, Home Depot, and Trader Joe's have recently announced they are dropping health insurance for part-time employees.[50]

#7) Obamacare is intended to make the IRS and government employees' unions even more powerful. Obamacare adds thousands of new IRS agents. It puts the IRS in charge of overseeing 15 percent of the U.S. economy. Because of Obamacare the IRS has the right to snoop into every aspect of your life, to withhold your tax refund, to fine you, to frighten you, to intimidate you. *Brilliant.*

If the IRS oversees healthcare, what stops them from refusing to pay the bills of the political opponents of the president? Will they let Obama's critics like me die—by refusing to pay for the proper medical tests, drugs, or surgery? Will the bills just happen to get lost in the mail? Will they intimidate and persecute a sick Tea Party activist until he or she dies from the stress? This is the same IRS that tried to ruin the lives of Tea Partiers with audits. This is the same IRS that audited a Stage-4 terminal cancer victim after he appeared on Fox News to criticize Obamacare. Do you trust that they won't harass, intimidate, and persecute sick conservatives?

#8) Obamacare is intended to make doctors "agents of the state." Doctors will now be in charge of asking questions about your health and sexual history. Guess who wants those answers? Government. That information is now in the hands of Obama and his cronies, who can use it to blackmail critics, or persuade dangerous opposition candidates to withdraw from the race, or force Republicans in Congress to support bigger government. *Brilliant.* If you don't think this could happen, you are naïve.

#9) Obamacare is intended to unionize 15 million healthcare workers. Fifteen million new union workers produces $15 billion in new union dues. That money goes to fund Democratic candidates and socialist causes, thereby guaranteeing Obama's friends never lose another election. *Brilliant.*

#10) Obamacare is about creating an elite privileged class, blessed by Obama with special rules. Select government employees, senators, congressmen, congressional staff, big business, big donors, and big unions all demanded (and most got) exemptions or huge subsidies in Obamacare.[51]

But the middle class and small business have no exemptions, choices, no options, no way out. If we don't pay, we are fined and the IRS can grab our tax refund. Different sets of rules for different people.[52] *Brilliant.*

#11) Obamacare is intended to make government more powerful than religion. Government replacing religion is a key feature of every socialist or communist society. So Obamacare is demanding that even religious institutions must pay for abortion-causing morning-after pills and other services to which they are morally opposed—under penalty of law.[53] *Brilliant.*

I'm not here to lecture about morality. But I am here to tell you that government has no right to force a church, religious institution, or private business owner to provide or pay for services that they find immoral and against everything in which they personally believe. Obama says otherwise. It is obviously his opinion that government rules supersede private religious beliefs. Obama is putting government above God.

#12) Finally, Obamacare puts government in control of our lives through regulation. Obama has perfected a novel and insidious form of socialism. There is no need for government to "socialize" the economy or to take ownership of your business. Obama has figured out how to control business through onerous regulations. You may own it, but the government controls your every move. *Brilliant.*

The massive wave of Obamacare regulations already implemented to take control of 15 percent of the U.S. economy is just the start. The worst is yet to come.

As I was writing this book a new report warned of the "avalanche" of regulatory burden still to come. There are twenty-eight major Obamacare regulations that have not yet been finalized. Their cost in time and money? 45.7 million burden hours, meaning it would take 22,800 employees working full time at 2,000 hours per year to deal with this blizzard of paperwork. The cost will be $1.4 billion.[54]

And that doesn't include the armies of new lawyers, government bureaucrats, and new IRS employees to police it, who will try to fine you to justify their jobs.

You might ask, "If these are the hours and cost for twenty-eight new regulations, what is the total cost of all Obamacare regulations?" In a previous analysis prepared by the American Action Forum, the facts are that Obamacare imposes 645 million hours of paperwork, 4,116 new federal forms, and $35.3 billion in costs.[55]

Folks, do you get it? This is a Marxist nuclear weapon that's going to explode in a mushroom cloud that will destroy our lives, our jobs, our businesses, our healthcare, and our capitalist economic system. Obama learned well from Saul Alinsky. Even Lucifer himself could not have invented such a perfectly evil weapon to murder the middle class.

Postscript: The Collapse of America Accelerates

No sooner had I finished writing this chapter than the CBO (Congressional Budget Office) released a devastating report. A report that proves true everything I've ever predicted about Obamacare. That was just the start of a frightening, shocking, sickening month that revealed Obama's cards. The mask is off. If this doesn't define "accelerated collapse," I don't know what does. Obama is obviously in a rush to finish the job.

First, let's examine that report from the non-partisan CBO. They courageously unmasked Obamacare as the perfect job-killing machine. Millions have already been downsized from full-time to part-time work, and now we know from the CBO that an additional 2.3 million full-time jobs will be eliminated over the next decade.[56]

But it is the reaction of Obama's defenders to the CBO report that tells us all we need to know about Obama's goals. The CBO courageously pointed out that Obamacare makes it less likely millions of Americans will want to work. Obama's defenders actually celebrated that "choice." They painted it as a wonderful development that middle class wage earners and small businesses would pay for all those who want to be freed from the need to work so they can enjoy their free time and pursue their hobbies.[57] I call it what it is...Marxism and *theft*.

The cat is out of the bag. It's time to stop treading lightly and being politically correct. Join me in calling Obama's murder of the middle class what it is. This is communism, pure and simple. Anyone who thinks "the American Dream" is to choose not to work and collect a government check is reading directly from Karl Marx. Anyone who thinks some people should have a "choice" not to work, by stealing the money of hardworking taxpayers, is reading directly from *The Communist Manifesto*.

But the month from hell was only getting started. Next Obama illegally rewrote his own Obamacare law *again*. He gave a one-year exemption to businesses with fifty to ninety-nine employees, conveniently postponing the cancellation of millions of employee health insurance policies until after the 2014 elections.[58]

Mimicking the traits of communist dictators, Obama obviously believes he can change any law he wants, at any given hour, of any given day. The Constitution says only Congress makes laws. But Obama doesn't care.

But it gets worse. As part of this new illegal Obamacare directive to postpone the law for businesses with fifty to ninety-nine employees, Obama put the IRS in direct control of critical U.S. business decisions. He demanded that businesses must justify hiring and firing decisions to the IRS to qualify for the exemption. Employers must swear on penalty of perjury that they didn't fire anyone to get under the ninety-nine-employee metric.[59]

Plain and simple, putting government in charge of the business decisions of private companies is the very essence of communism. It is how communist economies like North Korea, Cuba, the old Soviet Union, and East Germany have always been run—and run into the ground.

Later that month we found out that health insurance premiums are up more since Obamacare took effect than in the previous eight years COMBINED.[60]

And we're only getting started. Health insurance industry officials report some premiums will double again in 2014 and 2015.[61]

This was just one month in early 2014. The terrible news is coming in waves. Our president is hardly hiding the fact that he is a tyrant, dictator, and communist, who hates capitalism, Judeo-Christian values, and America.

The mask is slipping. The murderer of the middle class is revealed, and we know exactly how he's committing the crime. Obama no longer cares to hide his radical Marxist ideology. From here on out it's "pedal to the metal" in the destruction of America.

The question is... *Who will stop him?*

CHAPTER 10

Braveheart:
Forward to the Past

There's a difference between us. You think the people of this coun-
try exist to provide you with position. I think
your position exists to provide those people with freedom.
—Sir William Wallace in *Braveheart*

I've said it before, let me say it again. History repeats, and those who fail
to study history are destined to fail.

This past holiday season I sat with my sons to watch a "guys'
movie." It's our annual holiday tradition. We chose the movie *Braveheart*.
It's my favorite movie of all time, but this was the first time I had watched
Braveheart since Obama became president. It was an eerie experience
because I realized that we are watching history repeat. *Braveheart* is the
story of America today—the middle class fighting for its very survival.

The plot of *Braveheart* is the story of Scotland's battle for freedom and
self-determination against the powerful British empire. It's the same battle
America's middle class and small business are fighting today against Washington, D.C.

The hero of *Braveheart* is Sir William Wallace, a passionate, enthusiastic, heroic, and principled leader and warrior. Wallace didn't fight for
personal gain. He fought only to achieve freedom for his people and he was

willing to die for that cause. **The Tea Party is today's embodiment of Sir William Wallace.**

The Tea Party does not fight for corporate interests, but only for the people. The Tea Party believes in limited government; believes that people should keep more of their own money (that they earned); believes the people shouldn't have to work until they are dead just to pay off the government's debt; and believes in giving more power to the people.

The evil villain of *Braveheart* is the king of England, Edward Longshanks. **Today the embodiment of King Edward is Barack Obama.**

Just like Obama today, King Edward was out to control the people lock, stock, and barrel. Just like Obama, King Edward believed his subjects' money was his money. Just like Obama, he believed that every decision should be made by government, every conversation should be listened to, and the people's rights and weapons must be confiscated as a threat to his rule.

And just like Obama, King Edward was arrogant, egomaniacal, and vicious. King Edward stopped at nothing to hide his true intentions. He repeatedly broke his word to set up his enemies for defeat (and death).

King Edward was a liar—just like Obama:

- "If you like your health care plan, you can keep your health care plan."[1]
- "I can assure you that I certainly did not know anything" about the IRS persecuting conservative and Tea Party groups.[2]
- Obama "did not know" that the U.S. Ambassador in Benghazi had requested more security.[3]
- Obama on what caused Benghazi: "Here's what happened.... You had a video that was released by somebody who lives here, sort of a shadowy character who—who made an extremely offensive video directed at—at Mohammed and Islam. . ."[4]
- Obama on Fast and Furious: "I heard on the news about this story that fast and furious, where allegedly guns were being run into Mexico and ATF knew about it but didn't apprehend those who had sent it."[5]

- Obama's NSA "did not discuss with President Obama" the fact that they were snooping on world leaders.[6]
- The White House website: "President Obama is committed to helping America's small businesses grow and prosper."[7]
- Obama: "What matters most to me right now is the impact that rising [gas] prices have on you."[8]
- Obama's press secretary: "Other than press reports, we have no knowledge of any attempt by the Justice Department to seek phone records of the A[ssociated] P[ress]."[9]
- Obama: "I'm a warrior for the middle class."[10]
- Obama: "This is the most transparent administration in history."[11]

Obama puts King Edward to shame. Obama must have been the model for the old joke about lawyers: "What's the definition of a good lawyer? He can tell you his client is innocent without smiling."

Our own King Obama must have taken notes from King Edward. He tells the people anything to distract them while he takes control of our lives and livelihood. He uses the power of government to get his way, to silence dissent, to steal our property, to control our lives. Obama uses the government as a weapon to intimidate and persecute his own people. The IRS, NSA, EPA, SEC, FDA, ATF, DOJ, DHS—you name the three-letter government agency and it is at war with the people it is supposed to serve and protect. The "civil servants" have become the masters.

Like King Edward, Obama's every policy is aimed at creating a two-class society—leaving only the super-rich (in the king's days called "royalty" or "nobility") and the masses ("serfs"). Tyrants can only survive in a two-class society where the super-rich are easily bribed and the poor are beholden to government for survival.

The super-rich will sell out the middle class for an extra dollar in a nanosecond. And of course tyrants love the masses of poor folks—because, ironically, keeping them helpless, hopeless, and clueless makes them dependent on government, the very institution that destroyed their middle class life in the first place. The poor huddled masses and serfs now have little choice but to vote for the tyrant who keeps the government checks coming.

A smart king keeps his supporters happy. He makes the richest richer. He hands out checks to the poor. Desperate people thank him for the crumbs.

The only group a tyrant can't abide is the middle class. It has to go. Just like in *Braveheart*, the middle class doesn't fit into the plans of a tyrant like Obama. The middle class is not easily bribed. They believe in personal responsibility. They will stand and fight for things like God, country, the Constitution, American exceptionalism, and Judeo-Christian values. They are willing to die for those principles.

Obama knows that. Remember his words during the 2008 presidential primaries. Obama said, "You go into these small towns in Pennsylvania and, like a lot of small towns in the Midwest, the jobs have been gone now for 25 years and nothing's replaced them.... it's not surprising then they get bitter, they cling to guns or religion or antipathy toward people who aren't like them or anti-immigrant sentiment or anti-trade sentiment as a way to explain their frustrations."[12]

Just like King Edward in *Braveheart*, Obama must eliminate the middle class, the "bitter clingers" to the rights and freedoms that made the country great. They must be driven into poverty. That's how you get them to cling to government, instead of guns or religion.

Braveheart is like today's America in one other important way. For hundreds of years the noblemen of Scotland sold out their own people through "negotiating" and "compromise." The excuse of these frightened cowards, traitors, and sellouts was that the Scottish people could never defeat the powerful British army. Or so they justified their cowardly actions. *Why try? We're better off compromising. It's better for the people.*

That was the excuse. But in reality these noblemen sold out the people for their own personal gain—titles of royalty, land, and fancy estates. **The noblemen of *Braveheart* are embodied today by establishment GOP leaders in Washington, D.C.**

Just like today's GOP leadership, the Scottish rulers cut deals and "compromised" with the king of England to turn the people (the middle class) into serfs. The people got nothing, while the noblemen got rich and fat, all the while acting like they were the friends of the people. History repeats.

The good news is that *Braveheart* had a happy ending. After centuries of slavery, cowardice, and traitorous behavior by their leaders, the Scottish people rose up and defeated the British. Starving, outmanned, and out-numbered, the peasants defeated the "unbeatable" British army and won their freedom—inspired by Sir William Wallace.

With the Tea Party leading the charge, the same outcome is possible today, but only if it leads with the same passion, intensity, enthusiasm, and principles of Sir William Wallace.

Only if we defeat the negotiating, compromising, country club Repub-licans (i.e., noblemen) who sell us out every day in D.C. and shudder, shake, and genuflect whenever King Obama walks into the room.

These are the same country club Republicans who show up at a gunfight with knives. They are the same people who sell out the middle class for a committee chairmanship, or millions of dollars in corporate campaign con-tributions. If they lose reelection after doing the bidding of the D.C. elite and crony capitalists, they get a lobbying job, law firm partnership, or millions deposited into a Swiss bank account. That's how the game is played today.

We will only win if we understand that our opposition is playing for keeps, with a purposeful plan to destroy our country, capitalism, economy, freedoms, and most importantly, the middle class. The American Dream is being extinguished; the middle class is being murdered.

And we must understand that our GOP "defenders" are too docile, fearful, or naïve to fight back; too "country club elite" to even understand what is happening to the middle class; or too concerned with amassing a fortune to secure their constituents' future (just like the noblemen of Scotland). In other words, they've sold us out.

As in the days of King Edward, the goal of this conspiracy is to enslave your children and grandchildren to big government, big spending, big taxes, and the loss of all privacy and civil rights.

So, just like William Wallace realized, it's time to fight back. That's what Part Two of this book is about.

It's time to fight fire with fire. It's time to find a Sir William Wallace for our times. A leader with passion, fire, and fighting spirit. A war leader. This is a war to save the heart and soul of America—the middle class.

It's time to stop bringing a knife to a gunfight—and bring a rocket launcher. It's time to call the people who are trying to take the American Dream away by their proper names: traitors, thieves, tyrants, elitists, Marxists, Fascists, socialists, and communists.

It's time to fight with passion and enthusiasm, and to throw caution to the wind. It's time to fight like a cornered wolverine. It's time to fight with a daredevil attitude that comes from knowing your freedom, your life, and your family's future depends on it.

Because it does.

Saving the Middle Class... the GOP...America... and *YOU*

When the solution is simple, God is answering.
—Albert Einstein

Now you understand Obama and the murder plot that's being carried out right in front of your eyes.

The crucial question is: Who will save the great American middle class...and our country?

YOU will. You and millions of middle class Americans like you...we just have to wake up in time and fight back! It may seem like a daunting task...but

I'm here to show you how we can get it done.

Part Two of this book is about solutions. This is the good news! You've already gotten the bad news under your belt. You've already taken the first step toward rescuing America—you've waded through the horrific FACTS about how and why our president and his allies are destroying the biggest, most productive, most prosperous middle class the world had ever seen.

Now I'll show you how to fight and WIN. How to take back America. How to take back the Republican Party and use it as the vehicle to save the middle class. And most important, how to save yourself and your family. Here comes the fun part!

This book is not just about the problems. It's about the solutions:

- Solutions for saving capitalism and the U.S. economy
- Solutions for saving and strengthening the Republican Party so it can save the country
- Solutions for saving and protecting the middle class and the individual—meaning YOU

Why the Republican Party? Because like it or not, I believe, at this time, the GOP is the only vehicle at the voting booth capable of keeping the OCF (Obama Crime Family) and its co-conspirators from succeeding at the murder of the middle class. Trust me, I don't have any illusions about the GOP. I'm well aware of the Republicans' flaws. I even ran as a third-party vice presidential candidate in 2008, for the Libertarian Party. But if the middle class and the economic freedoms that created it are going to be rescued from the murder Obama and his cronies are plotting, we are going to have to elect more Republicans—there is no other practical way to defeat Obama & Co. at the voting booth.

All the solutions I'm going to propose have one thing in common: they require action, individual action by YOU! I hope that after reading this book, you will understand your most dangerous course of action is to take no action. Now is not the time to get distracted. Now is not the time to "tune out" politics. Now is not the time to study the life of Justin Bieber. Now is not the time to get discouraged or give up because the situation appears hopeless. Most important, now is not the time to be complacent, or sit back and hope others will save you.

Now is the time to take action.

The solutions I'm about to present will empower you with the knowledge, passion, spirit, political know-how, inspiration, and financial wherewithal to save this great country...if you act on them. And at this point a little prayer wouldn't hurt either. God gave us the greatest nation in world history. God blessed America. He will be needed to help us take it back.

Many politicians, Democrats as well as Republicans, may bemoan what is happening to this country. But because they don't have the common sense, or the courage of their convictions, and don't want to risk offending any voting bloc, they speak in generalities, reluctant to offer specifics. What America needs now is not cowards and politically correct politicians afraid of offending someone and losing the election.

America needs bold, courageous risk-takers. *Leaders.* Small steps won't save America. Visionary leaders willing to face reality and take big, bold steps and political risks are what's desperately needed to save the middle class and the American Dream.

If we can't get leadership from our politicians, then it is time to VETO them all—Vote Every one of Them Out. It's time to find new leaders who fit the bill. The power to elect those leaders is in YOUR hands.

Here are the solutions. Buckle up. Snap your chin strap in place. Hold on for dear life. Some of you may be shocked. Some of you may be offended. I don't care. It's time to be bold, tell the truth, and take action.

CHAPTER 11

Your Elevator Pitch

I have never said that low-information voters are stupid. . . .
It's not that they're stupid or don't understand the issues.
They just haven't had it all explained to them.
—Rush Limbaugh

Are you ready to **take action**? In this chapter I'm going to lay out what you need to do to get started saving the middle class. I'm going to show you *exactly* how to take the first step to resist what Don Obama, the Obama Crime Family, and their willing co-conspirators in the media and big business are up to. But first, let me give you the reasoning behind that first step.

Most people who read my books are open-minded and ready to hear the truth. They already lean in my political direction and, for the most part, are informed voters.

Unfortunately, that means I'm preaching to the choir. I will have a very limited effect on the uninformed and closed-minded, who would rather watch *American Idol* and TMZ than think about the state of the country. They have more interest in Justin Bieber and Lindsay Lohan than in national healthcare, government spending, and taxes. Unfortunately those are the very people who need to be reached, if we're going to have any chance of saving the middle class. That means the job of reaching these uninformed voters is up to... YOU. The fact is, you are just as important as me. If America is to be saved, if our children are to be saved, you will have to be one of the saviors.

If all the time, thought, effort, and heart and soul that has gone into the writing of this book is to be effective, it will be up to you to go to your friends, family, and into your community at a grassroots level to pass on the truth. It will be up to YOU to inform and educate on a one-to-one basis. It will be up to you to evangelize with passion and emotion and stories that get people's attention, inform them, and change their minds. It will be up to YOU to stop "the murder of the middle class" and save the American Dream for your children and generations to come.

To help you accomplish your vital mission to save the middle class, I have written this short chapter to provide you with what we in sales and business call "The Elevator Pitch."

The point is... assume you find yourself in an elevator with Donald Trump, or Bill Gates, or Sir Richard Branson, or the guys from *Shark Tank*. This is a once-in-a-lifetime opportunity. But you only have one to two minutes to make your case. If you succeed, they'll fund your business plan, and your life will change forever. But if you fail to move, interest, and excite them, your life goes back to exactly where you were two minutes ago, and the opportunity is gone forever.

Politics is no different. You have one to two minutes (max) to make your pitch. But instead of Donald Trump, it's the average voter. They have a short attention span. But if you succeed in convincing them of the value of your view, candidate, or party, it changes your life, your children's future, and your country forever. ***You'd better sharpen your pitch!***

Democrats excel at sales. Let's face it, their sales pitch is an easy one to put over: "Whatever you want, I'll give it to you FREE!" If dentists were Democrats they'd tell kids, "You can eat all the candy and junk food you want, from breakfast through dinner. Have a good time." Boy, that's a tough sell. If parents were Democrats they'd tell kids, "School is boring. Skip school today and go smoke some pot, get drunk, and pick up girls. Hang out at the park with your friends, or go to the mall. You're only young once. Here's $100." Tough sell, huh?

Your sales pitch is a little more difficult. You need to be the adult in the room. You need to point out there is no such thing as a "free lunch." There's always a price. Sometimes accepting "free" goodies or doing the "easy thing" damages or ruins your life. You need to be able to say "No" and present a commonsense solution that is best for everyone, not just today, but for the future. Long term...eating sugar all day isn't a good plan. Long term...smoking pot, drinking, and picking up gals or guys at the mall isn't a good plan. It doesn't end well. And neither will the free-goodies-for-everyone path that Obama has put our country on.

Remember, the attention span of the audience you are trying to reach is very short, so tailor your pitch accordingly—direct and to the point. I can assure you it will do no good to get into arguments with the closed-minded. All you can do is present the FACTS...the truth...the emotional stories that leave them with an impression...and hope they see the light themselves.

It is a daunting task, but if we are to save the middle class and the American Dream, it is a task to which we must all commit ourselves. We all have to "get in the game." We all have to wear out the shoe leather. You have to put in the same kind of effort that made you the winner you are today into this rescue mission for the middle class. Don't sit silently by and watch the murder of the middle class or the enslavement of your children and future generations to a life of shared misery because you were tired, or bored, or depressed, or worn out. You are the last hope for America and your family.

So for your never-say-die sales pitch, here are ten important "Talking Points" that you can use on those around you from the time the elevator door closes, until it opens at its destination.

Talking Point #1: The progressive policies of the past five years have murdered the middle class. Under Obama the net worth of the average American is down 40 percent and average income is down more than $4,000 per year. Even worse, gas, electricity, grocery, health insurance, and education costs are all exploding while your income is shrinking (with no end in sight). That's *if* you still have a job. Is this the American Dream? Is this what you want for your children's future? If this keeps up, will there even be a middle class left? **Throw the bums out!**

Talking Point #2: Ten million Americans have left the workforce since Obama became president. Over 100 million Americans are receiving some form of welfare. More Americans collect government checks than work full time year round. Real unemployment (counting those under-employed and those who have given up) is in the range of 15 to 20 percent. Obama spent a shocking $3.7 *trillion* on welfare in the past five years. How is this plan working for the middle class? **Throw the bums out!**

Talking Point #3: "If you like your doctor, you will be able to keep your doctor, period. If you like your health care plan, you'll be able to keep your health care plan, period." *Sure you will*! Obama stole your healthcare and your money to redistribute to his voters. He blatantly lied and committed fraud. Now your premiums are higher, if you still have insurance at all. The insurance industry says premiums will double *again* later this year or next. This is exactly how you murder the middle class. **Throw the bums out!**

Talking Point #4: Detroit has been under Democrat rule, with Obama's exact progressive game plan, since 1962. It is a bankrupt, abandoned, violent, poverty-stricken, debt-ridden, uneducated third world hellhole. The middle class of Detroit has been destroyed. Implementing this same strategy nationally will turn America into one big Detroit. Do you want Detroit to come to a city near you? **Throw the bums out!**

Talking Point #5: Debt is the primary weapon for the murder of the middle class. It's a silent killer. You can't see it, or feel it, or hear it. But it's like rising water threatening to overwhelm the economy and drown you—and your children's future. Every child is now born owing over $400,000.[1] This debt is due to unsustainable government spending, entitlements, corruption, and lies from the politicians. Bush added $4 trillion to the national debt; Obama will add $12 trillion by the time his second term is up.[2] Isn't it time to stand up for your children? **Throw the bums out!**

Talking Point #6: The stock market is up. Happy days are here again, right? *Except they're not*. The government is printing trillions in fake money to make stocks go up. But all that fake money is debt, owed back by our children. Your future is wrecked in the name of corporate welfare, bribery to the biggest political campaign contributors, and crony capitalism. The rich get richer, but the middle class is stuck with the bill. This is what socialists do to murder the middle class. Look no further than Venezuela. Their economy is a carbon copy of what's in store for America.

The Venezuelan stock market is enjoying all-time record highs, while the people are starving in the streets amidst food and toilet paper shortages. The middle class and small business have been wiped out. Is this the future you want for America's middle class? **Throw the bums out!**

Talking Point #7: Spain turned itself into "The green energy capital of Europe." The result: a collapsing economy, massive debt, no jobs, no future. Green energy and greenhouse standards have so destroyed the European economy that the EU just dropped its "renewable energy" requirements. It sounds nice to "protect the environment" and "go green" and "help the kids." But the results are proven. Instituting draconian environmental regulations and a "green economy" is the murder of the middle class. Are you ready to sacrifice your job, triple your energy bills, and destroy your middle class quality of life in order to "go green"? All of this to make some politically connected crony billionaires richer, while the rest of us lose everything? **Throw the bums out!**

Talking Point #8: Obamacare is succeeding—at driving premiums and deductibles sky high, denying patients access to their doctors, un-insuring Americans who used to have insurance that they were perfectly happy with, and putting us in the fast lane to socialized (i.e., really terrible) medicine. **Throw the bums out (along with Obamacare)!**

Talking Point #9: States with the big government, big taxes, and big spending—e.g., New Jersey, New York, Connecticut, and Massachusetts—are plagued by unemployment, poor economic growth, and moving vans moving out. Why? Because big government, big spending, and big taxes always murder the middle class. Do you want your state to continue on this path? You already know the results. **Throw the bums out!**

Talking Point #10: Single moms tend to vote Democrat.[3] Many of these women have stories about men who lied to them or mistreated them. Well a man has lied to you again. A man has mistreated you again. Is the economy better? Are there more jobs? Is your salary higher? Are your health insurance costs down? Is your life better? How's your job security? More of the same policies will not help. With the lies Obama has told and the results his policies have produced, you have to be suffering from "Bat-tered Spouse Syndrome" to continue voting for more of this. **Throw the bums out!**

This is your elevator pitch. Pick the one or two points that apply most to those you're trying to save from their own ignorance, lack of information, or media brainwashing. Memorize them. Practice them. Rehearse them. Sell them with PASSION. Start spreading the news!

God Bless you and your families. God Bless America.

You're off to a running start at saving the country, the, economy, the GOP, the middle class, and YOU!

CHAPTER 12

The Seinfeld Strategy

If every instinct you have is wrong,
then the opposite would have to be right.
—Jerry Seinfeld to George Costanza

DID YOU KNOW?

- Obama spent almost a trillion dollars on a failed stimulus package that failed to stimulate the economy
- 14.7 million more Americans were on food stamps in the month of Obama's reelection than in January 2009, when Obama became president. Only 194,000 net new jobs were created
- Obamacare is the biggest tax increase in history

Remember *Seinfeld*? It was one of the most successful TV series in the history of American television. The show revolved around Jerry Seinfeld and his buddy George Costanza. George was the ultimate loser. Everything he did was a colossal failure.

One day that all changed. George was hired by George Steinbrenner and the world champion New York Yankees. He had hit the lottery—overnight he had a great job, power, money, and beautiful girlfriends. Jerry is in shock. George explains how he turned his life around overnight from complete loser to incredible winner. I'll quote directly from the script of the *Seinfeld* episode titled "The Opposite":

> It all became very clear to me sitting out there today, that every decision I've ever made in my entire life has been wrong. My life is the complete opposite of everything I want it to be. Every instinct I have in every aspect of life, be it something to wear, something to eat…It's often wrong.…
>
> …. A job with the New York Yankees! This has been the dream of my life ever since I was a child, and it's all happening because I'm completely ignoring every urge towards common sense and good judgement I've ever had. This is no longer just some crazy notion, Elaine, Jerry. This is my religion.[1]

As one of America's strongest critics of President Obama, I am constantly asked, "What would you do differently if you were president? Do you have any solutions?"

The answer is simple. *EVERYTHING.*

I'd do everything differently from President Obama. It's the Seinfeld strategy. *Do the OPPOSITE!*

Obama is George Costanza. Every decision he makes poisons America, capitalism, and the middle class. Obama is killing the American Dream. The solution is so simple. To save America we only have to do the opposite of everything Obama is doing.

Obama's agenda of big government, big spending, big unions, and big debt is driving the American economy to never-before-imagined levels of economic disaster, debt, unemployment, and small business failure. After reading this book, you now know that this is not due to inexperience, amateurism, incompetence, or ineptitude. (Well, maybe a little incompetence is thrown into the mix. See the defective, dysfunctional Obamacare website.)

Instead, it is due to a well-conceived and well-executed plan to destroy capitalism, the great American middle class, and the American way of life. Therefore the answer to saving America and turning around this economy is simple: do the EXACT OPPOSITE of everything Obama does.

Obama spent almost one trillion dollars on a stimulus package and billions more on bailouts. The middle class somehow missed being bailed out, and the economy doesn't seem all that stimulated. But the spending covered Obama's priorities: bribing the poor voters addicted to government checks, paying off his political donors, and bribing big business to support bigger government. We need to do the opposite. It is time to ban all versions of stimulus, bailouts, earmarks, and corporate welfare. They are nothing more than pork barrel spending to buy votes and reward the cronies of the political class. Even as I'm writing this, Congress has just passed another $1-trillion-per-year "Farm Bill." Eighty percent of the spending goes to food stamps.[2] The balance is simply pork (pure bribery) to ensure the special interest political donations keep pouring in.

From the month Obama became president up until November 2012, on net, *seventy-five* new people started getting food stamps for every *one* new job that was created. That's 14.7 million more Americans on food stamps versus 194,000 new jobs.[3]

We should do the opposite: cut waste, spending, corporate welfare, and political bribery. And get people off food stamps!

Obamacare is imposing the biggest tax increase in history[4] and placing most of the tax burden on small business owners and the middle class. Opinion? No, it's fact. Remember, Obamacare has now increased health insurance premiums more in one year than the eight years previous *combined!* All that pain falls on middle class families.[5]

We should do the opposite. Middle class taxpayers and small business owners are the heroes of our economy—they create most of the jobs (that generate most of the taxes). My plan (which you'll soon be reading about) includes rewarding the taxpayers and job creators with a one-year NITV (National Income Tax Vacation). The cost would be about the same as Obama's failed stimulus fiasco, and it will turn this economic bust into one of the great booms in world history—just as Reagan overnight turned the disastrous Jimmy Carter economy into the greatest economic expansion in world history.

Obama has named czars to oversee every aspect of Americans' personal and business lives. We should do the opposite: fire them all…and ban czars from our government forever.

Obama has dramatically increased the size, scope, power, and spending of government, through so-called "reform" of healthcare and banking. We should repeal those fraudulent "reforms" and do the opposite—dramatically decrease the size of government and put more money and power in the hands of the citizens (and the states—where power and decisions are closer to the people). We should cut overpaid government employees by the millions, freeze all raises, and cut their obscene salaries and pensions. They are bankrupting America.

Obama and his Marxist cabal would say, *It's impossible to cut spending or the size of government without damaging the economy.* Well, perhaps they should ask Canada about that. In the 1990s Canada was in major economic trouble, with huge deficits and debt. Their solution? Canada dramatically cut spending, reformed "untouchable" entitlement programs, downsized government (from 53 percent to 39 percent of GDP), laid off tens of thousands of government employees, and turned their government finances around without any tax increases. The budget deficit was eliminated and turned to surplus, the national debt was cut in half, the economy exploded, and Canada led all the G7 nations in job creation. That led to tax cuts. Today Canada's economy is humming. Like I say, we should always do the opposite of Obama.[6]

Obama is spending billions on our failing public education system to reward his teachers union campaign contributors. We should eliminate the Department of Education, move education funding to the state and local level, and encourage vouchers to give parents the freedom to pursue alternatives such as home-schooling and private, charter, and religious schools. We must restore power to administrators to hire, fire, and grant raises to teachers based on performance, not tenure. We should pay teachers more—but only the good ones!

Obama supports the Federal Reserve and encourages them to print ever more money, devaluing our currency and stealing every American's savings. We should do the opposite: audit the Fed, make it transparent and accountable to the people—with an eye to eliminating it as soon as possible.

Against all reason, Obama has stalled the Keystone Pipeline for five years and counting.[7] He has made millions of acres of land off-limits to oil drilling.[8] He responded to the Gulf of Mexico oil disaster with an oil-drilling moratorium costing thousands of good jobs.[9] As I was finishing up this book, Bloomberg reported, "EPA Takes First Step Toward Regulating Fracking Chemicals."[10] Get ready for Obama's Environmental Protection Agency to regulate fracking out of business—just like they're doing to the coal industry.

If we want to save the middle class, we should do the opposite of every decision Obama makes about energy.

The Texas Oil & Gas Association just reported that the AVERAGE salary for their 416,000 employees in 2013 was $120,000 per year.[11] This is how you save the middle class—by creating high-paying energy jobs and at the same time dramatically reducing energy bills. Only if you wanted to murder the middle class would you reject the Keystone Pipeline, ban drilling, fight fracking, and regulate coal into extinction.

Obama is adding thousands of new IRS agents[12] as taxes, regulations, and IRS audits become ever more burdensome for small business owners. We should aim to streamline government bureaucracy, dramatically cut regulations, encourage and reward small business job creators, and make sure no politician can ever again use government agencies like the IRS to reward their friends or punish their foes.

Obama has treated friends such as Israel harshly, while treating evil rulers that support terrorism (in Iran, North Korea, Syria, Cuba, Venezuela, Muslim countries) with kid gloves. We should do the opposite—treat friends with respect, and not give enemies the time of day. We should also eliminate foreign aid to despots and adversaries of America across the globe.

I'm the Founder of AARP—Americans Against Rotten Politicians. Congress has become a home for career politicians like Pelosi, Reid, McConnell, and Boehner who care more about their position and power than the welfare of this country. We should support term limits and throw all the lifetime politicians out of D.C. It's time to start over.

Finally, Obama has continually violated the Constitution, governing by executive order without and even against the will of the legislature. We should ensure that the U.S. Constitution—the greatest governing document ever created—is respected and followed.

Yes, Obama is our very own George Costanza, the lovable loser of *Seinfeld* fame. Except that Obama is a Marxist and he's not lovable. Obama is leading America toward tragedy, insolvency, and bankruptcy. The answer to saving America is clear, simple, and effective: **START BY DOING THE OPPOSITE OF EVERYTHING OBAMA DOES.**

But to do that—in order to have the chance to turn America around the way George Costanza's life was miraculously transformed when he quit following his wrong-every-time instincts—we are going to have to start winning elections. And take it from me, Wayne Root, former Libertarian Party vice presidential candidate: whether we like it or not, the only practical vehicle for doing that is the Republican Party. So let's look at how we can save the GOP from its worst instincts and turn it into the perfect Tea Party–infused vehicle for winning elections, turning the country around, and saving the middle class!

CHAPTER 13

Saving the Republican Party from Itself

Courage is not simply one of the virtues
but the form of every virtue at the testing point.
—C. S. Lewis

DID YOU KNOW?

- Seventy percent of the $10 billion bet on the 2014 Super Bowl was bet on the Broncos, but I advised my clients to bet on the Seahawks—because of the "12th man"
- Obama's poll numbers have sunk to Richard Nixon levels
- Chris Christie became an Obama pal and attacked Ted Cruz, Rand Paul, and the Republican Congress—only to be investigated by the Obama administration for "misusing" storm Sandy relief money

I t's time to save the Republican Party. Why? We cannot save the middle class or change America without a vehicle for winning elections. The GOP is that vehicle.

The problem is the GOP is a flawed vehicle. The Republican Party has lost its way. Worse than that, the Democrats have taken the initiative and the high ground by defining the GOP as "the party of the rich." It's a brilliant strategy to incite class warfare, hate, and jealousy; divide the electorate; and fool the middle class. And they have executed it well.

But as my father told me so many years ago, *"The GOP is not the party of the rich; it is the party of anyone who wants the opportunity to be rich and successful, or wants their children to have the opportunity to be rich and successful."*

In other words, we are the party of unlimited opportunity. We are the party of economic mobility. We are the party that allows everyone to dream big. We are the party that gives your children the opportunity to do better than you. That, folks, is a positive message to win elections. And winning elections and putting the right people in important positions of national leadership is the only way to save the middle class and the American Dream.

Winning with the Tea Party— the 12th Man of the GOP

The Seattle Seahawks won this year's Super Bowl in one of the most lopsided beatings in sports history. Few saw it coming. Over 70 percent of the $10 billion bet on the Super Bowl in Las Vegas (and illegally across the USA) was bet on Peyton Manning and his Denver Broncos. But I knew better.

Perhaps many readers don't know that I began my career as a Las Vegas oddsmaker and sports handicapper. I was so successful the media dubbed me "the King of Vegas" and I was awarded my own 180-pound granite star on the Las Vegas Walk of Stars. This was before my political career ever began.

Today my career centers on politics, but I still have a thriving sports prediction business with thousands of clients who pay for my advice. This past February 2 I gave my clients my strongest possible "play" on the Seattle Seahawks to win the Super Bowl. Why was I so confident the Seahawks would win? Well there is a fantastic lesson here for the GOP.

Politics has more in common with sports than most people realize. In both politics and sports, winning is everything. And in both these endeavors, winning is about energy and enthusiasm. There are thirty-two teams in the NFL. The difference between winning and losing is razor thin. How did one team—the Seattle Seahawks—rise above the battlefield and dominate this season? The Seahawks are a model for the valuable and unique role of energy and enthusiasm providing a winning edge.

Seattle gets its energy and enthusiasm from "the 12th man"—their crazed fans. Each football team has eleven men on the field. The "12th man" is an invisible energy force produced by the fans—giving a team energy, inspiration, and momentum. It is a well known fact in sports that fan intensity creates momentum. It changes the outcome of games.

Seattle has the loudest, proudest, craziest fans in all of sports. The Seattle fans are so loud they once caused an earthquake—literally.[1]

They own the Guinness Book of World Records for loudest fans. Their cheering is as loud as a jet's engines. Prolonged exposure at this level can cause hearing damage.[2]

The Seahawks are the only NFL team to fly a "12th man" flag—to represent and acknowledge the importance of their fans.[3] Boeing has even created a "12th man" 747 airplane.[4] Seattle celebrates and embraces its most loyal fans. The Seahawks understand that without the energy of their crazed fans, they'd be just another NFL team. That "12th man" is the razor thin "winning edge" Seattle needed to win the Super Bowl and become one of the great teams in NFL history.

Who is the GOP's 12th man? Well it sure isn't the green-jacket-wearing country club Republicans... or the "moderate" wishy-washy stand-for-nothing Northeast Republicans... or the cowardly Washington, D.C., Republicans who want to apologize to Obama every time he walks in the room... or the fat-cat Republican consultants who tell their candidate clients not to personally attack their opponents for fear of being called "racist" or "extreme."

To paraphrase the famous line from the days of Bill Clinton, "It's the Tea Party, stupid." The GOP's energy, enthusiasm, and courage are found in the true-blue, patriotic, conservative base called the Tea Party. The GOP's "12th man" has the same qualities as the Seattle Seahawks fans—a faith in victory…a belief in the right principles…a love for party and country…a passion for the fight to save America…an intensity and energy found nowhere else. The Tea Party is the razor thin "winning edge" that can make the Republican Party winners.

Like in the NFL, winning is very difficult in American politics. We are living in a nation sharply divided. Every election is decided in a few key districts and battleground states. Elections are won based on intensity, energy, and turnout.

Like Seattle's "12th man" the Tea Party led the GOP to an earthquake win—literally. In 2010 the GOP shocked the experts by winning a historic record-setting landslide victory. It was due to the incredible energy and intensity of the Tea Party.

But this is where the stories diverge. The GOP needs to learn a lesson from the Seahawks. Seattle embraces their most loyal and intense fan base—whereas the GOP establishment does not.

The biased leftist mainstream media worked hard at branding the Tea Party as "extreme," "radical," "crazy," and even "terrorists." This was a purposeful plan right out of the Saul Alinsky playbook. The left knew they needed to slander, denigrate, and destroy the Tea Party before the Tea Party could stop Obama's agenda.

Obama and the Democrats weren't alone in this goal to destroy the GOP's "12th man." Big business was central to the plan too. As outlined earlier, big business loves big government and the crony capitalism that comes with it. Big business loves corporate welfare and the thousands of draconian regulations that make it difficult for small business (without big business's armies of lawyers, lobbyists, and accountants) to compete. So big business, their lobbyists and lawyers, and the Chamber of Commerce all got into bed with Obama and the mainstream media to try to slander and ruin the Tea Party.[5]

But it doesn't stop there. GOP establishment leaders like John Boehner, Mitch McConnell, John McCain, Karl Rove, and Chris Christie openly show their contempt for the Tea Party as well. At best, this is because they believe the GOP can win only if they run moderate, compromising, establishment candidates. At worst, the GOP establishment is scared stiff that the Tea Party will throw these compromising RINO Republicans out of office by running true patriotic fiscally conservative constitutionalists against them in primaries.

The problem is, the GOP can't win elections without their "12ᵗʰ man." We are the GOP's "winning edge."

The GOP needs to learn a lesson from the Super Bowl champion Seattle Seahawks. The GOP must celebrate and embrace their loyal base of fans. Love your "12ᵗʰ man." Feed off our intensity. Only our energy, enthusiasm, and passion will lead you to victory. We are the GOP's pounding heart...*on steroids.*

Without us, you're just another losing party.

Wanted: GOP Leaders with Guts

All the GOP leadership needs at this juncture in history is some courage. To win, the GOP needs the enthusiasm of millions of true-blue conservatives energized about the sorry state this county is in—i.e., the Tea Party. So the GOP needs leaders who are brave enough to embrace the Tea Party, instead of quaking in their boots about associating with people the Democrats and the mainstream media call "extreme" or clinging to their own positions and perks at the expense of victory. Without courage, your good intentions and even your principles are useless—you'll give them up as soon as you're in a tight spot.

I have two great examples of how you take victory. You don't wait for it. It will not be handed to you. You can't wish or hope for it. You must take it. BOLDLY.

Let's start with the Civil War. More specifically, with the Battle of Gettysburg. I'm a war buff. And there is no greater story of "seizing victory" than that of Colonel Joshua Chamberlain.

What makes the story so remarkable is that Chamberlain was just a college professor from Maine, with no military experience. Yet he led a regiment into battle at Gettysburg. He was ordered to defend a small hill named "Little Round Top." What he did that day helped turn the tide for the Union. His efforts led to the victory at Gettysburg, which in turn changed the course of history. The North won the Civil War and Chamberlain's actions were the catalyst.

With union forces under heavy attack and about to falter...with his men outnumbered, in disarray, running out of ammo and about to retreat, Chamberlain ordered a counterattack with only bayonets. He was surrounded and outnumbered, yet rather than retreat, he ATTACKED! This crazy bold move emboldened his own troops, while it shocked and confused the Confederate forces. The small unit under Chamberlain's command charged right at the larger force. Down to their last men, without even ammunition to fire at the enemy, this small force turned the tide. The shocked Confederates were caught off guard and captured.

The Union went on to win the battle of Gettysburg. It was the turning point of the Civil War. Chamberlain received the Medal of Honor, the highest award for bravery in the United States military. He was promoted to brigade commander and then general. Chamberlain served in twenty battles and numerous skirmishes, was cited for bravery four times, had six horses shot from under him, and was wounded six times, even once given up for dead by surgeons.

Chamberlain's heroism, bravery, and tenacity were recognized by General Grant. Chamberlain was given the honor of commanding the Union troops at the surrender ceremony for the infantry of Robert E. Lee's army at Appomattox Court House, Virginia. He then went on to a successful political career as the four-term Republican governor of Maine.

What the GOP needs today is 535 Joshua Chamberlains in the United States Congress. We need 535 leaders with the spirit, boldness, bravery, tenacity, and heroism of that Maine college professor. We need leaders willing to attack when surrounded, out-flanked, and out-numbered. We need leaders who never give up. We need leaders who are RELENTLESS.

Instead we have John Boehner and Mitch McConnell. Are you kidding me?

Now to an example of how boldness works today. No, it's not another story from a battlefield. It's a story of war on a football field. Still it's more proof positive that boldness carries the day.

We've already seen how the Seattle Seahawks' "12th man"—their bold, enthusiastic, committed fans—helped turn the tide in this past Super Bowl on February 2, 2014. In that game the Seattle Seahawks dominated the Denver Broncos in one of the most lopsided beatings in sports history. It was pure domination from start to finish. And few saw it coming. As you already know, I gave my strongest possible "buy" on the Seattle Seahawks to win the Super Bowl that day. It was one of the great wins of my career.

There are some fantastic lessons for the GOP to learn from the Super Bowl–champion Seattle Seahawks. Because politics, just like football, is about the art of war. And the leaders of the GOP—who too often *don't* recognize the value of the "12th man" Tea Party's enthusiasm and energy— have a lot to learn if they're going to make the Democrats look like the hapless, intimidated Denver Broncos.

Let's start with the obvious.

First, Denver looked unbeatable coming into the Super Bowl. Led by perhaps the greatest quarterback of all time, Peyton Manning, the betting in Las Vegas (and across the country with bookmakers) was over 70 percent on Denver. No one thought Seattle's defense could stop the great Peyton Manning.

That situation mirrors Barack Obama and the GOP. Like Peyton Manning, Obama looks unbeatable, invincible, formidable. Intimidation is Obama's game. Ask the former governor of Virginia, now indicted by the federal government. Ask Dinesh D'Souza, the producer of the anti-Obama hit documentary *2016*—now indicted by the federal government. Ask the ratings agencies that dared to downgrade America's debt... you remember, charged with fraud by the feds.

Obama rules by intimidation. He has even bragged in his State of the Union address about his executive orders that are violating the Constitution, daring the GOP to stop him. There is no debate or compromise with Obama. He refuses to compromise on the budget, spending, or the debt ceiling—it's his way or the highway. He dares the GOP to shut down government if they don't like it. He names his own political donor to investigate his IRS scandal. He's laughing in the GOP's face.

No wonder the GOP is scared to death to challenge Obama. They're visibly intimidated. They're still playing by old-fashioned rules: "We must show respect to the president of the United States." But that's not how you win football games or political campaigns. If Seattle had played that way,

Peyton Manning and the Broncos would be the champions of the NFL—just the way the Democrats and Barack Obama won the 2012 election and run the country.

Seattle didn't worry about respecting Manning. Their goal was to annihilate him. They played with swagger and bravado. They weren't afraid of the big bad Denver Broncos. They didn't care about Peyton Manning's

Lessons from Super Bowl XLVIII

Lesson One: Attack, attack, and keep attacking viciously and relentlessly like Seattle's defense. Never let your foot off the pedal.

Lesson Two: Play the game with swagger and bravado. If you're going to win the championship, don't wait for it, SEIZE IT. Obama's not going to give it to you. He isn't a gentleman. He's playing for keeps, because he understands what's at stake. He said he was going to fundamentally change America... and he is doing it. This isn't a game we're playing, it's a battle for the future of America.

Lesson Three: No one is invincible. The whole world bet on Peyton Manning. Over $10 billion was bet on this one game. Over 70 percent ($7 billion) of it was bet on Peyton. But Seattle didn't fear Peyton. They came to take him down. They came to take the prize away from him. Obama isn't invincible either. Don't back down. Don't respect him. That's the big mistake of the GOP. If you want the championship, hit him in the mouth, kick him in the gut, and take it from him.

Lesson Four (the most important lesson of all): Energy and enthusiasm win championships. Seattle gets its energy and enthusiasm from "the 12th man"—their crazed fans. Without the energy of their passionate and loyal fans, Seattle would be just another good football team. It's the energy and intensity that made Seattle the world champions. The GOP needs to embrace and encourage the Tea Party, their 12th man.

résumé or storied history. Like Colonel Joshua Chamberlain at the battle of Gettysburg, they didn't wait for victory, they seized it.

Seattle attacked viciously and aggressively. They stripped the ball. They pounded Peyton's receivers. They "ball hawked." They forced fumbles by ripping at the ball. They demanded Peyton respect *them*.

Obama has no heart, no mercy. He sent the IRS to destroy critics (like me). He sent the IRS to destroy the Tea Party. His IRS even tried to intimidate a Stage-4 terminal cancer victim who criticized Obamacare on Fox News. His U.S. Attorney indicted Dinesh D'Souza.

We can't afford "civility," compromise, or any kind of weakness—our opponent has no pity or compassion. Just like Seattle relentlessly and viciously intimidated and annihilated the Denver Broncos on Super Bowl Sunday, we need to give 200 percent and never let up.

The GOP must learn lessons about what it takes to win from Joshua Chamberlain and more recently from the NFL champion Seattle Seahawks. If you want to win, be bold...show courage...show swagger...charge right at the heart of the enemy...and SEIZE VICTORY!

Cut the Crap!

What the GOP needs are more Republicans like Richard Sherman, the talented, cocky cornerback of the Seattle Seahawks. Sherman trash talks and intimidates and humiliates his critics and opponents. He gets inside your head. He plays to win. The game of Seattle's opponents is completely thrown off by Sherman's antics.

In other words, he gets under their skin—just like Ted Cruz gets to President Obama and the Democrats. One of the best things to happen to the GOP in decades was Ted Cruz filibustering the debt increase. It gave millions of responsible taxpayers hope that at least some politicians might put America's well-being ahead of their own.

The following is an editorial I wrote that was published at many conservative websites shortly after Boehner and the old guard Republicans once again "compromised" and gave Obama exactly what he wanted—an obscene debt ceiling increase with no strings attached.

The Debt Ceiling Is a Load of Crap

The debt ceiling debate is upon us again. And once again you are being fed a line of crap. Obama is full of crap. The media is full of crap. Congress is full of crap. John Boehner and the establishment GOP are full of crap. And the debt ceiling itself is one big load of crap. It's all a big lie. Let me explain in simple terms anyone can understand.

Have you ever had a sewage pipe break? If the raw sewage kept pouring out and piling up to your ceiling, would you hire contractors to raise your ceiling? Or would you ask them to correct the problem—to fix the broken pipe and clean the piles of crap out of your home?

Raising the ceiling of your home would be incredibly stupid—it would cost hundreds of thousands of dollars. It would change the entire construction of your home. Most importantly, it wouldn't solve your problem. If you raised the ceiling but didn't fix the broken pipe, you'd spend $100,000 on the higher ceiling, but weeks later, they'd have to raise it again...and again...and again. Until you'd spent over $1,000,000 on ceiling raises on a $100,000 home that is *still* full of crap.

Right now, I'm sad to say America is full of crap.

The Republican chief coward House Speaker John Boehner just gave in to Obama again (as he always does) and got nothing in return (as he always does). It's as if this debate is actually a choreographed acting performance. The loser is America. You've been fed a load of crap.

They're all lying to you, trying to distract you from the truth. The issue isn't the debt ceiling. That's only the result. The actual problem is out-of-control government spending. Obama has added almost $7 trillion to the national debt. Debt is like sewage. It is bad stuff. It carries disease. It stinks. It's a cancer or a curse upon whoever touches it.

Here's what this so-called debt ceiling fight is about. Government has a sewage leak. Raising the ceiling is a big mistake. Because no one is fixing the problem. The problem is stopping the raw sewage before it spreads fatal disease and causes a catastrophic epidemic that brings about an economic collapse.

Debt has already destroyed the so-called PIIGS of Europe—countries like Greece, Italy, Spain, Portugal. They are drowning in debt. By raising our debt ceiling we are making the exact same mistake, heading in the exact same direction. We are Greece, except much bigger. Debt will destroy us too, but our collapse will take the entire world down with us. The debt ceiling is a ticking time bomb. Each time we raise the debt ceiling we are closer to the implosion.

Raising the ceiling again PROVES that Obama is a failure. It proves that Obama is reckless and irresponsible. It PROVES that Obama is spending us into bankruptcy. It PROVES that Obama is once again (what a surprise) a liar. He claims to have cut spending. But the fact we are at the debt ceiling again proves we actually raised spending. It PROVES that even the infamous "sequester" that Obama claimed cut too much spending...actually never cut enough. If we actually cut any substantial spending, why would we need to raise the debt ceiling? Obama and the media don't want you to ask that question. They need to distract you.

Back to this analogy of a house with a broken sewer pipe. What if your plumber allowed 50 percent more sewage to pour out of the pipe, into your house...but told you that's better than 100 percent more sewage? What if he bragged that he'd slowed the sewage leak into your house? Would that work? Or would your home still be destroyed by sewage—just a little more slowly? Would you want to sleep in a bedroom covered in two feet of raw sewage, instead of four feet? Would you sleep soundly? Of course not, because that didn't solve the problem.

That's what is happening to America. We are over-loaded with crap. And our ceiling is going to soon explode and take the economy (and your job) with it. The very act of raising the debt ceiling means you're spending and printing too much money. You're in debt. And because you're spending too much, soon you'll need to raise the roof again.

The politicians tell us about all the threats to our country if we don't raise the ceiling. But the reality is that the ultimate national security threat is out-of-control debt. Raising the ceiling doesn't solve the problem, it allows the problem to get worse. It encourages more spending. It delays the inevitable—a massive debt crisis that causes the collapse of America.

The politicians desperately need the reckless spending to continue—to bribe their voters. That's how they stay in office, by perpetuating a massive

Ponzi scheme. They desperately need to distract you from seeing the truth— that government spending is the problem. The way to solve the problem isn't raising the ceiling, it's fixing the pipe.

How do we fix the pipe? We slow the spending. We cut government. We actually...get ready for this...must spend less than we take in. No one in the hysterical media has ever mentioned this simple alternative solution.

Raising the ceiling is one way to go, fixing the pipe is the other. Which one would you go with in your own home?

This is the simplest and most obvious solution, in my book. It's the exact same solution recommended by debt experts to consumers who are heavily in debt and spend more than they take in. They advise you to cut up your credit cards, slow your spending, and start saving and paying down your debt. Why would a country act any differently? Cutting our national debt responsibly is the number one way to save the middle class.

Stop Listening to Democrats and the Media

If I could get one message through the skulls of the D.C. establishment Republican leaders, it would be: stop listening to the propaganda of Obama and his Marxist cabal. Stop listening to the mainstream media. Stop listening to big business, lawyers, lobbyists, and the big money consultants. They are not looking out for your best interests—or the best interests of the American people. They are looking out only for themselves. Big government proponents (progressives) have one goal: keep the status quo, so they keep getting elected, keep getting richer, and keep amassing more power— while America, and specifically the middle class, gets screwed.

The strategy of the Democrats who suck the blood of the middle class like ticks is to silence anyone who threatens their power. And their willing accomplices in the media fall all over themselves to back that strategy up. That's why the Democrats so viciously attack the Tea Party and other principled conservatives. That's why these powerful insiders work so hard to intimidate and silence us. That's why the press does everything they can to destroy our brand and slander and demonize us with bad names. That's why they try to frighten the public by calling us "radical," "extreme," "terrorists," and "racist," when we are anything but.

Conservatives aren't "radicals" or "terrorists" any more than the Founding Fathers. America was founded on the exact things the Tea Party believes in: limited government, power to the people, and individual freedom. We are the ones fighting to defend the Constitution that created the foundation for the greatest middle class in world history. We are not "radicals" or "extremists"; we are patriots. We are the heroes and good guys riding to the rescue of women, children, and apple pie. We wear the white hats. We are the thin blue line—the last hope to save the greatest country in world history.

So GOP, listen up. Please stop shaking in your boots every time true principled conservatives actually stand up and attempt to fight back against Obama, or demand the repeal of Obamacare (the centerpiece of the plan to murder the middle class). Stop trying to impress the media by agreeing that principled conservatives are "radical" or "extreme" for supporting the same principles as the Founding Fathers and the United States Constitution.

And here's a big one. Learn to laugh in the leftists' face when they call us racists. First of all, the very definition of racism is voting for a black candidate because... *he's black.* That's racism. The fact that 93 percent of black voters voted for Obama and 96 percent of black women voted for Obama[6] is nothing but voting based on race.

White voters have abandoned Obama in droves, but it has nothing to do with the color of his skin. It has to do with the color of his policies—red, as in communist red. We hate his policies, not the color of his skin.

We hate the fact he has ruined our children's future quality of life with the record-setting $12 trillion in debt he'll have piled up by the time his second term is finished.

We hate his tax increases on the middle class and small business[7] that haven't helped the economy or created new jobs—because the money was handed to his voters for more entitlements and to his donors for more bribes and payoffs such as the stimulus and green energy boondoggle.

We hate the fact that millions of jobs have been lost and the economy is in ruins under his leadership. Except (of course) for Wall Street, which only goes up because Obama has used the Fed to turn the stock market into a rigged craps game (with our money).

We hate the fact that Obama ruined the finest healthcare system in the world. We hate the fact that he is a liar and fraud, who promised "if you like your health care plan, you can keep your health care plan." Now we either don't have insurance, or as middle class taxpayers our costs have gone through the roof to subsidize Obama's voters.

He has damaged our lives beyond belief. The color of his skin has nothing to do with it.

Over the years I hated the policies of George McGovern and Jimmy Carter. They were both white. So did that mean I hated whites?

Today I hate the policies of Nancy Pelosi and Harry Reid. Does that mean I hate Italians and Mormons?

I hate the policies of Hillary Clinton. Does that mean I hate women?

I hate the policies of Congresswoman Debbie Wasserman Schultz and Senator Chuck Schumer. Does that mean I hate Jews? Well guess what? I'm Jewish. There goes that argument.

And I hate the policies of Joe Biden. Does that mean I hate idiots? I'm just kidding... *kind of.*

The point is, in every case, it's the politics and policies that we hate. Not the person, or the race. It comes down to common sense. Middle class Americans (regardless of race) are suffering because of the policies of an incompetent, fraudulent, lying Marxist.

Unlike so many Democrats and members of the media, we're not in delusion or in denial, because we're *not* the ones blinded by the color of his skin. We see the cold, hard truth. Obama's policies are murdering the middle class and killing the American Dream.

So the GOP needs to wake up! As I write this book the non Kool-Aid-drinkers, those not blinded by the color of his skin, have given Obama his lowest poll numbers in history. His numbers have sunk to Richard Nixon levels.[8]

It's time to take a stand. Fight back. Stop acting like a doormat. Stop elevating "compromise" to the level of sainthood. You can't save America by compromising with the devil. Nor can you ever impress the leftist media, or Obama and his crowd of Chicago thugs. To them "compromise" means you fold up and agree to whatever they want.

Ask New Jersey Governor Chris Christie. He embraced Obama in the fall of 2012. He practically French-kissed Obama on the airport tarmac in New Jersey. *Yuck!* Christie courted the liberal media by being friendly to Obama and being outright hostile to his fellow Republicans. Christie denigrated Tea Partiers. He went out of his way to bad-mouth Rand Paul and Ted Cruz. Instead of reserving his anger and passion for pointing out the damage Obama's taxes, spending, and regulations are doing to America, Christie kissed Obama's ring in order to get billions of dollars in disaster aid for New Jersey. What an embarrassment.

But Obama must have told him ring kissing alone wasn't good enough—you've also got to sell out your fellow Republicans. Because Christie went after Rand Paul, Ted Cruz, and the GOP Congress with fervor. Why was he mad at the GOP Congress? Because they showed fiscal restraint and refused to pass a superstorm Sandy relief bill loaded with waste, bribery, and obscene spending having nothing to do with storm relief (the exact kind of pork spending that led to our country's $17 trillion debt).

Commandments for Republicans

Ronald Reagan's so-called 11th commandment was "Thou shalt not speak ill of any fellow Republican." I'd like to revise that rule with three new updated commandments:

- 12th Commandment: Thou shalt not sell out principled, heroic fiscal conservatives in favor of radical leftists or outright communists. You cannot win by doing that.
- 13th Commandment: Thou shalt reserve thy most passionate and fiery vitriol for radical leftists and outright communists, not fellow Republicans. You cannot win elections by being nice to Democrats and the media, but vicious to conservatives.
- 14th Commandment: Thou shalt not side with bigger government, bigger spending, or bigger taxes. First of all, government, spending, and taxes are all too big already. Second, if you support making them bigger, who needs you?

What did Chris Christie get in return for selling out his fellow Republicans? Investigated. As I write this book he is under investigation by the Obama administration for supposed misuse of Sandy relief funds.[9] That's what a Republican gets for trying to cut a deal with the devil. The devil hates you, uses you, and thinks nothing about double-crossing you.

Maybe Governor Christie should have read the dedication to *Rules for Radicals*.

Why should Republicans worry about what Democrats have to say about them? Do Yankees fans worry about what Red Sox fans are saying? Do Pittsburgh Steelers fans worry about what Baltimore Ravens fans are saying? Did Reagan worry about what Jimmy Carter was saying about him? Does Apple worry about what Microsoft says about their products? Do dogs worry about what cats are thinking?

If the GOP is ever going to take back this nation and save the middle class, they'll have to learn confidence, independence, and contrarian thinking. They'll have to learn to think for themselves. Most importantly, they'll have to grow a pair of cojones!

CHAPTER 14

Make the GOP the Party of the Middle Class

Republicans... are for both the man and the dollar;
but in case of conflict, the man before the dollar.
—**Abraham Lincoln**

DID YOU KNOW?

- Democrats are using fraudulent "1 percent vs. 99 percent" rhetoric to divide and conquer the middle class
- Illegal immigrants who never paid taxes are collecting billions in "tax refunds" via the "Earned Income Tax Credit" (EITC)
- Wisconsin governor Scott Walker turned a $3 billion state budget deficit into a surplus by getting government employee benefits under control

Big business and the mega-wealthy have abandoned the American middle class and succumbed to big government's bribes. It is time for the GOP to abandon big business and billionaires and become the party of small business and the middle class.

The .01 Percent

Obama's "pet billionaires" like Warren Buffett are feeding so deeply at big government's trough that I say it's time for the GOP to sacrifice the billionaires to save small business and the middle class.

We've seen that Warren Buffett is not the sweet, humble old man he portrays himself to be. To the contrary, he's a phony, hypocrite, and tax avoider. Yes, he portrays himself as fair and generous, gladly willing to pay more taxes. It's time to call his bluff.

Buffett and his friend Obama are one hell of a wrestling tag team. They misdirect, distract, and divide with class warfare. The truth is the so-called "1 percent" that Obama is so keen on taxing aren't billionaires with yachts and private planes. Tax increases on "the rich" are primarily aimed at a bunch of hard-working small business owners who are struggling and already over-taxed.

I've been screaming about this scam from the highest rooftops for five years now. But until now it was only my gut instincts telling me that the "tax the rich," anti-"1 percent," rhetoric was a fraud to fleece small business owners for the benefit of the *really* rich. Just as I finished writing this book the facts came in. My argument has been that the top 1 percent is mostly upper middle class small business owners. And even the *New York Times* now admits that the "1 percent" includes small business owners working hard to make $380,000 per year.[1]

But now the cat is out of the bag. Those small business owners working around the clock to build a business that pays them $380,000 a year aren't getting richer while the poor get poorer. It turns out that their slice of the pie hasn't gotten any bigger since the 1960s! According to the March 30, 2014, edition of *Atlantic* magazine,

> . . . the gain in wealth share is all about the top 0.1 percent of the country. While nine-tenths of the top percentile hasn't seen much change at all since 1960, the 0.01 percent has *essentially quadrupled* its share of the country's wealth in half a century.
>
> It turns out that wealth inequality isn't about the 1 percent v. the 99 percent at all. It's about the 0.1 percent v. the 99.9 percent

(or, really, the 0.01 percent vs. the 99.99 percent, if you like). Long-story-short is that this group, comprised mostly of bankers and CEOs, is riding the stock market to pick up extraordinary investment income. And it's this investment income, rather than ordinary earned income, that's creating this extraordinary wealth gap.[2]

In other words, it's the 1/10 of 1/10 of the 1 percent that make up the tiny sliver at the top, the billionaires like Warren Buffett and Bill Gates and George Soros, who have made a fortune because of the Fed policies that have enriched the richest among us, that are getting richer. The rest of us are lucky if we're treading water.

How can you lump billionaires like Buffett, who made almost $13 billion last year,[3] in with a small restaurant owner who makes $380,000 a year? The "99 percent" are supposed to be angry at the small restaurant owner, whose income is about seven and a half times the median family household income in the U.S. (which was $51,017 in 2012, the last year the U.S. Census Bureau has released figures for).[4] But Warren Buffet's income (disguised as capital gains) is more than *thirty-three thousand times* the small restaurant owner's income, and more than *two hundred and forty thousand times* the median income. See the scam Obama and his co-conspirators are running? They're playing "divide and conquer" with the middle class. Under the pretense of taxing "the 1 percent" and "the rich," they're raising taxes on the middle class small business owners who are struggling, who create most of the jobs, and whose incomes are a heck of a lot closer to the incomes of the "99 percent" than they are to Warren Buffett's.

The scam is that they lump the billion dollar incomes of the tiny .01 percent sliver at the top of the 1 percent into the entire 1 percent, to make it look like everyone in the 1 percent is getting rich. Not true. It's only a handful of oligarchs distorting the entire picture. The real theft is the .01 percent versus the 99.99 percent. Warren Buffett and a handful of bankers, investment gurus, private equity CEOs, and Wall Street CEOs are the only ones benefiting. The rest of us schmucks haven't seen income growth in the last fifty-plus years. Small business—even in the $250,000 to $500,000 income range—is treading water. Meanwhile the .01 percent are making out like bandits. And the gain comes from investment income, not from earned income. The .01 percent make their fortune from corporate welfare and stock gains created by Fed money printing, off the backs of the middle class.

Do Buffet and other billionaires have the ability to pay more taxes? Absolutely! So why does Buffett pay his secretary with income that will be taxed at higher rates, yet convert all his own income to capital gains so that he pays the lowest rate and smallest amount? He could change that voluntarily any time he wants. What a hypocrite!

I've already told you about Buffett's $1 billion tax bill owed to the IRS for many years. Buffett has paid the best tax law firm that money can buy to *not* pay a billion dollars owed by one of his companies to the United States. If you're rich, generous, and intent on paying more, why not just pay what you owe? After all, as he and his ilk are so quick to say, "the rich can afford it."

Of course, the reason Buffet doesn't pay more (or even what he owes) is that all his talk about people like him paying more is just a smokescreen for his real agenda. He wants *you and me* to pay more.

He doesn't care about you and me. He cares only about the next sweetheart deal he can get (while still owing a billion to the IRS). Check out his Goldman Sachs deal, or his B of A deal, or the railroad profits he made when Obama rejected the Keystone pipeline deal (the first time).[5]

Buffett is just playing the *tax-the-rich* con game. What he really means is *keep your hands off my billions of dollars of assets, but tax the income of those damned small businesspeople to make sure they never have the capital to compete with me. And, by the way, where's my next government contract?* How dare he?

Buffett and Obama are trying to sideline the GOP, painting them as the "party of the rich" and driving a wedge between small business owners and the rest of the middle class. The GOP must break that strategy by positioning itself as the *protector* of small business (the sweet spot where the jobs are created is small business and independent contractors earning $250,000 to $500,000)—and of professionals and hard-working wage earners, and the entire middle class.

To get the U.S. economy moving again and keep it going, the GOP needs to become the courageous fighter for the middle class—including small business and the self-employed—against the obscenely super-rich cronies of Obama who are his accomplices in murdering the middle class. In the process, the Republican Party will be defending ECONOMIC FREE-DOM, which our Founding Fathers wrote into the Constitution to nurture and grow the great American middle class in the first place. Everyone in the middle class, from hard-working sales reps and self-employed profes-sionals to independent contractors and small business owners, wants more economic freedom. The super-rich .01 percent want regulation, crony capitalism, and special deals from the government.

As far as the idea of taxing billionaires like Buffett...let him pay more. He's willing to throw the rest of us under the bus. Now it's time for the middle class and small business to sacrifice him and billionaires like him. They're not on our side, folks. The GOP can show that it's really the Dem-ocrats who are the party of the rich by proposing a deal to raise tax rates on incomes starting at $5 million, $10 million, and $20 million per year. Add a special tax increase on incomes over $100 million per year to be used specifically to pay down the national debt. Hit Buffett where it hurts. Let's see if the hypocritical old geezer agrees to that one. I'm betting he blows a gasket. So will every other billionaire, even though 5 percent of a billion dollars is like me pulling a $5 bill out of my wallet. They want to keep every last penny, while the rest of us pay all the bills.

If the GOP is serious about winning elections, sacrifice the *truly* rich—the ones who are raking in the dough from the "too big to fail" bank bailouts and the Fed manipulating interest rates. If the Democrats won't agree, then they're the enemy of small business and the protector of fat cat billionaires. Which means the secret is out of the bag: Democrats are lead-ing **The Murder of the Middle Class**.

By fighting for small business tax cuts, not big business bailouts, stim-ulus, and corporate welfare, the GOP will show they are the true "Party of the Middle Class."

Instead of giving billions in handouts (i.e. "bailouts") to banks and businesses "too big to fail," the GOP should be finding ways to encourage banks to give loans to small business owners and homeowners.

Two Birds with One Stone:
Fixing Unemployment and Immigration

Instead of joining Democrats to give amnesty (and welfare benefits) to millions of illegal immigrants so that big business can profit from low-wage workers, the GOP should be encouraging businesses to hire unemployed Americans. By getting the Americans unable to find jobs back to work, the GOP can become the party of small business and the middle class—and win elections.

There is no bigger issue than jobs. Yet the GOP joins big business and the Chamber of Commerce in trying to legalize twelve million illegal immigrants, plus bring in more guest workers. This is insanity squared. The reason that business desperately needs foreign guest workers...the reason that homeowners need foreign maids, nannies, and gardeners...the reason farmers need foreign workers...is because almost 100 million able-bodied, working-age Americans are sitting home collecting dozens of different entitlement checks. One third of America is not working! That group isn't motivated to take gardening, farming, or housekeeping jobs.

Shouldn't we put our own unemployed to work before we legalize illegal immigrants, or invite in "guest workers"? The reason we need immigrants to do these low-wage jobs is because too many Americans are fat and happy sitting home collecting welfare, food stamps, and disability for mild back aches. If we took their checks away, they'd be lined up to do those jobs. Everyone likes to eat. Sometimes they just need a little incentive.

Once they found out what it was like to work for a living again, these folks would rediscover the self-respect that made the American middle class great. Once they get going, many of them won't stay in minimum-wage jobs. They'll work themselves back into responsibility for their lives and discover that the sky is the limit when you take charge of the future for yourself and your family—and both they and the country will be better for it.

My plan is to spend billions as an "investment" in putting Americans to work. Provide mandatory job training for every single American who collects a government check. If after training, they refuse a job, they lose their check. Period. It is our duty to instill work ethic and discipline. It is our duty to help Americans living in poverty learn a trade and to put them to work. It is not our duty to provide for life for those unwilling to at least try to provide for themselves.

Train them, find them work, or if there is no work, put them to work (in government jobs). That should be the new GOP mantra. It is a mantra that would make the GOP the majority party in America again.

Solving our illegal immigration problem is easy and simple. All it takes is three simple, commonsense steps. The GOP needs to have the brains and the courage to present this plan.

Step 1: Demand we secure the border before anything else gets done. Period. Without securing our porous, crime-ridden, drug-smuggling border first, I'd agree to nothing. Zero. Zip. There is no negotiation.

Obama and his amnesty crowd don't want a secure border. It's bad business for Democrats, who rely on poor, uneducated, helpless, dependent voters who support big government. Obama and his socialist cabal want millions of additional illegal immigrants to keep crossing the border, simply because they see them as millions of future Democratic voters.

Obama's mentor, Saul Alinsky, famously taught that the ends justify the means.[6] So Democrats distract us from the truth by claiming a wall is too expensive and can't work. Really? Why don't Republicans point to Israel's wall? Before the wall was built Israel suffered from nonstop terror-ist attacks and cross-border killing rampages. Since the wall was built, Israel is safe again.[7] The citizens can sleep at night. It's a fantastic success, proof that a wall works.

Now let's respond to the argument that a wall is too expensive to build. Welcome to the year 2014—we don't need to build a real wall. We can cre-ate a VIRTUAL WALL with high-tech surveillance. All we need is drones and cameras. Not one person could cross a border protected by drones— with border patrol, or National Guard, or U.S. military positioned to swoop in the moment anyone crosses the border.

Obama has created a Soviet-style surveillance state that snoops on his own law-abiding citizens. The NSA can listen in to all our communications without a warrant, and the IRS intimidates the president's political oppo-nents. Soon our skies will be filled with drones. Funny, and telling, how when it comes to protecting our border the president suddenly forgets how to put the same high tech tools to use. Drones can create an impenetrable virtual wall, at a fraction of the cost of a brick-and-mortar wall.

Step 2: Let's see how much Democrats really care about illegal immigrants. Because I don't think they give a damn about them, other than as future voters. Let's test my theory.

After the border with Mexico is secured by a virtual wall (and ONLY after), let's give illegal immigrants still living in this country the chance to become permanent legal residents (over a long period of time, meeting certain strict conditions), but NOT voting citizens.

They've broken the law. They've given up the right to become citizens. Millions of people around the world apply to become legal citizens of the United States. Many never get in. So the compromise is that those who are already here get the break of a lifetime. They get in. They never have to fear that knock on the door in the middle of the night. They are free to work and live their lives as legal residents. What a gift. But they can never be citizens, they can never vote. Period. They gave up that privilege when they broke the law. But they can live with the knowledge and pride that their children born here will be full American citizens.

"The American Dream" is simple. It's about working, raising a family, having economic opportunity, and enjoying our unique freedoms. It's not about voting. People from other countries don't dream of voting in America. They come here for a better life. No one comes here to vote. So under this plan, illegal immigrants gain the opportunity to stay and achieve the American Dream. They just can't vote. Will Democrats support that? My bet is they won't. Let's call their bluff.

Step 3: Here's the big one. Here's where the GOP is disconnected from its own voters. Conservatives welcome immigrants. We have no problem letting immigrants who want to work and contribute into America. A major problem with our immigration policy, or at least the way it is implemented, is that there is too little differentiation between those applicants who are willing and able to work and contribute...and those who aren't.

Real immigration reform must deal with this head on. Here is the simple solution: New immigrants must give up the right to welfare and government subsidies. *Forever.* That's the agreement. You can become a legal resident, and if you came into the country legally, you can become a citizen, but only if you give up any right to food stamps, housing allowances, aid to dependent children, free meals at school, and free healthcare. Did you come here to work, or to collect handouts? That's the key question we should be asking before we let *anyone* into America.

America is generous, but let's not be stupid. We'll let you in, but only if you're here to work. We won't let you in, if you're here to mooch off us.

Why would taxpayers invite strangers into our country to collect handouts that raise our taxes and debt? Why would we invite you in so you can lower our quality of life, and that of our children? We're not THAT dumb, are we?

Well, actually, under President Obama, we are. The Republican Party should be leading the charge for immigration reform that bans welfare in return for working and living in this great country. That has to include the "earned income tax credits" that have allowed billions in tax refunds for illegal immigrants who never paid income taxes in the first place.[8]

Immigrants who are here to work and contribute will welcome this gift of a lifetime and thank those who propose and support it. So would Democrats...if they actually cared about the well-being of immigrants. That's a big "if."

So, here is the plan that will fix our immigration problems, expose the Democrats as the hypocrites they are, and win elections for the Republican Party. Secure the border forever; allow into our country only those who want to work, as demonstrated by their willingness to give up government handouts; give them legal residency but not voting rights; and we have a deal. I'd let millions of immigrants in under those terms. By any measure, I'm pro-immigrant. As long as they are "working immigrants."

Call the Democrats' bluff. I'm betting they will pass.

Why is this issue so important? Because letting in millions of new illegal immigrants is a disaster for the middle class. It suppresses wages (by adding millions to the workforce); it takes away jobs from Americans (who would want those jobs if they had no other choice because they weren't able to collect government checks); and it adds a tremendous tax burden to the middle class to pay for the free healthcare, welfare, entitlements of all kinds, education, and prison costs of 12 million (or more) illegal immigrants (and many more to follow). This problem is crushing the middle class.

Illegal immigration, our porous border, and amnesty are turning America into a Third World country divided between elite super-rich government cronies and the poor peons who do their yard work and nanny their children. But we can stop that. All we have to do is go back to the work ethic and patriotism—the values that prevailed when the millions of immigrants who came through Ellis Island were assimilated into the great American middle class.

Eliminate Government Employee Unions and Reform Pensions

Besides the super-rich and the welfare-dependent, there's another class of people living at the expense of the middle class in America today. We've seen that government employees are paid TWICE what Americans in the private sector make, and that they have insanely bloated benefits and pensions—all paid for by the middle class. We've got to rein this runaway spending in because if we don't stop it, it will bankrupt the country—and because these "swarms of officers" who "harass our people, and eat out their substance" are threatening the well-being and very life of the middle class.

Many cities have so inflated the pay and benefits of city employees that they will have no choice but to declare bankruptcy and declare their contracts with public employees null and void, or at least drastically renegotiated and downsized. There is no debate. It's all happening in front of our eyes.

As I was about to finish this book, the credit rating of Chicago (Obama's hometown) was downgraded to just slightly above "junk status." More downgrades are on the way.[9]

What caused this downgrade of Chicago's credit by Moody's Investors Service? Moody's blamed it on "massive and growing" pensions for government employees, which undermine "the city's fiscal solvency." This pension funding hole is about $20 billion (for just one city). And Chicago is right behind Detroit). I have no doubt that the Windy City will eventually be forced to follow Motown into official bankruptcy.

And some states are not far behind. Congress should change the law to allow states to declare bankruptcy, so they too can have the ability to renegotiate and restructure government employee contracts. If not, you know who is on the hook to pay for these taxpayer-guaranteed pensions— YOU. If the GOP doesn't come out strong against them, bailouts of whole states could be next on the agenda otherwise known as *The Murder of the Middle Class.*

Not all government employees are created equal. I appreciate policemen and firemen. I call them heroes. As I pointed out in *The Conscience of a Libertarian,* I'd give government employees who risk their lives special compensation, i.e. "combat pay." Police, fire, and law enforcement personnel deserve extra pay for the risks they take (if they are in fact out in the streets, not sitting behind a desk). But regardless of hero status, not every policeman or fireman can retire on a six-figure pension. Teachers, firemen, and police who have provided real service to their communities should be able to retire in modest middle class comfort—not on pensions worth millions of dollars, which are bankrupting their communities.

Ironically, I'm trying to save the pensions of government employees. The present system is unsustainable. If it is to be saved, the system must be changed, at least for new hires. Following is a five-step solution that the GOP should propose in its new role as the party of the middle class:

1. Peg government employee salaries to private sector salaries. No government job should pay more than its equivalent in the private sector.
2. Government employee wage increases must be tied to performance. Why should anyone in America receive automatic salary increases just for showing up? Isn't that what you're supposed to do? Isn't that why they call it a job? You've already been paid for showing up. Raises and bonuses should be paid only for exemplary work.

3. Government employees, at least new hires, must be put on a "defined contribution" plan, to replace their present unaffordable and unsustainable "defined benefits" plan.

   This ensures government employee pensions are fully funded during the employment period. The taxpayers are off the hook, and the age of retirement is no longer an issue. A government employee can retire at forty-five, or fifty-five. I don't care. It's none of my business, as long as your retirement plan is fully funded during your time of employment—you're taking out of the system only what you invested in it, and the proceeds from that investment.

4. Collective bargaining for government employees must be eliminated. It's a con job. There is no "bargaining." It's extortion. Collective bargaining in government employment is like a chicken negotiating with a pack of wolves. Of course the chicken will give the wolves whatever they want, or he's dead.

   Government employee unions donate millions to Democrat candidates, walk door to door, send out mailers, man phone banks, and actively work the campaign. After that Democrat is elected, he or she is a pawn, beholden to the union.

   After the election, it's time for contract negotiations—except we the taxpayers aren't represented. Sitting at the table are the union representatives, union lawyers, and the politician who owes his job and political life to the union that elected him. The fraud begins in that room. A gun is put to the politician's head by the union that elected him and threatens to make sure he is never elected again unless he gives them what they want. That's called extortion. When the "bargaining session" is over, government employees walk out with unaffordable salaries and obscene pensions. Everyone smiles and says, "No problem. Why worry? It's not our money." But whose money is it? The middle class taxpayers'. *Yours.*

5. While I would be in favor of immediately changing all government employees to a fully funded "defined contribution" retirement as opposed to an open-ended "defined benefit"

pension, the best we can probably hope for is that this reform be implemented for new hires. If that is the case, there are several tweaks that need to be implemented for current employees still on defined-benefit retirement pensions.

a. Set a minimum age for public employees to start collecting their pensions. They can retire at any age, but they can't collect a pension until age sixty-five (or the same age as Social Security).

b. Ban double dipping. You can take another government job after retirement, but you can only collect one pension.

c. Pensions must be based only on the employee's base salary— eliminating the scam of using overtime and unpaid sick leave to inflate pensions.

d. Base the pension on the average salary for the last ten years, not on the last two or three years.

e. Ban the practice of public employees cashing out their vacation and sick days. In many cases, employees are getting cash lump sum payouts of $250,000 or more upon retirement. The only reasonable answer is to use those sick and vacation days, or lose them. You shouldn't be paid in cash for unused sick or vacation pay.

f. Require public employees to pay substantially higher contributions for pension and health benefits than the small percentages they pay now. NOTE: Wisconsin Governor Scott Walker has already proven this works. He made government employees pay just a little bit more for their own healthcare and retirement. Overnight, like magic, a massive Wisconsin budget deficit of $3 billion turned into a surplus, and as I write this book, Walker is proposing to give back almost $1 billion to taxpayers.[10] Amazing. Can you imagine what we could do on the national level with the same small tweaks to government employee benefits? Could we save $1 trillion and pay down the debt? As they say in the Midwest, *"You betcha!"*

Government employees' ridiculous benefits are lifeblood being squeezed out of the middle class. If the GOP wants to win elections, it needs to follow Scott Walker's lead, get those pensions and unions under control, and become the true party of the middle class.

The middle class is the productive class in America. Despite the depredations of Obama and his cronies, the American middle class is still brimming with energy, entrepreneurship, patriotism, and a deep sense of responsibility for themselves, their families, and their country. If the GOP truly became the party of the middle class, Republicans would win.

CHAPTER 15

Tea Party Infusion

I have a message. A message from the tea party.
A message that is loud and clear and does not mince words.
We've come to take our government back.
—Rand Paul[1]

DID YOU KNOW?

- It's more crucial to vote Democrats out of office than to vote Tea Party candidates in
- A winning strategy supports Tea Party candidates in the GOP primary and Republicans in the general election
- A Tea Party candidate was just elected to the Pennsylvania state senate as a write-in candidate

We've seen that the Republican Party needs to be bold enough to embrace the Tea Party and become the true party of the middle class. This chapter will explain exactly how synergy between the Tea Party and the GOP can put the middle class—and its values of hard work, patriotism, financial discipline, and personal responsibility—back in the driver's seat in America

The Perfect Tea Party Election Strategy

Let me begin by making something perfectly clear. Establishment Republicans may be cowards, weaklings, and compromised, but they are still in almost all cases better than Democrats. Yes, I want to cut government, cut spending, cut entitlements, and cut taxes. Establishment sellouts like John Boehner and Mitch McConnell will usually settle for slightly bigger government, slightly higher spending, slightly higher entitlements, and slightly higher taxes. That's how we got into this mess.

But they're still a hell of a lot better than Democrats like Obama, Harry Reid, and Nancy Pelosi who support insane, irrational, unsustainable levels of government, spending, entitlements, and taxes, coupled with a Big Brother IRS used to destroy critics and bleed dry business owners. There is just no comparison.

I don't want my taxes raised one dollar. I'm "Taxed Enough Already." But $1 of higher taxes is better than $10,000 of higher taxes. The first option means discomfort, but survival. The second option means destruction and bankruptcy.

We can save America with a Republican president, Republican Senate, and Republican House, if a portion of those Republicans are Tea Party influenced and inspired. We don't need all of them to be Tea Party Republicans.

However, we cannot save America—CANNOT—if Democrats are in power. So electing as many Tea Party candidates as possible is a priority for everyone who wants to save the middle class. But it's not the only priority. Electing solid GOP majorities across the board from statehouses to Congress is crucial too. The real #1 goal should be defeating socialist, progressive Democrats who have never met a large tax increase or large spending increase or onerous regulation they don't like. That's the #1 priority above all else, if we're going to save the middle class—keeping *really* bad people away from power.

All for One and One for All

So here's my unique Tea Party compromise strategy. Yes, I'm willing to compromise, as long as it is a reasonable, commonsense compromise.

Every business owner understands there are times we need to compromise to succeed.

So my "compromise" is to work hard for, promote, and donate to principled fiscal conservative Tea Party candidates. I will work in the primaries to defeat RINO Republicans in every precinct, district, city, and state in the country. If given a choice, I will always support the Tea Party candidate. I will fight to elect as many "perfect candidates" as possible. I will fight to defeat the RINO establishment in GOP primaries. I will fight with passion to put principled conservatives in the leadership of Congress. I will fight to replace the John Boehners and Mitch McConnells.

But...

If the moderate establishment GOP candidate wins the primary, I will support him or her in the general election over any Democrat. And I will do it with all the enthusiasm and cash I can muster. Today's Democratic Party is extreme. It stands for socialism, class warfare, punishing and demonizing success, theft of private property, addicting voters to welfare, allowing teachers unions to damage our children's future with inferior education, allowing government employees to bankrupt taxpayers, dangerously weakening the military, and in many cases complete surrender to our many enemies around the world. If you've read this far you know just how dangerous Democrats are to America's future. Democrats must be defeated at all costs before we can worry about electing only "perfect" Tea Party candidates.

This is the perfect Tea Party strategy (even though it won't always elect the perfect candidate). We fight the GOP establishment with everything we've got, but when the fight is over, we come together as teammates. When the fight is over, we fight just as hard for each other. At this point saving America is more important than perfection.

I hope every reader of this book realizes electing GOP politicians now, right now, regardless of how perfect they might be, is our only hope of saving America and stopping *The Murder of the Middle Class*.

But the key to this compromise election strategy is that it has to be a two-way street. The establishment GOP has to be "all in" too. They can fight us in the primary, but if we win, they must rally the troops too. They must circle the wagons and fight with passion for the Tea Party candidate in the general election. It's one for all and all for one.

It's funny how the GOP establishment (Exhibit A is Karl Rove) hates the Tea Party and calls principled conservatives too radical or "extreme." Rove seems to forget it was the Tea Party that saved the Republican Party's bacon in 2010 and showed the GOP the perfect strategy for winning elections.

Victory Is in the Air

Literally as if on cue, the very month I handed this book in to the publisher, something special happened. I'm calling it a sign of things to come in November.

First, Tea Party candidate David Jolly won a special Congressional election in Florida against Alex Sink. It was a huge upset. Democrat Alex Sink out-spent Jolly on TV ads by more than 3 to 1. The district had not only voted for Obama in 2008 and 2012 but also voted for Sink in her race for governor in 2010. The GOP establishment abandoned Jolly and even badmouthed him in the media, the way they too often do to Tea Party candidates. Yet against all odds, Jolly won.[2]

Then came the really big news! In Pennsylvania, a Tea Party conservative was elected to the state senate . . . **as a WRITE IN candidate.**[3]

Businessman Scott Wagner defeated both the Democrat and establishment Republican candidates, even though he wasn't on the ballot. Voters had to choose to physically write in his name on a piece of paper. Yet he beat them each by a margin of 2 to 1. WOW! The Tea Party rides again. Of course the mainstream media didn't even mention this shocking victory.

I know something special is in the air again—just like in 2010. I predict another historic landslide GOP victory in November of 2014. Once again it will be led by Tea Party candidates, principles, intensity, and PASSION!

The Perfect Tea Party Issues

No matter how many times Obama, Democrats, establishment Republicans and their consultants, or the mainstream media badmouth the Tea Party, it was the Tea Party who figured out the way for the GOP to win a

Republican landslide. That way is to focus on fiscal, pocketbook issues along with limiting government intrusions into personal and constitutionally guaranteed freedoms.

There is nothing extreme or "radical" about Tea Party views on the issues. Our views are the views of a majority of Americans. Principled conservatives are on the same side as the majority of Americans on the issues of limiting the size of the federal government; reducing government spending; reducing the power of government over our lives; streamlining government by eliminating waste and earmarks; reducing welfare and other entitlement spending; reducing taxes; reducing regulations; reducing the national debt; reforming government employee pensions; balancing the budget; expanding energy exploration to achieve energy independence; opposing and repealing Obamacare; banning corporate welfare, bailouts, and stimulus; returning power to the states and the people; and following the U.S. Constitution. That is a winning platform, supported by the vast majority of Americans.

Tea Party views on each of these issues are in the mainstream. That makes us moderate and popular, not "extreme" or "radical." It's Obama and his Marxist cabal who are the "radical" and "extreme" ones.

Feel free to add the issues of school choice (the civil rights issue of the twenty-first century), right to work, gun rights, and increased border security. These are all winning issues.

As far as foreign policy, I'd report the Tea Party consensus is for reasonable, rational, commonsense support of limited foreign intervention and reduced foreign aid (especially to countries like Egypt, Pakistan, Afghanistan, Syria, and Libya that aren't our friends). On most other foreign policy issues you will not find unified agreement. That's why, at election time, foreign policy is a secondary issue.

That's it. Those are the winning issues for the GOP. That is a winning strategy. Giving major importance to social issues is negative and divisive. It loses elections again and again. Social issues not only divide the general electorate, they divide conservatives and the GOP itself.

I understand that many conservatives are conservative about social issues, as well as fiscal issues. I have my own personal social beliefs and will stand up and defend them at any time. But they are NOT the issues around which the GOP should run national campaigns. For the foreseeable future, the winning issues for the GOP are fiscal responsibility, spending, debt, restoring the Constitution, and protecting economic and personal freedoms.

To the prospective candidate who is on record as talking about "legitimate rape" or calling homosexuality the work of the devil: please don't run. You're not going to win, you'll just divide the party and bring ridicule upon yourself.

If, like me, you believe in the Constitution of the United States, then you understand what the Founding Fathers intended. Moral and social issues are the province of the states, not the federal government. As someone running for U.S. Representative or Senator, you must stand by your personal beliefs. However, that must be followed by a very clear statement that those are state, not federal issues, and you will do everything in your power to ensure that the federal government stays out of both the bedroom and boardroom.

There is a huge bonus to this brilliant Tea Party strategy. The bonus is these views do not turn off the two blocks of voters the GOP desperately needs to win elections and save America: women and young people. The goal of the GOP should be broadening the tent to attract female and youth votes.

If you disagree with me, please see the results of the straw poll at the most recent CPAC, the annual gathering of true principled conservatives in Washington, D.C., each March. Almost half of the audience in 2014 was between the ages of eighteen and twenty-five. These aren't just Republican youth, they are passionate true believers. They are the future of the GOP.

Who did this crowd vote for in the CPAC presidential poll? Senator Rand Paul, a libertarian-leaning Republican just like me. What else did this crowd of young Republicans vote for? Legalization of marijuana for both recreational and medical purposes, as well as less foreign military intervention.[4]

On the question of political philosophy, 78 percent chose as their most important goal "promote individual freedom by reducing the size and scope of government and its intrusion into the lives of its citizens." Whereas only 12 percent chose "promote traditional values by protecting traditional marriage and protecting the life of the unborn," and only 7 percent chose "to secure and guarantee American safety at home and abroad regardless of the cost or the size of government."

In other words, the future of the GOP is moderation on social and foreign policy issues.

A majority supported the following statement, "Nearly 70 years after the end of World War II, it's time for our European, Asian and other allies to provide for their own defense."

And a huge 78 percent opposed NSA data collection—i.e., government spying on American citizens.[5]

Day and night the mainstream media, which hates the GOP, tells us we must change our views to attract minority support. I disagree. Latino voters, especially, are family-oriented and very concerned about the future they can provide for their children. They would welcome a party that wanted to help their families make it into the great American middle class. The GOP simply needs to find a powerful way to convey its message of economic freedom, opportunity, and upward mobility to win more Latino support. My strategy of fiscal conservatism, capitalism, and moderate libertarianism on personal freedoms and social issues is a winning strategy to dramatically increase GOP vote percentages among women and young voters.

Colorado is the perfect bellwether state. Its population is youthful, entrepreneurial, health-oriented, both pro-gun and pro-pot, and evenly divided between Republicans, Democrats, and independents. Every statewide race is wide open. Yet according to Fox News, "Democrats have won every top-of-the-ticket race in the state since 2004," in part by attacking Republicans as out of the mainstream, in particular on issues important to moderate suburban women who often determine the winner of elections.[6] If we start moderating on bedroom issues, focusing on economic and personal freedom, and finding charismatic candidates with bigger-than-life personalities... then the GOP can win any race, anywhere in this country. Appeal to suburban women and young voters, and every election will swing Republican, even without adding a single minority voter. However I have a plan to win over minority voters too (coming up).

This is not your grandfather's GOP. If the GOP is interested in winning elections and saving America it must embrace the views of the Tea Party. Fiscal conservatism combined with moderate, libertarian views on social, bedroom, and foreign policy issues is what will attract strong support among future generations. The road map for victory is there. All the GOP has to do is follow it.

CHAPTER 16

The First Plank in the Platform

*I am in favor of cutting taxes under any circumstances
and for any excuse, for any reason, whenever it's possible.*
—**Milton Friedman**

DID YOU KNOW?
- Ronald Reagan reduced the top income tax rate from 70 percent to 28 percent, turning the Carter malaise into an economic boom
- Reducing all income taxes to zero for a year would cost about the same as President Obama's failed "stimulus package"
- Hong Kong, the most dynamic economy in the world, has a flat 15 percent tax rate with deductions for mortgage interest and charitable donations

To win elections, a Tea Party–infused GOP needs a winning platform. And the very first item in that platform should be tax relief for the overburdened middle class. Because we need to start out by showing that we can reverse the wholesale destruction of jobs, the decline of the economy, and the death of opportunity that the Obama administration has brought to middle America.

We have a massive, pork-laden, unfair tax system in America today. It is such a convoluted mess of handouts, punishments for hard work, and rewards for special interests that there is no option but to throw it in the trash and start over. There are a number of reasonable plans out there, known by names such as "flat tax," "fair tax," and the like.

My personal preference is what I've named the 0-15-0 tax plan. It is designed to turn bust into boom, creating the greatest economic explosion and economic expansion in history—and produce it F-A-S-T.

Where is the Ronald Reagan we need in today's GOP? Reagan boldly cut top tax rates from 70 percent to 28 percent, driving an economic resurgence that quickly created 20 million jobs and turned Jimmy Carter's economic bust into boom times. The 0-15-0 tax plan is a plan to make that happen again.

Today's GOP is neither radical nor revolutionary. Mitt Romney's tax proposals maintained "revenue neutrality"—in other words, no net tax cut for the American people.[1] How pathetic.

The liberal media called Romney's idea "radical."[2] How is "revenue neutral" radical? Try winning an election with this slogan: "A Tax Plan That is Revenue Neutral!" Oh right, we already did that. Romney proved that a tax plan that is "revenue neutral" doesn't win elections.

Today's GOP is filled with funeral directors re-arranging deck chairs on the *Titanic*. In the face of massive deficit and debt, economic collapse, chronic unemployment, and a "misery index" rivaling that of the Great Depression, the GOP's answer is to recommend either the status quo, or tax and spending cuts so small it takes a microscope to find them.

Here's the problem: Obama wants to raise taxes and punish business owners. The alternative is the GOP, which wants to keep things where they are, or nibble around the edges at best. America is facing a lose-lose scenario.

That's why we need a new winning platform for a Tea Party–infused GOP. We need a contrarian new vision. We need a bold, game-changing, conversation-changing tax plan. We need 0-15-0.

The NITV

GOP, take notes. This is my plan:

First…

A NATIONAL INCOME TAX VACATION (NITV).

That's right—everyone gets a holiday from paying taxes. For one year you keep 100 percent of what you earn. *Your money belongs to YOU.*

To Obama and his socialist cabal, the idea of a "tax cut" is to cut the taxes of only those with little or no income—including giving out tax "refunds" to people who never paid taxes in the first place. The group that is left out in the cold in that kind of "tax cut" just happens to be the economic engine of the U.S. economy—middle class taxpayers, private sector employees, and small business owners. Like it or not, you cannot turn around an economy by giving "tax cuts" to people who don't pay taxes, who have no idea how to create jobs, who are not "rainmakers."

The NITV aims the tax cut directly at the only people who can ignite the economy and dig us out of this hole—the innovators, rainmakers, and entrepreneurial risk-takers. Or as I call them **"FINANCIAL FIRST RESPONDERS."**

The NITV incentivizes the people who start the businesses and create the jobs. This plan doesn't just refill their fuel tanks; it puts racing fuel into a turbocharger. It's Ronald Reagan… *on steroids.*

Stand back and watch the economic explosion when taxpayers and small business owners capitalize on this once-in-a-lifetime opportunity. They will do what all smart and ambitious entrepreneurs do with money— spend it, invest it, and risk it to start new businesses or expand old ones. And they will do it QUICKLY because for the first year they get to keep all of it. That's all you have to tell entrepreneurs—and they are off and running, with a smile and a gleam in their eyes! Democrats claim rich people are "greedy." Well guess what? This plan capitalizes on that greed. It forces rich people to spend their money like never before, to create jobs, manufacture products that make customers' lives better, and open up new business opportunities for others—all in order to take advantage of the greatest opportunity of their lifetimes.

Obama and his Marxist cabal will scream, *But how can we run government without taxes?* Notice how that question never bothered Obama when he spent almost $1 trillion on his stimulus plan. Actually the true cost has risen to the range of $2 trillion.[3]

The cost of my NITV plan is about $1.2 trillion (the total of annual personal income taxes). It's about the same amount (or less) than Obama wasted on his stimulus plan to nowhere.

The difference is that Obama's trillion dollars created nothing, inspired no one, did not create one job, and added almost $1 trillion in debt for our children to pay. Oh and Obama lied. He later made a joke out of the fact that there were never any "shovel-ready" jobs.[4]

Why did the stimulus never work, never improve the economy, never create any large number of jobs? Because the money was handed to the wrong people—Democratic voters, Democratic donors, welfare addicts, and unions. None of those groups could find a job if it hit them in the face.

But my NITV (National Income Tax Vacation) empowers the right people by allowing them to keep 100 percent of their income for one year. Who are the right people? Small business owners and small investors. This is exactly what Reagan did when he cut tax rates from 70 percent to 28 percent—he helped only those who paid taxes in the first place.

Reagan's idea worked because it empowered the people who knew how to use the money to start businesses and create jobs. Brilliant. My 0-15-0 tax plan is a double dose of Ronald Reagan tried and true medicine, for an economy that is even sicker than Jimmy Carter's. This plan is like a defibrillator jolt for the heart of the economy. At this point, nothing less will do.

Simply put, taxpayers will be so excited by the NITV that they will begin an investing spree that will create millions of jobs, and quickly increase tax revenues. If critics are worried about the cost, then we can always find corresponding spending cuts. That's even better!

Obama's Marxist cabal will scream, *This can't be done. You can't give people a tax vacation.* Well we can debunk that idea by simply looking at the "sales tax holidays" used by many blue Democratic states over the years.[5]

These sales tax holidays encourage consumers to spend loads of money (usually the week before school starts), thereby jump-starting the economy and helping small businesses. Why do these tax holidays work so success-fully? Obviously the governors of those blue states understand that con-sumers will be driven by "greed" to spend more than they normally would, to take advantage of a "tax holiday." But how can governments afford the lost tax revenue? When consumers spend all that money, businesses gain. With all those increased profits, businesses pay more taxes in the long run. Everyone wins!

That's the exact same theory as my NITV. With all the extra money in the hands of taxpayers for the next year (because they owe no income taxes), consumers will go on a spending and investing spree.

The results? Businesses will have to hire new employees. So that creates lots of new jobs for the middle class. That increases payroll taxes. And all those new employees will spend their money. All that increased spending will add up to dramatically increased taxes paid by business. Everyone wins.

Now ask yourself what Obama's stimulus did with the same (or larger) amount of money? Nothing. Zero. Zip. Nada.

Let's look at another example. Many blue states (like Michigan) offer large "tax credits" for anyone making a movie in their state. Why? To capitalize on the "greed" of Hollywood movie producers. It works like magic. Today most movies are made in states with income tax credits. Of the twenty-six big budget movies made in 2013, only two were made in California.[6]

California has lost most of the movie production business because they refuse to give tax breaks to moviemakers. How utterly stupid. Tax holidays and tax credits are a proven success. Why else would anyone leave sunny beautiful California to make a movie in cold, gray, ugly Detroit? Because money always speaks louder than words, or sunshine, or anything else. In the end human behavior is driven by money. Allow people to keep more of it (or in this case, all of it) and watch the explosion of happiness, excite-ment, risk, and "greed."

NOTE to the GOP: This is how you change the conversation. This is how you use boldness and courage to turn a historic bust into a boom. This is how you inspire voters. Reagan gave us the greatest tax cut in history to save us from Jimmy Carter. Today we need to cut taxes to *zero* for a year (or two) to save America from Obama, because the Obama economy is that much worse than the Carter economy. So the defibrillator jolt must be that much stronger. An income tax vacation will start a revolution to save capitalism and take back our country.

I can feel Ronald Reagan looking down from above and saying, *"Let's get this revolution started."*

The 0-15-0 Tax Plan

And the NITV is only a small start. Here comes the next important part of the plan. In 2012 GOP presidential candidate Herman Cain proposed a 9-9-9 tax plan that was attacked and denigrated by his conservative opponents. Liberals had a cow. The media was up in arms. It seemed everyone was upset. Not me—I was *inspired.*

The only way you know something works in D.C. is when it makes all sides angry. Cain stirred a hornets' nest because he created a winning idea. Of course the lawyers, lobbyists, and bureaucrats knew it had to be discredited and killed.

9-9-9 was simple...it was memorable...it opened the conversation...and it reminded me of Ronald Reagan's plan to cut taxes from 70 percent to 28 percent. That, too, was laughed at and denigrated as "simplistic." No one believed it would work.

But it did. All it took to revive the American economy was unleashing the power and motivating the great American middle class—and especially the people that start, invest, and run small businesses. If they're inspired, rewarded, and energized they can get America going again. That's the group Reagan always played to. Smart. Ironically, that is the same group that Obama spends his time denigrating, demonizing, and punishing.

Herman Cain's 9-9-9 plan was creative, daring, and interesting. It was made up of 9 percent income taxes, 9 percent capital gains tax, and 9 percent sales tax. But that last 9 percent of 9-9-9 represents a dangerous precedent. It's not a good idea to introduce a national sales tax unless you first get rid of the income tax completely through a constitutional amendment. Still, Cain should be applauded. He was headed in the right direction. We need to inspire and reward the job creators, flatten the tax code, and eliminate capital gains to encourage investment and financial risk-taking. Herman Cain inspired me to create an even better idea.

My 0-15-0 Tax Plan keeps the best of Cain's plan (low rates and simplicity), while eliminating the worst (a national sales tax). And, it starts with the supercharged attention-getter that, we've seen, will create jobs like no tax plan in U.S. history: the NITV (National Income Tax Vacation).

But the NITV is just the start.

Now comes part two, the "15" of the 0-15-0 Plan. U.S. taxpayers will be welcomed back from their one-year income tax vacation with a 15 percent flat tax on personal and business income starting on any amount over $40,000 a year. This replicates the most successful economic model in the world—Hong Kong, with a booming economy and 3.5 percent unemployment. Unlike Cain's plan, we don't rely on a national sales tax. We just keep the income tax flat and simple—15 percent for everyone, individuals and business.

Unlike the Cain tax plan, instead of a 9 percent rate we make ours 15 percent (just like Hong Kong), but allow three deductions: mortgage, charitable, and health and medical expenses.

Why allow a mortgage deduction? Real estate is the foundation of America (and any economy). Without a housing recovery and stability there can be no recovery; there can be no healthy retirement for older Americans; and there can be no investment in small business. The equity in our homes fuels the entire economy.

Hong Kong gets it—that deduction is part of their income tax system. Yet every time the blind, deaf, and dumb GOP mentions a "flat tax"...not only is it not really flat (there are always two or three rates), but it also eliminates or greatly reduces the home mortgage deduction. Hong Kong keeps the mortgage interest deduction, and their economy is booming! That's because real estate is the straw that stirs the drink. Homeownership is the foundation of a capitalist society. It's how the middle class accumulates wealth. Taking it away is just plain stupid.

Charity must be deductible because private charities undoubtedly do a much better job, at a much lower cost, of providing for the needy than government bureaucracy does. Hong Kong gets it—that deduction is also part of their income tax system.

Finally, with the healthcare deduction we can repeal Obamacare and institute a free market approach that will dramatically cut healthcare costs while continuing to provide American citizens the best healthcare in the world.

So the end result is a flat tax with three simple deductions—mortgage, charitable, and healthcare. Period. You can fill out your taxes on a post-card. As a bonus, this would save untold billions a year in accounting and tax attorney bills, freeing up money for more productive investment and job creation. Small business people, of course, would still be able to deduct the costs of their businesses before paying tax on their income, just like any corporation. The accountants who no longer have work filing tax returns could do work for all the productive, growing new small businesses.

Now to the final 0 of the 0-15-0 Plan. That zero stands for the elimination of taxes on capital gains, dividends, and interest—also replicating the Hong Kong tax system. Eliminating capital gains taxes is how you motivate Americans to put their money where it best helps the economy and creates jobs: into stocks, real estate, small business startups, and other investments. Hong Kong gets it. They have a zero capital gains tax. But more important, so does our number one economic competitor in the world—China. To compete, America must end these taxes on business growth and job creation that make us uncompetitive in the world economy.

The bonus of zero capital gains taxes is that it helps solve a growing crisis: providing for America's retirees. With my plan saving for retirement is so much faster and easier—when you know your capital gains, stock dividends, and bank interest are tax-free for the rest of your life. We'll see an explosion among those sixty-five and older in investing, charitable giving, and paying for the college educations of their grandchildren.

Middle class people, not the rich, benefit the most from the 0-15-0 Plan. First, they'll have new jobs by the millions. Second, the income tax vacation applies to everyone (including every middle class taxpayer). Third, the 15 percent flat tax is a win for every middle class taxpayer. The mortgage and charitable deductions are great for the middle class homeowners and church-goers. The healthcare deduction solves the disaster caused by Obamacare. Finally, the zero capital gains tax applies to every home, stock, and small business sold by middle class Americans. It applies to their savings and dividends. And when grandpa dies he leaves you all the extra money he saved over the years from this 0-15-0 Plan. What a bonanza for the middle class. What a boom for the economy!

There you have it. The 0-15-0 Plan will create an economic miracle. Sincere thanks to Herman Cain and Ronald Reagan for providing the inspiration for this 0-15-0 tax plan. It is *REAGAN SQUARED!*

CHAPTER 17

A Middle Class Contract with America

Daring ideas are like chessmen moved forward.
They may be beaten, but they may start a winning game.
—**Johann Wolfgang von Goethe**

DID YOU KNOW?

- Raul Castro's Cuba is cutting 1 million government jobs
- The cost of new federal regulations in just one *year* of Obama's presidency was more than the total cost of new regulations in the *two first terms* of Bill Clinton and George W. Bush combined
- U.S.-based big business has $1.95 trillion in offshore bank accounts that they're keeping outside the U.S. to avoid paying our high tax rates

A one-year income tax vacation; followed by a flat tax (modeled after Hong Kong); along with zero capital gains tax (modeled after Hong Kong) all add up to a great start. But we must deal with many other aspects of this failing American economy, and we need a complete platform to show America how a Tea Party–infused GOP will put the middle class back in the driver's seat and turn this country around.

So in this chapter I propose a commonsense contract to protect, save, and serve America's middle class. This "Middle Class Contract with America" has three main goals: **support, stimulate, and reward job creation.**

As James Carville might put it, "It's about the jobs, stupid!"

How do you empower the middle class to prosper? With plentiful jobs by the millions, much smaller government, less government spending, fewer regulations, and unleashing energy independence. This "Middle Class Contract with America" is the polar opposite of the Obama socialist plan. It also differs from typical Republican plans because it involves both economic and personal freedom, as well as spending cuts (in order to rein in the size, scope, and power of government). Because tax cuts are useless and temporary without corresponding spending cuts. So it's the opposite of everyone. George Costanza and Jerry Seinfeld would be proud.

Can it be done? Look south to communist Cuba. Raul Castro cut one million government employees, privatizing vast swaths of government, and encouraging Cubans dependent on big government to find a private sector job, or start a small business. Even communists are getting the message.[1]

Or look north to our neighbor Canada. As noted earlier, in the late 1990s, facing economic disaster and debt, the Canadians pulled off an economic miracle by dramatically cutting spending and laying off government employees. Canadians turned a large deficit that threatened to destroy their economy into a budget surplus. But don't forget Canada's economy is built around energy production. They drill, drill, and drill some more. Smart.

If Cuba can do it, if Canada can do it, America (the greatest nation in world history) can do it bigger, better, and quicker. So here is the plan:

The Middle Class Contract with America

1) **Step One—the NITV—National Income Tax Vacation.** (See chapter sixteen above.)

2) **Step Two—The 0-15-0 tax plan** modeled after the most successful economy on earth—Hong Kong. (See chapter sixteen above.)

For those critics who believe an immediate cut of taxes to a flat 15 percent is too drastic, I offer a two-step process. Start the flat tax at 20 percent, to be reduced to 15 percent when the budget deficit is reduced to no more than 3 percent of GDP. This two-step process will stimulate taxpayers to elect politicians who will rein in spending, deficit, and debt. Don't say I'm not willing to compromise.

3) Jumpstart Jobs. America desperately needs jobs. Two of every three new jobs are created by small business.[2] We need to encourage more startups.

First, offer an "Angel Investors Tax Deduction." Under my plan investors receive a dollar-for-dollar tax credit for up to 50 percent of their income tax bill, up to $50,000, for investments in new business startups, as well as IPO and secondary offerings for small companies. This isn't for millionaires. It's tailor-made just for middle class investors.

Think what this means for jobs. A middle-income taxpayer can invest $5,000 or $10,000 or $25,000 on up to $50,000 in a small business startup, instead of giving the money to the IRS. Once you give $25,000 to Uncle Sam, it's gone forever. At the end of ten years you've thrown away $250,000. But if you could choose to invest $25,000 in a business every year for the next ten years (all tax deductible) and it works, you could have $1 million sitting around at the end of the decade. WOW! This is a middle class retirement plan.

Not only will this idea generate billions of start-up investment dollars for entrepreneurs, it will create millions of jobs and build wealth and retirement income for the middle class.

Second, create a "Small Business Payroll Tax Vacation" by suspending the employer's FICA Payroll Tax for two years. Obama (as usual) got this one backward. It's not the employees who should have gotten this break— it's the employers. Obama gave employees a small payroll tax cut of about $500 to $1,000 each. The results are in. What exactly did that do for the economy? Nothing. Did it create jobs? No. What we needed to do was motivate small business owners to hire more employees by giving *them* a payroll tax vacation. Cut the payroll taxes owed by small business owners (who create a majority of jobs) and you've just created the solution for our jobs crisis. Only businesses with two hundred employees or under qualify. If you want new jobs, always inspire the people who create jobs. Common sense.

The savings will be invested by small business owners in new job creation, expansion of businesses, new startups, or capital improvements, creating millions of new jobs. This is how you save the middle class, instead of murdering them.

Third, experts estimate American corporations (as in "big business") have over $1.95 *trillion* earned offshore that they're keeping parked there because of high U.S. corporate tax rates.[3] Along with lowering the corporate rate to a flat 15 percent, my plan allows companies to bring their foreign earnings back to America with only a small 10 percent tax. Companies will rush to take advantage—thereby instantly producing $195 billion in new tax revenues (10 percent of $1.95 trillion) to be applied to debt reduction. But, better yet, $1.95 trillion will be pumped into the U.S. economy, creating hundreds of thousands of new jobs.

However, while I've just cut corporate tax rates to a flat 15 percent and allowed corporations to bring all their offshore money back into the USA at an even cheaper tax rate, the Middle Class Contract with America would also eliminate corporate welfare—all the tax loopholes, credits, specially targeted deductions, subsidies, and bailouts. It ends corporate welfare as we know it.

We must support free market capitalism—not a "crony capitalist" system that picks winners and losers while awarding favors, subsidies, and sweetheart deals to the biggest campaign contributors. Think Solyndra, Obama's $500 million bust.

4) Freeze and Cut Regulations. It's not just taxes and spending that destroy economic growth and jobs. It's actually a three-headed monster, and the third head is regulations. Obama creates new government regulations by the thousands every year. The cost of his new federal regulations, just in the year 2012, was more than the cost of all new regulations in the entire first terms of George W. Bush and Bill Clinton *combined.*[4]

The staggering cost of complying with regulations is like a doubling of business taxes. And the cost gets passed to middle class consumers in the form of higher prices. A recent study by the Competitive Enterprise Institute estimates annual regulatory compliance costs for U.S. businesses at $1.8 trillion—more than the entire GDP of Canada, or Mexico.[5] Just imagine how our economy could boom if the dead weight of all that regulation were lifted.

First and foremost, all regulation must be frozen in place. No new regs until the national unemployment rate hits 6 percent or lower.

Second, let's create a commission filled with small business owners to streamline regulations and reform and repeal unnecessary and harmful regulations. Obama's Jobs Council (which rarely ever met) was filled with the CEOs of billion-dollar multi-national corporations. Those guys don't know how to create good-paying American jobs. They only know how to offshore good jobs. We need the input of small business owners, not big business CEOs.

Big business loves regulations. But small business creates most of the jobs. What do they think? Sixty-nine percent of small business owners report that regulations are hurting their business. Sixty-two percent of small business owners say taxes and regulations do more damage to their business than foreign competition. Fifty-four percent say China and India are more supportive of small business than America.[6]

Last, demand that the CBO (Congressional Budget Office) price out the cost of every proposed federal regulation before it goes into effect. This allows Congress and the public to see the actual cost of every bill. Now Congress passes laws (see: Obamacare) that are blank checks for executive agencies to force enormous compliance costs on the American people, and Congress never even sees what those costs are. The fact is there are 283,615 full-time government employees drafting and enforcing regulations, while fewer than fifty employees at the OMB (Office of Management and Budget) are reviewing the new regulations.[7]

5) Seal the Border and Reform Immigration Policy. (See chapter fourteen above.)

6) Reform Social Security, Medicare, and Medicaid for the future. These programs will consume the entire budget within twenty years. Social Security can be secured and the debt reined in with an *immediate* rise in the age of retirement to age sixty-eight for anyone younger than fifty-five. Then, just like automatic adjustments for inflation, the retirement age should be pegged to average lifespan and be regularly adjusted accordingly. This phase-in secures Social Security for decades to come *without* raising taxes. It's simple logic. People are living longer. We must adjust the age of retirement to keep America from going bankrupt.

Combine this age raise with a *partial* privatization of Social Security for younger workers. This gives younger Americans ownership of their own retirement accounts. Your retirement belongs to you—not a bunch of bureaucrats in D.C. who can change the rules at any time. More important, upon death your retirement account belongs to your family. As usual, this was never properly explained by Republicans. Social Security privatization is about economic freedom and ownership. Social Security should be your private property. When you die, why should government steal your retirement back from your family? It belongs to you, not the government. When you die, you can leave it to your grandkids. But the key here is "partial." There is nothing radical or frightening. For the most part, Social Security remains "as is."

Convert Medicare and Medicaid into block grants with the entire budgets controlled by the states. Constitutionally, these are issues for states to handle. Let's take advantage of fifty laboratories of experimentation and innovation. Let each state determine the best way to serve their citizens and save money on medical care. This will turn the states into competitors, fostering fierce competition to attract new residents and taxpayers.

7) Reform the Student Loan Program. Put the responsibility for student loan repayment where it should be—on the colleges. Social Security, Medicare, and Medicaid are huge contingent future liabilities of which most of us are aware. Few taxpayers are aware we are facing a huge contingent future liability from student loans too. These loans are now larger than total consumer credit card debt and are guaranteed by YOU, the taxpayer. With the highest default rates in almost twenty years, taxpayers are facing an exposure of over $1 trillion and growing rapidly.[8]

I propose we take this burden off the taxpayer and put it squarely where it belongs—on the educational institutions that took the money. They didn't have to take it, but since they did, as with any contractual obligation, by accepting a student's loan money the institution also accepted the responsibility to train that student to be a productive citizen, capable of repaying that loan. If they fail in that task, the educational institution (not the taxpayer), should be responsible for the debt. If the institution is not up to the task, they should not have taken the money in the first place. This will motivate schools to help students get jobs, so the debt is paid off. Who got the money? The colleges. So why shouldn't they get the bill if things go wrong?

This requirement should apply whether the institution is an auto-body repair school, beauty salon school, community college, or Ivy League university. If you take the money, you are responsible. A college's job is not to take the money for four years, then dump the student at the curb and walk away. If the student did not learn the skills required to get a job, the college has failed. If students can't find a job then colleges will have to cut $250,000 and $400,000 salaries to professors and administrators. Poor babies!

8) Reasonable, Fair, Commonsense Entitlement Reform.

A) Emulate England by putting a limit on the TOTAL amount of entitlement dollars each family can receive. It is only common sense. There are so many different welfare and entitlement programs that "playing the system" can become a full-time job and a huge disincentive for productive work and self-reliance.

This also stops welfare recipients from having more babies to receive more money. You want six kids, fine. This is America. You can have six kids. But we're not going to bribe you to have more kids by paying three times as much for six kids as for two. Like people who work for a living, you'll have to figure out a way to manage the family size you choose on your income.

B) Ban welfare recipients from voting while they are on the government dole. This is the ultimate conflict of interest. Why should someone burdening their fellow citizens, adding to the debt, and contributing nothing toward paying the bills of America, be entitled to vote themselves more welfare? I'm not discussing Social Security or Medicare here, which should not be considered welfare. People paid into those programs. The fact both those programs lose money is the fault of our elected officials, not those receiving benefits for which they already paid.

Progressives often claim that conservatives want to starve poor people. Well here's a reasonable, commonsense solution. We aren't starving anyone.

If you need help, you'll still get your checks. But you can't vote too. You can vote again as soon as you're off the government dole. Voting should be a privilege for those that pay into the system.

A quick commonsense answer for those who think this is "extreme" or "racist." These are the favorite arguments of Democrats. You know the definition of a racist? *Anyone winning an argument with a liberal.* There is nothing "extreme" about this idea. The private sector operates profitably. Government is a failure. Government operates at a huge loss. Under Obama that loss has been averaging about $1 trillion per year.[9] Do you consider that a success? Any private sector CEO would have been fired long ago.

Can you imagine letting people who owe large credit card debt to American Express or Visa vote on the terms of repayment? Do banks allow the customers with car loans and home loans to vote on the repayment schedule? Does Walmart allow the people who shop at Walmart to determine the prices they pay for goods? Of course not. These are all recognized as conflicts of interest. So why would people who collect welfare payments from government be allowed to vote for politicians who promise to pay bigger checks? That's like letting me run up a big Visa credit card bill and then vote for a new rule that reduces my Visa interest rate to zero.

C) All those who get welfare must work. Once again, no one is taking your checks away. But no one should get something for nothing. Why should anyone live off government checks and contribute nothing, while those of us paying our bills have to go to work every day?

Demand that anyone who collects a government check must perform a job for government. No exceptions. That means we can save billions by not having to hire expensive government employees. Let the welfare recipients do simple jobs. As an example, why shouldn't we assign welfare recipients to sort and deliver mail, thereby saving the Postal Service from losing billions of dollars per year?

Here's another example. America needs infrastructure rebuilding. Welfare recipients can flag traffic, dig ditches, or place orange cones on the road just as easily as highly paid union workers. Or let one single welfare mother manage a day-care center, so ten other welfare mothers can work at a government job.

Clearly people on welfare need jobs. I was recently in Washington, D.C., on business and took a jog outside my hotel. I was amazed at all the healthy, able-bodied young men sitting on stoops outside their buildings, laughing, playing, and drinking. Clearly they get checks from government. Why shouldn't they work for those checks?

Don't get me wrong. This is America and no one should go hungry. If you require welfare or charity, you'll get it. But no one should get it, unless they agree to perform a job. These are reasonable, moderate, fair reforms. No one will starve in the streets.

9) Pass a Balanced Budget Amendment to the Constitution, to take effect after the end of the National Income Tax Vacation.

10) Cut Spending! Put a plan in place to get "there" (to a balanced budget) from "here" (our national debt crisis). A balanced budget can only be accomplished by cutting government spending. We have a spending addiction problem in this country. It's time for rehab. Cutting spending helps the middle class, simply because they always get stuck with the bill. Here is what I propose:

a.   Immediately freeze spending at last fiscal year's level. Is that draconian? Last year we spent a *lot*. So we'll still be spending a lot. Let's keep it simple and use $3.5 trillion as our baseline (give or take, that was the 2013 figure). Total incoming tax revenues were about $2.8 trillion, leaving a deficit of over $600 billion.[10] That's simple math. So let's keep the solution simple too.

b.   Cut spending 10 percent each year. With this simple plan, cuts of $350 billion and $315 billion in the first two years would balance the U.S. budget—*without a tax increase*. Then we can start to pay down our debt.

c.   After a balanced budget is achieved, limit increases in government spending to the simple formula of "population growth plus inflation."

d.   Give the president the line item veto to carve additional waste out of each and every spending and budget bill passed by Congress.

e. Audit all federal agencies and programs and immediately eliminate all spending that is not constitutional. This would automatically result in the banning of stimulus, bailouts, corporate welfare, and green energy "investments" by government.

Obama, the media, and most politicians (both Republicans and Democrats) will call my plan "extreme" and "radical."

It is anything but. We're starting with a massive, bloated federal budget and our spending cuts are not draconian. The 10 percent spending cuts don't add up to $1.2 trillion until the end of four years. That's about the same as the "sequestration" agreed to by Congress as a last resort to lower the national deficit and debt.[11]

What makes my plan "radical" in their minds is that mine demands real spending cuts, not the usual Washington, D.C., fraud of cutting only the future increase in projected spending—and pushing all the painful cuts into distant future years, when a different set of politicians will be in office, and the cuts will never actually happen. The sequestration cut only the increase in spending for future years, but it never made a dent in the actual spending.[12]

On some issues I disagree with Republicans too. The reality is we can't get "there" from "here" without cutting defense spending. The exact amount of cuts can be a matter of debate. But in this plan ALL departments get cut.

11) Pay Down the Debt. Once we get the annual deficits under control, it is time to pay down the accumulated national debt. Remember a "balanced budget" means we are paying all our current bills. We have eliminated the deficit. It does nothing about the national debt. That hasn't been reduced one cent.

So in addition to spending cuts, I propose the following programs be targeted specifically to reduce the national debt. These ideas will pay down our debt and free up tens of billions of dollars in interest payments that can be used more productively.

a. It's time for a yard sale. The U.S. government is the biggest landlord in America, with billions in assets. Just like any other debtor, the government should sell assets to reduce its debt. The deficit commission identified sixty-four thousand buildings owned by the federal government that are "excessive, underutilized or vacant." Altogether, the federal government owns or manages nine hundred thousand buildings, 630 million acres of land (worth almost $1 trillion), and the mineral rights under that land. Put out a "Yard Sale" sign and start unloading—all of it must go to pay down the debt. As a side benefit, the cost of managing all these assets will be dramatically reduced.[13]

b. Allow Americans on their tax returns, and recipients of Social Security and other benefits, to check off a "pay down the debt" box. If citizens truly believed the money was only going to reduce the debt on their children and grandchildren, I believe the media would be amazed at how many Social Security recipients would gladly donate $5, $10, or even $25 per month to the cause.

12) Scale Back Our Military Adventurism. Wind down the wars around the world and require Congress, unless responding in self-defense, to issue a formal declaration of war before going to war.

That includes dramatically cutting military bases across the globe—specifically in Japan, Germany, and South Korea. It is time for our rich friends to pay their own way. If they want us to stay and provide their national security, they can pay for it. That way our military around the world can become a profit center. We'll defend anyone in the world—*if* the price is right.

That also includes implementing a rational foreign aid policy. Why are we sending money to countries that don't like us? Talk about the definition of "fiscal insanity." Why do we continue to give billions to countries like Pakistan (that hide and protect Osama bin Laden)...or the Palestinians (who name streets after terrorists that murder women and children)...or any one of the twenty or so countries in the United Nations that vote against us virtually 100 percent of the time? It is insanity to use taxpayer money to pay countries to hate us, and borrow forty cents of every dollar from China to do it!

I propose a very simple two-phase foreign aid plan.

- Phase I: Immediately stop foreign aid to countries that hate and mock us. At the very least, all payments must be tied to very specific, measurable actions that support America's interests.
- Phase II: Over a reasonable amount of time—thereby giving our good friends time to prepare—phase out the rest of foreign aid by 10 percent per year over 10 years. As a prime example, once we defund Israel's enemies, we can slowly wean Israel off foreign aid too, without any repercussions to our friend and special ally.

13) Repeal and Replace Obamacare. See the details below in chapter eighteen.

14) Reform Education. The current system is clearly a disaster where the worse the performance, the more money teachers unions and bureaucrats demand. My plan includes the following elements:

a. Get the federal government out of the education business. Education is not a responsibility delegated to it by the Constitution. Eliminate the Department of Education and redirect the funds to the state and local level.
b. Ban unionization of teachers. A well-educated country is essential to the economic future of America. Teachers unions have damaged education almost beyond repair.
c. End tenure. Teacher job security and compensation must be based on performance.
d. Encourage competition through school choice and offering parents vouchers at the state and local level. If competition works for Coke vs. Pepsi and Apple vs. Microsoft, it will certainly work to improve the quality of public schools.

15) Legalize and Tax Sin. I'm a proud card-carrying Reagan fiscal conservative. But Reagan once said, "I believe the very heart and soul of conservatism is libertarianism." Here's where I showcase my true libertarian bona fides. Prohibition has never worked—anywhere, at any time. People always find a way to do what they want. I say we capitalize on their "sins" by legalizing them. If it's necessary to regulate and tax them, do it at the state level. America is, after all, a Republic. Keep the federal government out of it—as per the Constitution. By now you know I'm not a big fan of taxes. But legalizing and taxing sin sure beats throwing Americans in jail for making personal choices that harm no one but themselves.

Nevada, my home state, is a laboratory for the national experiment and Nevada has proven it works. Taxes on legal gambling and now legal medical marijuana help fund our state government. "Sin taxes" allow us to have no personal or business income tax, no capital gains tax, no death tax, and the sixteenth-lowest property taxes in America.

Does legalization of "sin" hurt religious people? Nevada may be the "sin capital" of America, but you will undoubtedly be surprised that Las Vegas leads the nation in churches per capita.[14]

The Nevada model proves allowing more personal freedom does not interfere with the lives of religious people. Ironically it helps law-abiding, church-going citizens lead a much better quality of life. The taxes that gamblers and other "sinners" pay in Nevada, allow the "moral" church-goers to keep more of our own money and lead a better life. What if one man's choice to gamble or smoke marijuana allows you to pay lower taxes, thereby paying for your child's college education, or your retirement at age fifty-five. Is that bad? It's time to get our heads out of the sand.

Studies prove that the legalization of marijuana generates billions in new tax revenues nationally.[15]

Marijuana has been legalized in Colorado. As I was finishing this book the results came in. Colorado is on pace to haul in about $40 million in taxes in 2014. For a state budget, that's a huge chunk of change. That first $40 million is earmarked for school construction. That's $40 million paid for by pot users, not taxpayers. That's great news![16]

It's time to legalize, regulate, and tax sin, just as we already do alcohol. Billions in new tax revenue will be generated; and billions more in police, court, and prison costs reduced. That's not conservative or liberal politics. It's just smart economics.

16) Drill, Drill, Drill. Let's take the shackles off the U.S. energy industry. We should be encouraging drilling, natural gas, clean coal, nuclear, and fracking for shale gas. This is the opportunity of a lifetime. Because of technological advances, America is in the middle of an energy revolution. If only the Obama administration would take the shackles off, America could become the energy capital of the world. This issue is not just about economic growth. The energy industry has more of a direct impact on middle class Americans than any other issue.

We need to approve the Keystone Pipeline— instantly creating thousands of high-paying jobs. Keystone is also America's "best revenge" on Russia. According to the *New York Post*, "Together, the US and Canada have more oil and natural-gas reserves than Russia or the Middle East." We need an energy policy that exploits that advantage.[17]

We should expedite the approval of liquefied natural gas (LNG) plants and exports—so we can start supplying the EU with all of their energy needs (thereby taking away Russia's business). There are more than twenty LNG projects awaiting approval in the U.S.[18] Approving them would punish Russia (which supplies natural gas to the EU) and reduce Japan and India's dependence on Russian natural gas too. We also need to streamline regulations that have prevented the building of a single new oil refinery in the United States since 1976.[19]

An energy program that encourages oil drilling, fracking, clean coal, natural gas, and nuclear will create hundreds of thousands of middle class jobs and billions in new tax revenues, while dramatically reducing gas and electricity bills for middle class Americans. This is quite simply the greatest opportunity to improve the lot in life of the middle class *ever*.

17) Encourage New Sources of Energy. I propose we close the Department of Energy and use the $27 billion annual savings as a prize to the company or companies that find an economical, domestically-sourced replacement for fossil fuel. Taxpayers will save hundreds of billions in future spending, and once a company succeeds and claims the prize, we eliminate the motivation for going to war to secure access to foreign oil. This "open source problem solving" should be used to solve many of the biggest challenges facing our country.

18) Limit the Power of Congress and All Branches of the Federal Government. Note: Some of the key points below are covered in more detail in a later chapter.

a. Institute term limits.
b. Limit the amount of time Congress can meet to four months per year. The less time they meet, the less damage they can do to the American people and the U.S. economy.
c. Limit Congress to passing only bills that are PROVEN constitutional (as in the "Enumerated Powers Act").
d. Place a three-year moratorium on passing any new rules, regulations, or mandates on the American people or American business.
e. Ban members of Congress and their staff from serving if they have outstanding tax debts or liens. If the people that run the country can't or won't pay their tax bills, they have no right to ask us to pay ours.
f. Require that all bills be read out loud in front of a fully assembled Congress before they vote on them. This will put an end to two-thousand-page laws that no member of Congress ever reads, but all Americans are required to follow.
g. Post all bills online at least two weeks before voting on them, for public vetting.
h. Mandate that all laws passed by Congress also apply to members of Congress.
i. Allow the legislatures of two-thirds of the states to overturn any federal law or regulation. It's time to provide states with a check on a runaway Congress.

See chapter twenty-one below for how we can implement these constitutional reforms.

That's my "Middle Class Contract with America"—a platform that a Tea Party–infused, middle class–champion GOP can win on. This plan will put the U.S. economy back in high gear, while it puts the American middle class back to work (with high-paying jobs). It creates millions of jobs—just as Reagan's tax cut did in the 1980s. It restores economic freedom. It rewards entrepreneurship. It stimulates small business job creation. It limits the power of government—just as the Constitution demands. It puts the power back in the hands of the people. Most importantly, it stops *The Murder of the Middle Class.*

CHAPTER 18

Three Necessary Fixes

*Obamacare comes to more than two thousand pages
of rules, mandates, taxes, fees, and fines that have
no place in a free country.*
—Paul Ryan

DID YOU KNOW?

- One hepatitis pill that costs $1,000 in the U.S. costs $10 in Egypt
- Though "defensive medicine" may be responsible for as much as a third of healthcare costs, our lawyer president's healthcare "reform" doesn't include malpractice lawsuit reform
- Fraud involving hundreds of voters who may have voted in the 2012 presidential election in two different states has been uncovered in North Carolina

ith my "Middle Class Contract with America" we've got a great platform to run on—and a program for turning America back into the most prosperous nation with the greatest middle class in the world. But before we can restore the middle class to security, prosperity, and freedom, there are three important tasks we have to accomplish.

We can't begin building until we clear the ground—by getting rid of three pernicious institutions that are giving our own home-grown socialists the power to squeeze the life out of the middle class—and turning America into a Banana Republic. There are three things terribly wrong in America today, so wrong that if left unchecked they could undermine all our other good work and guarantee that *The Murder of the Middle Class* succeeds after all.

Those three insidious problems in Obama's America are 1) Obamacare, 2) the Fed's reckless creation of fiat money, and 3) voter fraud. We must repeal and replace Obamacare, rein in the Fed, and stamp out voter fraud with effective voter ID laws if we're going to take this country back for the middle class.

Repeal and Replace Obamacare

Capitalism and the U.S. economy cannot be saved without dealing with the ten-ton whale in the room: Obamacare. You saw in chapter nine how Obamcare is a ticking time bomb poised to definitively destroy the American middle class. Obama and Democrats constantly claim there is no better alternative. Really? Here is a simple and commonsense ten-point plan to repeal and replace Obamacare. Note that most, if not all, of these points have been proposed by other conservatives. I believe, however, that this is the first time they have been put into a comprehensive easy-to-implement plan...and, of course, they have my own "Capitalist Evangelist" twist.

HEALTH FREEDOM, allowing the marketplace to control costs and quality, is the alternative to inefficient, high-cost, low-quality, government-controlled Obamacare.

1) Make health insurance and medical costs tax-deductible from dollar one for individuals. Currently, businesses are allowed to deduct all the costs of the health insurance they provide their employees. For 2013 the only medical expenses most individuals could deduct were those that exceeded 10 percent of their adjusted gross income. One hundred percent of medical expenses should be deductible for individuals, putting individuals on par with corporations.

2) Encourage a free market in healthcare. Allow consumers to buy health insurance anywhere—including across state lines. If there are better and less expensive policies in New Hampshire than Nevada, why shouldn't the consumers in Nevada—and forty-eight other states—be allowed to buy them?

3) Encourage prevention over treatment. It's time to put prevention and healthy choices on par with the high costs of medicine and surgery after you've gotten sick. Make healthy alternatives tax-deductible just like health insurance, doctor visits, and drugs. Allow consumers to deduct the cost of vitamins, herbs, holistic doctors, gym memberships, and home gym equipment from their taxes. A healthy, fit America will save both consumers and government billions in healthcare costs.

4) Allow consumers to buy cheaper drugs from outside the U.S. Why can't we buy drugs at much cheaper prices across the border? Because Obama blocked our access as a bribe to Big Pharma (in return for their support for Obamacare). That bribe is costing Americans billions. How much can American consumers save? One pill for hepatitis costs $1,000 in America. The same exact pill costs $10 in Egypt.[1]

5) Seal the borders to prevent more illegal immigrants from coming to America to obtain "free" healthcare. We can't afford the healthcare costs of American citizens, so how can we pay for millions of new arrivals looking for "free" healthcare? Why would any country allow people in to get services for free? You'd have to be an idiot, insane, or looking to overwhelm the system and bankrupt taxpayers, right?

6) Implement tort reform and a "loser pays" malpractice system. U.S. medical costs are being driven through the roof by the powerful one-two punch of lawyers and lawsuits. Not just any lawsuits, but frivolous, ridiculous, and outrageous lawsuits. It's no coincidence Obamacare never addressed the number one problem in the healthcare system: tort reform. Obama is a lawyer, Michelle Obama is a lawyer, the White House staff is packed with lawyers,[2] trial lawyers are some of the Democrats' biggest donors.[3] Because the American political system—and especially the Democrats' electoral victories—are built on a foundation of legal bribery, the best possible solution for lowering healthcare costs was never even considered for Obamacare: tort reform was left on the cutting room floor.

The answer is quite simple: America needs to copy Texas. Texas has instituted major tort reform. The results are outstanding. Insurance rates for Texas doctors have dropped dramatically and thousands of new doctors moved into Texas. Then Texas went a step further. They became the first state to pass a "loser pays" system. That means anyone can still sue, but the plaintiff better have a good case, because a loss means the loser pays the attorney fees of both sides.

It's a simple, mainstream solution. Every major industrialized nation except America has a "loser pays" legal system. Somehow Obama and Obamacare left out the one idea that could have actually reduced our healthcare costs.

7) **Cap damage awards.** Putting caps (limits) on damage awards for pain and suffering will drive the cost of medical care down. It can be a fair cap, say $500,000, not the tens of millions of dollars often awarded in a single case. This would curb trivial lawsuits and stop the expensive practice of medically unnecessary "defensive medicine"—where doctors prescribe tests to defend against possible lawsuits (up to a third of healthcare costs may be attributable to this cause)[4]—while still holding doctors liable for real negligence.

8) **Medicaid recipients should be required to pay something, even if only a small co-pay.** If the patient pays no cost, it encourages over-utilization and waste. Everyone needs to have "skin in the game."

9) **Raise the eligibility age for Medicare.** Life expectancy is much longer than when Medicare was created. The original intent of Medicare was to ensure care during the last few years of life. As life expectancy moves upward, the age at which coverage begins should automatically be adjusted on a regular basis. The changes and timing should be left up to actuaries, not politicians.

10) **Give states more responsibility and flexibility for their social safety nets.** The Founding Fathers created a Constitution that left power in the hands of the states—where decisions could be made closer to the citizens. States are ultimately responsible for the healthcare of their poor

and indigent citizens and should each decide how best to handle those costs. These fifty "laboratories of innovation" will find the solutions that will help improve the healthcare system with the best solutions being adopted by others.

Rein in the Fed with a Gold Standard

We've already seen, in chapters five and fourteen, how the Fed's reckless money-printing is driving the middle class into poverty while the richest .01 percent make out like bandits. Without the Fed's fiat money, Obama and his cronies would have to stop charging their reckless spending spree to our children and grandchildren.

Cutting spending is hard to do. It takes discipline. In many cases, people must be forced into doing it. It's often the last possible choice. So here's how you force a reckless irresponsible government to cut taxes: with a gold standard.

I spend a lot of time attacking Democrats (because it's so easy to do), but it's often Republicans who abandon their principles and make the really big mistakes. In 1971 it was Republican President Richard Nixon who removed the dollar's link to gold.

This final deathblow to "real" U.S. money created the fiat currency (paper notes) that we all use today. With this decision, the Fed could now print unlimited amounts of inherently worthless paper dollars, and be immune from any (immediate) consequences.

Why did Nixon do it? Primarily to hide his out-of-control spending on the Vietnam War. Bombers, bombs, and tanks cost big money. When the government wants things it can't afford, the Fed covers the actions of big-spending politicians by creating fake money out of thin air. But who has to pay back all that debt eventually? The middle class.

Needless to say, since 1971 inflation has soared, thereby robbing the hard-working middle class of their savings. Wall Street fraudster Bernie Madoff has nothing on the U.S. government. Our government runs the biggest Ponzi scheme on earth.

Politicians despise the gold standard because it keeps their greed in check. With a gold standard in place, a central bank cannot create money out of thin air to fund any and all government pet projects and earmarks. With a gold standard in place, politicians can't just bribe voters with promises of more spending, entitlements, and poverty programs.

It is time we put common sense and sanity back into our monetary system and return to the gold standard, which will create a stable, credible, reliable money supply and a true free market economy. The gold standard ensures that you can't spend what you don't have. The gold standard protects the middle class from liars, frauds, reckless spenders, and corrupt politicians.

A return to the gold standard will prevent politicians from inflating the money supply. They will no longer be able to hide from the American public the actual costs of the welfare state, corporate bailouts, entitlements, stimulus packages, and wars across the globe. Remember the old saying, "A billion here, a billion there, and pretty soon you're talking real money!" That's exactly what politicians want to spend. Spending serious money makes them feel important. Just keep in mind that serious money comes from you and me.

It is this simple: a return to the gold standard will force politicians to live within their means. For that very reason fiscal conservatives like me love the gold standard. We want the size of government and the imaginations of politicians *limited*. The gold standard is a fiscal conservative's dream come true. Let me summarize. The gold standard:

- Prevents out-of-control deficit spending;
- Prevents runaway, unlimited hiring of government bureaucrats and the pension liabilities that come with them;
- Hinders government's ability to dole out massive welfare and entitlement programs; and
- Stands in the way of government's ability to redistribute wealth and pursue economic re-engineering.

Plus, under the gold standard, money regulates itself.

With the gold standard in place, government automatically becomes more open, honest, and transparent. It either lives within its means or has to raise taxes—instead of simply printing more money and therefore creating a *stealth* tax (inflation) that robs the savings of the middle class.

New York Senator Elihu Root realized all this back in 1913. It's a shame we didn't listen. The Fed is now the biggest buyer of new American debt.[5] Why? Because there aren't enough investors out there willing to take the risk of buying our debt. With $17 trillion in debt (and counting), any major rise in interest rates would eat up the entire U.S. budget. There'd be no money left for national defense or entitlement programs. The Fed's solution? Print more and print faster. It is a vicious downward "death spiral."

As the man who jumped from the roof of a thirty-story building yelled as he passed the fifteenth floor: "So far, so good!" The splat has yet to come, but it will come. And it will be devastating.

The solution is simple. First, we must audit the Fed. As unbelievable as this may seem, the Fed has never been audited since it was founded in 1913. The American people have no idea what the Fed has been up to for the last century. Isn't it time we took a look under the hood?

Then, with the audit information in hand, we should next develop a plan to eliminate the Fed and restore the gold standard. It is the only way to stop the insanity and protect America from an economic disaster that will make the current economy look like boom times.

To put it bluntly, it's time to end the Fed, before the Fed ends the middle class.

Bust the Voter Fraud Scam with Voter ID

As I was finishing this book, hundreds of cases of possible voter fraud in the 2012 presidential election were uncovered in North Carolina. It appears that a large number of people voted twice in the election—in North Carolina and in another state.[6]

Folks, we are being scammed. Democrats are winning elections through what appears to be massive voter fraud.

Many citizens may not realize most national elections are won by a sliver of votes in only a few key battleground states. Change the vote totals by a small bit in a few states—Ohio, Florida, Virginia, Colorado,

Nevada, New Mexico, Wisconsin, Iowa, Pennsylvania—and Romney is the president.

Why did Obama and the Democrats win (by just a sliver) in those few battleground states? In 2012 it was a powerful one-two punch, both of which were out-and-out election fraud.

First, Obama used the IRS as his personal mafia thug enforcers to persecute, intimidate, and destroy his political opposition—ranging from Tea Parties, to conservative fundraising organizations, to top GOP donors, to high-profile outspoken critics like myself.

Obama's IRS killed enthusiasm and intensity, dampened energy, silenced free speech, and prevented fundraising through a witch hunt. This changed the outcome of the 2012 election, and Obama should be impeached for it.

If you think impeachment can't happen, study Ukraine. One day the arrogant president was mocking protestors and sending police to kill them. The next day he was abandoning his palace, impeached by Congress, running for his life ahead of mobs and police, and the military was hugging the citizens in the streets.

It can all change quickly. What was once considered impossible or unrealistic can quickly become reality.

The IRS scandal is a very "teachable moment." Impeach Obama and no president will use the IRS for political purposes ever again. Problem solved. If the GOP can win the Senate in 2014 it may be possible for congress to credibly investigate and tie Obama to the IRS scandal.

But an even more widespread problem involves voter ID (or the lack of it). Without voter ID, Democrat voters across this country could be voting four times, five times, ten times each. There is no way to prevent it, and the facts indicate that is exactly what happened in 2012.

Take Philadelphia as just one example. There were voting precincts in Philly where the combined vote was Obama over Romney by more than 19,000 to 0.[7] GOP poll watchers were forcibly removed from voting places in Philadelphia for several hours, until a judge ordered them back in.[8] During those hours were the ballot boxes stuffed? Did Democrat voters vote ten times each? As absurd as 19,000 to 0 is (it's just statistically impossible), maybe the right vote total was closer to 6,000 to 100. It makes a big difference in the final vote total in a close race.

If I'm wrong, why did the wolves want the chicken coup left unguarded?

How easy is it to cheat? Even left-leaning Politico reported the U.S. voter registration system "is in chaos." Millions of dead people are still on the voter rolls, 24 million registrations are no longer valid, 12 million have incorrect addresses, and 2.75 million people are registered to vote in more than one state.[9]

The obvious solution? Voter ID.

But Democrats *hate* voter ID. It's one of their biggest issues. But that's ridiculous. You need an ID to do most anything: cash a check, buy cigarettes or alcohol, buy groceries, board a plane, get food stamps, or get any government benefits. You even need ID to get into government buildings! But here's the best one of all: protestors were asked to bring photo ID to a recent NAACP event in North Carolina protesting Voter ID.[10] Voter ID is a no-brainer.

So why are Democrats so intense and passionate about such a commonsense issue? *Methinks thou doth protest too much.*

This is a much bigger issue than meets the naked eye. Democrats are losing their minds over voter ID because they know they can't win elections without fraud. Obama and his socialist cabal are making a mountain out of a molehill because this issue is their edge. This is how they win elections when their policies are a failure, when they've ruined the economy, when they've spent the country into bankruptcy, when they've killed millions of jobs. Voter fraud is their secret weapon. They stuff the ballot box. *They cheat.*

I dare Democrats to prove me wrong. But of course they won't. They don't dare agree to voter ID because with voter ID we would be able to stop voters from voting multiple times, in different precincts, using false names, or the names of dead voters, or the names of voters who have moved, or using illegal immigrants to illegally vote across this country.

There is finally proof positive that the Democrats' objections to voter ID are a complete scam. Obama's Democratic Party argues against voter ID because:

A) It's racist,

B) It's meant to stop people from voting, and

C) It's too big a burden for poor and minority voters to obtain photo ID.

I just returned from two doctor visits for a checkup and a follow-up test. These were my first doctor visits since Obamacare took effect in 2014. Guess what both medical offices asked me for before any doctor could see me, or any medical test could be done?

Official government-issued photo ID.

You cannot see a doctor or receive your Obamacare benefits without ID to prove it's really you. A health insurance card won't do the trick; the medical office needs to prove you are in fact the person whose name is on the insurance card.

I questioned the nurses at both offices. They verified no one is able to collect their Obamacare benefits from any doctor or medical office without showing ID. And since everyone is now required by law to have health insurance (or is given free insurance), the government is requiring that EVERYONE have a photo ID.

Does that make Obama and the Democrats racists? No, what it makes them is hypocrites who are shaking in their boots in fear of fair elections. Because fair elections (without massive voter fraud) mean Democrats will have a harder time winning. Don't look now, but Obamacare just destroyed the Democrat argument against voter ID. If you have photo ID for your Obamacare, then you already have it to present at the voting booth.

The Democrats are BUSTED!

Their hypocrisy is unbelievable. Every single Democrat voter must be lining up to get their photo ID so they can get their Obamacare. The argument that poor and minority Democrat voters don't have ID, or shouldn't be "burdened" to get it, is out the window. The idea that asking for ID is racist is out the window.

That leaves only one possible reason to oppose photo ID for voters…so the Democrats can preserve their ability to cheat and steal elections!

President Obama, you are BUSTED.

It was recently reported by the media that an Ohio woman who was convicted of voter fraud because she voted for Obama SIX times in the 2012 election sat on the board of an environmental group that received an Obama administration EPA grant and attended a conference with Obama's Labor secretary Hilda Solis.

It's important to note that after she served time in prison for her crime, her sentence was reduced because of a George Soros–funded group's intervention. Then, upon release from prison, she was hugged on stage by Al Sharpton at a Democrat party rally.[11]

Are you starting to get the picture? Connect the dots. Important Democrats, with important careers, sitting on boards of influential organizations that receive government funding, are voting six times. She's just the one who got caught. How many more are there? Just think how many anonymous Democrat voters across this country, with nothing to lose, are voting six or ten or twenty times. Think of the importance of national Democrat figures like Al Sharpton publicly congratulating a criminal released from prison for voter fraud. Think of the importance of Soros-funded groups fighting on her behalf. There is no doubt that elections are being stolen across this country in order to advance *The Murder of the Middle Class.*

CHAPTER 19

The Most Important Sales Job in History

Facts tell, stories sell.
—old adage often quoted in sales,
advertising, and Hollywood

DID YOU KNOW?

- Every U.S. presidential election since 1960 has been won by the candidate who smiled more
- Barry Goldwater and George McGovern had the same agendas as Ronald Reagan and Barack Obama—but not the personality to win elections
- Congressman Steve Pearce represents a majority-Hispanic district on the Mexico border—as a conservative Republican

W e know what to do. We've got the perfect platform for saving the middle class and making America a great, free, and prosperous nation again. But the best ideas in the world don't mean anything if we can't actually win elections. And without winning the Congressional election in 2014—and more crucial, and much more difficult—the presidential election in 2016—it will be too late. *The Murder of the Middle Class* will have succeeded.

To win those elections, we need the right candidate, the right sales techniques, and the right attitude—the relentless energy to keep pushing through to VICTORY. In this chapter I address the question of the practical steps we need to take to boot the socialist-fascist-totalitarian frauds (i.e., the Democrat Party) out of office and put the new and improved Republican Party, infused with Tea Party energy and ideals, and ready to champion the middle class, in charge.

Finding the Right Candidate

The GOP is mistaken. They keep looking for a presidential candidate with the right pedigree and credentials. What they should be looking for is a messenger, a charismatic salesman. The fact is, in politics the messenger (like it or not) is more important than the message.

Barack Obama is 100 percent about sales. He sells 24/7/365. He sells to win elections, and to win public opinion on issues too. Obama may have disdain for business, but he sure understands the art of the sale.

The GOP thinks facts win elections. Madison Avenue and Hollywood know better. "Facts tell, stories sell." The GOP has facts on its side. What we need is a storyteller. We need emotion and passion. We need to win hearts and minds. Blandly recited facts won't do that. Emotional stories will. Because of Obamacare, we have great material to work with! In the next few chapters I'll give you the details about how Obama and Obamacare stories can win elections.

For now, let's focus on the need for a talented, dynamic, charismatic messenger and salesman to sell these stories to the voters. Barack Obama is an outstanding example on the Democrat side. Ronald Reagan is the GOP's best example.

Reagan was a Barry Goldwater protégé. They had the same views, opinions, and policies. Reagan gave the speech that many believe won the 1964 Republican convention for Goldwater.

In 1964, Goldwater lost in a landslide. Yet sixteen years later in 1980, with the exact same message Reagan won in a landslide, then won again in 1984. What was the difference?

The difference was the communicator. Reagan was a salesman extraordinaire. He was funny. He was telegenic. He had a great big smile. He was charismatic. He told great stories. He spent decades honing his craft as a Hollywood actor. Acting, sales, ability to communicate, those are the ingredients of a winning political candidate.

The GOP has spent three decades looking for "another Reagan." But they have been looking in the wrong place. They are looking for someone with the same message when what they need is the same quality of messenger. The GOP message has really never changed. But without a great messenger, it has fallen on deaf ears.

This is not just the GOP's problem. The exact same thing has happened on the Democrat side. Barack Obama has the exact same views, opinions, and policies as George McGovern. They were both ultra-leftist, socialist, anti-business apologists, and weak on foreign affairs and national defense. Yet Obama won two presidential elections while McGovern, like Goldwater on the GOP side, lost in a historic landslide.

What was the difference? The messenger, not the message. Personality…communication…sales skills…charisma…emotional stories. Obama has those things. McGovern didn't. McGovern was bland, just like Goldwater, No personality. No charisma. No stories. No smile.

Obama has much in common with Reagan. Not his views, those are obviously polar opposites. But Reagan and Obama have similar personalities. Obama, like Reagan, smiles all the time. He tells stories, not facts. He appeals to emotion, not reason. He makes people feel good. Obama is a quintessential salesman.

Still not convinced? How about the study by two scientists who proved that every U.S. presidential election since 1960, when a television was in every living room, has been won by the candidate who smiled more. That's over half a century of solid proof.[1]

All these years of intellectual debates, serious speeches, thousands of hours of campaigning and billions of dollars spent on advertising…and it turns out it always came down to who smiled the most. Smile, you're on candid camera!

But I think the difference goes much deeper. Whoever smiles the most also has the bigger personality, the better salesmanship skills, the most charisma, and the better storytelling skills. It's a package deal.

And I'll take it one step further. I believe virtually every election in America from school board and town council up to Congress and president is determined by who smiles the most and tells the best stories. Republicans need to understand this isn't only about message, or principles, or policies. It never has been. Tea Party principles won't win elections, unless they are accompanied by big bright pearly whites. We have to learn to choose candidates who smile and sell in order to win elections. Find me a great message coming from the smiling mouth of a great messenger and salesman and I'll show you the winning candidate.

So GOP, stop looking for another candidate with Reagan's message and start looking for a great messenger and salesman (or saleswoman) with Reagan's smile, personality, charisma, and stories! That's how the GOP will win back the White House and every other political office.

The Ground Game

The GOP must find salesmen and women to sell conservatism. But winning elections isn't just about the candidate and his or her personal ability to sell, communicate, and smile. Although a critical ingredient, that alone does not guarantee success. It's also about the database, sales force, and "ground game." It's about all the things that are geared to motivating the customer to take action, get off the couch, and vote.

Today, successful companies have detailed databases of customers, as well as teams of tech-savvy whiz kids who analyze the data. They break down the demographics and identify the buyers—where they come from, why they buy, what motivates them—and determine how we can reach them to make a sale today. Once that information is in place, the sales force goes to work—attacking, pushing, prodding, hounding, and motivating the customers and potential customers to buy the products.

How a Successful Company Builds a World-Class Business

1. Build a massive database.
2. Know everything about your customers' habits.
3. Repetition, repetition, repetition. Make sure customers hear from you again and again (with TV, radio, emails, and direct mail). Put your company name or product name in front of them every day in every way. The more they see it, the better the chance they'll take ACTION and buy something.
4. Have your sales force make nonstop personal contact with customers.
5. Finally and most importantly, never forget that loyal, repeat customers are the base of your business. It is far easier and much less expensive to retain a loyal customer than to find a new one.

Did you think that people buy on their own, without prodding? If that is the case, why do companies hound you with calls, emails, direct mail, catalogs, and special offers: "free, half off, two for the price of one, special price today only"? It's all about getting you to take action. You show me a successful "best in its industry" company, and I'll show you a company that understands the customer is everything. These companies use advertising to build a detailed database of potential customers. From that point on it's all about the GROUND GAME— in other words, attack, attack, and attack relentlessly.

Team Obama understands that the rules of business are the exact same rules of politics. For some strange reason, the GOP doesn't. That is how Obama won reelection. Team Obama built the most detailed database in the history of politics, then they put in place a relentless "ground game" to get out their voters.

First they maintained constant contact through emails, direct mail, and phone calls.

Second, Team Obama knew where the most likely Democratic voters were—down to the voting precinct, each block in the precinct, each building on the block, and each apartment in each building. Then they hounded them, cajoled them, motivated them, and relentlessly pushed them to get out and vote.

Last, they concentrated on their loyal, repeat customers—i.e., "likely Obama voters."[2] The media talks all day about how the GOP needs to have a "big tent" and "reach independent voters," but all that pales in importance compared to getting your own "most likely" voters to the polls. Whoever does that best usually wins the election. Obama didn't win because of his message or policies. He merely got every one of his likely voters to the polls by pulling them, pushing them, prodding them, tackling them, lassoing them, pointing them, or driving them there. Just as any great sales organization does in the business world.

To win elections you must start with a smile and great salesmanship. But that's only the start. Getting out every last vote—the ground game—is even more important. Team Obama mastered both of those strategies.

The GOP's get-out-the-vote effort in 2012 wasn't just pathetic, it was non-existent. The GOP tried to build a database to get out the vote for Romney on election day. It was small and not nearly as detailed as the database of Team Obama, but it was at least something…until it crashed the morning of the election! The software had never been beta-tested until election day.[3] And at that crucial moment it crashed. Republicans had no ground game on election day to compete with the most sophisticated get-out-the-vote effort in political history by Obama. And *still* Obama won the election by only a sliver of votes in a few key battleground states.

Even with all the smiling, communicating, and salesmanship, Obama still needed the high-tech sophisticated database and "ground game" to seal the deal. Despite all this, I predict a GOP landslide this fall. Why? Because this is a mid-term election. Without Obama on the ballot, Democratic voters will not turn out in big numbers. Only super-committed Tea Party conservatives are dedicated enough to come out in big numbers in a Congressional election year. That and, of course, the devastating failure of Obamacare will motivate Republicans to vote this fall.

But 2016 is a different story. The GOP must develop a database and demographic software to compete with Democrats for the presidency. Then they must perfect the "ground game." That's how you win elections.

Always remember the sales model from successful companies in the business world. People don't vote on their own, just as few customers in the business world buy without prodding. It's all about sales—you must give them a reason to buy, or a reason to vote. Then you must hound them with calls and emails to force them to follow through. Most people (no matter how well intentioned) are procrastinators. They make excuses. They get busy. They just don't care enough. They're lazy. Whatever the reason, it takes pushing, prodding, and motivating to get them off the couch.

The GOP must follow the Obama model. Find candidates who are great salespeople…who smile…who communicate…who can sell a conservative message. Then run a 24/7 sales campaign supported by a sophisticated high-tech database and demographic models. Then hire relentless salesmen to coordinate an intensive ground game to get out the vote. Winning is about pushing every last supporter on your side to the polls by 8:59 p.m. on election night. Policy is secondary. Get-out-the-vote is the biggest factor in winning elections. Go after the people who are already committed Republicans and give them a hundred good reasons to vote.

Politics is all about motivating the customer to take action.

Let's Show Minority Voters We Give a Damn

Let me give you a couple of examples of how salesmanship can make a difference in politics.

Our candidates need to give 110 percent. They need to out-work their Democratic opponents. They need to reach out and touch someone, actually *everyone* in their district. They need to wear out the leather on the soles of their shoes. That is what is missing in so many GOP candidates—a willingness to give 110 percent. We need to meet the people, show we give a damn, show we really care about their problems, and offer real solutions.

Exhibit A is Republican Congressman Steve Pearce of New Mexico. He is the model for the new Republican Party. Congressman Pearce is the only GOP Representative with a district on the U.S.-Mexico border—a rare white, non-Hispanic voted into Congress by a Hispanic-majority district.

I keep hearing that the GOP needs to change its views to appeal to minority voters. Not true. We just need to campaign door to door in minority districts and show we give a damn. We need to show the voters we are willing to work hard to win their votes.

How does Congressman Pearce do it? In an interview in the *National Journal* he described his advantage.[4] He simply out-works his opponents. He wears out his shoe leather. His district is the largest in America—a district bigger than the state of Florida with eighteen counties and over seventy thousand square miles. Yet he is reelected every year. When he stepped down to run for the U.S. Senate and lost, he came back in 2010 and beat the incumbent Democrat. Let that sink in…a white Republican beat an incumbent Democrat in a Hispanic-majority district.

Is he a liberal? Is he pro-amnesty? To the contrary, Pearce is a principled conservative and opposes amnesty for illegal immigrants. So how could he win that district? The answer is that his constituents like him. He works hard, attends meetings, knows their names, allows voters to question him at numerous town hall events across the district. In other words, he is INTERACTIVE.

We have a problem. Too many Republican candidates are country club Republicans. They don't go door to door in minority neighborhoods. They are afraid or unwilling to bring their message to the neighborhoods of Democrats. Pearce brings his message unapologetically to every corner of his district. Showing you care is often just about showing up.

Pearce knows that Hispanics will vote for him if he works hard for them: "they're looking for people who understand their desire for better education for kids, jobs, and safety in the streets."[5]

Amen.

Few people know that I first ran for political office at the age of twenty-one. I proved Congressman Steve Pearce's theory correct back in 1983. I was a kid, just days out of college. But I'd been in politics all my life. My parents were two of the original founders of the New York State Conservative Party. They showed up at the first meeting in 1962 and were leaders for thirty years in Westchester County, N.Y. My political career began at age three, in my dad's arms, handing out political literature for Barry Goldwater in front of a supermarket in Mt. Vernon, N.Y. I grew up campaigning for Republicans across New York State. Every GOP leader in the state knew my parents had raised me to become a future GOP star.

So in the spring of 1983, Republican leaders asked to meet with me. They asked if I would run against the most unbeatable Democrat incumbent in New York State for the office of Westchester County legislator. Since it was impossible to beat this candidate, no one else would run. In previous races she had won by embarrassing margins. The New York GOP leadership would watch how I fared. It would be a "trial run" to gauge my future as a statewide GOP candidate.

I agreed. At the time I believe I was the youngest Republican candidate in the history of New York. Why was the Democrat so unbeatable? First, she was a very good campaigner. Second, she out-worked every opponent by tenfold. Third she was in an overwhelmingly Democratic district. It was primarily black and Jewish, lifelong Democrats.

Into the fray I stepped—white Republican, twenty-one years old, only days out of college. My opponent never knew what hit her.

I campaigned as hard then as I work today running my businesses—sixteen to eighteen hours a day. I ate, slept, and lived my campaign. I walked the entire district from top to bottom. I met every voter. I put my campaign literature under every door. Most of the voters I met were lifelong Democrats and therefore hated me for being a Republican. But they all respected me. The single response I got the most was pure shock to actually see a Republican candidate at their door.

I walked up and down every public housing project building in New Rochelle, N.Y. These buildings were 100 percent black, with graffiti on the walls, gangs hanging out in the hallways, drug deals going on in the stairwells. Many times I knocked on doors in these buildings and black women would say, "Are you crazy? What are you doing here? You're going to get yourself killed." Then they insisted on walking door to door with me, to keep me safe. I'll never forget what those nice women did for me. I never got a scratch. Soon I was respected. Gang members walked up to me to say, "You're one brave white boy. You are under my protection from now on."

I campaigned a dozen times in each building from June through November. By election day, I was known by every tenant of those buildings as "that crazy white boy... who has *balls*... who cares about us... the only white Republican who has ever stepped foot in these buildings."

I didn't win the election, but my "unbeatable" Democrat opponent was forced to campaign harder against me than anyone she ever ran against in her life. After the campaign she called me to say, "I'm exhausted. I've never seen a Republican like you in my life...and I hope I never see one like you ever again. I can't do this a second time."

A black Democrat district leader came up to me on election day, as I directed my team of a hundred young volunteers to fan out across the district for last-minute campaigning. He said, "I've been doing this for twenty-five years, and I've never seen a better run campaign in my life. Not from a Democrat. Not from a Republican. And you're twenty-one years old? I'd be proud to work on your next campaign. You will be the first and only Republican I'll ever support in my life." It brought tears to my eyes.

I lost that night, but I gave my opponent the scare of her life.[6]

Steve Pearce is right. Republicans need to bring our message to the people—black people, Hispanic people, Asian people, Jewish people, gay people. They want you to care enough to show up. They want to shake your hand—even if they disagree with your views. They want to feel you give a damn. They want to vote for the politician that works the hardest to get their vote. Do that...and Hispanic Democrats will vote for a Republican who opposes amnesty for illegal immigrants. Do that...and black Democrats will vote for a Republican who wants to cut spending and the size of government.

The problem is black voters have never seen a white Republican in their district. They've never met one in the lobby of their building. They've never seen one in front of their supermarket. They've never shaken the hand of a white Republican asking for their vote.

Steve Pearce proves it works. He wins year after year in a Hispanic-majority district. I proved it works in a 100 percent black urban housing project in 1983.

Republicans need to outwork our opponents, wear out our shoe leather, and show people, all people, that we give a damn.

CHAPTER 20

The Magic of Branding

. . . embrace the first principles of marketing, which involves
brand definition and consistent storytelling.
—**Simon Mainwaring**

DID YOU KNOW?

- This administration that claims it's "committed to" small business proposed over 6,000 new rules, regulations, and mandates in a single quarter
- Obama's NIH gave scientists $1.5 million to research why lesbians are fat
- The White House bragged about photos of Americans *standing in line* to sign up for government-mandated healthcare

O bama was the right candidate for the Democrats, but they also did an outstanding job of "branding" the GOP. By "branding," I mean planting in the voters' minds what your opponent stands for. The Democrats have branded the GOP as anti-minority and anti-women. They have done an even better job of branding conservatives and the Tea Party as "extremists," "radicals," and "racists." If the GOP is to win elections, we must go on the attack. That attack must include branding the Democrats and their policies.

It was easy for the Democrats to brand the GOP, because they have the mainstream media as their partners. The GOP doesn't have that advantage.

Since we know the media hates Republicans, conservatives, and the Tea Party, we must find another way to get our branding messages out. We need to ignore the mainstream media. Go over their heads, directly to the American people, with **INFOMERCIALS.**

Infomercials have sold hundreds of millions, undoubtedly billions of dollars of products and services over the years. Personally, TV and radio infomercials have been my most successful marketing tools, reaching millions of Americans.

You don't need the media to love and adore you; you don't need their approval. All you need to do is open your checkbook and pay for the media time. Using this model for over twenty years, I aired a Saturday morning football pregame show that got as many as *fifteen thousand* consumers to call and order my products on a typical Saturday morning. Yes, I said FIFTEEEN THOUSAND on one morning.

What I'm trying to say is: **SCREW THE MEDIA.** This is the model for the GOP. Go over the media's head. Buy thirty-minute blocks of time on cable TV on weekday nights, late night, early mornings, and weekends. Blanket cable TV channels that conservatives, gun enthusiasts, business owners, patriots, hunters, fishermen, independents, and other target audiences like youth, women, and Hispanics like to watch. Blanket Christian television too.

Also buy thirty-minute blocks of time at night and on weekend mornings on radio across the USA. Then create, produce, and air thirty-minute TV and radio programs explaining why Americans need to vote Republican and vote out Obama and his Marxist cabal.

Why is a thirty-minute infomercial so effective? Because:

A) A thirty-minute infomercial allows Republicans to answer the questions the media refuses to allow us to answer. We need to specifically answer the hard questions that independents, young adults, college students, women, and minorities might ask. We need to show them charts and facts (like Ross Perot did) that prove Obama's ideas and policies have damaged their lives, ruined their careers, killed their jobs, and taken away their freedom.

B) Thirty-minute infomercials will give us the time to explain the IRS scandal, Benghazi, Obamacare, and Obama's other criminal actions.

C) Thirty-minute infomercials allow us to showcase average middle class Americans and their personal stories—up close and personal. We can sit in the living rooms and kitchens of real people who have gut-wrenching stories of how Obama's policies have damaged their lives, or their small businesses, or their farms, or forced them to fire employees, or downsize their company...how Obamacare has hurt them.

D) Thirty minutes allows us to show the real stories of what one man with radical Marxist ideas has done to real middle class Americans in five years.

E) You can get points and facts across that are impossible to convey in a one-minute commercial on prime time TV or radio. A one-minute commercial is perfect for the Democrats, who have nothing to say. A one-minute commercial is perfect for Obama, who campaigns with no facts, just as a celebrity. A one-minute commercial is perfect for the low-information voters of the Democratic Party. They won't pay attention for more than one minute anyway!

F) Last and most important, if you want to change people's minds, educate them, and fill them with facts, you need thirty minutes.

Show those stories during a thirty-minute program, blanket the airwaves for sixty days in the run-up to the election, and it's GAME, SET, & MATCH for the GOP.

Brand Obamacare

I travel the world lecturing about branding. I recently returned from a sixteen-day, four-city tour of South Africa where I taught "Branding, American Style." Branding works. The bestselling products in America owe their success to branding. Apple. IBM. Coca-Cola. Pepsi. Disney. McDonald's. Microsoft. Merrill Lynch. Mercedes.

The Republican Party needs to start branding too. The first thing to brand is Obamacare. It should be the easiest law to brand and destroy in the history of American politics—right up there with Prohibition. How? By telling real-life, dramatic, and emotional stories about and by American families just like you...suffering because of Obamacare. Show what Obamacare has done to their lives...and why you, the viewer, may be next. This is a reality show combined with a horror movie.

Once the truth is out, Obama and the Dems will be dead at the polls. All you have to do is show real-life interviews and testimonials like the following:

- Americans with terminal cancer who have lost their health insurance, because of Obamacare.[1]
- Americans with terminal cancer who have lost their trusted doctor who has kept them alive for years, because of Obamacare.[2]
- American parents of little children with cancer who have lost their insurance or doctor, because of Obamacare.[3]
- Americans who signed up with Obamacare, were told they were insured, then had a heart attack, and now have $400,000 in medical bills because the Obamacare exchange never signed them up for an actual insurance policy.[4] This is directly because of one man—Barack Obama.
- Average American middle class families in anguish who have lost their health insurance—and they are scared.[5]
- Average American middle class families in anguish whose insurance rates have skyrocketed[6]—and they can no longer afford to be insured.
- Average middle class Americans who have lost their job, because of Obamacare.[7] Health insurance is now the least of their worries.
- Average middle class Americans who had their job downsized to part-time hours, because of Obamacare.[8]
- Average middle class Americans who are angry because they supported Obamacare, but now have to live with the disastrous results: unaffordable policies, long waits, poor care, and bureaucratic indifference.[9]

- Small business owners who can't afford the new Obamacare law and simply dropped all insurance.[10]
- Small business owners who have laid off employees or downsized their staff to part-time because of Obamacare.[11]
- Small business owners who are closing their business because of the combination of Obamacare taxes and the nightmare Obama economy.[12]
- Internet experts based in America who can't understand why Obama hired a foreign firm to design a defective Obamacare website—thereby costing American jobs.[13] Bring in experts to estimate how many U.S. jobs were lost.
- Internet experts testifying that they could have built the exact Obamacare website for $10 million, and wondering where the other $990 million went.[14]
- Business experts testifying that a $678 million contract should never have been awarded NO BID to a college classmate of the president's wife.[15] Bring in law professors to discuss if this was a criminal action.
- Business experts wondering why the "fix" of this Obamacare website was awarded to a firm based for tax purposes outside the USA, who uses non-American employees at a fraction of the cost.[16] Experts should estimate how many U.S. jobs were lost.
- Constitutional law experts and professors testifying that the president has no right to make or change laws—yet Obama has broken the law and violated the U.S. Constitution numerous times by changing, delaying, or exempting firms from Obamacare.[17]

Intersperse every single tragic personal story with a video of Obama saying, "If you like your insurance plan, you will keep it." Then have multiple experts testify that at the moment Obama traveled the nation repeating that statement, internal White House documents made it clear he knew 47–60 percent of Americans with individual health insurance policies and more than 50 percent of Americans with coverage through their jobs would lose their insurance because of Obamacare.[18]

Finally, close the case with interviews of prosecutors and former U.S. Attorneys testifying that the statement "If you like your health care plan, you can keep your health care plan" is out and out fraud and criminal misrepresentation.

If after these thirty-minute TV and radio show segments are aired for sixty days in a row before the election, the GOP doesn't win in a land-slide…America is lost.

If this game plan is ignored by the GOP, every member of the GOP leadership in Washington, D.C., should be fired, sued in court for breach of fiduciary duty, and banned from politics for life.

Brand Obama

It's time to stop being politically correct and afraid to make our case. Obama is a Marxist. His policies are Marxist. Many of those in his admin-istration are Marxists. America is headed the way of Cuba, Venezuela, Argentina, and the socialist-run states of Greece, Italy, Spain, and France. Polls show a majority of Democrats have a positive view of socialism.[19] So why hide it? Why let them deny it?

We need to be "in your face" making our case. Politics isn't badminton with Muffy at the country club. There are no gentlemen here. This is a battle for the soul of America. It is a battle to save capitalism and Judeo-Christian values. A battle for your children's future. Throw out the nice guy's rules. Nice guys finish last.

Obama and his Marxist cabal hate to be called socialists, communists, or Marxists. They run from those names like cockroaches run from light. They are afraid those names might stick. That's exactly why we need to brand them for who they truly are. It's time to stop letting them get away with calling themselves "liberal" or "progressive."

We need to practice the same strategies from Saul Alinsky's *Rules for Radicals*, as Obama does. Be bold. Be brave. Tell Americans what Obama stands for. Publicly discuss *The Communist Manifesto* and compare each plank with Obama's policies. Define him as radical and extreme. Brand him as the Marxist he is.

And if that doesn't get the point across, then use humor. Sometimes a little humor is the best way to prove your point.

So let's look at the facts up close and personal, *Jeff Foxworthy–style*. Comedian Jeff Foxworthy proved with his humor—without a doubt—who might be a redneck. Let us leave no doubt about who our president really is . . . what he really stands for . . . what his true agenda is . . . and who is the real "radical" in the room. Read it and weep Obama—the truth hurts!

You Might Be a Marxist If. . . .

If you are proud that we're handing out the most welfare and food stamps in history, but don't realize that the National Park Service orders tourists, "*Do not feed the wildlife.* When you feed animals they may become dependent on handouts and fail to survive. . . ."[20] . . . **YOU MIGHT BE A MARXIST.**

If you created "Cash for Clunkers" . . . yet you don't realize the $3.7 trillion in welfare, food stamps, and handouts[21] you've given to your most loyal Democratic voters should be called "Cash for Flunkers" . . . **YOU MIGHT BE A MARXIST.**

If you don't understand that the reason babies scream hysterically the moment they are born is because they instantly realize they are facing a future of no job prospects and a debt of $400,000 per every member of the population[22] . . . **YOU MIGHT BE A MARXIST.**

If you think anyone who doesn't read the *New York Times* is dumb and ignorant . . . but you think it's okay that the Democrat-controlled Congress passed a two-thousand-page healthcare bill without reading it . . . **YOU MIGHT BE A MARXIST.**

If you think the "White House Party Crashers" are terrible people because they crashed your White House state dinner without an invitation, but you want to give amnesty to millions of uninvited illegal immigrants who crashed our border . . . **YOU MIGHT BE A MARXIST.**

If you think food stamps, welfare, disability, and unemployment checks are "economic stimulus"... **YOU MIGHT BE A MARXIST.**

If you think our economy is in "recovery" when food stamp growth is seventy-five times as high as job growth[23]... **YOU MIGHT BE A MARXIST.**

If you think giving F-16 jets for *free* to the Muslim Brotherhood of Egypt is okay,[24] at the same time you're considering gun control for Americans[25]... **YOU MIGHT BE A MARXIST.**

If you think there's nothing to cut in the budget but military veterans' pensions,[26] while we spend $300 million to pay mortgages for Palestinians[27]... **YOU MIGHT BE A MARXIST.**

If you think it's perfectly fine for government to listen in on all of our phone calls without a warrant, but you believe a corporation doing a criminal background check on job applicants is racist and discriminatory[28]... **YOU MIGHT BE A MARXIST.**

If your administration fights hard to deport a German home-schooling family with six kids who don't want welfare, and who have never committed a crime and who just want to be left alone[29]... but you want to give amnesty to millions of illegal aliens,[30] most of whom expect entitlements and tax refunds (even though they've never paid taxes)... **YOU MIGHT BE A MARXIST.**

If your IRS targets and persecutes Tea Party groups and conservative critics, but lets illegal aliens steal billions by claiming dozens of children who don't exist to get a tax "refund"[31]... **YOU MIGHT BE A MARXIST.**

If the only thing you, your cabinet members, and czars know about business is from books you read at Harvard or Columbia that were written by Karl Marx... **YOU MIGHT BE A MARXIST.**

If you called this country's debt crisis "the fiscal cliff" and you announced with pride that you "solved" it by adding $2.1 trillion in new debt[32]... **YOU MIGHT BE A MARXIST.**

PLUS, IT'S OBVIOUS YOU LEARNED MATH IN A PUBLIC SCHOOL.

If your TSA humiliates cancer patients[33] and molests three-year-olds in wheelchairs[34] in their haste to avoid "racist" profiling of Muslims (who are of all different races) but your IRS profiles and targets your conservative critics for destruction... **YOU MIGHT BE A MARXIST.**

If you think it's racist to ask for voter ID,[35] but not to require the exact same photo ID every time people access their Obamacare benefits[36]... **YOU MIGHT BE A MARXIST...**

AND A HYPOCRITE, TOO.

If you think denying Americans a job, government contract, or entry to college because of the color of their skin is immoral and criminal... but GIVING someone a job, government contract, or college admission because of a different color of their skin is "social justice"[37]... **YOU MIGHT BE A MARXIST.**

If you think it's okay to meet with dictators, tyrants, communists, America-haters, and terrorist sympathizers (and bow down to some of them),[38] but have no interest in meeting with Republican leaders in Congress[39]... **YOU MIGHT BE A MARXIST.**

If you can't find the money for White House tours,[40] or to pay air traffic controllers,[41] or to keep illegal aliens in jail,[42] but you have $100 million sitting around for a presidential visit to Africa[43]... where you pledge $7 billion from the U.S. taxpayers for electricity access for Africans[44]... **YOU MIGHT BE A MARXIST.**

If you think it's terrible that a law school student has to pay $9 per month for her own contraception,[45] but you see no problem with colleges and law schools (run by your most loyal leftist intellectual supporters) charging that same student $60,000 per year to attend that school[46]... so ultra-liberal professors can be paid more than $300,000 per year[47]... **YOU MIGHT BE A MARXIST.**

If you think *New York Times* columnist Paul Krugman deserves a Nobel Prize for economics, and you deserve a Nobel Peace Prize, even though neither of you ever created a job or did anything to produce one minute of peace in the world... **YOU MIGHT BE A MARXIST ...**

AND AN EGOMANIAC, TOO.

If you think it was a good idea to steal $10 billion from U.S. taxpayers to save the bloated pensions of union workers in the auto bailout,[48] but it was just fine to allow the non-union workers to lose their pensions...**YOU MIGHT BE A MARXIST.**

If you talk about "fairness" all the time,[49] but you closed down GM and Chrysler dealers based on their contributions to the Republican Party[50]...**YOU MIGHT BE A MARXIST.**

If you want to allocate millions of dollars to the IRS to go after tax cheats, even though your administration is filled with tax cheats...including the first guy you put in charge of America's taxes (Treasury Secretary Timothy Geithner)[51]...**YOU MIGHT BE A MARXIST.**

If you condemn anyone (like Mitt Romney) that holds their money in the Cayman Islands,[52] but you just named a guy as the new Treasury Secretary (Jack Lew) who keeps his money in the Cayman Islands[53]...**YOU MIGHT BE A MARXIST.**

If you believe it's greedy for taxpayers to want to keep more of their OWN money, that they earned[54]...but it's not greedy to demand government confiscate other people's money and redistribute it to those who didn't earn it (i.e., YOUR voters)[55]...**YOU MIGHT BE A MARXIST.**

If your tax policies are so onerous that even Denise Rich, one of the leading contributors to the Democrats for the past three decades...renounces her U.S. citizenship...to move to *London*[56]...**YOU MIGHT BE A MARXIST.**

If you think Bush adding $3.5 trillion to the national debt in five years was an embarrassment, a travesty, and a disgrace[57]...but you have no problem adding nearly $7 trillion to the national debt in the same time[58]...**YOU MIGHT BE A MARXIST.**

If you actually said "you didn't build that" to business owners...because you think the credit for their success goes to bridges, roads, highways, airports, schools, and hospitals built by government...but you don't understand that business owners and taxpayers paid all the taxes that allowed government to build all those things in the first place[59]...**YOU MIGHT BE A MARXIST.**

If your White House website says you're "committed to" small business,[60] while in just one quarter you proposed *over six thousand* new rules, regulations, and mandates[61] that are making it impossible to run a lemonade stand in America anymore...**YOU MIGHT BE A MARXIST.**

If you promised to cut the average family's health insurance bill by $2,500 annually, but instead you raised it by $3,000[62] ... **YOU MIGHT BE A MARXIST...**

AND YOU'RE A LIAR.

If you promised "If you like your health care plan, you can keep your health care plan," while your own White House reports concluded that 93 million Americans would lose their plans[63] ... **YOU MIGHT BE A MARXIST...**

AND A CON MAN, TOO.

If you want to convert America to a "green economy" to create millions of "green jobs"[64] ... even though Spain has proven the green economy destroys more than twice as many jobs as it creates and leads to 27 percent unemployment... and 58 percent youth unemployment[65]

...YOU MIGHT BE A MARXIST...

AND AN IDIOT, TOO.

If your wife thinks, "we are in the midst of a huge recovery. Right? Because of what this president has done."[66] ... and you think the economy is "moving in the right direction,"[67] even though almost 100 million working-age Americans are not working[68] ... and the labor participation rate for men is the lowest ever recorded[69] ... **YOU AND YOUR WIFE MIGHT BOTH BE MARXISTS.**

If you send out your press secretary to paint you as a fan of oil drilling[70] ... while oil drilling permits are actually down 36 percent under your administration[71] ... **YOU MIGHT BE A MARXIST...**

AND A DAMN LIAR, TOO!

If you want to abandon capitalism and put the economy under the control of government bureaucrats, even though virtually every city, county, state, and federal department run by those same bureaucrats is bankrupt and heavily in debt... **YOU MIGHT BE A MARXIST.**

If you favor "transparency"[72] ... and then hand out hundreds of billions of dollars in "stimulus" to unions, leading Democrat bundlers and contributors, and "green" boondoggles[73] ... and hide your tracks by refusing to disclose who got the money, or how much[74] ... **YOU MIGHT BE A MARXIST...**

AND A CROOK, TOO.

If you think putting the same government that brought us the U.S. Postal Service that can lose $15.9 billion in a year[75] without competition in charge of our healthcare will SAVE us money[76]... **YOU MIGHT BE A MARXIST ...**

AND AN IDIOT, TOO.

If your solution to Medicare driving the country into bankruptcy is passing Obamacare so we can expand government-run healthcare to *everyone*[77]... **YOU MIGHT BE A MARXIST...**

AND I'M BETTING YOU FLUNKED MATH AT YOUR PUBLIC SCHOOL.

If you can't seem to find anything to cut from your budget...yet you just gave a $1.5 million research grant to scientists to find out why lesbians are fat[78]... **YOU MIGHT BE A MARXIST.**

If you want to take guns away from law-abiding Americans because a mentally ill nutcase went on a killing rampage at a school designated as a "GUN FREE ZONE"...which advertised that everyone inside was a helpless, defenseless, sitting duck[79]... **YOU MIGHT BE A MARXIST.**

If you blame guns for killing children in Newtown, Connecticut[80]...but it doesn't occur to you that you sold guns to Mexican drug lords in the "Fast and Furious" scandal that resulted in three hundred murders, including of a U.S. border agent[81]... **YOU MIGHT BE A MARXIST...**

AND A GUN RUNNER TOO.

If your administration says global warming is a national security threat, but you ignore the fact that scientists studying global warming in Antarctica were stranded by too much ice[82]... **YOU MIGHT BE A MARXIST.**

If you say you want to lower the cost of healthcare...but purposely left malpractice suit reform out of your signature healthcare reform... **YOU AND YOUR WIFE MIGHT BE MARXIST LAWYERS.**

Finally, and I hope against hope that it doesn't come to this, if in your last year in office, the citizens are waiting in line for toilet paper and Bangladesh is hosting "Aid America" concerts... **WE DEFINITELY HAVE A MARXIST PRESIDENT!**

Thank heavens we can still buy toilet paper in the stores—for now. But Americans are already waiting in line for government-mandated healthcare. *Literally.* And the Obama administration is BRAGGING ABOUT IT. The

White House blog actually featured a picture of Americans waiting in line to sign up for Obamacare. The post is titled "This is What an #ACASurge Looks Like."[83]

.I think it's safe to say... THERE IS A MARXIST IN THE WHITE HOUSE.

Brand the Democrats as the Party of Economic Suicide

In their blind denial, the Democrats are driving America off a cliff. They're repeating the exact same mistakes that have destroyed socialist economies around the world again and again: big government, big taxes, big spending, big regulations, big entitlements, big unions, and free healthcare have never worked in any country, *ever.*

All the GOP needs to do is compare Democrat policies to those imposed in the old Soviet Union, the old People's Republic of China, and the old East Germany. Or look at North Korea, Cuba, Venezuela, Zimbabwe, Greece, Italy, Spain, Portugal, France, or Argentina today. Or look at Detroit. (See chapter two above.) Government control of anything is always a failure. To deny that is the definition of denial.

But the best issue of all that the GOP should use to brand Democrats 24/7 is "global warming," a.k.a. "climate change." Throw it back in their faces. Don't be scared or intimidated to address the issue. The leftist solution to "global warming" is worse than the supposed crisis. The "cure" will kill you faster than the disease. Democrats are in denial about what is happening across the globe. Green energy is a PROVEN economic disaster. Right now. *Everywhere.*

The EU stands out as Exhibit A for branding Democrats as the Party of Economic Suicide. The EU started earlier than we did with this leftist obsession that everything had to "go green." They're bankrupting their entire continent with this madness. So as of February of this year the EU has thrown in the towel, dropping their mandatory "renewable energy" targets. They have to, or skyrocketing "green" energy prices will drive them out of business.[84]

Only a madman would see the economic suicide of Europe and want to follow their path.

Solar, wind, biofuels, electric cars—they are all wonderful ideas. But they are not ready for prime time. At this point in their development they are too expensive. The math doesn't add up for green energy. Middle class taxpayers are left holding the bag—paying much higher taxes and much higher energy bills. It is economic suicide.

We've already seen how Spain converted to green energy and destroyed their entire economy. There are no jobs. Spain may never recover—certainly not for a generation, or two, or three.

Now the rest of Europe just put up the white flag before the same thing happens to them. This is what a "green" economy looks like: Businesses are out of business. Consumers can't afford to heat their homes. Home prices have collapsed. Tax revenues have disappeared. It's a vicious toxic cycle.

So the EU Commission started 2014 by announcing they'd scuttled all the greenhouse gas emission standards. Gone. Up in smoke (excuse the pun).[85] The EU is in a race to save their economies, before green energy destroys what little hope is left.

Yet at the exact moment of Europe's capitulation, Obama and the Democrats doubled down. Secretary of State John Kerry called climate change "perhaps...the world's most fearsome weapon of mass destruction."[86] Senate Democrats held an all-night vigil on the Senate floor to praise green energy and sing the song of "climate change."[87] Even with the proof staring them in the face, Democrats want to ignore the economic disaster caused by green energy and double down on insanity and bankruptcy.

Green energy is the biggest scam in world history. It is the very definition of "economic suicide"—and the GOP must brand it as such. Brand the Democrats with their own insanity and dysfunction. Point out the reality of what green energy is. Point out that the jury is already in. Green energy has ruined the EU economy. No matter how many times we try it, the results will be the same. Don't be afraid to repeat these themes day and night.

Point out that Obama's policies are economic suicide. Obama's high taxes are economic suicide. Obama's spending is economic suicide.

Obama's regulations are economic suicide. Obama's debt is economic suicide. Obamacare is economic suicide. We can "Saul Alinsky" them.
The only difference is… we're just stating the truth.

Brand the Democrats as Criminals

Who would have believed it? Democrats aren't worried about the GOP, but they're scared to death of RICO (Racketeer Influenced and Corrupt Organizations Act).

The very week I was finishing this book, we experienced a Democratic crime spree. Democratic politicians were arrested all over the country. The arrests came fast and furious—all in one week. There were so many arrests, it almost made you think the Democratic Party was one big widespread organized crime gang.

Keep in mind the Democrats are the ones always claiming to care about women, children, minorities, and the poor. It turns out this is all a cover for "Show me the Money!"

While they are busy painting Republicans as "mean-spirited," "racist," "radical," and "extreme" for wanting to cut spending, reduce the debt, and allow taxpayers to keep more of their own money, Democrats are busy orchestrating criminal schemes of bribery, fraud, theft, extortion, and gun-running. What a great "cover"! Al Capone and John Gotti would be proud of this scam.

The crime spree started with Charlotte, North Carolina, mayor Patrick Cannon. He resigned after being arrested on corruption charges in an FBI sting operation.[88]

According to the FBI, Mayor Cannon wanted far more than to help the poor in his city. Apparently he was trying to line his own pockets by demanding bribes from developers for the right to build in his town. The Democratic mayor was charged with theft, bribery, fraud, and extortion.

Just a few days earlier Gordon Fox, the Democratic speaker of the Rhode Island House, abruptly resigned after an FBI raid on his State House office.[89]

This should have come as no surprise to Rhode Island citizens. Right next door in Massachusetts, the last three speakers of the Massachusetts

House were convicted of felonies. Would it surprise you to learn they were all Democrats? They were Democrat Salvatore DiMasi, Democrat Thomas Finneran, and Democrat Charles Flaherty.[90]

Meanwhile, back to that late March 2014 crime spree among Democrat office-holders. In California, powerful Democratic State Senator Leland Yee was arrested alongside his partner in crime, a gangster known as "Shrimp Boy."[91]

Yee was charged with wire fraud, conspiracy to deal firearms without a license, and illegally importing firearms. Yee allegedly accepted $42,000 for introducing an arms buyer to an arms dealer. Investigators said Yee was helping the arms buyer obtain weapons, such as shoulder-fired missiles, from a Muslim separatist group in the Philippines, in order to pay off campaign debts. WOW.

Keep in mind that Yee was a big gun control advocate—meaning his goal was to take guns away from honest law-abiding citizens. That's quite a scam. Democrat politicians disarm the citizens, leaving them helpless at the hands of heavily armed thugs—who buy their illegal weapons with the help of the Democrat politicians. I think Democrats have been watching too many re-runs of *Goodfellas*.

But Yee was only one of three Democrat Senators suspended that week from the State Senate in Sacramento.[92]

Democrat Senator Rod Wright faces voter fraud charges. Democrat Senator Ron Calderon faces federal charges for accepting $100,000 in bribes for passing bills.

Just the week before the Democrat politician crime spree, the *Philadelphia Inquirer* reported that the Pennsylvania attorney general had caught four leading Philadelphia Democrat politicians (members of the Pennsylvania House delegation) red-handed accepting bribes, but the entire investigation was shut down when a new Democrat attorney general took office.[93]

Democrat attorney general Kathleen G. Kane claimed the investigation was "tainted by racism." Funny, that's the word Democrats always use when Democrat politicians are caught with stacks of bribe money in FBI stings.

Because all those allegedly accepting the bribes were members of the Pennsylvania Assembly's Black Caucus, the Attorney General was able to claim "racism." But sources familiar with the sting in Philadelphia say offers of bribes were made to both Republicans and Democrats, but only Democrats took the money.

And the same week that news broke, Pennsylvania Democratic State Senator LeAnna Washington was charged with corruption.[94]

It was also disclosed that Nevada Democratic senator Harry Reid gave $31,249 in campaign funds to his granddaughter Ryan Elisabeth Reid for "holiday gift" charges. Nice job if you can get it.[95]

Reid claims there was nothing wrong with what he did. It's funny, though, that the recipient of the $31,000 in "holiday gift" disbursements was listed on his Federal Elections Commission form as "Ryan Elisabeth." Senator Reid conveniently left off his granddaughter's last name, which happened to be "Reid." Using campaign funds for personal use (such as enriching family members) is a crime. Ask Jesse Jackson Jr. You can reach him at the Federal Correctional Complex in Butner, North Carolina.

Keep in mind this was just a *one-week* Democratic crime spree. One week of "business as usual" for the party that claims to care so much about the poor and minorities. One week for the party that claims to care about "fairness," "equality," and "social justice."

I have advice for the GOP in 2014 and 2016. We don't need good candidates to defeat the Democrats...**we need good prosecutors.**

How does the GOP take advantage of this Democrat crime spree? Once again, the GOP has been handed a branding gift (i.e., "manna from heaven"). The GOP's job is to remind voters about the crimes committed by Democrats across this country, twenty-four hours a day, in TV commercials headed into the November elections. Brand the Democrats as "The Party That Makes Crime Pay."

Like it or not, voters just don't seem to care about traditional GOP issues like out-of-control government, out-of-control spending, or taxes. Why? Maybe because the typical voter isn't paying taxes, so they don't care about the taxpayers. Maybe because the average voter is collecting a government check (or two), so they don't mind the spending. But we know all voters get upset over politicians who are crooks. Even voters who pay no taxes hate crooked politicians. Even voters who collect welfare hate crooked politicians. Everyone gets riled up over corrupt politicians stealing the citizens' money. That's a fact. Even in Chicago they put Democrats in jail if they are caught stealing from taxpayers. *This, folks, is a winning issue!*

So here is a story that absolutely resonates with voters. Everyone hates crooks. Run TV ads showing a montage of Democrat politicians' faces as they are led away in handcuffs. Show it in slow motion. Put bright red stamps over each new face that says "DEMOCRAT." Then end with "Send a message from the taxpayers to the crooks: Crime Doesn't Pay."

That's how you brand Democrats and win elections.

Brand Hillary

Finally we come to Hillary Clinton. I reserve a special place in this book (and in my heart) for Hillary because she is the key to winning in 2016. Beat Hillary, and the GOP controls the keys to the kingdom.

My message to the GOP: *Brand Hillary Clinton right now.* Do it before she becomes too big to fail, before it's a foregone conclusion that the first female president will follow the first black president.

First let's look at the polls. Hillary Clinton is not only the frontrunner for president...it isn't even close.[96] This is the branding opportunity of a lifetime for the GOP. Hillary isn't formidable or unbeatable. If the GOP has even a clue about branding, Hillary is a gift from heaven!

This is such a great opportunity for the GOP because Hillary is the "A Team"—and there is no "B Team." There is no bench. It's Hillary or bust for the Democratic Party in 2016. She has a sixty-one-point lead—the biggest lead in Democratic presidential poll history.[97]

Destroy Hillary now and it's over. What are the Democrats left with? "Crazy Joe" Biden? Elizabeth "I swear I'm an American Indian" Warren? Take Hillary down now, *before* she gets started—and the GOP is in the driver's seat for 2016.

Branding works. Ask Mitt Romney about that. "Team Obama" poisoned Mitt Romney's brand early in 2012. He never recovered from being branded as a rich, mean-spirited, out of touch CEO.

But hey, that's okay. All is fair in love, war, and politics. That's what branding is for. So what is the GOP waiting for? Hillary (just like Mitt) is a big fat sitting duck.

The Democrats are facing a landslide defeat in 2014 because of Obamacare. If Hillary is defeated now, the Democrats will be out of luck in 2016 too.

What do we brand Hillary with? You don't brand her with Monica Lewinsky or old Bill Clinton scandals. Karl Rove is right.[98] That's old news. The voters don't care about what happened in the 90s.

But I know exactly how to brand Hillary.

Do you remember her Congressional hearings over the Benghazi disaster? Hillary famously said, "what difference at this point does it make?" Make her own that brand. "What difference does it make?" should become Hillary's middle name.

Run "What difference does it make?" advertisements on TV and radio twenty-four hours a day, seven days a week. Repeat it so much that you can't say "Hillary," without finishing the sentence with "What difference does it make?"

Boy is there a lot to work with! The State Department "misplaced" $6 billion of your taxpayer money. SIX BILLION. $6 billion is unaccounted for at the State Department—almost all of it on Hillary's watch.[99] According to the U.S. Inspector General there weren't enough "internal controls," causing "conditions conducive to fraud." Meaning no one cared what happened to $6 billion of your taxpayer money.

This is what Madison Ave. advertising executives call "pure gold." All the GOP has to do is run TV and radio ads twenty-four hours a day stating that $6 billion of your taxpayer money is missing. Who was in charge? Hillary. Who was the CEO? Hillary. Where does the buck stop? Hillary. Then show Hillary's testimony saying, "What difference does it make?"

Next hit Hillary with a series of Benghazi-themed ads. Once again, Hillary was in charge. During the Benghazi attack the red phone rang at 2 a.m., just like her 2008 presidential campaign ads warned it would. The U.S. Embassy was under attack, and Americans were about to die. Show Hillary saying, "What difference does it make?"

The branding campaign should ask, "Where was Hillary when the embassy desperately needed a military rescue? Why did Hillary refuse to mount a rescue? Why did Hillary let those four brave heroes die?" If those boys were her sons, would she say, "What difference does it make?"

Don't forget the cover-up. Hillary and everyone at the State Department knew Benghazi was a planned al Qaeda attack, not a spontaneous protest.[100] A cover-up is a crime. Ask President Richard Nixon. The GOP ads should interview the parents of the four dead American heroes and ask them, "What difference does it make if Hillary participated in a cover-up of your son's death?"

Then it's time for round three. Hillary was in charge of America's foreign policy when the world fell into chaos. Show scenes of the entire Middle East in flames. Tahrir Square in Cairo burning. Libya in flames. Syrian children lying dead in the streets. Venezuela's leader laughing at us. North Korea negotiating with...*Dennis Rodman*. That all happened with Hillary as secretary of state. Ask voters "What difference did Hillary make as secretary of state?"

Then move on to round four—Obamacare. Millions of Americans have lost their insurance.[101] Millions will see their insurance premiums dramatically increased.[102] The CBO predicts 2.3 million jobs will be lost.[103] The middle class is being annihilated. Cancer patients are losing their health insurance, or their doctors, or the drugs that keep them alive. Ask, "What difference does it make?"

Ask Hillary where she stands on Obamacare? Does she support it? Does she want government to get even more intrusive? How intrusive? Like a proctologist with his finger up our...wallet? Let's ask America, "What difference does it make, if government gets even more involved in healthcare under Hillary Clinton?"

Brand that all over national TV and radio now. That's how you use branding to destroy Hillary's campaign *before* it even starts. That's how you poison Hillary's brand.

Make Hillary run on her record of accomplishments: $6 billion missing on her watch; four dead American heroes; a criminal cover-up; the world in crisis, chaos, and flames while she was in charge of foreign policy; the miserable failure of Obamacare (which is a *mild* version of the government takeover of healthcare she proposed in the 1990s); and the U.S. economy in severe decline under the leadership of an administration she endorsed and supported. "What difference does it make?" Hillary will soon find out.

When it comes to the presidency...branding makes all the difference in the world.

In short...

Branding is the only way to elect Republican candidates who can save the middle class.

CHAPTER 21

Constitutional Convention

The cowardice of career politicians governing to win the next election above all else made me sick. I don't think Washington can fix Washington.... I don't think you fix this place until you have a convention of the states. Only America can change Washington.
—**Senator Tom Coburn, announcing his retirement,**
Wall Street Journal, February 1, 2014[1]

The last eight chapters of this book have laid out a winning strategy for electoral victory. But in Obama's America we've reached a point where winning elections may not be enough.

To stop ***The Murder of the Middle Class***, we are going to have to go further than that. So this chapter and the next are devoted to reform proposals over and above putting a new Tea Party–infused GOP, devoted to rescuing the middle class, in political office.

In *The Liberty Amendments: Restoring The American Republic*, Mark Levin points out that since this concentration of power and theft of individual liberties by a "political class" was exactly what the Founding Fathers were fighting against, they provided a means in the Constitution to restore sanity and save the Republic. As Levin points out, the Founders provided two methods for amending the Constitution. The first method provides for two-thirds of the elected Congress to propose amendments to the Constitution. The Constitution has been amended by this method twenty-seven times.

Since the Founders recognized elected politicians would have no interest in proposing amendments limiting their own power, however, they wisely provided a second method.

That method empowers the States to call a convention for amending the Constitution. It is this second method that Levin rightfully argues gives citizens our best opportunity to restore our freedoms from the tyranny of the political class. Note that both methods for amending the Constitution require the approval of three-fourths of the states.

America is supposed to have a republican form of government. Those of us who are news and political junkies often report on violations of the Tenth Amendment, which best describes exactly what a Republic is:

> Amendment X: The powers not delegated to the United States by the Constitution, nor prohibited by it to the States, are reserved to the States respectively, or to the people.

The fact is, the Constitution's primary purpose is to *limit* the power of the federal government. The problem is not that the powers enumerated in the Constitution are too broad, it is that the "political class" (empowered politicians and judges) has so distorted and ignored the Constitution to increase their own power that state and individual freedoms have been severely and unconstitutionally eroded.

For those interested in exploring the specifics of this abuse of the Constitution, I refer you to Levin's book. In addition to calling for the States to convene a Constitutional Convention, Levin outlines ten specific amendments he proposes, to restore the American Republic. I recommend you read them all.

Here are a few of my own ideas:

1) Limit Terms: Serving in Congress should be the honor of a lifetime, not a lifetime job. Term limits for politicians are probably the single most important constraint we citizens can impose on the political class. The ideal term limit would be one where no politician ever runs for reelection.

(For example, one four-year term for a member of Congress and one six-year term for a senator and the president). With these limits, every two years, half of the Congress and one-third of the Senate would be newly elected. This would allow our elected representatives to focus solely on doing the will of the people who elected them, rather than the will of the people contributing to their reelection campaign. But let's be "fair" and "moderate" and "compromising," as the media demands. I'd accept a three-term limit for the House (six years total) and two-term limit for the Senate (twelve years total).

2) **Stamp Out Conflict of Interest:** Prohibit lawyers from running for Congress. The greatest conflict of interest in all of politics is that lawyers are allowed to be legislators, thereby making laws that they will profit from. Politicians are required to put their investments into "blind trusts" so their decisions are not biased by personal financial gain. But lawyers benefit from virtually every law passed by Congress—which is mostly made up of lawyers! This is precisely why Obamacare does not include one word about medical lawsuits or tort reform. Good luck in getting this one passed, because the politicians voting will be mostly...*lawyers.*

3) **Get Lobbying under Control:** Anyone serving in Congress must be banned from working as a lobbyist for a minimum of ten years after leaving Congress. That way every decision our representatives make would not be based on a million-dollar job working for big business waiting on the other end.

4) **Close the Capitol Building and Work from Home:** In today's high-tech communication world there is no longer a need for members of Congress or senators to meet together in a big room in Washington, D.C. How 1800s. Legislators should maintain offices in their home districts and conduct the business of Congress from there. They can meet once every two years in D.C. for a three-month session (the same way it's done in Nevada and Texas—two states with no state income tax). This will ensure that senators and Congressmen stay in touch with their constituents and the issues that matter back home. This is how you keep your pulse on the people, not the lobbyists. It also makes it more difficult to be swayed by the money and bribes of D.C. lobbyists and power brokers. Congressional votes, face-to-face meetings, and even debates with fellow legislators can

easily be handled with technology installed in the legislators' home district offices—like Skype (which is 100 percent free), or video teleconferencing. Currently 90 percent of a senator's or congressman's time is spent in D.C., away from his own constituents. Flip that percentage and put him back in his district 90 percent of the time.

5) Block Grants: Much of the growth and power of the federal government has come from implementing programs for the so-called "public welfare." These include bureaucracies such as Education, HHS, Agriculture, Labor, and the Interior. My first preference is to simply close them since, in a Republic, the activities they support are the responsibility of the states. They were NOT granted to the federal government by the Constitution.

If, in today's world, this is "a bridge too far" once again let me be "fair" and "moderate" and "compromising." As an alternative, let's run these programs as block grants to the states, which would decide how to spend the funds. That would get the federal government out of the unconstitutional business of dictating to the states and would allow these departments, at the federal level, to be managed by a small handful of bureaucrats whose sole role would be to distribute funds to the states.

6) Rein in Regulations: All regulations (for example, by the EPA) and executive orders must be confirmed by vote of the majority of both houses of Congress, or they will be automatically void in ninety days.

7) State Legislature Veto: The legislatures of two-thirds of the States would be able to overturn any federal law or regulation. It's time to provide states with a check on a runaway Congress.

8) English as the National Language: I'm sure many of you thought that English was already the national language of the United States. It is not, but it is time for it to be.

When my ancestors emigrated from Germany and Russia I am sure they struggled with the English language. But you can be sure their children did not. Their immigrant parents would never have allowed it. How can you hope to prosper and succeed if you can't speak the language? My reason for advocating this can be summed up in one word—assimilation.

Making English the official language and doing away with bilingual EVERYTHING will be a major step in the right direction. If you can't speak

English, learn. We'll provide you the tools. If you can't swim, and you're thrown into a pool, you'd better learn fast. It's sink or swim. Is it "racist" to force Americans to learn English? Actually it's "racist" to allow kids from other countries and cultures to ruin their lives by not gaining proficiency in English. Poor kids are being condemned to lives of despair by political correctness.

9) No Pensions for Congress. Congressmen and Senators have every right to earn a nice living while they are working. But few Americans (outside of government employees) get a pension anymore. The days of paying people to not work are long over. The economics make no sense. Politicians should learn to live like the rest of us. You get paid while in office. After you leave office, you find a job.

10) Congress Must Live by the Same Laws They Impose on the American People. Period.

In his book, Mark Levin outlines a number of specific amendments he advocates for "Restoring The American Republic." Mr. Levin, count me in as a strong supporter and please consider how a few of my suggestions might be added to your list of amendments.

CHAPTER 22

Impeach Obama!

 nough said.

CHAPTER 23

Saving *YOU* from the Murder of the Middle Class

Buy the truth, and sell it not; also wisdom,
and instruction, and understanding.
—Proverbs 23:23

DID YOU KNOW?

- Since 1970, gold has risen in value by 3,500 percent
- In 1954, the average price of a new home was $19,499
- Since 2011, the price of bacon has gone up 23 percent, ground beef 17 percent, and chicken 18 percent, while incomes have risen only 1 percent a year

In this book I have **exposed** *The Murder of the Middle Class* …

…**fingered the perpetrator,** his accomplices, his unindicted co-conspirators in this insidious attack, and revealed where the plot was first hatched, and …

…**provided a detailed playbook** of strategies for rescuing the middle class from the plot: reviving the Republicans with a Tea Party infusion, making the GOP the party of the middle class, winning elections, turning the economy around, and putting the greatest middle class the world has ever known back in the driver's seat of a free, happy, and prosperous America.

Now it's time to save YOU. To put you (the dear reader) into the driver's seat—no matter what happens to the world around you. Because I need you healthy and financially stable, so you are mentally and physically strong enough to lead this desperate fight to save the middle class. You bought this book because you believe the middle class is worth saving, and you want to know how. You want to follow my model. Well here is my model. These ideas make up the foundation of my life.

I've saved the best for last. These last two chapters are special chapters of my book that I hold near and dear. This is the core of my plan to save YOU—the individual—from the murder of the middle class. Here I turned to three of America's greatest experts to help me unearth and explain the crucial facts you need to know. For financial advice, I turned to Swiss America, America's leading authorities on precious metals. My trust in Swiss America's integrity and expertise is so solid that I have actually come on board with them as a spokesman for the company. There's no better place to turn for advice and service when it comes to investing in precious metals. For staying healthy, I turned to Wayne Gorsek, one of America's leading authorities on vitamins and nutrition. "The other Wayne" has agreed to special promotional pricing for YOU, my readers. (Details below.) And for pure survival in times of crisis, tragedy, terrorism, or collapse, I turned to a U.S. Special Forces operative and member of the Joint Special Operations Command. (This section could literally save your life!)

The Middle Class Weapon
of Self-Defense

"He can take his players and beat yours, and he can take your players and beat his!"

That quote about the legendary college football coach Bear Bryant is also the perfect description of gold. It doesn't matter if you are comparing

gold's rate of return to stocks, bonds, or real estate. Just like Bear Bryant—
Gold can beat 'em all!

In my opinion gold and silver (a.k.a. precious metals) are the foundation of any attempt to save the middle class. What is strange is how few
Americans know anything about owning precious metals. Not a word is
spoken or taught about gold in school, or college, or even graduate school.
Rarely is a word spoken about gold on financial TV networks like CNBC
or Bloomberg TV. Rarely is gold mentioned in the *Wall Street Journal* or
other financial publications. On the rare occasions gold is mentioned by
financial experts in the media, it's almost always negative. They disparage
gold. They scare the middle class away from owning gold. They make it
clear that gold "makes no sense" as an investment.

That's bizarre, because gold is a financial foundation for many of the
wealthiest investors in America. Gold is a staple for central bankers all
over the world. Gold is being bought in record quantities by the middle
class of China and India, but not by the American middle class. In this
country big government, big business, and big media don't want you to
know about it, or consider it as an investment (let alone your financial
foundation).

Why? What are they afraid of? Are they worried the middle class might
achieve financial security? Are they worried you might become more
confident, self-sufficient, and independent…and less dependent on politicians, big government, and big business?

Once you hear the remarkable record of gold over time you'll understand why this is such a bizarre omission by the media and financial
experts. The performance of gold is so remarkable, this can only be a
purposeful omission, a conspiracy to keep you blind, deaf, dumb, and
always dependent on big government and big business.

In my last book, *The Ultimate Obama Survival Guide*, I detailed the
remarkable appreciation of gold for the past century.

Even the mass media confirms that gold is the best long-term asset to
hold in the twenty-first century:

- "Gold price has soared by some 3,500pc since 1970" —*The
  Telegraph*[1]

- "Gold has risen 37.43 fold since 1967" —Seeking Alpha[2]
- "Gold *has dramatically outperformed* the stock market for the better part of 40 years" —Zero Hedge[3]

Why the forty-year demarcation line? Because up until 1967 world currencies were pegged to gold. Once that ended (France dropped the gold standard in 1967), gold has outperformed stocks in every period in the past forty-seven years, except for the tech bubble (1997–2000). Overall since 1967 stocks are up 18.45 fold versus gold's rise of 37.43 fold.[4]

From January 1, 2000, to December 31, 2013 (fourteen years), gold outperformed every other asset class by a mile. Gold beat stocks, bonds, real estate, and even inflation. By how much? The NASDAQ was up over those fourteen years by 16.40 percent. The S&P 500 was up by 56.50 percent. Gold bullion was up by 446 percent.[5]

What accounts for this phenomenal success? It's actually pretty simple. Gold is WEALTH INSURANCE. You don't expect to die today, yet you pay for life insurance. You don't expect to be sick today, yet you pay for health insurance. You don't expect to wreck your car, yet you pay for auto insurance. These are all ways to protect yourself from disaster.

Well, buying gold is "wealth insurance"—it protects you from economic disaster. There are many forms of economic disaster. The most obvious is crisis of all kinds: wars, panic, tragedy, terrorism, or cyber attacks. But over time there's a subtle form of economic disaster: reckless, irresponsible, spendthrift, corrupt politicians and governments. The more they spend, the more debt they create. That debt destroys economies and creates economic crises that erode the value of paper money (the dollar) and eventually lead to the collapse of even dominant empires.

Gold is your hedge. While paper money issued by reckless governments declines in value, gold holds its value. That's what has happened since 1913, the year the Federal Reserve was founded. But that's all short-term thinking. Gold has served as wealth insurance for thousands of years. It has successfully held its value during major wars, economic collapses, debt crises, hyperinflation, and unrest in the streets.

In 2013 gold prices had their first down year in over a decade. That was to be expected. After all, gold went up for twelve years in a row—experts call that "one of the most impressive bull-market runs for any asset class in history. " Even gold needs to rest sometime.[6]

But while Wall Street investors were liquidating their "paper gold," the demand for physical gold (the kind you can hold in your hand) didn't slow down in 2013. *It went up!* Here are the cold hard facts:

While ETF investors and COMEX commodity exchange speculators were selling "paper gold" on Wall Street last year (2013), physical demand for gold coins and bars was the highest in history, up 28 percent. Private investors in China, Japan, and India drove most of that buying.[7]

China consumed and imported more gold in 2013 than any country in the history of the world.[8]

From 2012 to 2013 China imported a staggering 1,400 physical tons of gold. That's $70 billion worth of gold consumed by one country.[9]

But China isn't alone. Central banks around the world bought an average of twenty-seven metric tons of physical gold a month in 2013.[10] All that buying by central banks in 2013 followed a record buying spree in 2012 that saw central banks buy more gold that year than in all the years since 1964 *combined.*[11]

So why isn't any of this in the news? Why isn't it a headline at CNBC? Why isn't it taught in high school or even college? What do central bankers know what you don't? What does China know that you don't? Why does the Chinese middle class desperately want to own all the gold they can get their hands on, while the American middle class is completely and utterly ignorant about gold? The powers that be in America obviously want it that way.

Gold is the best way for middle class Americans to protect themselves from the Obama model of economic disaster. Gold protects against government over-spending, debt, corruption, and crises of confidence. Gold is the ultimate middle class weapon of self-defense.

The Real Cost of Living

In 2013, the Federal Reserve turned one hundred. But there is no cause for celebration. One result of Federal Reserve policy throughout its lifetime has been a huge increase in the cost of living for the average American. Since 2011, the price of bacon has gone up 23 percent, ground beef 17 percent, and chicken 18 percent, while incomes have only risen 1 percent a year.[12]

Most Americans now have no choice but to run up huge levels of debt to purchase items they used to be able to afford without credit cards and loans. No matter what period of time is examined, over the long term, gold prices have always offered protection from a declining dollar, runaway debt, inflation, stagflation, etc. Those who bought and held gold over the last ten, twenty-five, or fifty years have maintained their purchasing power and far outpaced the rising cost of living.

For example:

In 1954 ...
> Average Household Income $4,167
> New Car $1,700
> New Home $19,499
> Gold $35/oz.
> Silver $1/oz.

Now ...
> Average Household Income $51,017
> New Car $30,000
> New Home $158,722
> Gold $1,300/oz.
> Silver $20/oz.[13]

And in between 1954 and 2014 we've seen the rise in two-income families. Now you need two incomes to qualify for the mortgage that your grandparents qualified for with only one! No wonder owning a home is such a struggle. Inflation has taken a bitter toll on families' cohesiveness and created generations of "latch key children."

In *The Inflation Deception: Six Ways Government Tricks Us…and Seven Ways to Stop It!*, Craig R. Smith, chairman of Swiss America, writes,

> Inflation…is quietly being used as a tool, an ideology, and a form of taxation that secretly extracts the earnings not only of Americans but also of unsuspecting people in other countries. It has also become a means of wealth redistribution, a mode of social engineering, a device to weaken some and strengthen others both within our nation and in the global community of nations, and a way to seize and exercise power.

All of this has occurred because of Fed policies that have debased the value of the U.S. dollar over time. One of the world's most successful investors, Jim Rogers, warned that the Fed's policies have set the stage for a new economic crisis and even a collapse of the Federal Reserve itself in the next ten years. Rogers is bullish on the long-term prospects for gold and prefers physical gold over gold equities. "Gold will become one of the only refuges around," he says.[14]

Rogers recognizes that gold is inherently the best hedge against a falling dollar. Currently, the U.S. dollar is the world's reserve currency of choice. When world investors lose confidence in the dollar, the first place they usually turn is gold. When the value of the dollar declines, the price of gold tends to increase.

Dean Heskin, the CEO of investment firm Swiss America, reminds gold owners that the physical gold market is still alive and well, despite ETF liquidations from major banks, brokerages, and traders: "This flushing out of weak-handed, short-term gold speculators will prove a valuable entry point for those who have felt they missed the gold rush over the last few years," says Heskin.

The recent price dip offers wise buyers the ninth major gold buying opportunity since 2004. The average price rebound following major price dips is 36 percent. And this is the first time in a decade that gold prices have dipped nearly 20 percent.[15] When a valuable commodity that has been proven over time is down, think of it as a gift from heaven. Buy more every time the price goes lower and smile at your good fortune. The sharpest, smartest, wealthiest investors in the world have been buying gold on every dip for decades. Emulate their success and learn from their wisdom…**PUT YOURSELF ON A PERSONAL GOLD AND SILVER STANDARD.**

How do you get started? You can simply purchase precious metals and take physical delivery, or have them stored by a private depository outside of the traditional banking system (and if you choose, outside the United States), or open a precious metals IRA. Over the past decade, Precious Metal IRAs have outperformed all other asset classes.

Who You Gonna Trust?

I want to take a moment to discuss the importance of who you buy your precious metals from. Here are some simple steps I advise taking before buying or selling precious metals from anyone:

1. Buy from a recognized national broker/dealer with at least a ten-year track record.
2. Be sure the coins you want can be bought and delivered at the prices quoted.
3. Be sure the broker/dealer offers you a two-way market.
4. Reputable companies should settle a trade within seventy-two hours and deliver coins within fourteen days.
5. Insist on truthful disclosure of both the upside potential and downside risks. All investments have risk.
6. When buying collector coins, buy only coins certified by independent grading firms PCGS or NGC.

If you follow these simple steps, you too can build a golden legacy for your retirement and for your children and grandchildren's future.

My years of painstaking research have shown that one firm stands head and shoulders above the rest because of their integrity, customer service, and fair prices: Swiss America, at www.swissamerica.com/gold. That's why

I'm on board with the company as an official spokesman for their great products and services.

A Final Note of Urgency

These are not normal times. The U.S. debt is increasing by more than $58,000 a second![16] And Congress just keeps raising the debt ceiling again and again—making it more likely we will experience a debt crisis and bringing us closer to a future economic collapse.

In a word, the U.S. is broke. It may seem unlikely to most, but we are one bad headline away from economic chaos. Any major catastrophe could sink the entire fragile and weakening paper-based, debt-over-loaded global economy overnight (by leading to panic, unrest, bank runs, etc.). Think *Titanic*.

Gold offers protection from runaway government spending by maintaining your buying power. Gold promotes long-term thinking and financial planning. Gold offers freedom from currency devaluation and higher inflation. Gold is "the golden secret" of economic survival.

But most of all gold is "wealth insurance" against the arrogance, ignorance, stupidity, recklessness, and corruption of our politicians. Gold is the ultimate middle class weapon of self-defense.

SOURCE for Gold and Other Precious Metals:

I recommend contacting Swiss America for the answers to your questions about gold, silver, precious metals, U.S. rare coins, or setting up a Precious Metals IRA via info@swissamerica.com or 800-519-6270.

Your Prescription
for Beating Obamacare

The Murder of the Middle Class has no more important central character than Obamacare. The costs of Obamacare will very likely bankrupt the middle class. Perhaps even worse is the decline in the quality of care. You don't want your family in this system. Once you're in a government-run bureaucratic maze, your life becomes a living hell.

Does the prospect of putting the people who run the post office in charge of your healthcare make you tingle all over? As I was writing this book it was announced that the U.S. Postal Service was $100 billion in debt, in "serious financial crisis" with "insufficient revenue to cover its expenses."[17] Proving once again that putting government in charge of anything, including healthcare, will not end well.

Like it or not, Obamacare could be with us long term. In case you get sick and have no choice, I'll give you a variety of ways to maneuver within the healthcare system. But here I want to focus on my most important solution to beating Obamacare: staying healthy and never having to enter the healthcare system.

Let me start by giving you some information about two important studies you need to know about.

First, in a recent report the WHO (World Health Organization) predicts cancer will rise by 57 percent worldwide over the next two decades. They call this "an imminent human disaster."[18]

As devastating as that prediction is, the report also contains very good news: half of all cancers are preventable. The operative word here is "preventable," very different from "treatable." The WHO reports four simple changes can dramatically prevent cancer:

- Diet
- Exercise
- Quit smoking
- Reduce alcohol consumption

But it's not just cancer that is preventable. A healthy lifestyle can prevent or reduce the severity of heart disease, diabetes, strokes, and Alzheimer's disease.

The second study is by the Credit Suisse Research Institute. This 2013 study concluded that 30 to 40 percent of all U.S. healthcare expenses are for diseases directly related to overconsumption of sugar. Since America spends almost $3 trillion per year on healthcare, more per capita than any other nation, yet we are among the most unhealthy nations in the world (dead last in most categories), something is very wrong. This may be one of the answers.[19]

Based on this math, we are spending over $1 trillion annually fighting the damaging effects of sugar. Obesity equals illness and sugar directly causes obesity.

These studies form the basis for how I plan to beat Obamacare: by practicing a healthy lifestyle. I've been practicing this my entire adult life. I eat a healthy, mostly organic diet; exercise one to two hours every day (seven days per week); start most days with a healthy walk in the sunshine (thereby filling my body with natural Vitamin D); supplement with the right vitamins (including mega doses of Vitamin C); don't smoke, don't drink, don't use drugs, don't eat junk food. I limit my sugar/fructose and gluten/grain carbs intake. I also meditate, pray, read the Bible, practice yoga, affirmations, visualizations, and positive thinking. I call my program "Positive Addictions."

The result is that I'm rarely sick; never get the flu (even though I've never had a flu shot); have incredible levels of energy; put in sixteen-hour days running multiple businesses; give speeches and media interviews, write books and commentaries; serve on multiple Boards of Directors; and serve as spokesman for several companies. And I'm the father of four children ranging in age from six to twenty-two. I owe my success and world-class energy level to a healthy lifestyle and vitamins. I pop vitamins all throughout the day and I can literally feel the difference in my energy, clarity, and creativity.

Doctors, drug companies, and the media (bribed by drug company advertising) tell you *vitamins don't work*. Or *vitamins are a waste of money*. Or *we get all the vitamins we need in our food*. I believe my personal experience shows they are DEAD WRONG.

Staying healthy isn't about doctor visits. I respect doctors. But doctors don't prevent illness, they treat it. Just like policemen who often arrive after the robbery or murder has already taken place. Doctors are the same. Once a doctor runs the tests and reports you have cancer, heart disease, diabetes, or Alzheimer's, it's often too late.

Do you think prescription drugs are the answer? Have you ever heard the numbers? More people are killed by prescription drugs than car accidents. Annually, over 2 million Americans suffer adverse reactions to prescription drugs and over one hundred thousand die, most because of the toxicity of the drugs. Another hundred thousand die from accidental overdose of prescription drugs. Prescription drugs are the fourth leading cause of death in America, behind only heart disease, cancer, and strokes.[20] You've probably never heard those dismal statistics. Could it be that Big Pharma spends so much money on media advertising that the media won't tell you the truth (for fear of losing those advertising dollars)?

So what's the answer? It's certainly not big government, big business, Big Pharma, big insurance, or the AMA (American Medical Association). The answer is YOU. You need to take personal responsibility for your own health. This is a perfect prescription for conservatives. We normally think of personal responsibility as applying to business or career. Well it's high time to think of personal responsibility in terms of our health and what we put in our bodies. If you want to live a long, healthy life, you are responsible—not doctors, drugs, and hospitals.

Let me add one other aspect to health—ENERGY. It is a valuable commodity. I've been called a "Human Energizer Bunny." I get my energy from the synergistic effect of my "Positive Addictions" program. But the single most important piece of the program is vitamin supplementation. I plead guilty as charged—"I am a vitamin addict!"

As with almost every product, vitamins come in all grades and quality levels. After years of research, I've come to trust one man, Wayne Gorsek, founder and CEO of DrVita.com and my personal health guru and "fountain of youth" adviser.

I believe in "the DrVita difference." When I believe in something, I go "all in." That's why for the first time ever, I've agreed to put my name behind the vitamin products of DrVita.

Wayne is an authority, not just on vitamins and nutrition, but the right vitamins, in the right doses. DrVita is one of America's leading online vitamin retailers (found at www.DrVita.com/911).

Before DrVita.com, Wayne founded what became the #1 online vitamin retailer. Under his leadership, the vitamin company he founded was inducted into *Inc.* magazine's "Inc. 500 Lifetime Hall of Fame" for being one of America's five hundred fastest growing companies for five consecutive years. He is a remarkable man.

Like me, the other Wayne is healthy and filled with energy. "Wayne & Wayne" make a dynamic duo! We are teaming up here to make sure conservatives are healthy, so we have plenty of focus, creativity, energy, and passion to fight Obamacare!

I asked Wayne, the man who formulates all the unique vitamins at DrVita, how to educate my readers. Here is what I learned.

Wayne Gorsek was adopted and raised by his grandparents. It was their aging as they entered their seventies and eighties and their related illnesses that inspired him to make a difference. It didn't take long to learn that doctors, drugs, and surgeries were not preventing or curing his grandparents' diseases.

Wayne began studying in a medical school library on nights and weekends trying to help his grandparents. He was both shocked and excited to learn there are thousands of studies proving hundreds of nutrients and foods are safe and effective to naturally keep us healthy.

Sadly, he also learned this information is not taught in medical school. Rather than preventing disease, medical school training focuses primarily on disease diagnoses and treatment via expensive tests, drugs, and surgeries. The fact is, the sicker you get, the more money the hospitals, drug companies, and doctors themselves earn.

Wayne learned that eating healthily and exercising moderately will allow us to stay healthy without drugs and surgery. Plus as a bonus, healthy living provides a huge cost savings—think of the money you'll save by not needing doctors, surgeries, or expensive drugs.

Wayne and Wayne want to make a difference. I'm a vitamin enthusiast; Wayne Gorsek is a vitamin *authority*. So I'm going to let Wayne Gorsek take it from here. In his own words, here is the advice of Wayne Gorsek about how dietary supplements support health.

The Truth about Multi-Vitamins, by Wayne Gorsek

For many decades doctors and healthcare professionals have recommended multivitamins to their patients, realizing the standard American diet (SAD) is lacking essential vitamins and minerals required for optimal cellular, immunity, bone, cardiovascular, and brain health. Sadly, these typical multivitamins claiming to be "complete" and sold in retail stores and pharmacies are formulated by large drug companies based on RDAs (Recommended Daily Allowances, now called DVs—Daily Values) that have not been kept current based on the most recent science.[21]

In fact, studies looking at Vitamin D levels clearly prove the diet and supplements people are consuming are providing inadequate levels of this nutrient. The effective level to achieve optimal blood levels of vitamin D is 4,000 to 10,000 IU per day of Vitamin D3, whereas typical multivitamins have worthless 400–600 IU ranges.[22]

Another powerful example of why typical multivitamins do not work is the lack of Lutein. The simple math with Lutein is that it requires about 2,400 percent higher levels than what is in the typical multivitamin to actually work. Why is this? The primary ingredient in a typical multivitamin is calcium carbonate, the same ingredient used to make concrete. It only costs a few dollars per kilo, whereas the Lutein costs several hundred dollars per kilo.

One may ask, "Why do the drug companies fail to improve their formulas?" I can only speculate, but the fact is they generate $260 billion a year selling drugs to sick people. They own patents that create a monopoly for a drug that can generate billions in sales and massive margins (up to 1,000 percent higher than a typical vitamin). Clearly their focus and priority is selling drugs to sick people, not making vitamins that actually work. Sadly, vitamin brands produced by drug companies control the shelf space at most mass-market retailers.

Very sadly the typical multivitamin sold at health food stores is only slightly better (and very expensive).

Also important, capsules provide an easier way to swallow and quicker-to-digest delivery, versus rock-hard tablets which are full of artificial chemicals. In fact the typical tablet contains up to eight chemicals that I personally would not consume.

This is why I started my first vitamin company over twenty years ago—to formulate an effective multivitamin that actually works. To help improve the lives of people like my wonderful grandparents. I'm blessed that I have been able to change the lives of millions of people over the last twenty years. I'm very proud of DrVita.

Let's talk about my top ten recommended nutrients and supplements you should consider to maintain robust health, plus help support high energy:

1) A high-quality multivitamin that is free of copper and toxic chemicals and easy to swallow and digest in an all-natural capsule is essential. Look for far higher than RDA/DV levels of vitamin D3 (minimum 4,000 IU); B-Complex including the Methyl form of B12; K1/K2; 200 mcg selenium; grape seed; CoQ10; green tea standardized for EGCG; alpha lipoic acid; quercetin; and 6 mg of lutein for healthy vision.

2) Coenzyme Q10 (CoQ10) is one of the first nutrients I studied, over twenty years ago, because medical studies indicated excellent benefits for heart function and brain health. There is also a newer more active form of CoQ10 now available called Ubiquinol (CoQH is the brand). How do CoQ10 and CoQH work? From moment to moment, we are burning energy and aging. As a result, free radicals are produced in our bodies. Additionally, environmental toxins enter into our bodies.

Despite the aging process, every cell in the body is in the business of producing energy to keep you vital and healthy. The energy each cell produces is in the form of a molecule called ATP, which is made in the energy powerhouses of the cell known as the mitochondria. CoQ10/CoQH promotes ATP production in the cell's power plants.[23]

The typical diet only provides 2–5 mg of CoQ10 and typical multivitamins provide ZERO. Look for a multi with 100 to 200 mg per day.

3) Magnesium is involved in more than three hundred essential metabolic reactions, including energy production. The metabolism of carbohydrates and fats to produce energy requires numerous magnesium-dependent chemical reactions. Numerous studies now indicate that magnesium supports heart health and helps maintain normal blood pressure levels. The average American diet is very deficient in magnesium. Choose a multivitamin that has at least 400 mg per day.[24]

I'm also very excited about Magtein, a new form of magnesium that may provide enhanced brain health. A study with this new magnesium showed that by increasing the brain's magnesium level, Magtein (Magnesium-L-threonate) could increase the learning ability, working memory, and short- and long-term memory in young and aged rats. It also showed that common magnesium compounds do not effectively improve brain magnesium levels, which is required to improve memory and cognitive functions.[25]

4) **Turmeric** (standardized for 95 percent Curcuminoids) is an herb from the ginseng family popular in India. When used as a supplement in the 1,000-mg range combined with 5 mg of black pepper for enhanced absorption, turmeric has powerful antioxidant benefits and it appears to promote healthy brain aging. Turmeric also increases the antioxidant called Glutathione, which helps eliminate toxic compounds in the body.[26]

5) **Fish oil** containing Omega-3s (in the range of 1,000 to 3,000 mg of EPA and DHA) has numerous benefits. Sadly, most people take only 300 mg of EPA and DHA and there may be little to no benefit at this level. Omega-3s are essential for good mood, cognitive, memory, and joint and cardiovascular health. Look for the "next generation" triple-strength fish oil that contains 750 to 1,000 mg of EPA and DHA per softgel.[27]

6) **Resveratrol and grape seed** should be a central part of your vitamin regimen. Only the very best multivitamins will contain these nutrients. Studies report incredibly powerful antioxidant and health benefits from taking these. There are several good human studies showing grape seed promotes healthy blood pressure and maintains healthy cholesterol levels that are already within the normal range. Resveratrol tricks the cells at the DNA level to think they are in starvation mode and activates DNA repair enzymes that regenerate cells for producing the ATP energy molecule. Cell and animal studies with Resveratrol indicate extension of life and lean body mass. The only prior method to achieve similar results for extending a healthy lifespan was severe calorie restriction (about 1,200 calories per

day). Yet the average American consumes triple this amount of calories. Supplementation with 250 to 500 mg of Resveratrol and 150 to 300 mg of grape seed are my recommendations.[28]

7) Glucosamine, chondroitin, and MSM are great nutrients to take in combination for good joint and skin health. I must admit I have switched to a new and more powerful patented nutrient complex called Biocell Collagen. It has a natural synergy unlike any other containing a natural matrix of Hydrolyzed Collagen + HA (Hyaluronic Acid) + Chondroitin Sulfate = BioCell Collagen. This combination is essential for healthy joint, skin, and connective tissues. Human clinical studies indicate Biocell:

- Supports skin and joint collagens (type I, II, and III)
- Reduces skin dryness by up to 76 percent
- Reduces fine lines and wrinkles Promotes joint comfort and mobility

I find 1,000 mg per day is an effective dosage and when combined with a triple strength fish oil, you will be amazed at how great your joints feel and how healthy your hair, nails, and skin look.[29]

8) Alpha Lipoic Acid (ALA) and Acetyl L-Carnitine (ALC) are powerful brain and memory nutrients. A combination of Alpha Lipoic Acid (ALA) and Acetyl L-Carnitine (ALC) made research headlines when it was given to old lab rats, which began acting like young lab rats. In the words of the lead researcher, they "got up to do the Macarena." This amazing study provides evidence about the benefits of these key nutrients on the brain.

Supplementing with ALA/ALC has also been shown to improve spatial and temporal memory in persons with mild memory loss associated with aging. The combination of ALA and ALC are 100 to 1,000 times more powerful than taking each nutrient individually.[30]

Combining these two miracle nutrients with CoQ10 actually creates a brain and energy nutrient trifecta combination.

9) Probiotics are the natural solution to building a healthy GI tract and good digestion, plus the bonus of a strong immune system. Probiotics are essential friendly bacteria living in your GI tract that number in the hundreds of billions to trillions. I recommend supplementing with a probiotic supplement containing at least ten strains of friendly bacteria, the food that feeds the friendly bacteria called FOS, and a potency of at least 50 billion CFU. Yogurt contains probiotics, but may only have a few strains and potency is well under one billion (or even as low as tens of millions CFU).[31]

10) 7-Keto® is another nutrient that I am excited about. This substance is found naturally in the body. It is metabolized from the hormone DHEA. By the time we reach the age of forty, our production of natural 7-Keto has dropped by 40 percent, and this decline continues through the rest of our lives. Supplementing with 7-Keto® is simply putting back what time and Mother Nature have taken away. 7-Keto® plays an important role in your body's ability to maintain healthy fat levels. Research shows that it is involved in activating three important enzymes that influence your metabolism. When added to a moderate diet and exercise program, 7-Keto® can help accelerate weight loss.[32]

That's my best advice for healthy living and a LONG life!

—Wayne Gorsek

Thank you, Wayne Gorsek. You are "America's King of Health." The other Wayne is too nice and humble to say it, but there is exactly ONE multivitamin I know of that follows the latest science and contains the effective doses of many of the cutting edge nutrients we have discussed. It is called the DrVita Six Daily Advanced Multivitamin. You can find it, along with all of the remarkable products discussed above (based on the most recent and advanced science), at DrVita.

I take a plethora of vitamins, minerals, and other supplements every day. I exercise every day, 365 days a year. I eat healthy and organic. I am not part of Obama's healthcare system. I want you to aim for that same outcome. If you're healthy and don't need doctors, or drugs, or surgery…Obama loses, Big Pharma loses, and America gains. That's the point.

The best way to beat Obamacare is by never becoming dependent on the healthcare system. Don't trust in big government, big business, Big Pharma, and big media. Those are all BIG mistakes!

SOURCE for Vitamins:

For any and all of your vitamin, nutrition, and supplement needs, go to www.DrVita.com/911, and use promo code "WAYNE" to get your special discount, free gifts, free vitamins, free DVD, and free shipping for orders over $49.

Take Ownership of Your Family's Health: Part II of Your Prescription for Beating Obamacare

Clearly, your best defense against Obamacare is to stay healthy. Unfortunately, some people get sick and cannot avoid the system. So here are some unique suggestions, tailored for the individual, to help you manage the costs of medical treatment. I know you won't be surprised that all my solutions are based on freedom and personal responsibility—the true hallmarks of the great American middle class!

1) Consider a concierge or "direct pay" physician. If you can afford it, go outside the system and hire the best physicians money can buy. Concierge medicine, also called "direct pay" medicine, establishes a relationship between patients and a primary care physician in which the patient pays an annual fee of about $3,000. For that fee, doctors provide individual enhanced care. One way to afford this is to set up an HSA (Health Savings Account).

2) Pay cash for most of your medical needs. Whether it's a doctor visit, dentist visit, chiropractor, or special tests (like MRIs), many doctors have a cash price that is considerably lower than what they bill the insurance company. With the higher deductibles and co-pays under Obamacare, more and more doctors and medical experts recommend this as your best choice.

3) Consider "medical tourism." For years, knowledgeable consumers have been traveling to countries like Panama, Thailand, and Costa Rica where they have well-trained doctors, modern hospitals, and much lower costs for surgery and other medical procedures. It is possible to get your medical needs taken care of and enjoy a beautiful vacation for considerably less than the medical costs here. You might ask, "Why would I need that? After all, under Obamacare our medical care is free." In reality, what's "free" might very well be sub-standard care, combined with long waits, or outright denial of necessary surgery or other treatment.

Medical tourism has long been the choice of those living in countries with socialized medicine like Canada and Europe. A friend who lived in Panama for several years tells me that on almost every trip back to the States he would meet a Canadian who had gone to Panama for a hip or knee replacement. The story, he said, was always the same. Yes, the surgery in Canada would be done for "free." BUT, they had been on a waiting list for over a year with no idea how much longer they would have to wait. If they went to the U.S. it would cost them over $30,000. In Panama the cost was less than $10,000 and the doctors and hospitals were of equal quality.

So if you can't get the quality of care inside America under Obamacare, or the wait is just too long, it may very well pay to have your medical or dental procedures done outside the USA. It's important to deal in reality, and know your options.

4) "Healthcare sharing ministries" are exempt from Obamacare. A century ago, churches understood they were called to care for the sick and needy, and so they founded hospitals. Today churches are reviving that heritage with "health sharing ministries." This is a way for individuals and families with a common set of religious beliefs to band together to share medical bills.

The sharing ministries are not insurance: there's no guarantee that a given bill will be covered. It's more like a co-op, where members decide what procedures to cover, and then they all pitch in to cover the cost as a group. Members put aside a certain amount of money every month, which then goes to others in the ministry who need help paying their medical bills. The Christian health ministries of which I'm aware require that in addition to being a Christian you must also agree to live a Christian lifestyle (no smoking, drugs, or alcohol abuse).

Here are a few choices of health sharing ministries:

- Medi-Share: http://mychristiancare.org/how_does_it_work. aspx
- Samaritan Ministries: http://samaritanministries.org
- Christian Healthcare Ministries: http://www.chministries. org
- Alliance of Health Care Sharing Ministries: http://www. healthcaresharing.org/hcsm

5) If you own a business, set up a self-insurance plan. This is the biggest Obamacare loophole available for small businesses and can result in considerable savings. Note that it must be professionally administered by a health insurance company, so be sure it is properly established. For more information about how to set up a plan contact the Self-Insurance Institute of America at http://www.siia.org/i4a/pages/Index.cfm?pageID=4546.

Beating Obamacare is all about claiming personal responsibility and ownership of your body, mind, spirit, and health. It's about taking control over your own healthcare to live a longer life, without government involved.

Take Personal Responsibility for Your Family's Survival

Now that we've shored up your finances and your health, let's turn to something a bit more frightening—your survival if things go very badly for America. The topic here is survival preparation, as defined by a Special

Forces expert. While I hope and pray it never happens, a worst-case scenario is possible.

If there is a complete collapse—of the U.S. economic system, monetary system, or the global financial system, or as a result of terrorism or war—we will all have much bigger worries than preserving our incomes, assets, or health. We'll be concerned about our physical survival amidst unrest and anarchy.

Will it ever get that bad? Who knows? But I believe in being prepared—especially when the lives of my family are involved. So I turned to one of my close friends, a former elite U.S. Special Forces operative who served in intelligence, in counterterrorism, and as a member of the Joint Special Operations Command (JSOC). He is also an expert in biometrics and nonlethal defense technology. He is a man we can reliably turn to for professional advice on how to prepare for disaster. Because of his career connections to the military and the government, he chooses to write anonymously.

Here is his exclusive and valuable advice, in his own words, excerpted from *The Ultimate Obama Survival Guide*.

Increasing Your Odds of Survival

For the next few pages let's focus on defining survival at its most basic level—staying alive.

It is paramount to be prepared and have options when a national emergency or act of God occurs. We have no control over events unfolding globally or nationally, just as we have no control over catastrophic events. However, I can tell you, without a doubt, if you don't have a contingency plan that will allow you to execute a step by step process when the unthinkable occurs, you and your family are doomed to disaster.

Please listen to my advice now. You'll believe me later after a catastrophic event: **THE GOVERNMENT WILL NOT COME TO YOUR RESCUE.**

Let me say it another way. Any significant event will result in the immediate stoppage of food, fuel, and essential services to which you are so accustomed. You, and you alone, will be responsible for yourself and your family. There will be no FEMA, no fuel, no food, no garbage collection and very likely, no electricity or water.

What's your plan?...Time is of the essence. Within the first ninety minutes after an emergency, while the masses are waiting for help to arrive, you must be proactive and put your plan into action. Your contingency plan is now your roadmap to survival.

What's included in your roadmap? Do you have an exit strategy to get out of the affected area? Are you prepared to hunker down and protect your fortress? The first and most important requirement is food and water—followed by shelter, heat, power, and self-defense. If you do not have at least a thirty-to-ninety-day supply of basic, easy-to-fix meals for yourself and your family, now is the time to start putting that in place. At the end of these pages I will provide a few websites where you can obtain key elements to your contingency plan.... I'm prepared and I hope you are. But, you have to take responsibility to "pack your own parachute."

If your plan includes departing your location, be sure you have a safe location already identified. Then, you must be prepared to leave in ninety minutes or less.... Your family members must be aware of the plan and have a rally location or return immediately to aid in the loading and move out order....

Trust me when I say the operational security of your plan is essential to your survival....

As part of your plan, know who your threats are and identify the potential they have to derail your plans.... Hesitation will get you killed! ...

What else does it take to put together a cohesive and doable plan?...The most important part is to practice and rehearse.

U.S. Special Operation forces are so effective in combat because of:

1. Highly Intelligent Operators
2. Best Equipment in the World
3. Training, Training, and More Training

Training is everything in life. Just as you practice a sport or study for a test, you must practice your plan to be ready to put it into action. You will learn during these exercises what works and doesn't work. You will improvise the plan so that it becomes seamless. It has to be second nature. . . .

When developing a plan, understand your surroundings and also your end-game location. If your plan is to ride things out at home, then prepare for that. Are you going to secure the entire home or just a couple rooms? Who will be in your neighborhood network of trusted parties? Where will your water come from? Your swimming pool? How will you filter it? How will you dispose of your waste? Are you prepared to share with those who were not prepared? Do you have auxiliary power generation? Fuel generator? Solar power? And the last and probably the most important question to ask yourself is once you have the logistics and plan for your family in place, how are you going to defend and protect your fortress?

Know that, however much you might want to, you are not going to be able to reason or negotiate with those in dire straits. You must be prepared to provide security by force. And, by force I mean you need fire-power. . . . Many families today have guns. However, I can assure you they are not well trained, and they don't possess sufficient quantities of munitions to sustain a fight. Don't be one of those. If you are prepared, they will move on to some other soft target to get what they need. So in your plan you must have a defense component that includes training, a sufficient quantity of weapons, and an over-supply of munitions.

It is not my intent to put the fear of God in you. It is my intent to open your eyes to the possibility of a major disruption of essential needs. I see people living their lives every day and how they react when their cellular service goes down. Imagine what happens when you can't procure food and fuel! Imagine no electricity, and no communications. . . .

I've traveled the world, lived life, and endured hardship. I've defended my country with my life and love America with all my heart. I know I must be prepared to defend what is mine and what is near and dear to me! That is my family, loved ones, and my team members. We have a bond. . . . It is our hope that disaster never comes, but we would be naïve to think it won't. We will be prepared and we will practice. It is infinitely better to be prepared and never have to implement than to not be prepared at all!

.... Do you really want to put your lives in the hands of others? ...

Let me walk you through what you will need. Establishing your minimum requirements is dependent upon your needs and experience....

As I stated earlier you must address your human priorities as follows:

1. Food and water
2. Shelter
3. Heat
4. Power
5. Self-defense

Self-Defense

I choose to start with what I feel most comfortable with and that is, at a minimum, having one weapon for each individual capable of providing support. I recommend a handgun and would also suggest one shotgun for every two individuals. Shotguns are perfect for home and close quarter protection and you don't have to be a marksman to take down or ward off an aggressor. In the event you're looking for standoff protection, acquire a rifle or assault weapon.

Here are your weapons requirements in a snapshot:

1. .40 Caliber hand gun (Glock Model 22, 27 or equivalent)
2. Shotguns (Mossberg Model 500 Series)
3. Optional: assault weapons (XCR-L Series)
4. Ammunition (as much as each person can carry)

To make life easier you should also have some type of backpack system. The choices are MOLLE or ALICE:

- MOLLE = Modular Lightweight Load-carrying Equipment
- ALICE = All-purpose Lightweight Individual Carrying Equipment

My recommendation is MOLLE Large, as it is the most modern and allows you to add and subtract pouches as needed; it offers the ability to add Commercial Off The Shelf (COTS) sleep systems.... for value it is the perfect bug-out bag that facilitates "grab and go" scenarios, saving precious time. Each member in your team should be fitted and equipped. You should have the contents of the bag fully defined and packed. It should at a minimum include:

1. Food (3 Days)
2. Water and water purification systems
3. Medical kit
4. Extra set of clothes, socks, etc.
5. Knife and entrenching tool
6. Chem (snap and shake) flashlights
7. Fire starter
8. Sleep system
9. Flares
10. Ammunition

Special Note: Have a supply of cash, silver, and gold and an emergency hand crank AM/FM radio....

Now, you are asking, "If I'm basing my survival from my existing domicile, why would I need the bug-out bag?" Quite simply, it is vital for many reasons. I keep mine in the trunk of my car and if I have to abandon my vehicle during a time of crisis, I have the essentials to get home. What happens if your home gets overrun? Even if your plan is to stay put, plan an exit strategy to a predetermined safe haven...just in case.

Food and Water

Have sufficient supplies of both food and water. "Sufficient" depends upon your location. If you lose power, utilize food on hand that will spoil first. Save the recommended freeze-dried foods for later.

Fill your bathtubs and other containers with water. Do this first. You never know how long city water sources will be available. If you have access to a stream, river, lake, or swimming pool, make sure you have adequate filtration equipment.

Ration your food and become disciplined from day one. Above all, do not panic and NEVER communicate your food supplies to anyone. Operational security is paramount to your survival. The last thing you want is to make your location a target.

Shelter, Heat, and Power

Wherever you are, step one is to limit access. Board up all first floor windows and reinforce doorways. There are simple ways to do this without a major renovation. Place lookouts on the second floor to ensure these areas are not breached.

Have a supply of firewood if you have a fireplace, or space saver heaters in the event that you don't. Acquire a gas-powered generator to be used only to power essentials and locate it on a secure balcony with an adequate supply of fuel.

This is all about prior planning; dress rehearsals, and trial and error from these practice rounds....

My intent here is simply to open your eyes, give you a brief overview, and let you determine how much or how little you will be prepared....

Ayn Rand's *Atlas Shrugged* is a work of fiction quickly becoming reality.

Who is John Galt? Wayne Root, is it you? <u>I hope so.</u>

Author's Note from Wayne

First, I want to thank my Special Forces buddy who wrote this section. You are my rock!

It's time to start preparing. You and I know in our hearts that protection will come late, be insufficient when it comes, or never come at all. Ask the people of New Orleans how quickly help came after Hurricane Katrina. Ask the people of the Philippines how quickly help came after Typhoon Haiyan. Ask the people of Thailand how quickly help came after the massive tsunami.

Everything you'll need to put yourself at an advantage is listed in this chapter. Read it, study it, and memorize it. Then see the links at the end of this chapter.

Don't wait, hesitate, or procrastinate. Order the things you need and store them in a safe place so they are safe and ready to use when you need them. I personally recommend you buy a minimum of two years' supply of freeze-dried food (that lasts up to twenty-five years) for every family member, a minimum of 1,500 calories per person per day. It is important to buy several survival stoves to boil water and cook food. It is also a good idea to buy GMO FREE seeds in long-term storage containers.

DrVita has vitamins that are nitrogen flushed like freeze-dried foods, to extend shelf life for many years. I recommend a two-year supply of DrVita multivitamins and triple-strength fish oil.

I also recommend you purchase several water filters that can remove harmful organisms from thousands of gallons of water. DrVita also has a new product called the Aquapod, which will turn any bathtub into safe and clean drinking water that can save the lives of your loved ones.

It is also important to stock up on solar recharging panels and devices for batteries along with rechargeable batteries. Emergency LED lighting, communication devices, and radios are very important.

You cannot survive without clean water, food, protection, light, and communications. Further, these are items you can use for barter, as you should expect your credit cards, checks, and cash to be worthless in a serious or prolonged crisis. This commonsense strategy could be the difference between life and death.

SOURCES for Survival Supplies, Food and Vitamins, Water Filters, Solar Energy Resources, and Stoves:

www.DrVita.com/911

Use promo code "WAYNE" to get your special discounts, gifts, free DVD, and free shipping on orders over $49.

Weapons:

http://us.glock.com/
http://www.mossberg.com/
http://xcr.robarm.com/

Survival Websites:

http://www.tacticalintelligence.net/blog/top-10-most-influential-survival-and-preparedness-blogs.htm

CHAPTER 24

Take Ownership of Your Future

*All that is necessary for the triumph of evil
is that good men do nothing.*
—**Edmund Burke**

DID YOU KNOW?

- Owning your own business is a great *legal* tax shelter
- Home-schoolers are more likely to attend college, more likely to graduate, and have higher college GPAs than other students
- In 2012, only 7.5 percent of families headed by two married parents lived in poverty

Rescuing the middle class depends on YOU. Only YOU can take responsibility for your own personal prosperity. Only YOU can save yourself and your family from the depredations of *The Murder of the Middle Class*. Only YOU can work harder, work smarter, take the right risks, and ensure that you get rewarded for your efforts. And I'm here to show you how you can do that.

I've shown you how to prepare financially with "wealth insurance." How to build robust health. How to prepare for your family's survival. Here are some additional practical solutions for YOU, the individual reader, with some heartfelt advice. I know how difficult it is to step out of your comfort zone and make significant changes. However let me assure you that being proactive and "ahead of the curve" is far better than sitting tight paralyzed by fear and being forced to be reactive as your world crumbles around you. We are at a time in history where waiting for others or taking no personal action will very likely result in the loss of your current lifestyle and could potentially even cost you and your family their lives.

Build Your Life around Ownership and Personal Responsibility

Ownership equals power. America has always been about ownership, opportunity, and freedom. In many other countries you don't own or control your life. The government controls everything. That's precisely what makes America different ... and great. We all have a shot at ownership and upward mobility because of the economic and personal freedoms guaranteed in the Constitution and the opportunity those freedoms provide for everyone willing to risk and work.

My dad the butcher pointed it out on his deathbed in 1992. "I've never been rich, if the definition of rich is money. But I got to own my own business. I've called my own shots for twenty-five years. That's rich."

I guess I turned out to be a chip off the old block. My whole life is about ownership. I want to breathe freedom with every breath I take. Take away our freedoms, put big government in charge of our lives from cradle to grave, and it's no longer America. It's no longer special. It's no longer exceptional. Take ownership away from the individual ... and America might as well be Mexico, or Cuba, or Spain, or Argentina. Those are all countries with failing socialist-type economies and people living in abject poverty with little or no hope of better.

In America we own and control our lives. Our destiny is in our hands. We call the shots, not government. My dad was right, that's the true definition of "rich."

This book is dedicated to saving the American middle class, and this chapter is dedicated to personal advice that can help save the great American middle class way of life for YOU. Think hard about each recommendation below—they all revolve around *ownership and empowerment*.

Author's Note: Many of the recommendations presented here are explained in greater detail in my last book, *The Ultimate Obama Survival Guide*. If you read that book and took action, congratulations! If you haven't read my last book (with valuable advice from eighteen of the wealthiest businessmen in America), get a copy and start reading. All that advice still holds true today. Hopefully this chapter will be the motivation and inspiration you need to start taking responsibility to protect yourself and your family from **The Murder of the Middle Class**.

Take Ownership of Your Career

Having your own business is the ultimate form of ownership. No matter how much tyrants like Obama hate small business owners, you are always better off owning your own business—simply because your career and earnings are in your hands, not someone else's. Not a boss's, not government's, not a big faceless corporation's. Owning a business gives you control.

Business owners attract the brunt of the Democrats' ire because we are independent. We don't want or need government to help us. We don't want what government is selling. Obama resents that attitude. So he desperately wants to put us out of business.

But everyone reading this book already understands the importance of defying big government tyrants who want to control your life. If tyrants like Obama don't want you to be a small business owner, then your goal should be to become a small business owner. If Obama wants to stop you, it must be the escape route from government control—the route to wealth, financial freedom, and independence.

I can tell you from experience … **IT IS!**

Ironically, owning your own business is the best way to solve the problem Obama constantly talks about—inequality. You want to be poor, helpless, and dependent? Then work for someone else. Accept a safe (but inadequate) paycheck. You want to be paid what you're worth? Then become the boss!

This is how you beat Obama. By building your own business you remain independent and never rely on government.

More small business owners means more people who want nothing from government. This is the combination that will drive Obama and his big business co-conspirators crazy.

For more specific advice on practical steps toward owning your own business, see my last book, *The Ultimate Obama Survival Guide*, where you'll learn:

- Why owning your own business is a *legal* tax shelter
- A great resource on the art of the legal tax deduction for business owners, professionals, and independent contractors
- Why as long as Obama and the Democrats are in power, most businesses cannot afford to hire full-time employees
- Four options for business ownership that are still viable even under Obama Great Depression conditions: the One-Man-Army business; the Web-Based Business; the Franchise; and Multi-Level Marketing (MLM)
- Why the lucrative opportunities in Multi-Level Marketing are despised by liberals
- Twelve advantages of owning your own businesses
- How to benefit from the opportunities of small business ownership while at the same time preserving your family's security

Take Ownership of Your Child's Education

School choice, charter schools, tuition vouchers, alternative education, and in particular home-schooling are all about ownership of your children's future. You need to take control out of the hands of teachers unions and government bureaucrats. Your children are the most valuable thing on this earth. Why would you leave the corrupt, failed, incompetent public school bureaucracy and teachers unions in control of their future?

Education is vitally important if we're going to rescue the middle class. For most of this country's history, Americans worked their way into the middle class by availing themselves of every educational opportunity. They bettered themselves by learning the skills they would need to produce goods and services that would make them a decent living, improve the lives of their fellow citizens, and contribute to the growing prosperity of their communities.

Today, the public school system cannot be counted on to provide the educational opportunity our children need.

That's a huge problem for your children's future. Education is an economic issue. If your kids are not being properly educated, their future income potential is limited and damaged. But education is not *just* an economic issue. It's also the civil rights issue of the twenty-first century. It is your child's God-given right to have a first class education. That right is being violated every day in America's public schools.

The dumbing down of America is at the very heart of **The Murder of the Middle Class**. Are your children being taught lies about American history, being taught the individual is subservient to the collective, and that equality is more important than opportunity and individual achievement? Are biased, leftist teachers brainwashing your children with guilt and lies to love and support Obama and his socialist policies? If so, and if it is allowed to continue, there is no hope for the future of America.

Plain and simple—our children are the future of America. They are the workforce, the entrepreneurs, the job creators, the inventors, and the CEOs of the future. Just like virtually every political, economic, or social issue in this country, less government and more freedom is the solution. If our children are being taught to be obedient order-followers, not business owners, leaders, and decision makers, America is doomed.

The freedom to live the American Dream starts with a quality education. The pursuit of happiness in the Declaration of Independence is dependent upon a quality education. And a quality education is dependent upon parents having the freedom to choose the best education for their children.

Our government-run public school system means one thing: "Every Child Left Behind." Education spending since 1975 is up. Meanwhile, SAT scores are the lowest in history, reading scores have gone down 25 percent, and American students' math and science scores are in the bottom third of developed nations.[1] If you're interested in a boatload of statistics about just how bad public education in America is today, you can find them in *The Ultimate Obama Survival Guide*. Suffice it to say that the education system in this country is a disgrace. And it's killing the American Dream.

No wonder Glenn Reynolds (the University of Tennessee law professor of Instapundit fame) regularly asks "Is sending your kids to public school parental malpractice?"[2]

But what can you do? Elite private schools—like Sidwell Friends in Washington, D.C., where the president's daughters are being educated ($24,545 for one year of high school)[3]—were quite a stretch for a middle class budget even before this Obama Great Depression.

Fortunately, today there are also much more affordable alternatives— from lower-priced Catholic schools to voucher programs to publicly funded charter schools to magnet schools to home-schooling.

Any of these could be a great choice for you as a parent determined to take ownership of your child's education. The crucial decision you need to make is the realization that your children's education is your responsibility. You can't just blindly hand your kids over to public school bureaucrats and trust

For more specific advice on practical steps toward taking ownership of your children's education, see my last book, *The Ultimate Obama Survival Guide*, where you'll learn:

- The Department of Education reports a 74 percent increase in home-schooling since 1999
- Home-schoolers score 72 points higher than the national average on the SATs. They're also more likely to attend college, more likely to graduate, and have higher college GPAs than other students
- How we fostered an ambition for a Harvard education in our daughter, Dakota
- How we set the bar high early
- How Dakota learned to relish competition while her peers were becoming expert "partiers"
- How crucial it is to make sure a parent is home with children every day

that they'll come out at the other end as well-educated, competent adults. It may be possible for your kids to get a decent education in a public school system, depending on where you live. But it's up to you to monitor the situation, marshal resources, and make it your business to see that your children are actually being educated—not indoctrinated, or neglected, or both.

Let me put in a special word for home-schooling. My wife and I have home-schooled our four children—with pretty remarkable results so far. Our daughter Dakota is a graduate of Harvard (where she got straight As), and our three younger children are following in her footsteps with similar results on national exams. They're on a path to be productive and independent members of the great American middle class.

Escape from States That Are Hostile to the Middle Class

If you want to escape *The Murder of the Middle Class*, it may be time to consider a radical option to protect yourself, your family, and your assets—MOVING. To a state that's more friendly to the middle class.

If you live in California, New York, New Jersey, Illinois, Maryland, Massachusetts—or any other Democrat-ridden state where the politicians see middle class taxpayers as marks to fleece—consider getting out now. "Blue" states persecute their middle class citizens and tax-paying, job-creating business owners in myriad ways, from sky-high tax rates to regulations that make life miserable for anyone who is trying to run a business.

Moving to a low-tax state is all about ownership and empowerment. It's pretty simple. In places like Texas, Florida, Nevada, Utah, Wyoming, and South Dakota taxes and regulations are lower, so you get to keep more of your own income and assets. That gives you freedom. Wealth gives you options in life. The more money you make and keep, the less dependent you'll be on government.

And separate from taxes and regulations, there are other wonderful bonuses in these less-government, more-freedom states. You'll have cheaper energy bills and a lower probability of getting hit with lawsuits. And with the money you save you can live in a bigger home; drive a newer, safer car; pay for private school; and spend more time with your family. In other words, your life belongs to you ... not big government, big business, lawyers, unions, and environmentalists.

For more specific advice on practical steps toward relocating to a middle class–friendly state, see my last book, *The Ultimate Obama Survival Guide*, where you'll learn:

- How technology makes it easier than ever to run your business from a low-tax, low-regulation, high-freedom state
- The top fifteen fastest-growing states (all low-tax, no-tax, business-friendly, and/or Republican red states)
- The states losing the most population (all high-tax states)
- Which states the happiest people live in
- How the money I saved by moving from New York to Nevada boosted my family's standard of living—and paid for the tutors who helped get my daughter into Harvard

One Final Recommendation

I've got one remaining piece of advice about ownership and personal responsibility: **GET MARRIED!**

Obama talks day and night about "income inequality." It dominates his every move. There's a simple solution that will dramatically reduce your odds of living in poverty, protect your middle class lifestyle, and even give you a fair shot at happiness. I can't guarantee you'll be rich, but the facts pretty much guarantee you won't be poor if you make one decision—to get married. The facts show that marriage, and having children only after marriage, prevents poverty.

Ari Fleischer, a prominent Republican media personality and former presidential press secretary presented some facts about marriage in a recent *Wall Street Journal* editorial.[4]

According to the Census Bureau's own statistics, among families headed by two married parents in 2012, only 7.5 percent lived in poverty. When families are headed by only a single mother, poverty increases to 33.9 percent.

Obama blames poverty on "racism" because of the dramatic difference in poverty rates among whites versus blacks and Hispanics. Those poverty rates don't come from racism. They correlate exactly to the disintegration of the married family in America. In white families, 28.6 percent of children were born outside of marriage, versus 52.5 percent of Hispanics and 72.3 percent of blacks. Fleischer points out that "marriage inequality," not income inequality, produces poverty.

Conversely Fleischer reported on a Heritage Foundation study that shows white married couples have a poverty rate of 3.2 percent versus 22 percent for non-married white families. For black married couples the poverty rate was 7 percent, but for non-married black families the poverty rate was 35.6 percent.[5] Clearly, poverty is more related to marriage (or the lack thereof) and the stability missing in homes without fathers present, than it is to race.

The statistics are clear. If you want a good chance at a middle class lifestyle, get married. And, if you wait to have children only after marriage, you'll also give them the best opportunity for opportunity and mobility.

By the way, how would you define marriage? I'd define it as taking ownership of your future together. Dating someone is like renting. Marriage is joint ownership of your relationship, children, and financial future. And as usual, ownership produces fantastic results!

Marriage is part of the middle class culture of ownership. That ownership culture is part of what made the middle class great. Thinking in terms of ownership accomplishes a whole lot of good things:

It gives you great goals to aim for. Everyone should aim to become an owner, not renter. Everyone should aim to control their own destiny.

Science proves that the way you think helps to produce the outcomes you're visualizing. So if you think like a frightened helpless person who needs government to save you, that's exactly what you'll become. But if you think like an owner, there's a high probability you'll make it happen. It all starts with mindset.

Even if you work for others, the middle class ownership mindset works like a charm. The employee who takes control, personal responsibility, and ownership of his or her job, will not only be the one that keeps his job in tough times, but the one who gets promoted by a thankful boss.

And there's an ADDED PLUS. This kind of empowerment, ownership thinking drives big government tyrants and control-freaks (like Obama and his big business co-conspirators) absolutely crazy. They can't stand independent thinkers, who want nothing from big government or big business. That alone makes it worth its weight in gold!

Now you know about *The Murder of the Middle Class*. And now you know what you need to do to stop it—to rescue the greatest country in world history, the economy, the GOP, and YOU! Go out there and do it!

Good luck, and God bless you and your families.

God Bless America.

WAR
Wayne Allyn Root
Las Vegas, Nevada 4/15/14

We hope you enjoyed Wayne's book.

To contact Wayne Allyn Root:

Email: Wayne@ROOTforAmerica.com

PH: 888 444-7668(ROOT) or (702) 407-5548

Mailing Address:

Wayne Allyn Root
c/o ROOT for America
2505 Anthem Village Drive, Ste. 318
Henderson, NV 89052

To receive Wayne's FREE weekly commentaries via email, please sign up at:

ROOTforAmerica.com

To add your name to Wayne's list of volunteers for a future ROOT Campaign for political office, please sign up at:

ROOTforAmerica.com

To book Wayne for a political or business speech, please go to:

ROOTofSuccess.com

or call (888) 444-7668(ROOT)

Notes

Epigraph

1. Cornelius Tacitus, *The Life and Character of Agricola*, Loeb Library ed., vol. 35, p. 80, purporting to quote the British chieftain Calgacus. See Scott Horton, "Tacitus and the Costs of War," *Harper's*, November 26, 2007, http://harpers.org/blog/2007/11/tacitus-on-the-costs-of-war/.

Introduction

1. Palash R. Ghosh, "Native Americans: The Tragedy of Alcoholism," International Business Times, February 11, 2012, http://www.ibtimes.com/native-americans-tragedy-alcoholism-214046.
2. "Alcohol and Native Americans," Wikipedia, http://en.wikipedia.org/wiki/Alcohol_and_Native_Americans, citing "Fetal alcohol syndrome–Alaska, Arizona, Colorado, and New York, 1995–1997," *Morbidity and Mortality Weekly Report* 51, no. 20 (2002): 433–35.
3. Stephanie Woodard, "Suicide Is Epidemic for American Indian Youth: What More Can Be Done?" *American Renaissance*, October 10, 2012, http://www.amren.com/news/2012/10/suicide-is-epidemic-for-american-indian-youth-what-more-can-be-done/.
4. Ghosh, "Native Americans: The Tragedy of Alcoholism."
5. Sari Horwitz, "The Hard Lives—and High Suicide Rate—of Native American Children on Reservations," *Washington, Post*, March 9, 2014, http://www.washingtonpost.com/world/national-security/the-hard-lives--and-high-suicide-rate--of-native-american-children/2014/03/09/6e0ad9b2-9f03-11e3-b8d8-94577ff66b28_story.html.

6. "Challenges Facing American Indians," in "A Reporter's Guide to American Indian Law," Reporters Committee for Freedom of the Press, http://www.rcfp.org/reporters-guide-american-indian-law/challenges-facing-american-indians.
7. "Alcohol and Native Americans," Wikipedia, http://en.wikipedia.org/wiki/Alcohol_and_Native_Americans.

Chapter 1: The Evidence for the Crime

1. Tami Luhby, "America's Disappearing Middle Class," CNNMoney, January 28, 2014, http://economy.money.cnn.com/2014/01/28/middle-class/?iid=HP_LN.
2. David Leonhardt and Kevin Quealy, "LOSING THE LEAD: The American Middle Class Is No Longer the World's Richest," *New York Times*, April 22, 2014, http://www.nytimes.com/2014/04/23/upshot/the-american-middle-class-is-no-longer-the-worlds-richest.html?hp&_r=1.
3. Joshua Gardner and Associated Press, "Death knell rings for 142 years of American dominance as China prepares to leap into first place as world's largest economy," *Daily Mail*, April 30, 2014, http://www.dailymail.co.uk/news/article-2616806/American-dollar-hits-wall-China-prepares-leap-place-worlds-largest-economy-end-year.html.
4. Christopher Ingraham, "U.S. businesses are being destroyed faster than they're being created," *Washington Post*, May 5, 2014, http://www.washingtonpost.com/blogs/wonkblog/wp/2014/05/05/u-s-businesses-are-being-destroyed-faster-than-theyre-being-created/?hpid=z5.
5. Terence P. Jeffrey, "86M Full-Time Private-Sector Workers Sustain 148M Benefit Takers," CNS News, April 16, 2014, http://www.cnsnews.com/commentary/terence-p-jeffrey/86m-full-time-private-sector-workers-sustain-148m-benefit-takers.
6. Ali Meyer, "1,148,000 Fewer Americans Have Jobs Today than 7 Yrs Ago," CNSNews.com, December 6, 2013, http://cnsnews.com/news/article/ali-meyer/1148000-fewer-americans-have-jobs-today-7-yrs-ago.
7. Tyler Durden, "The Number of Working Age Americans without a Job Has Risen by Almost 10 Million under Obama," Zero Hedge, January 13, 2014, http://www.zerohedge.com/news/2014-01-13/number-working-age-americans-without-job-has-risen-almost-10-million-under-obama.
8. Susan Berry, "Rasmussen: Only 31% of Americans Work 40-Hour Week," Breitbart, December 15, 2013, http://www.breitbart.com/Big-Government/2013/12/15/Rasmussen-Only-31-Of-Americans-Work-40-Hour-week?utm_source=twitterfeed&utm_medium=twitter.
9. Michael Snyder, "10 Facts about the Growing Unemployment Crisis in America That Will Blow Your Mind," The Economic Collapse, November 10, 2013, http://

theeconomiccollapseblog.com/archives/10-facts-about-the-growing-unemployment-crisis-in-america-that-will-blow-your-mind.

10. Ibid.

11. Katie Sanders, "Labor Force Participation Is at Lowest Point since 1978, Says Texas Sen. Ted Cruz," PolitiFact, January 26, 2014, http://www.politifact.com/truth-o-meter/statements/2014/jan/26/ted-cruz/labor-force-participation-its-lowest-point-1978-sa.

12. Jodie Gummow, "Shocking Stat: 70% of Americans Not in the Labor Force Are under 55 Years Old," AlterNet, March 6, 2014, http://www.alternet.org/economy/shocking-stat-70-americans-not-labor-force-are-under-55-years-old.

13. Terence P. Jeffrey, "Men Who Work Full-Time Earn Less Than 40 Years Ago," CNS News, April 28, 2014, http://cnsnews.com/news/article/terence-p-jeffrey/men-who-work-full-time-earn-less-40-years-ago.

14. "Employment Data Show Low Labor-Force Rate for Men," *Wall Street Journal*, September 7, 2012, http://live.wsj.com/video/employment-data-show-low-labor-force-rate-for-men/B47D73B9-EEA5-4217-B0BF-738A2414FFA6.html#!B47D73B9-EEA5-4217-B0BF-738A2414FFA6.

15. Nin-Hai Tseng, "More Americans Are Working, but Pay Is Still Low," CNNMoney, December 6, 2013, http://finance.fortune.cnn.com/2013/12/06/more-americans-are-working-but-pay-is-still-low/?iid=HP_River.

16. Michael Grabell, "The Expendables: How the Temps Who Power Corporate Giants Are Getting Crushed," ProPublica, http://www.propublica.org/article/the-expendables-how-the-temps-who-power-corporate-giants-are-getting-crushe.

17. Ashe Schow, "Recovery Woes: America's Second-Largest Employer Is a Temp Agency," *Washington Examiner*, July 8, 2013, http://washingtonexaminer.com/recovery-woes-americas-second-largest-employer-is-a-temp-agency/article/2532778.

18. "Wage Statistics for 2012," Social Security Online, May 2, 2014, http://www.ssa.gov/cgi-bin/netcomp.cgi?year=2012.

19. Tyler Durden, "40% of US Workers Now Earn Less than 1968 Minimum Wage," Zero Hedge, August 5, 2013, http://www.zerohedge.com/news/2013-08-05/40-us-workers-now-earn-less-1968-minimum-wage.

20. "Average (Mean) Duration of Unemployment," available on the Federal Reserve Bank of St. Louis website, http://research.stlouisfed.org/fred2/data/UEMPMEAN.txt.

21. Ibid.

22. Tyler Durden, "What Happens to America's Long-Term Unemployed (Spoiler Alert: Nothing Good)," Zero Hedge, March 24, 2014, http://www.zerohedge.com/

news/2014-03-24/what-happens-americas-long-term-unemployed-spoiler-alert-nothing-good.

23. Alan B. Krueger, Judd Cramer, and David Cho, "Are the Long-Term Unemployed on the Margins of the Labor Market?" Brookings, March 20–21, 2014, http://www.brookings.edu/about/projects/bpea/papers/2014/are-longterm-unemployed-margins-labor-market.

24. "Alternate Unemployment Charts," ShadowStats.com, http://www.shadowstats.com/alternate_data/unemployment-charts.

25. "Job at McDonald's Harder to Get than Acceptance to Harvard," The Traders Crucible, April 29, 2011, http://traderscrucible.com/2011/04/29/job-at-mcdonalds-harder-to-get-than-acceptance-to-harvard/.

26. "Walmart and Harvard: Which Is More Selective?" e21, December 9, 2013, http://www.economics21.org/commentary/walmart-and-harvard-which-more-selective.

27. Michael Snyder, "Employment Recovery? 1,600 Workers Apply for Just 36 Jobs at an Ice Cream Plant in Maryland," The Economic Collapse, January 7, 2014, http://theeconomiccollapseblog.com/archives/employment-recovery-1600-workers-apply-for-just-36-jobs-at-an-ice-cream-plant-in-maryland.

28. Tyler Durden, "It Is Five Time [sic] More Difficult to Get an Attendant Job at Delta Airlines than Enter Harvard," Zero Hedge, December 22, 2012, http://www.zerohedge.com/news/2012-12-22/it-five-time-more-difficult-get-attendant-job-delta-airlines-enter-harvard.

29. Victoria Barret, "Getting a Job Washing Cars Is Harder than Getting into Harvard," Forbes, May 10, 2012, http://www.forbes.com/sites/victoriabarret/2012/05/10/getting-a-job-washing-cars-is-harder-than-getting-into-harvard/.

30. "Harvard, Prison, or McDonald's: Which Is Harder to Get Into?" ESL Podcast Blog, June 2, 2011, http://www.eslpod.com/eslpod_blog/2011/06/02/harvard-prison-or-mcdonalds-which-is-harder-to-get-into.

31. Claire Gordon, "Target Is Hiring: Harder than Getting into Yale?" Aol Jobs, August 31, 2012, http://jobs.aol.com/articles/2012/08/31/target-is-hiring-the-inside-scoop-on-getting-a-job.

32. Kenneth Bozarth, "All Unemployed People in the United States Would Constitute the 68th Largest Country in the World!!" Greater Phoenix Tea Party Patriots, September 5, 2011, http://phoenixteaparty.ning.com/profiles/blogs/all-unemployed-people-in-the-united-states-would-constitute-the?xg_source=activity.

33. Sherle R. Schwenninger and Samuel Sherraden, "The American Middle Class under Stress," New America Foundation, April 2011, http://growth.newamerica.net/sites/newamerica.net/files/policydocs/26-04-11%20Middle%20Class%20Under%20Stress.pdf.

34. Martha C. White, "Facing Cuts, Long-Term Unemployed Brace for Grim New Year," NBC News, January 5, 2014, http://www.cnbc.com/id/101307964.

35. Michael Snyder, "53 Percent of All Young College Graduates in America Are Either Unemployed or Underemployed," The Economic Collapse, April 22, 2012, http://theeconomiccollapseblog.com/archives/53-percent-of-all-young-college-graduates-in-america-are-either-unemployed-or-underemployed.

36. Michael Bastasch, "Report: Private Sector Shrank in 41 States under Obama," Daily Caller, December 6, 2013, http://dailycaller.com/2013/12/06/researchers-private-sector-has-shrunk-in-41-states-under-obama/#ixzz2mjz7BAAe.

37. Tyler Durden, "It's Official: The US Created Less Jobs in 2013 than 2012," Zero Hedge, January 10, 2014, http://www.zerohedge.com/news/2014-01-10/its-official-us-created-less-jobs-2013-2012.

38. Martha C. White, "Facing Cuts, Long-Term Unemployed Brace for Grim New Year," NBC News, January 5, 2014, http://www.cnbc.com/id/101307964.

39. Tyler Durden, "The Good and the Bad News for the Future of America's Jobs," Zero Hedge, January 10, 2014, http://www.zerohedge.com/news/2014-01-10/good-and-bad-news-future-americas-jobs.

40. Ben Bullard, "More Americans on Government Entitlement than Working Full Time," Personal Liberty Digest™, October 25, 2013, http://personalliberty.com/2013/10/25/more-americans-on-government-entitlement-than-working-full-time/.

41. Daniel Halper, "Report: U.S. Spent $3.7 Trillion on Welfare over Last 5 Years," *Weekly Standard*, October 23, 2013, http://www.weeklystandard.com/blogs/report-us-spent-37-trillion-welfare-over-last-5-years_764582.html.

42. Terence P. Jeffrey, "Census on Obama's 1st Term: Real Median Income Down $2,627; People in Poverty Up 6,667,000; Record 46,496,000 now Poor," CNS News, September 17, 2013, http://cnsnews.com/news/article/terence-p-jeffrey/census-obama-s-1st-term-real-median-income-down-2627-people-poverty.

43. Ibid.

44. Michael B. Sauter, Alexander E. M. Hess, Samuel Weigley, "Cities Where Suburban Poverty Is Skyrocketing," 24/7 Wall St, May 28, 2013, http://247wallst.com/special-report/2013/05/28/cities-where-suburban-poverty-is-skyrocketing/.

45. Ibid.

46. Ibid.

47. Jeryl Bier, "Gov't Report: Food Stamps Participation at Historic High, Even as Unemployment Rate Falls," *Weekly Standard*, February 20, 2014, http://www.weeklystandard.com/blogs/govt-report-food-stamps-participation-historic-high-even-unemployment-rate-falls_782712.html.

48. Terence P. Jeffrey, "23,116,928 to 20,618,000: Households on Food Stamps now Outnumber All Households in Northeast U.S.," CNS News, September 17, 2013, http://cnsnews.com/news/article/terence-p-jeffrey/23116928-20618000-households-food-stamps-now-outnumber-all-households.

49. Elizabeth Harrington, "Food Stamp Rolls in America now Surpass the Population of Spain," CNS News, February 11, 2013, http://cnsnews.com/news/article/food-stamp-rolls-america-now-surpass-population-spain.

50. Tyler Durden, "The Number of US Citizens on Disability Is now Larger than the Population of Greece," Zero Hedge, May 9, 2013, http://www.zerohedge.com/news/2013-05-09/number-us-citizens-disability-now-larger-population-greece; Michael A. Fletcher, "U.S. Disability Rolls Swell in a Rough Economy," *Washington Post*, September 20, 2013, http://www.washingtonpost.com/business/economy/us-disability-rolls-swell-in-a-rough-economy/2013/09/20/a791915c-1575-11e3-804b-d3a1a3a18f2c_story.html.

51. Mamta Badkar, "Mary Meeker's Definitive Guide to the American Public Debt Crisis," Business Insider, February 25, 2011, http://www.businessinsider.com/mary-meeker-usa-inc-february-24-2011-2.

52. Terence P. Jeffrey, "Census: 49% of Americans Get Gov't Benefits; 82M in Households on Medicaid," CNS News, October 23, 2013, http://cnsnews.com/news/article/terence-p-jeffrey/census-49-americans-get-gov-t-benefits-82m-households-medicaid.

53. Michael Snyder, "Obamacare Is Going to Be the Biggest Expansion of the Welfare State in U.S. History," The American Dream, November 21, 2013, http://endoftheamericandream.com/archives/obamacare-is-going-to-be-the-biggest-expansion-of-the-welfare-state-in-u-s-history.

54. Michael Snyder, "More than 100 Million Americans Are on Welfare," The American Dream, August 8, 2012, http://endoftheamericandream.com/archives/more-than-100-million-americans-are-on-welfare.

55. Terence P. Jeffrey, "Census Bureau: Means-Tested Gov't Benefit Recipients Outnumber Full-Time Year-Round Workers," CNS News, October 24, 2013, http://cnsnews.com/news/article/terence-p-jeffrey/census-bureau-means-tested-govt-benefit-recipients-outnumber-full.

56. Jeffrey, "Census: 49% of Americans Get Gov't Benefits."

57. Jordan Weissmann, "The Kids Are Not Alright: Nearly Half of Public School Students Are Low Income," Yahoo! Finance, October 17, 2013, http://finance.yahoo.com/news/kids-not-alright-nearly-half-212100193.html.

58. Associated Press, "'Dismal' Prospects: 1 in 2 Americans Are Now Poor or Low Income," NBC News, December 15, 2011, http://usnews.nbcnews.com/_

news/2011/12/15/9461848-dismal-prospects-1-in-2-americans-are-now-poor-or-low-income.

59. "US Hits Record Number of Homeless Students," First Focus Campaign for Children press release, October 24, 2013, http://www.firstfocus.net/news/press_release/us-hits-record-number-of-homeless-students.

60. Alyssa Brown, "More Americans Struggle to Afford Food," Gallup, September 12, 2013, http://www.gallup.com/poll/164363/americans-struggle-afford-food.aspx?utm_source=add_this&utm_medium=addthis.com&utm_campaign=sharing#.UjG.

61. Jeryl Bier, "Gov't Report: Food Stamps Participation at Historic High, Even as Unemployment Rate Falls," *Weekly Standard*, February 20, 2014, http://www.weeklystandard.com/blogs/govt-report-food-stamps-participation-historic-high-even-unemployment-rate-falls_782712.html.

62. Harry Bradford, "Nearly Half of Americans Have Less than $500 in Savings: Survey," Huffington Post, updated October 23, 2012, http://www.huffingtonpost.com/2012/10/22/americans-savings-500_n_2003285.html.

63. Charles Riley, "Family Net Worth Plummets Nearly 40%," CNN Money, June 12, 2012, http://money.cnn.com/2012/06/11/news/economy/fed-family-net-worth/index.htm.

64. Wynton Hall, "Census: Typical Family Makes Less Today than in 1989," Breitbart, September 17, 2013, http://www.breitbart.com/Big-Government/2013/09/17/Census-Typical-Family-Makes-Less-Than-It-Did-In-1989.

65. Dave Umhoefer, "Romney Says Median Income Has Dropped 10 Percent in Last Four Years," PolitiFact, June 18, 2012, http://www.politifact.com/wisconsin/statements/2012/jun/27/mitt-romney/romney-says-median-income-has-dropped-10-percent-l/.

66. Constantine Von Hoffman, "Most Americans Adding Debt Faster than Savings," CBS News, October 29, 2013, http://www.cbsnews.com/news/most-americans-adding-debt-faster-than-savings.

67. Raven Clabough, "Official ObamaCare Launh: More Insurance Cancellations than Enrollments," New American, January 3, 2014, http://www.thenewamerican.com/usnews/health-care/item/17309-official-obamacare-launch-more-insurance-cancellations-than-enrollments.

68. Blake Ellis, "Retirement Scare: 60% of Workers Have Less than $25,000 Saved," CNN Money, March 13, 2012, http://money.cnn.com/2012/03/13/retirement/workers-confidence/.

69. Tyler Durden, "If You Have Children, You Need to See These Numbers," Zero Hedge, December 17, 2013, http://www.zerohedge.com/news/2013-12-17/if-you-have-children-you-need-see-these-numbers.

70. Tyler Durden, "Real Disposable Income Plummets Most in 40 Years," Zero Hedge, January 31, 2014, http://www.zerohedge.com/news/2014-01-31/wtf-going-real-disposable-income-plummets-most-40-years.

71. Tyler Durden, "The Fourteen Year Recession," Zero Hedge, March 24, 2014, http://www.zerohedge.com/news/2014-03-24/fourteen-year-recession.

72. Ibid.

73. "Home Ownership Rate for the United States," available on the Federal Reserve Bank of St. Louis website, http://research.stlouisfed.org/fred2/data/USHOWN.txt.

74. Terence P. Jeffrey, "Christmas Lights? Electricity Price Index at All-Time High in U.S.," CNS News, December 23, 2013, http://www.cnsnews.com/news/article/terence-p-jeffrey/christmas-lights-electricity-price-index-all-time-high-us.

75. Christopher Matthews, "Nearly Half of America Lives Paycheck-to-Paycheck," *Time*, January 30, 2014, http://business.time.com/2014/01/30/nearly-half-of-america-lives-paycheck-to-paycheck.

76. Durden, "If You Have Children."

77. Halah Touryalai, "Work until You Die? More Middle Class Americans Say They Can Never Retire," Forbes, October 25, 2013, http://www.forbes.com/sites/halah-touryalai/2013/10/25/work-until-you-die-more-middle-class-americans-say-they-can-never-retire.

78. Dan Weil, "Wells Fargo Study: 37 Percent of Middle-Class Americans Say They Never Will Retire," Newsmax, October 24, 2013, http://www.newsmax.com/Personal-Finance/middle-class-retire- work/2013/10/23/id/532672?ns_mail_uid=27641677&ns_mail_job=1543152_10242013&promo_code=154A5-1.

79. Rich Miller and Michelle Jamrisko, "Americans on Wrong Side of Pay Gap Run Out of Means to Cope," Bloomberg, December 30, 2013, http://www.bloomberg.com/news/2013-12-30/americans-on-wrong-side-of-income-gap-run-out-of-means-to-cope.html.

80. Bruce Bialosky, "The New Welfare State," Townhall, October 20, 2013, http://townhall.com/columnists/brucebialosky/2013/10/20/the-new-welfare-state-n1727168/page/2.

81. Michael Snyder, "They Are Murdering Small Business: The Percentage of Self-Employed Americans Is at a Record Low," The Economic Collapse, May 2, 2013, http://theeconomiccollapseblog.com/archives/they-are-murdering-small-business-the-percentage-of-self-employed-americans-is-at-a-record-low.

82. Reporting by Lucia Mutikani and editing by Lisa Von Ahn, "U.S. Business Startups Rate at Record Low," Reuters, May 2, 2012, http://www.reuters.com/article/2012/05/02/us-usa-economy-businesses-idUSBRE84113G20120502.

83. Wayne Allyn Root, "Small Businessman to Obama: Liar!" Fox News, October 25, 2012, http://www.foxnews.com/opinion/2012/10/25/small-businessman-to-obama-liar/.

84. Henry I. Miller, "New Regulations Batter the Middle Class. Obama Changes the Subject," Forbes, July 29, 2013, http://www.forbes.com/sites/henrymiller/2013/07/29/new-regulations-batter-the-middle-class-obama-changes-the-subject.

85. Barbara Hollingsworth, "In 2013, Regulations Cost Americans $447 Million Each Day Government Was Open," CNS News, January 9, 2014, http://www.cnsnews.com/news/article/barbara-hollingsworth/2013-regulations-cost-americans-447-million-each-day-government.

86. Laura Hazard Owen, "New Report Shows Huge Drop in Startup Jobs (but Don't Just Think Tech)," Gigaom, September 15, 2012, http://gigaom.com/2012/09/15/new-report-shows-huge-drop-in-startup-jobs-but-dont-just-think-tech/.

87. Catherine Rampell, "A Look behind the U.S. Decline in Global Competitiveness," *New York Times*, September 6, 2012, http://economix.blogs.nytimes.com/2012/09/06/a-look-behind-the-u-s-decline-in-global-competitiveness/.

88. Timothy H. Lee, "2013 Index of Economic Freedom: U.S. Declines for Fifth Straight Year," CFIF (Center for Individual Freedom), January 17, 2013, http://cfif.org/v/index.php/commentary/43/1716-2013-index-of-economic-freedom-us-declines-for-fifth-straight-year.

89. Joel Gehrke, "55 Percent of Small Business Owners Would Not Start Company Today, Blame Obama," *Washington Examiner*, September 26, 2012, http://washingtonexaminer.com/55-percent-of-small-business-owners-would-not-start-company-today-blame-obama/article/2509069#.UNndYaVZ90f.

90. Humberto Sanchez, "Industry Study Shows Small-Business Pessimism," *Roll Call*, September 25, 2012, http://www.rollcall.com/news/industry_study_shows_small_business_pessimism-217813-1.html?pos=olobh.

91. Executive summary of survey conducted by Public Opinion Strategies on behalf of the National Federation of Independent Businesses and the National Association of Manufacturers, http://pos.org/documents/executive_summary.pdf.

92. Peter Schweizer, "IRS: The Small Business Bully," RealClearPolitics, October 25, 2012, http://www.realclearpolitics.com/articles/2012/10/25/irs_the_small_business_bully_115914.html.

93. Howard Portnoy, "83% of Doctors Say They Might Quit over Obamacare, According to New Poll," Examiner.com, July 11, 2012, http://www.examiner.com/article/83-of-doctors-say-they-might-quit-over-obamacare-according-to-new-poll.

94. "How Many People Will Be Newly Insured by Obamacare?" John Goodman's Health Policy Blog, October 11, 2012, http://healthblog.ncpa.org/how-many-

people-will-be-newly-insured-by-obamacare/; Kyle Cheney and Jennifer Haber-korn, "Report: Obamacare sign-ups cross 8 million," Politico, May 1, 2014, http://www.politico.com/story/2014/05/report-obamacare-sign-ups-106245.html.

95.   Mike Emanuel contributed to this report, "Second Wave of Health Plan Cancellations Looms," Fox News, November 20, 2013, http://www.foxnews.com/politics/2013/11/20/second-wave-health-plan-cancellations-looms/.

96.   "Average Wait Times to See Doctors in U.S.," Fox News, updated January 30, 2014, http://www.myfoxdc.com/story/24589786/average-wait-times-to-see-doctors-in-us#axzz2rpFqJe00.

97.   Terence P. Jeffrey, "In 23, Advanced Economies: U.S. Adults Rank 21st in Math Skills," CNS News, October 18, 2013, http://www.cnsnews.com/news/article/terence-p-jeffrey/23-advanced-economies-us-adults-rank-21st-math-skills.

98.   Tyler Durden, "Truly 'Exceptional' and Dumber than Ever: Verbal SAT Scores Plunge to Fresh Record Low," Zero Hedge, September 25, 2013, http://www.zerohedge.com/news/2013-09-25/truly-exceptional-and-dumber-ever-verbal-sat-scores-plunge-fresh-record-low.

99.   Nelson D. Schwartz, "The Middle Class Is Steadily Eroding. Just Ask the Business World," *New York Times*, February 2, 2014, http://www.nytimes.com/2014/02/03/business/the-middle-class-is-steadily-eroding-just-ask-the-business-world.html.

100.   Michelle Higgins, "Ultraluxury Apartment Sales Drive Records in Manhattan Real Estate," *New York Times*, April 1, 2014, records-in-manhattan-real-estate.html?_r=0.

101.   William A. Galston, "The Eroding American Middle Class," *Wall Street Journal*, November 12, 2013, http://online.wsj.com/news/articles/SB1000142405270230391430457919366381781 6486.

102.   Tony Lee, "Gap between Super Rich 0.1% and Poor Grows," Breitbart, April 1, 2014, http://www.breitbart.com/Big-Government/2014/03/31/Gap-Between-Super-Rich-0-1-and-Poor-Grows.

103.   Tyler Durden, "'The Cacophony of Fed Confusion' David Stockman Warns Will Lead to 'Economic Calamity,'" Zero Hedge, March 19, 2014, http://www.zerohedge.com/news/2014-03-19/cacophony-fed-confusion-david-stockman-warns-will-lead-economic-calamity.

Chapter 2: The Crime Scene

1.   Ezra Klein, "Inequality Is Highest in Democratic Districts," Vox, updated April 8, 2014, http://www.vox.com/2014/4/8/5591076/inequality-is-highest-in-democratic-districts.

2.　　Victor Davis Hanson, "Fish instead of People, Ideologies without Consequences," PJ Media, March 31, 2014, http://pjmedia.com/victordavishanson/ideologies-without-consequences/.

3.　　Jim Hoft, "Broke—after 50 Years of Democratic Rule Detroit Files for Bankruptcy," Gateway Pundit, July 18, 2013, http://www.thegatewaypundit.com/2013/07/she-broke-detroit-files-for-bankruptcy/. See Wayne Allyn Root, *The Ultimate Obama Survival Guide* (Washington, DC: Regnery Publishing, 2013), 51–57.

4.　　Nathan Bomey, Brent Snavely, and Alisa Priddle, "Detroit Becomes Largest U.S. City to Enter Bankruptcy," *USA Today*, December 3, 2013, http://www.usatoday.com/story/news/nation/2013/12/03/detroit-bankruptcy-eligibility/3849833/.

5.　　Micheline Maynard, "The $1.25 Billion Price Tag for Fixing Detroit," Forbes, June 15, 2013, http://www.forbes.com/sites/michelinemaynard/2013/06/15/the-1-25-billion-price-tag-for-fixing-detroit/.

6.　　Joel Schectman, "Detroit Asking for $80 Million IT Overhaul," *Wall Street Journal*, August 13, 2013, http://blogs.wsj.com/cio/2013/08/13/detroit-asking-for-80-million-it-overhaul/.

7.　　Charlie Leduff, "Detroit Paramedics Fear They're Losing the Battle to Save Lives," *Detroit News*, September 16, 2010, http://www.detroitnews.com/article/20100916/METRO08/9160409.

8.　　"Federal Judge Lets Detroit Move forward with Largest Bankruptcy in US History," RT, edited December 5, 2013, http://rt.com/usa/detroit-bancruptcy-court-ruling-653/.

9.　　"Detroit files for chapter 9 bankruptcy, read court filing document" WXYZ Detroit, July 19, 2013, http://www.wxyz.com/news/region/detroit/detroit-files-for-chapter-9-bankruptcy.

10.　　"Researchers: Detroit, Cleveland, Cincinnati, Buffalo, Milwaukee Lead Nation in Child Poverty," National Center for Children in Poverty, October 31, 2011, http://www.nccp.org/media/releases/release_136.html.

11.　　"United Van Lines' Annual Migration Study Reveals Oregon as Top Moving Destination of 2013," United Van Lines, January 2, 2014, http://www.unitedvanlines.com/mover/united-newsroom/press-releases/2014/2013-united-van-lines-migration-study.htm.

12.　　Estelle Sommeiller and Mark Price, "The Increasingly Unequal States of America," Economic Policy Institute, February 19, 2014, http://www.epi.org/publication/unequal-states/.

13.　　Troy Senik, "Land of Inequality," National Review Online, February 24, 2014, http://www.nationalreview.com/article/371796/land-inequality-troy-senik.

14.　　See Trading Economics," http://www.tradingeconomics.com.

15. Tyler Durden, "European Car Sales in 2013 Drop to 'Record', 23-Year Low," Zero Hedge, September 17, 2013, http://www.zerohedge.com/news/2013-09-17/european-car-sales-2013-drop-fresh-23-year-low.

16. Tyler Durden, "Spain Youth Unemployment Rises to Record 57.7%, Surpasses Greece," Zero Hedge, January 8, 2014, http://www.zerohedge.com/news/2014-01-08/spain-youth-unemployment-rises-record-577-surpasses-greece.

17. Lauren Frayer, "Help-Wanted Ad Shows Depths of Spain's Unemployment Problem," NPR, December 5, 2013, http://www.npr.org/blogs/parallels/2013/12/05/248903567/help-wanted-ad-shows-depths-of-spains-unemployment-problem.

18. Charles Penty and Angeline Benoit, "Spanish Bad Loans Ratio Rises to Record 13.6 Percent (1)," Bloomberg, February 18, 2014, http://www.businessweek.com/news/2014-02-18/spanish-bad-loans-ratio-rose-to-record-13-dot-6-percent-in-december.

19. Harold Heckle, "Details in Las Vegas Sands 'EuroVegas' Project Unveiled," Review Journal, February 9, 2013, http://www.reviewjournal.com/business/casinos-gaming/details-las-vegas-sands-eurovegas-project-unveiled.

20. "Sheldon Adelson Cancels $30 Billion EuroVegas Project in Spain," Jewish Business News, December 13, 2013, http://jewishbusinessnews.com/2013/12/13/sheldon-adelson-cancels-30-billion-eurovegas-project-in-spain/.

21. Ambrose Evans-Pritchard, "Citi Forecasts Greek Devastation, Unstoppable Debt Spirals in Italy and Portugal," *The Telegraph*, updated October 24, 2013, http://blogs.telegraph.co.uk/finance/ambroseevans-pritchard/100025913/citi-forecasts-greek-devastation-unstoppable-debt-spirals-in-italy-and-portugal.

22. Richard Palmer, "Greek Youth Unemployment Hits 62 Percent," theTrumpet.com, February 18, 2013, http://www.thetrumpet.com/article/10383.4.0.0/economy/greek-youth-unemployment-hits-62-percent.

23. Tyler Durden, "Peripheral Europe's New Normal: 50 Applicants for One Minimum Wage Job," Zero Hedge, December 13, 2013, http://www.zerohedge.com/news/2013-12-13/peripheral-europes-new-normal-50-applicants-one-minimum-wage-job.

24. Graham Ruddick, "France 'Totally Bankrupt', Says Labour Minister Michel Sapin," *The Telegraph*, January 28, 2013, http://www.telegraph.co.uk/finance/financial-crisis/9832845/France-totally-bankrupt-says-labour-minister-Michel-Sapin.html.

25. Tyler Durden, "France Unemployment Surges to 16 Year High," Zero Hedge, December 5, 2013, http://www.zerohedge.com/news/2013-12-05/france-unemployment-surges-16-year-high.

26. Tyler Durden, "French Joblessness Surges to New Record High (up 30 of Last 32 Months)," Zero Hedge, February 26, 2014, http://www.zerohedge.com/news/2014-02-26/french-joblessness-surges-new-record-high-30-last-32-months.

27. Régis Roussel, Valérie William, Alice Viélajus, Stéphane Héroult, ReferNet France, "France VET in Europe—Country Report 2012," Cedefop, 2012, http://libserver. cedefop.europa.eu/vetelib/2012/2012_CR_FR.pdf.

28. Henry Samuel, "François Hollande outlines manifesto for French presidency challenge," *The Telegraph*, January 26, 2012, http://www.telegraph.co.uk/news/ worldnews/europe/france/9042741/Francois-Hollande-outlines-manifesto-for-French-presidency-challenge.html; "François Hollande: Presidency through ambiguity," *Economist*, May 25, 2013, http://www.economist.com/news/ europe/21578445-normal-political-leader-who-having-grapple-unusual-times-presidency-through-ambiguity.

29. Craig S. Smith, "Letter from Paris: 4 simple rules for firing an employee in France," *New York Times*, March 28, 2006, http://www.nytimes.com/2006/03/28/world/ europe/28iht-letter.html?_r=0; Anne-Elisabeth Moutet, "Down and out: the French flee a nation in despair," *The Telegraph*, October 20, 2013,http://www. telegraph.co.uk/finance/10390571/france-hollande-taxes-socialist-farrage.html; Anne-Sylvaine Chassany and Jacqueline Simmons, "France Entrepreneurs Flee from Hollande Wealth Rejection," Bloomberg, May 10, 2012, http://www.bloom-berg.com/news/2012-05-10/entrepreneurs-in-france-flee-from-hollande-s-rejec-tion-of-wealth.html; "French-Property.com: Real Estate, Real Living, Real France," http://www.french-property.com/guides/france/finance-taxation/taxation/ wealth-tax/declarations/.

30. Moutet, "Down and Out; Bruce Crumley, "C'est It Ain't So Gégé: French Actor Depardieu Reportedly Seeks Tax Refuge In Belgium," *Time*, December 10, 2012, http://newsfeed.time.com/2012/12/10/cest-it-aint-so-gege-french-actor-depardieu-reportedly-seeks-tax-refuge-in-belgium/.

31. Tyler Durden, "If You Have Children, You Need to See These Numbers," Zero Hedge, December 17, 2013, http://www.zerohedge.com/news/2013-12-17/if-you-have-children-you-need-see-these-numbers.

32. Tyler Durden, "Poverty in Italy Rises to All Time High," Zero Hedge, December 31, 2013, http://www.zerohedge.com/news/2013-12-31/poverty-italy-rises-all-time-high.

33. Ambrose Evans-Pritchard, "Italy's President Fears Violent Insurrection in 2014 but Offers No Remedy," *The Telegraph*, December 17, 2013, http://blogs.telegraph. co.uk/finance/ambroseevans-pritchard/100026297/italys-president-fears-violent-insurrection-in-2014-but-offers-no-remedy/.

34. Konrad Kreft, "Poverty in German Hits New High," RINF Alternative News, January 6, 2014, http://rinf.com/alt-news/breaking-news/poverty-in-germany-hits-new-high/.

35. Raul Gallegos, "Venezuela Is Running out of Toilet Paper," Bloomberg, September 27, 2013, http://www.bloombergview.com/articles/2013-09-27/venezuela-is-running-out-of-toilet-paper-; Associated Press, "Venezuela Tackles Food Shortage with ID Card System," *The Guardian*, April 1, 2014, http://www.theguardian.com/world/2014/apr/01/venezuela-food-shortage-id-cards.

36. Associated Press, "Venezuelan Middle Class Seeks Refuge in Miami," *USA Today*, March 7, 2014, http://www.usatoday.com/story/news/nation/2014/03/07/venezuelan-middle-class-miami/6176793/.

37. Elizabeth Harrington, "Escape from New York? High-Taxing Empire State Loses 3.4 Million Residents in 10 Years," CNS News, May 29, 2012, http://cnsnews.com/news/article/escape-new-york-high-taxing-empire-state-loses-34-million-residents-10-years.

Chapter 3: The Victim

1. Roger Kimball, "Fundamentally Transforming the United States of America," PJ Media, September 8, 2013, http://pjmedia.com/rogerkimball/2013/09/08/fundamentally-transforming-the-united-states-of-america/.

2. Ansuya Harjani, "US No Longer among Top 10 for Economic Freedom," CNBC, January 13, 2014, http://www.cnbc.com/id/101332987.

3. "Freedom Is the Best Cure for Poverty," *Wall Street Journal*, March 13, 2014, http://online.wsj.com/news/articles/SB10001424052702304704504579431060896276916.

4. "Top 10 Percent of Earners Paid 71 Percent of Federal Income Taxes," and chart "Share of Federal Income Taxes and Income Earned in 2010," The Heritage Foundation, http://www.heritage.org/federalbudget/top10-percent-income-earners; Jane Wells, "The Rich Do Not Pay the Most Taxes, They Pay ALL the Taxes," CNBC, December 11, 2013, http://www.cnbc.com/id/101264757.

5. Wells, "The Rich Do Not Pay the Most Taxes, They Pay ALL the Taxes."

Chapter 4: The Chief Suspect

1. Tyler Durden, "The Number of Working Age Americans without a Job Has Risen by almost 10 Million under Obama," Zero Hedge, January 13, 2014, http://www.zerohedge.com/news/2014-01-13/number-working-age-americans-without-job-has-risen-almost-10-million-under-obama.

2. Tami Luhby, "America's Disappearing Middle Class," CNN Money, January 28, 2014, http://economy.money.cnn.com/2014/01/28/middle-class/?iid=HP_LN.

3. Melanie Hicken, "Moody's Downgrades Chicago amid Pension Crisis," CNN Money, March 4, 2014, http://money.cnn.com/2014/03/04/news/chicago-credit-rating/.

4. Aaron Klein, "Obama Quotes Alinsky in Speech to Young Israelis," WND, March 21, 2013, http://www.wnd.com/2013/03/obama-quotes-alinsky-in-speech-to-young-israelis/.

5. Jay Sekulow, "IRS Corruption Update—Three Key Revelations from Lois Lerner's Emails," Fox News, September 17, 2013, http://www.foxnews.com/opinion/2013/09/17/irs-corruption-update-three-key-revelations-from-lois-lerners-emails/.

6. Ben Bullard, "IRS Was 'Acutely Aware of Obama's Desire to 'Crack Down' on Tea Party," Personal Liberty Digest™, September 19, 2013, http://personalliberty.com/2013/09/19/irs-was-acutely-aware-of-obamas-desire-to-crack-down-on-tea-party.

7. Brett Logiurato, "Tea Party Group: The IRS Made Us Fill Out Endless Forms with Impossible Questions," Business Insider, May 13, 2013, http://www.businessinsider.com/tea-party-group-irs-targeting-conservatives-obama-2013-5.

8. Megyn Kelly with Dave Camp, "Rep. Camp Blasts Treasury, Lois Lerner for 'Off-Plan' Rules," Fox News, February 11, 2014, http://www.foxnews.com/on-air/the-kelly-file/transcript/2014/02/12/rep-camp-blasts-treasury-lois-lerner-plan-rules.

9. Becket Adams, "Congressman: IRS Demanded to Know Content of Pro-Life Group's Prayers," The Blaze, May 17, 2013, http://www.theblaze.com/stories/2013/05/17/congressman-irs-demanded-to-know-content-of-pro-life-groups-prayers/.

10. Mary Katharine Ham, "10 Crazy Things the IRS Asked Tea Party Groups," Hot Air, May 10, 2013, http://hotair.com/archives/2013/05/10/10-crazy-things-the-irs-asked-tea-party-groups/.

11. Billy Hallowell, "'Very Frightening': Prominent Catholic Prof. Claims IRS Audited Her after Speaking Out against Obama and Demanded to Know Who Was Paying Her," The Blaze, May 15, 2013, http://www.theblaze.com/stories/2013/05/15/exclusive-prominent-catholic-prof-claims-irs-audited-her-after-speaking-out-against-obama-and-demanded-to-know-who-was-paying-her/.

12. Douglas Ernst, "Dr. Ben Carson: 'I Had My First Encounter with the IRS' after Prayer Breakfast with Obama," *Washington Times*, October 1, 2013, http://www.washingtontimes.com/news/2013/oct/1/ben-carson-i-had-my-first-encounter-irs-after-pray/.

13. Christine O'Donnell, "Christine O'Donnell: I Was a Victim of the IRS," *New York Post*, February 22, 2014, http://nypost.com/2014/02/22/christine-odonnell-i-was-a-victim-of-the-irs/.

14. Evan McMurry, "Dinesh D'Souza Speculates on 'Retribution': 'Vindictive' Obama Sees Critics as Enemies," Mediaite, February 22, 2014, http://www.mediaite.com/tv/dinesh-dsouza-speculates-on-retribution-vindictive-obama-sees-critics-as-enemies/.

15. Documentary, 1982–Present, Total Grosses, Box Office Mojo, http://www.boxofficemojo.com/genres/chart/?id=documentary.htm.

16. Jerome R. Corsi, "Anti-Obama Filmmaker Charges Harassment by IRS," WND Politics, May 16, 2013, http://www.wnd.com/2013/05/anti-obama-filmmaker-charges-harassment-by-irs/.

17. "'Coincidence? You Decide': Sarah Palin's Father 'Horribly Harassed' by IRS under Probe Led by Obama Donor, Her Brother Claims," *Daily Mail*, January 15, 2014, http://www.dailymail.co.uk/news/article-2539976/Sarah-Palins-father-horribly-harassed-IRS-probe-led-Obama-donor-brother-claims.html.

18. Reid J. Epstein, "Franklin Graham: IRS Targeted Us, Too," Politico, May 14, 2013, http://www.politico.com/story/2013/05/franklin-graham-irs-targeting-91362.html; Dave Bohon, "IRS Targeted Billy Graham Ministry and Other Christian Groups," The New American, May 17, 2013, http://www.thenewamerican.com/usnews/item/15444-irs-targeted-billy-graham-ministry-and-other-christian-groups.

19. Matthew Boyle, "Romney Donor Vandersloot: I Was Audited Twice by IRS, Once by DoI & Investigated by Former Senate Staffer," Breitbart, May 19, 2013, http://www.salon.com/2012/02/17/billionaire_romney_donor_uses_threats_to_silence_critics/.

20. Lily Dane, "Tea Party Leader Is Harassed while Testifying about Being Harassed by the IRS," Infowars.com, February 11, 2014, http://www.infowars.com/tea-party-leader-is-harassed-while-testifying-about-being-harassed-by-the-irs/.

21. Wynton Hall, "Obama Met with IRS Union Boss Day before Tea Party Targeting Began," Breitbart, May 20, 2013, http://www.breitbart.com/Big-Government/2013/05/20/Obama-Met-With-IRS-Union-Boss-Day-Before-Tea-Party-Targeting-Began.

22. Vince Coglianese, "IRS's Shulman Had More Public White House Visits than Any Cabinet Member," Daily Caller, May 29, 2013, http://dailycaller.com/2013/05/29/irss-shulman-had-more-public-white-house-visits-than-any-cabinet-member/.

23. Patrick Howley, "IRS, White House Officials That Shared Confidential Taxpayer Info Had 155 White House Meetings," Daily Caller, October 10, 2013, http://dailycaller.com/2013/10/10/irs-white-house-officials-that-shared-confidential-taxpayer-info-had-155-white-house-meetings/.

24. Coglianese, "IRS's Shulman Had."

25. Ed O'Keefe and William Branigin, "Lois Lerner Invokes Fifth Amendment in House Hearing on IRS Targeting," *Washington Post*, May 22, 2013, http://www.washingtonpost.com/politics/lois-lerner-invokes-fifth-amendment-in-house-hearing-on-irs-targeting/2013/05/22/03539900-c2e6-11e2-8c3b-0b5e9247e8ca_story.html.

26. Lauren French, "IRS Workers Turn to Elite D.C. Lawyers for Defense," Politico, September 17, 2013, http://www.politico.com/story/2013/09/irs-workers-turn-to-elite-dc-lawyers-for-defense-96885.html.

27. Ed Morrissey, "Breaking: Senior IRS Officials Knew of Targeting Conservative Groups in 2011; Update: IRS Chief Counsel Knew in 2011," Hot Air, May 11, 2013, http://hotair.com/archives/2013/05/11/breaking-senior-irs-officials-knew-of-targeting-conservative-groups-in-2011/.

28. Drew MacKenzie, "IRS Targets Hollywood Conservatives," Newsmax, January 23, 2014, http://www.newsmax.com/Newsfront/friends-Abe-IRS-Hollywood/2014/01/23/id/548582.

29. Madeleine Morgenstern, "Cancer Patient Who Says Obamacare Canceled His Health Insurance Now Says He's Being Audited by the IRS," The Blaze, November 29, 2013, http://www.theblaze.com/stories/2013/11/29/cancer-patient-who-says-obamacare-canceled-his-health-insurance-now-says-hes-being-audited-by-the-irs/; C. Steven Tucker, "The TRUTH About Preexisting Conditions," C.Steven Tucker.WordPress.com, November 13, 2013, http://csteventucker.wordpress.com/2013/11/13/the-truth-about-preexisting-conditions/.

30. "Articles of Impeachment," Watergate.info, http://watergate.info/impeachment/articles-of-impeachment.

31. Jack Moore, "OSC Targets Hatch Act Violations at IRS, Improper Hiring at CBP," Federal News Radio 1500 AM, April 9, 2014, http://www.federalnewsradio.com/534/3599802/OSC-targets-Hatch-Act-violations-at-IRS-improper-hiring-at-CBP.

32. Bernie Becker, "Lerner Mentioned Organizing for Action Job," The Hill, April 9, 2014, http://thehill.com/blogs/on-the-money/domestic-taxes/203116-documents-lerner-references-organizing-for-action-job.

33. Katie Pavlich, "Breaking: Emails Show Lois Lerner Fed True the Vote Tax Information to Democrat Elijah Cummings," Townhall, April 9, 2014, http://townhall.com/tipsheet/katiepavlich/2014/04/09/new-emaisl-show-lois-lerner-fed-information-about-true-the-vote-to-democrat-elijah-cummings-n1822247.

34. Wayne Allyn Root, "I Am the Face of Team Obama's IRS Attacks," Fox News, May 13, 2013, http://www.foxnews.com/opinion/2013/05/13/am-face-team-obama-irs-attacks.

35. Frances Martel, "Obama Donor to Head IRS Tea Party Targeting Investigation," Breitbart, January 8, 2014, http://www.breitbart.com/Big-Government/2014/01/08/Frequent-Obama-Donor-Heading-IRS-Conservative-Targeting-Investigation.

36. Annalyn Censky, "September Jobs Report: Unemployment Rate Tumbles," CNN Money, October 19, 2012, http://www.breitbart.com/Big-Government/2014/01/08/Frequent-Obama-Donor-Heading-IRS-Conservative-Targeting-Investigation.

37. "'Jobs report truthers': The conspiracy theorists who claim the unemployment report is bogus," The Week, October 5, 2012, https://theweek.com/article/index/234397/jobs-report-truthers-the-conspiracy-theorists-who-claim-the-unemployment-report-is-bogus; Wayne Allyn Root, "Jobs Report Is Fraud, Greatest Ponzi Scheme in History Continues," The Blaze, December 9, 2013, http://www.theblaze.com/contributions/jobs-report-is-fraud-greatest-ponzi-scheme-in-history-continues/.

38. John Crudele, "Census 'Faked' 2012 Election Jobs Report," *New York Post*, November 18, 2013, http://nypost.com/2013/11/18/census-faked-2012-election-jobs-report/; Susan Ferrechio, "Darrell Issa Sends Letter to Census Demanding Info on Alleged Fake Jobless Data," Fox News, no date, http://nation.foxnews.com/2013/11/20/house-investigating-census-bureau-over-'fake'-2012-election-jobs-report; Peter Ferrara, "Did the BLS Give Obama a Major Election 2012 Gift?" Forbes, November 27, 2013, http://www.forbes.com/sites/peterferrara/2013/11/27/did-the-bls-give-obama-a-major-election-2012-gift/.

39. Andrew C. McCarthy, "Obama's '5 Percent' Con Job," National Review Online, November 18, 2013, http://www.nationalreview.com/article/364176/obamas-5-percent-con-job-andrew-c-mccarthy.

40. Sarah Hurtubise, "Report: Premiums Rising Faster than Eight Years before Obamacare Combined," Daily Caller, March 18, 2014, http://dailycaller.com/2014/03/18/report-premiums-rising-faster-than-eight-years-before-obamacare-combined/.

41. Tyler Durden, "Serfs up—Average Healthcare Premiums Have Soared 39–56% post Obamacare," Zero Hedge, March 19, 2014, http://www.zerohedge.com/news/2014-03-19/serfs---average-healthcare-premiums-have-soared-39-56-post-obamacare; Elise Viebeck, "O-Care Premiums to Skyrocket," The Hill, March 19, 2014, http://thehill.com/blogs/healthwatch/health-reform-implementation/201136-obamacare-premiums-are-about-to-skyrocket.

42. Drew MacKenzie, "Issa: Obamacare Navigators Put Americans at Risk from Identity Theft," Newsmax, December 16, 2013, http://www.newsmax.com/Newsfront/Obamacare-fraud-Issa-report/2013/12/16/id/542091?ns_mail_uid=32342417&ns_mail_job=1550424_12162013&promo_code=15F7D-1; Jillian Kay Melchior, "California's Obamacare Scandal," National Review Online, January 29, 2014,

http://www.nationalreview.com/article/369695/californias-obamacare-scandal-jillian-kay-melchior.

43. Patrick Howley, "Michelle Obama's Princeton Classmate Is Executive at Company That Built Obamacare Website," Daily Caller, October 25, 2013, http://dailycaller.com/2013/10/25/michelle-obamas-princeton-classmate-is-executive-at-company-that-built-obamacare-website.

44. Robert Oak, "ObamaCare Gets Outsourced amid Unemployment Crisis," *New York Post*, January 18, 2014, http://nypost.com/2014/01/18/obamacare-gets-outsourced-amid-unemployment-crisis/.

45. Jason Meisner, "TV Pitchman Kevin Trudeau Sentenced to 10 Years in Prison," *Chicago Tribune*, March 17, 2014, http://articles.chicagotribune.com/2014-03-17/business/chi-kevin-trudeau-sentenced-20140317_1_kevin-trudeau-global-information-network-guzman.

46. "The Budget and Economic Outlook: 2014 to 2024," CBO, http://cbo.gov/sites/default/files/cbofiles/attachments/45010-Outlook2014_Feb.pdf.

47. "Vegas Man Stuck with $407,000 Medical Bill after ObamaCare Breakdown," Fox News, March 18, 2014, http://www.foxnews.com/politics/2014/03/18/vegas-man-stuck-with-407000-medical-bill-after-obamacare-breakdown/.

48. Karen Peters, "President Obama, Executive Orders, and the EPA," Examiner.com, October 5, 2011, http://www.examiner.com/article/president-obama-executive-orders-and-the-epa.

49. Tabitha Hale, "Stupak: HHS Mandate Violates My Obamacare Compromise," Breitbart, September 4, 2012, http://www.breitbart.com/Big-Government/2012/09/04/Stupak-President-Played-Me-with-Obamacare-Deal; Matt Bowman, "Little Sisters of the Poor Case: The Administration's Position Goes from the Absurd to the Surreal," National Review Online, January 6, 2014, http://www.nationalreview.com/corner/367564/little-sisters-poor-case-administrations-position-goes-absurd-surreal-matt-bowman.

50. Jonathan H. Adler, "Another Day, Another Illegal Obamacare Delay," *Washington Post*, February 11, 2014, http://www.washingtonpost.com/news/volokh-conspiracy/wp/2014/02/11/another-day-another-illegal-obamacare-delay/.

51. Becket Adams, "The Moment a Prof. Warned That America Is at a 'Constitutional Tipping Point,'" The Blaze, February 27, 2014, http://www.theblaze.com/stories/2014/02/27/the-moment-a-prof-warned-that-america-is-at-a-constitutional-tipping-point/.

52. Matthew Burke, "Liberal Constitutional Professor: 'Framers Would Be Horrified' at Obama's Abuse of Power," Tea Party News Network, February 13, 2014, http://www.tpnn.com/2014/02/13/liberal-constitutional-professor-framers-would-be-horrified-at-obamas-abuse-of-power/; John Cusack, "John Cusack Interviews Law

Professor Jonathan Turley About Obama Administration's War on the Constitution," Truthout, September 1, 2012, http://truth-out.org/opinion/item/11264-john-cusack-and-jonathan-turley-on-obamas-constitution.

53. Mat Staver, "Harry Reid Uses 'Nuclear Option' to Stack Courts! (Liberty Counsel)," Liberty Counsel Connect, November 21, 2013, http://libertycounsel.com/2013/11/harry-reid-uses-nuclear-option-to-stack-courts-liberty-counsel/.

54. Compiled by General Paul Vallely, "List of Military Elite Purged and Fired under Obama," Rense.com, March 17, 2014, http://www.rense.com/general96/listof.html.

55. "Critics Want FCC Media Study Thrown on 'Trash Heap,' Skeptical of Changes," Fox News, February 20, 2014, http://www.foxnews.com/politics/2014/02/20/critics-want-fcc-media-study-thrown-on-trash-heap-skeptical-changes/?intcmp=latestnews.

56. Zachary A. Goldfarb, "S&P downgrades U.S. credit rating for first time," *Washington Post*, August 5, 2011, http://www.washingtonpost.com/business/economy/sandp-considering-first-downgrade-of-us-credit-rating/2011/08/05/gIQAqKeIxI_story.html; Aruna Viswanatha and Lauren Tara Lacapra, "U.S. government slams S&P with $5 billion fraud lawsuit," Reuters, February 5, 2013, http://www.reuters.com/article/2013/02/05/us-mcgrawhill-sandp-civilcharges-idUS-BRE9130U120130205.

57. William Bigelow, "ANOTHER CREDIT AGENCY DOWNGRADES US," Breitbart, April 6, 2012, http://www.breitbart.com/Big-Government/2012/04/06/USA-Credit-Rating-Downgraded; "Egan-Jones Rating Co. and Sean Eagan Charged with Making Material Representations to SEC," U.S. Securities and Exchange Commission press release, April 24, 2012, http://investor.gov/news-alerts/press-releases/egan-jones-ratings-co-sean-egan-charged-making-material-misrepresentation#.U2u1QPldV1A; William Alden, "Egan-Jones Barred for 18 Months on Some Ratings," *New York Times*, January 22, 2013, http://dealbook.nytimes.com/2013/01/22/egan-jones-barred-for-18-months-on-some-ratings/.

58. Tom Hamburger and Alice Crites, "Conservative Author and Pundit Dinesh D'Souza Charged in Campaign Finance Case," *Washington Post*, January 23, 2014, http://www.washingtonpost.com/politics/conservative-author-and-pundit-dinesh-dsouza-charged-in-campaign-finance-case/2014/01/23/69c67ee4-848a-11e3-bbe5-6a2a3141e3a9_story.html; Katie Pavlich, "Former Virginia Governor Bob McDonnell and Wife Maureen Indicted on Federal Corruption Charges," Townhall, January 21, 2014, http://townhall.com/tipsheet/katiepavlich/2014/01/21/former-virginia-governor-bob-mcdonnell-and-wife-maureen-indicted-on-federal-corruption-charges-n1782534.

59. Betsy McCaughey, "Obamacare Will Question Your Sex Life," *New York Post*, September 15, 2013, http://nypost.com/2013/09/15/obamacare-will-question-your-sex-life/.

Chapter 5: The Accomplices

1. Elspeth Reeve, "Rick Stengel Is at Least the 24th Journalist to Work for the Obama Administration, *Atlantic*, September 12, 2013, http://www.thewire.com/ politics/2013/09/rick-stengel-least-24-journalist-go-work-obama-administration/69362/; Jennifer Harper, "News Media's Revolving Door to Obama White House Blurs Lines of Objectivity," *Washington Times*, September 24, 2013, http://www.washingtontimes.com/news/2013/sep/24/news-medias-revolving-door-to-obama-white-house-bl/?page=all.

2. John Nolte, "CNN, CBS News, ABC News Honchos Have Obama Administration Family Ties," Breitbart, September 7, 2013, http://www.breitbart.com/Big-Journalism/2013/09/07/mainstream-media-honchos-related-towhite-house-officials.

3. Jill Colvin, "Bloomberg Sounds Alarm over 'Labor-Electoral Complex' in Final Speech as Mayor," *New York Observer*, December 18, 2013, http://politicker.com/2013/12/bloomberg-sounds-alarm-over-labor-electoral-complex-in-final-speech-as-mayor.

4. Ibid.

5. "Bankrupt cities, Municipalities List and Maps," GOVERNING: THE STATES AND LOCALITIES, December 3, 2013, http://www.governing.com/gov-data/municipal-cities-counties-bankruptcies-and-defaults.html.

6. Stephen Dinan, "77,000 Federal Workers Paid More than Governors," *Washington Times*, May 31, 2011, http://www.washingtontimes.com/news/2011/may/31/77000-feds-paid-more-than-governors/?page=all.

7. Dennis Cauchon, "Federal Workers Earning Double Their Private Counterparts," *USA Today*, updated August 13, 2010, http://www.usatoday.com/money/economy/income/2010-08-10-1Afedpay10_ST_N.htm; Chris Edwards, "Overpaid Federal Workers," Cato Institute, August 2013, http://www.downsizinggovernment.org/overpaid-federal-workers.

8. Joe Schoenmann, "Clark County Cost-Cutting Ideas Center on Salaries," *Las Vegas Sun*, December 30, 2009, http://www.lasvegassun.com/news/2009/dec/30/cost-cutting-ideas-center-salaries.

9. Trevon Milliard, "Leaders of Clark County Teachers Union See Big Jump in Pay," *Las Vegas Review-Journal*, February 26, 2012, http://www.lvrj.com/news/leaders-of-clark-county-teachers-union-see-big-jump-in-pay-140472673.html.

10. Jake Griffin, "How a Retired Teacher's Pension Adds Up to $400,000," *Daily Herald*, updated May 29, 2013, http://www.dailyherald.com/article/20130529/news/705299905.

11.   "9,900 Illinois Government Pensioners with Annual Pension over $100k," Taxpayers United of America, May 22, 2013, http://www.taxpayersunitedofamerica.org/uncategorized/9900-illinois-government-pensioners-with-annual-pension-over-100k.

12.   "Obama Jokes at Jobs Council: 'Shovel-Ready Was Not as Shovel-Ready as We Expected,'" Fox News, no date, http://nation.foxnews.com/president-obama/2011/06/13/obama-jokes-jobs-council-shovel-ready-was-not-shovel-ready-we-expected.

13.   Andrew Stiles, "CBO Director: 'Stimulus' Spending Bad for Long-Term Growth," National Review Online, November 15, 2011, http://www.nationalreview.com/corner/283250/cbo-director-stimulus-spending-bad-long-term-growth-andrew-stiles.

14.   "Despite Revenue Growth and Record Productivity, Postal Service Loses $5 Billion in 2013 Fiscal Year," United States Postal Service, November 15, 2013, http://about.usps.com/news/national-releases/2013/pr13_087.htm.

15.   Tom Schatz, "Amtrak: 40 Years, $40 Billion," National Review Online, May 6, 2011, http://www.nationalreview.com/articles/266575/amtrak-40-years-40-billion-tom-schatz.

16.   "The 'War on Poverty' Has Cost Three Times What All of America's Actual Wars Have Cost," Before It's News, August 10, 2012, http://beforeitsnews.com/politics/2012/08/the-war-on-poverty-has-cost-three-times-what-all-of-americas-actual-wars-have-cost-2447302.html; Elizabeth Harrington, "Welfare State Grows by Nearly 19% Under Obama—to Almost $1 Trillion a Year," August 9, 2012, http://cnsnews.com/news/article/welfare-state-grows-nearly-19-under-obama-almost-1-trillion-year.

17.   "What Country in the World Has Most Lawyers per Capita?" Wiki Answers, http://wiki.answers.com/Q/What_country_in_the_world_has_most_lawyers_per_capita.

18.   "Lawyers per Capita by State," The Law School Tuition Bubble, http://lawschooltuitionbubble.wordpress.com/original-research-updated/lawyers-per-capita-by-state/.

19.   Ali Meyer, "Bernanke Leaves Fed with Record Balance Sheet of $4,102,138,000,000," CNS News, January 31, 2014, http://www.cnsnews.com/news/article/ali-meyer/bernanke-leaves-fed-record-balance-sheet-4102138000000.

20.   Tyler Durden, "How the Fed Has Failed America, Part 2," Zero Hedge, March 12, 2014, http://www.zerohedge.com/news/2014-03-12/how-fed-has-failed-america-part-2.

21.   Robert Frank, "Does Quantitative Easing Mainly Help the Rich?" CNBC, September 14, 2012, http://www.washingtonsblog.com/2012/04/forget-competing-

theories-about-quantitative-easy-what-do-the-facts-show.html; "Does Quantitative Easing Benefit the 99% or the 1%?" Washington's Blog, April 29, 2012, http://www.washingtonsblog.com/2012/04/forget-competing-theories-about-quantitative-easy-what-do-the-facts-show.html.

22. *The Banking and Currency Bill: Speech of the Honorable Elihu Root of New York in the Senate of the United States, December 13, 1913* (U.S. Government Printing Office, 1913).

23. Bill McBride, "Bernanke: House Prices Unlikely to Decline," Calculated Risk, July 29, 2005, http://www.calculatedriskblog.com/2005/07/bernanke-house-prices-unlikely-to.html.

24. "Federal Reserve Board Chairman Ben Bernanke's Greatest Hits," Center for Economic and Policy Research, http://www.cepr.net/index.php/bernanke-greatest-hits.

25. ilene, "Bernanke Says That Any Criticism of the Federal Reserve Is Based on 'Misconceptions,'" Zero Hedge, November 11, 2011, http://www.zerohedge.com/contributed/bernanke-says-any-criticism-federal-reserve-based-%E2%80%9Cmisconceptions%E2%80%9D?page=2.

26. Associated Press, "Bernanke: Fed Ready to Cut Interest Rates Again," NBC News, updated January 10, 2008, http://www.nbcnews.com/id/22592939/ns/business-stocks_and_economy/t/bernanke-fed-ready-cut-interest-rates-again/#.U0H-d_ldVXk.

27. Associated Press, "Fannie Mae, Freddie Mac Not in Danger of Failure, Bernanke Says," Fox News, July 16, 2008, http://www.foxnews.com/story/2008/07/16/fannie-mae-freddie-mac-not-in-danger-failure-bernanke-says/.

28. John Carney, "Six Bad Calls by Ben Bernake," Business Insider, August 25, 2009, http://www.businessinsider.com/6-bad-calls-by-ben-bernanke-2009-8/-1?tru=Lb3io#predicting-no-economic-slowdown-to-come-3; David Zeiler, "7 Reasons Not to Trust the Bernanke Testimony to Congress," Money Morning, May 22, 2013, http://moneymorning.com/2013/05/22/7-reasons-not-to-trust-the-bernanke-testimony-to-congress/#.

29. Ben Swann, "Truth in Media: 100 Years of the Federal Reserve," BenSwann.com, December 19, 2013, http://benswann.com/truth-in-media-100-years-of-the-federal-reserve/.

30. Rohit Chopra, "Too Big to Fail: Student Debt Hits a Trillion," Consumer Financial Protection Bureau, March 21, 2012, http://www.consumerfinance.gov/blog/too-big-to-fail-student-debt-hits-a-trillion/.

31. Michael Snyder, "During the Best Period of Economic Growth in U.S. History There Was No Income Tax and No Federal Reserve," The Economic Collapse, August 8, 2013, http://theeconomiccollapseblog.com/archives/during-the-best-

period-of-economic-growth-in-u-s-history-there-was-no-income-tax-and-no-federal-reserve.

32. Tim Iacono, "Inflation—Before and After the Federal Reserve," 24hGold, March 4, 2013, http://www.24hgold.com/english/contributor.aspx?article=4269461978 G10020&contributor=Tim+Iacono.

33. Michael Snyder, "Where Does Money Come from? The Giant Federal Reserve Scam That Most Americans Do Not Understand," The Economic Collapse, June 26, 2012, http://theeconomiccollapseblog.com/archives/where-does-money-come-from-the-giant-federal-reserve-scam-that-most-americans-do-not-understand.

34. Anthony Watts, "Watch the Senate Pajama Party All-Nighter Live," Watts Up with That?, March 10, 2014, http://wattsupwiththat.com/2014/03/10/watch-the-climate-pajama-party-all-nighter-live/; Anthony Watts, "New Gallup Poll Shows Climate Change Near the Bottom of Things Worth Worrying About," Watts Up with That?, March 12, 2014, http://wattsupwiththat.com/2014/03/12/new-gallup-poll-shows-climate-change-near-the-bottom-of-things-worth-worrying-about/.

35. "Shocker: 5000 More 'Climategate' Emails Released!" EPA Abuse.com, November 22, 2011, http://epaabuse.com/3081/news/shocker-5000-more-climategate-emails-released/.

36. Bernard Goldberg, "When Is a Traffic Jame a Greater Threat to Democracy than an IRS Scandal?" BernardGoldberg.com, January 10, 2014, http://www.bernardgoldberg.com/traffic-jam-important-irs-scandal/.

37. "Hannity, Bozell Discuss Media Double Standard on Romney '47 Percent,' Obama 'Redistribution' Videos," NewsBusters, September 21, 2012, http://newsbusters.org/blogs/nb-staff/2012/09/21/hannity-bozell-discuss-media-double-standard-romney-obama-videotapes.

38. Hadas Gold, "Report: Univision, Telemundo Skew Liberal," Politico, March 31, 2014, http://www.politico.com/blogs/media/2014/03/report-univision-telemundo-skew-liberal-186084.html.

39. Matthew Philbin, "Shameless: NBC Never Tells Viewers It Smeared Zimmerman with Doctored Audio," NewsBusters, June 20, 2013, http://newsbusters.org/blogs/matthew-philbin/2013/06/20/shameless-nbc-never-tells-viewers-it-smeared-zimmerman-doctored-aud.

40. Chris Woodyard, "CBS' '60 Minutes' Admits to Faking Tesla Car Noise," *USA Today*, April 6, 2014, http://www.usatoday.com/story/money/cars/2014/04/06/tesla-motor-sound-cbs-apology/7320361/.

41. Benjamin Storrow, "Environmentalist Attempt to Block Oil, Gas Drilling in Key Wyoming Sage Grouse Area," *Casper Star Tribune*, October 29, 2013, http://trib.com/news/state-and-regional/environmentalist-attempt-to-block-oil-gas-drilling-in-key-wyoming/article_c0bce6ae-47f2-59c8-a3d9-3acfc040787c.html; Bob Price,

"Feds Push Anti-Oil Environmentalist Agenda over Prairie Chicken," Breitbart, March 30, 2014, http://trib.com/news/state-and-regional/environmentalist-attempt-to-block-oil-gas-drilling-in-key-wyoming/article_c0bce6ae-47f2-59c8-a3d9-3acfc040787c.html.

42. "Sage Grouse Rebellion," *Wall Street Journal*, March 11, 2014, http://online.wsj.com/news/articles/SB10001424052702304858104579262383209254934.

43. James Taylor, "As Its Global Warming Narrative Unravels, the IPCC Is in Damage Control Mode," Forbes, September 26, 2013, http://www.forbes.com/sites/jamestaylor/2013/09/26/as-its-global-warming-narrative-unravels-the-ipcc-is-in-damage-control-mode.

44. James Taylor, "Antarctic Sea Ice Sets Another Record," Forbes, September 19, 2012, http://www.forbes.com/sites/jamestaylor/2012/09/19/antarctic-sea-ice-sets-another-record/.

45. Robert, "2013 One of the Ten Coldest Years in US History," Ice Age Now, December 21, 2013, http://iceagenow.info/2013/12/2013-ten-coldest-years-history.

46. Anthony Watts, "New Study Suggests Global Warming Decreases Storm Activity and Extreme Weather," Watts Up with That?, January 25, 2014, http://wattsupwiththat.com/2014/01/25/new-study-suggests-global-warming-decreases-storm-activity-and-extreme-weather.

47. Steve Connor, "How Climate Change Helped Genghis Khan: Scientists Believe a Sudden Period of Warmer Weather Allowed the Mongols to Invade with Such Success," *The Independent*, March 10, 2014, http://www.independent.co.uk/news/science/how-climate-change-helped-genghis-khan-scientists-believe-a-sudden-period-of-warmer-weather-allowed-the-mongols-to-invade-with-such-success-9182580.html.

48. Laurie J. Schmidt, "Sensing Remote Volcanoes," Earth Observatory, July 13, 2004, http://earthobservatory.nasa.gov/Features/monvoc/.

49. Kendra Alleyne, "Oregon Man Sentenced to 30 Days in Jail—for Collecting Rainwater on His Property," CNS News, July 26, 2012, http://cnsnews.com/news/article/oregon-man-sentenced-30-days-jail-collecting-rainwater-his-property.

50. Tara Dodrill, "EPA Bans Most Wood-Burning Stoves," OffTheGridNews, October 2, 2013, http://www.offthegridnews.com/2013/10/02/epa-bans-most-wood-burning-stoves/.

51. Tom Borelli, "EPA's New Power Plant Rule Will Doom King Coal," RealClearEnergy, January 16, 2014, http://www.realclearenergy.org/articles/2014/01/16/epas_new_power_plant_rule_will_doom_king_coal_107470.html.

52. "900 New EPA Regulation n 90 Days, just Six Days after Elections," DamDems, November 13, 2012, http://damdems.wordpress.com/2012/11/13/2435/.

53. Ben Bullard, "How Much Influence Did Phone, Convicted EPA Leader Have over Environmental Policy?" Personal Liberty Digest™, March 20, 2014, http://personalliberty.com/2014/03/20/how-much-influence-did-phony-convicted-epa-leader-have-over-environmental-policy/; Brianna Ehley, "How John Beale Swindled the EPA Out of $1 Million," *The Fiscal Times*, December 17, 2013, http://www.thefiscaltimes.com/Articles/2013/12/17/How-John-Beale-Swindled-EPA-Out-1-Million; Michael Bastasch, "Report: EPA fraudster wrote the 'EPA's Playbook' on regulations," Daily Caller, March 20, 2014, http://dailycaller.com/2014/03/20/report-epa-fraudster-wrote-the-epas-playbook-on-regulations/; Jim McElhatton, "Fake CIA agent helped craft sweeping environmental rules while at EPA: Republicans seek review of John Beale's work while at agency," *Washington Post*, March 19, 2014, http://www.washingtontimes.com/news/2014/mar/19/republicans-seek-review-of-john-beales-work-while-/?page=all; "Vitter: DC Circuit MATS Rule Decision Further Facilitates EPA's Scientific Abuses" (press release), U.S. Senate Committee on Environment & Public Works, April 16, 2014, http://www.epw.senate.gov/public/index.cfm?FuseAction=Minority.PressReleases&ContentRecord_id=35b1f1d6-b859-653d-18be-a3df92dbf54b&Region_id=&Issue_id=; Lachlan Markay, "Report: Coal Power Plant Shutdowns to Accelerate: Industry, workers blame Obama EPA for layoffs as companies retire larger coal-fired plants," Washington Free Beacon, February 14, 2014, http://freebeacon.com/issues/report-coal-power-plant-shutdowns-to-accelerate/.

54. Dale Hurd, "Spain's Green Disaster a Lesson for America," CBN News, December 26, 2011, http://www.cbn.com/cbnnews/finance/2011/november/spains-green-disaster-a-lesson-for-america/.

55. Tyler Durden, "Spain Youth Unemployment Rises to Record 57.7%, Surpasses Greece," Zero Hedge, January 8, 2014, http://www.zerohedge.com/news/2014-01-08/spain-youth-unemployment-rises-record-577-surpasses-greece.

56. Luis Miranda, "Spanish Government Makes Official the Looting of Pension Funds," The Real Agenda News, September 29, 2012, http://real-agenda.com/2012/09/29/spanish-government-makes-official-the-looting-of-pension-funds/.

57. "Whistling Past the Wind Farm," *Wall Street Journal*, January 23, 2014, http://online.wsj.com/news/articles/SB10001424052702303947904579338253880436492.

58. Patrick Smith, "EU Drops 2030 Member State Renewables Targets," *Wind Power Monthly*, January 22, 2014, http://www.windpowermonthly.com/article/1228154/eu-drops-2030-member-state-renewables-targets.

59. Gianluca Baratti, "Job Losses from Obama Green Stimulus Foreseen in Spanish Study," Bloomberg, March 27, 2009, http://www.bloomberg.com/apps/news?pid =newsarchive&sid=a2PHwqAs7BS0.

60. Kenneth P. Green, "On Green Energy: Plainly Not Helping Spain," The American: The Online Magazine of the American Enterprise Institute, May 3, 2011,

61. Christine Lakatos, "Green Alert: Tracking President Obama's green energy failures, " The Green Corruption Files, October 20, 2012 with December 2012 update, http:// greencorruption.blogspot.com/2012/10/green-alert-tracking-president-obamas. html#.U29pZyh_i74.

62. Patrice Hill, "'Green' Jobs No Longer Golden in Stimulus," *Washington Times*, September 9, 2010, http://www.washingtontimes.com/news/2010/sep/9/green-jobs-no-longer-golden-in-stimulus/?page=all.

63. Vince Veneziani, "The Real Story of How George Soros Shorted the Pound, Etching His Name into Financial History Forever," Business Insider, June 4, 2010, http:// www.businessinsider.com/how-george-soros-shorted-the-pound-etching-his-name-into-financial-history-forever-2010-6.

64. "George Soros," DiscoverTheNetworks, http://www.discoverthenetworks.org/ individualProfile.asp?indid=977; Daniel Greenfield, "Obama Campaign Merges with George Soros," FrontPageMag, January 25, 2013, http://www.frontpagemag. com/2013/dgreenfield/obama-campaign-merges-with-george-soros/.

65. "George Soros," DiscoverTheNetworks.

Chapter 6: The Unindicted Co-Conspirators

1. "Pelosi: Republicans Are 'Legislative Arsonists' Trying to Burn Down the Government," RealClearPolitics, September 22, 2013, http://www.realclearpolitics.com/ video/2013/09/22/pelosi_republicans_are_legislative_arsonists_trying_to_burn_ down_the_government.html.

2. Michael Patrick Leahy, "Pat Caddell Says Establishment Republicans 'Want the IRS to Go After' the Tea Party," Breitbart, February 17, 2014, http://www.breitbart. com/Big-Government/2014/02/17/Pat-Caddell-Says-Establishment-Republicans-Want-the-IRS-to-Go-After-the-Tea-Party.

3. Sonya Sandage, "9 Generals Fired, 2 Military Leaders Suspended," BenSwann.com, October 23, 2013, http://benswann.com/9-generals-fired-2-military-leaders-suspended/.

4. Jonathan Weisman and Ashley Parker, "House Approves Higher Debt Limit without Condition," *New York Times*, February 11, 2014, http://www.nytimes. com/2014/02/12/us/politics/boehner-to-bring-debt-ceiling-to-vote-without-policy-attachments.html?_r=0.

5. Avik Roy, "The Inside Story on How Roberts Changed His Supreme Court Vote on Obamacare," Forbes, July 1, 2012, http://www.forbes.com/sites/aroy/2012/07/01/the-supreme-courts-john-roberts-changed-his-obamacare-vote-in-may/.

6. Ariane de Vogue, "Petraeus Investigation: When and How the FBI Can Access Email Accounts," ABC News, November 12, 2012, http://abcnews.go.com/blogs/politics/2012/11/petraeus-investigation-when-and-how-the-fbi-can-access-email-accounts/.

7. Les Leopold, "How Wall Street Devoured the Economy," Huffington Post, September 20, 2013, http://www.huffingtonpost.com/les-leopold/how-wall-street-devoured_b_3960271.

8. Glenn Greenwald, "Obamacare Architect Leaves White House for Pharmaceutical Industry Job," *The Guardian*, December 5, 2012, http://theantimedia.org/obamacare-was-written-by-big-pharma-lobbyists/.

9. Megan R. Wilson, "ObamaCare's Architects Reap Windfall as Washington Lobbyists," The Hill, August 25, 2013, http://thehill.com/business-a-lobbying/318577-architects-of-obamacare-reap-windfall-as-washington-lobbyists.

10. Edward Morrissey, "The Coming Obamacare Shock for 170 Million Americans," The Fiscal Times, April 3, 2014, http://www.thefiscaltimes.com/Columns/2014/04/03/Coming-Obamacare-Shock-170-Million-Americans.

11. Conn Carroll, "The Unaffordable Care Act: Obamacare Drives Up Premiums Nationwide," Townhall, December 26, 2013, http://townhall.com/tipsheet/conncarroll/2013/12/26/the-unaffordable-care-act-obamacare-drives-up-premiums-nationwide-n1768646; Tami Luhby, "Got Obamacare, Can't Find Doctors," CNN Money, March 19, 2014, http://money.cnn.com/2014/03/19/news/economy/obamacare-doctors/.

12. Kimberley A. Strassel, "Strassel: Big Business Sells Out Small Business," *Wall Street Journal*, December 20, 2012, http://online.wsj.com/news/articles/SB10001424127887324461604578189960633266322; Ben Hallman, "Business Roundtable Fiscal Cliff Proposal Bargains for Concessions on Corporate Rates," Huffington Post, December 12, 2012, http://www.huffingtonpost.com/2012/12/12/business-roundtable-fiscal-cliff-_n_2288683.html.

13. Wayne Allyn Root, "Who's Really Selling Out Small Business," The Blaze, January 10, 2013, http://www.theblaze.com/contributions/whos-really-selling-out-small-business/; "Crony Capitalist Blowout," *Wall Street Journal*, January 4, 2013, http://online.wsj.com/news/articles/SB10001424127887323320404578216583921471560.

14. "The 'War on Poverty' Has Cost Three Times What All of America's Actual Wars Have Cost," Before It's News, August 10, 2012, http://beforeitsnews.com/politics/2012/08/the-war-on-poverty-has-cost-three-times-what-all-of-americas-actual-wars-have-cost-2447302.html.

15. Jerome R. Corsi, "Poverty under Obama Rises to Alarming Level," WND Money, November 28, 2013, http://www.wnd.com/2013/11/poverty-under-obama-rises-to-alarming-level/.

16. Kit Daniels, "Wal-Mart: Food Stamp Cuts Hurt Our Profits," Infowars.com, January 31, 2014, http://www.infowars.com/wal-mart-food-stamp-cuts-will-hurt-our-profits/.

17. Reid Wilson, "State Republicans Making the Case for Internet Sales Tax to Congress," *Washington Post*, November 14, 2013, http://www.washingtonpost.com/blogs/govbeat/wp/2013/11/14/state-republicans-making-the-case-for-internet-sales-tax-to-congress/.

18. Timothy P. Carney, "Carney: Amazon Joins Walmart in Push for Online Sales Tax," *Washington Examiner*, August 1, 2012, http://washingtonexaminer.com/carney-amazon-joins-walmart-in-push-for-online-sales-tax/article/2503738.

19. Janet Novack, "While Congress Debates, Internet Shoppers Cough Up Sales Tax," Forbes, April 25, 2013, http://www.forbes.com/sites/janetnovack/2013/04/25/while-congress-debates-consumers-cough-up-internet-sales-tax/.

20. Janie Boschma, "Online Sales Tax Brings Powerful Interest Groups to the Hill," OpenSecrets.org, March 18, 2013, https://www.opensecrets.org/news/2013/03/online-sales-tax-brings-powerful-in.html.

21. Text of "H.R.684—Marketplace Fairness Act of 2013," available on OpenCongress, http://www.opencongress.org/bill/hr684-113/show.

22. Thomas Donohue, "A Steady Flow of Talented, Industrious Immigrants Can Fuel a Booming Economy," U.S. Chamber of Commerce, February 12, 2014, http://www.fresnobee.com/2014/02/13/3767153/a-steady-flow-of-talented-industrious.html.

23. George Borjas, "Immigration and the American Worker," Center for Immigration Studies, April 2013, http://cis.org/immigration-and-the-american-worker-review-academic-literature.

24. "Tax Credits for Illegal Immigrants," FactCheck.org, May 11, 2012, http://globaleconomicanalysis.blogspot.com/2013/06/irs-refunds-4-billion-child-tax-credits.html.

25. Paul Roderick Gregory, "Warren Buffett's Secretary Likely Makes between $200,000 and $500,000/Year," Forbes, January 25, 2012, http://www.forbes.com/sites/paulroderickgregory/2012/01/25/warren-buffetts-secretary-likely-makes-between-200000-and-500000year/.

26. "Report: Buffett's Berkshire Owes $1 Billion in Back Taxes, Newsmax, September 1, 2011, http://www.newsmax.com/Headline/buffett-irs-back-taxes/2011/09/01/id/409520.

27. Bonnie Kavoussi, "GE CEO Jeffrey Immelt Defends General Electric Tax Rate," Huffington Post, April 25, 2012, http://www.huffingtonpost.com/2012/04/25/ge-ceo-jeffrey-immelt-tax-rate_n_1451823.html.

28. Sean Higgins, "The Real Reason Warren Buffett Backs Estate Taxes," *Investor's Business Daily*, November 18, 2011, http://blogs.investors.com/capitalhill/index.php/home/35-politicsinvesting/5451-the-real-reason-warren-buffett-backs-estate-taxes.

29. Timothy P. Carney, "Industry, Not Environmentalists, Killed Incandescent Bulbs," *Washington Examiner*, March 3, 2014, http://washingtonexaminer.com/industry-not-environmentalists-killed-incandescent-bulbs/article/2541430; Timothy P. Carney, "How GE's Green Lobbying Is Killing U.S. Factory Jobs," *Washington Examiner*, August 27, 2009, http://washingtonexaminer.com/timothy-p.-carney-how-ges-green-lobbying-is-killing-u.s.-factory-jobs/article/36662.

30. William C. Triplett II, "Triplett: Railroading the Keystone XL Pipeline," *Washington Times*, June 19, 2013, http://www.washingtontimes.com/news/2013/jun/19/railroading-the-keystone-xl-pipeline/?page=all.

31. Tyler Durden, "Thanks Obamacare? Warren Buffett Cuts Health Benefits by over 57% at Heinz," Zero Hedge, December 24, 2013, http://www.zerohedge.com/news/2013-12-24/thanks-obamacare-warren-buffett-cuts-health-benefits-over-57-heinz.

32. Robert Frank, "Buffett's Wealth Soared $37 Million a Day in 2013," CNBC, December 18, 2013, http://www.cnbc.com/id/101282625.

33. "Does Quantitative Easing Benefit the 99% or the 1%?" WashingtonsBlog, April 29, 2012, http://www.washingtonsblog.com/2012/04/forget-competing-theories-about-quantitative-easy-what-do-the-facts-show.html.

Chapter 7: The Motive

1. Jazz Shaw, "A Younger Obama Considered His First Employer, 'the Enemy,'" Hot Air, July 28, 2012, http://hotair.com/archives/2012/07/28/a-younger-obama-considered-his-first-employer-the-enemy/.

2. Barbara Boland, "Pew Study: Christians Are the World's Most Oppressed Religious Group," CNS News, February 6, 2014, http://www.cnsnews.com/news/article/barbara-boland/pew-study-christians-are-world-s-most-oppressed-religious-group.

3. Stoyan Zaimov, "Obama Admin Criticized for Joke over Christians Attacked in Egypt," ChristianPost.com, August 26, 2013, http://global.christianpost.com/news/obama-admin-criticized-for-joke-over-christians-attacked-in-egypt-103059.

4. James Ball, "Obama Issues Syria a 'Red Lin' Warning on Chemical Weapons," *Washington Post*, August 20, 2012, http://www.washingtonpost.com/world/national-security/obama-issues-syria-red-line-warning-on-chemical-weapons/2012/08/20/ba5d26ec-eaf7-11e1-b811-09036bcb182b_story.html.

5. Todd Starnes, "Lawmakers Accuse VA of Disrespecting Christians," Fox News, January 6, 2014, http://www.foxnews.com/opinion/2014/01/06/lawmakers-accuse-va-disrespecting-christians.

6. Suzanne Hamner, "Muslim Mortgages Paid with More than $300 Million—Courtesy of US Taxpayers," Freedom Outpost, January 5, 2014, http://freedomoutpost.com/2014/01/muslim-mortgages-paid-300-million-courtesy-us-taxpayers/.

7. Todd Starnes, "Texas Lawmaker Calls for Congressional Probe into Ban of Christian Prayers at Military Funerals," Fox News, July 26, 2011, http://www.foxnews.com/politics/2011/07/26/texas-lawmaker-calls-for-congressional-probe-into-ban-christian-prayers-at/.

8. Katherine Weber, "Military Chaplains Banned from Using Jesus' Name, Reciting Bible; Lawsuit Filed in Calif.," ChristianPost.com, November 14, 2013, http://www.christianpost.com/news/military-chaplains-banned-from-using-jesus-name-reciting-bible-lawsuit-filed-in-calif-108734.

9. E. Turner Lee, "Obama Bans Ministers," Skinnyreporter.com, no date, http://skinnyreporter.com/clericsbanned.html.

10. "Pentagon Widens Chrstian Ban; Graham Says It's Anti-Relgion," Newsmax, April 26, 2010.

11. Todd Starnes, "Army: Don't Say Christmas," Fox News, December 24, 2013, http://www.foxnews.com/opinion/2013/12/24/army-dont-say-christmas/.

12. Ken Klukowski, "Air Force: Christians' Religious Speech Not Legally Protected Right," Breitbart, March 16, 2014, http://www.breitbart.com/Big-Peace/2014/03/16/Air-Force-Christians-Religious-Speech-Not-Legally-Protected-Right.

13. Todd Starnes, "Christians Vow Civil Disobedience if Home-School Family Is Deported," Fox News, March 4, 2014, http://www.foxnews.com/opinion/2014/03/04/christians-vow-civil-disobedience-if-home-school-family-is-deported/.

14. Judson Berger, "Administration Eases Restrictions on Asylum Seekers with Loose Terror Ties," Fox News, February 6, 2014, http://www.foxnews.com/politics/2014/02/06/administration-eases-restrictions-on-asylum-seekers-with-loose-terror-ties/.

15. Kenneth R. Timmerman, "Obama Administration Let Anti-Gay Muslim Leader into U.S.," *New York Post*, March 2, 204, http://nypost.com/2014/03/02/state-dept-lets-anti-gay-muslim-leader-into-u-s/.

16. "Controversial DOJ Nominee Fails to Clear Senate Test Vote," Fox News, March 5, 2014, http://www.foxnews.com/politics/2014/03/05/senators-clash-over-doj-nominee-work-on-convicted-cop-killer-case/.

17. Nick Wing, "Obama Africa Trip to Cost up to $100 Million: Report," Huffington Post, June 14, 2013, http://www.cnn.com/2013/06/30/world/africa/south-africa-obama-pledge/; Faith Karimi and Matt Smith, "Obama Pledges $7 Billion to Upgrade Power in Africa," CNN, June 30, 2013, http://www.cnn.com/2013/06/30/world/africa/south-africa-obama-pledge/.

18. Wayne Allyn Root, "The Party That Booed God," The Blaze, September 6, 2012, http://www.theblaze.com/contributions/the-party-that-booed-god/.

19. Ed Morrissey, "Iowa Democrat Prayer: Thank God for Abortionists!" Hot Air, August 29, 2013, http://hotair.com/archives/2013/08/29/iowa-democrat-prayer-thank-god-for-abortionists.

20. Steve Holland, "Obama National Security Aides Meet to Discuss Ukraine," Reuters, March 15, 2014, http://www.reuters.com/article/2014/03/15/us-ukraine-crisis-obama-idUSBREA2D15W20140315; Jennifer Burke, "Obama Blows Off National Security Meeting to Attend Film Festival," Tea Party News Network, March 2, 2014, http://www.tpnn.com/2014/03/02/obama-blows-off-national-security-meeting-to-attend-film-festival.

21. Sabrina Siddiqui, "Obama Too Busy to Meet with Jobs Council, White House Says," Huffington Post, July 18, 2012, http://www.huffingtonpost.com/2012/07/18/obama-jobs-council_n_1684221.html.

22. Josh Gerstein, "Obama Jobs Council Hits 1 Year without Official Meeting," Politico, January 18, 2013, http://www.politico.com/blogs/under-the-radar/2013/01/obama-jobs-council-hits-year-without-official-meeting-154524.html.

23. "Obama's Jobs Council Shutting Down Thursday," Fox News, January 31, 2013, http://www.foxnews.com/politics/2013/01/31/obama-jobs-council-shutting-down-thursday/.

24. "Did Barack Obama Hold 100-Plus Fundraisers while His Jobs Council Never Met?" PolitiFact.com, July 19, 2012, http://www.politifact.com/truth-o-meter/statements/2012/jul/19/republican-national-committee-republican/did-barack-obama-hold-100-plus-fundraisers-while-h/.

25. Terence P. Jeffrey, "Panetta and Joint Chiefs Chair: Obama Talked to Them Only Once on Night of Benghazi Attack," CNS News, February 7, 2013, http://cnsnews.com/news/article/panetta-and-joint-chiefs-chair-obama-talked-them-only-once-night-benghazi-attack.

26. Daniel Halper, "Panetta: Obama Absent Night of Benghazi," *Weekly Standard*, February 7, 2013, http://www.weeklystandard.com/blogs/panetta-obama-absent-night-benghazi_700405.html#.

27. Emily Miller, "Miller: No Worries! Obama Golfs 150th Round as Superstorm Devastates Philippines, Iran Deal Enrages," *Washington Times*, November 8, 2013, http://www.washingtontimes.com/news/2013/nov/8/miller-obama-plays-150-rounds-golf-president/?page=all.

28. See Obamagolfcounter.com.

29. "Obama's Quiet Yrs. In N.Y.C. Pol's Rise Stuns His Classmates from Columbia," *Daily News*, January 14, 2007, http://www.nydailynews.com/news/obama-quiet-yrs-n-y-pol-rise-stuns-classmates-columbia-article-1.261932.

30. Joel Gehrke, "Reid: Romney is guilty of tax evasion until he proves he's innocent," *Washington Examiner*, August 1, 2012, http://washingtonexaminer.com/reid-romney-is-guilty-of-tax-evasion-until-he-proves-hes-innocent/article/2503802; Ann Coulter, "Obama's Signature Move: Unsealing Private Records," Human Events, August 1, 2012, http://www.humanevents.com/2012/08/01/ann-coulter-obamas-signature-move-unsealing-private-records/.

31. BirtherReport.com, "Maddow Attacks Wayne Allyn Root over Birther Issue," Youtube, https://www.youtube.com/watch?v=A5IGaLTuIkg; Wayne Allyn Root, "Rachel Maddow—Your Attempt at Slander Failed," The Blaze, July 16, 2013, http://www.theblaze.com/contributions/rachel-maddow-your-attempt-at-slander-failed/.

32. Ibid.

33. Madeleine Morgenstern, "Report: Obama's 1991 Literary Agency Described Him as 'Born in Kenya and Raised in Indonesia and Hawaii,'" The Blaze, May 17, 2012, http://www.theblaze.com/stories/2012/05/17/report-obamas-1991-literary-agency-described-him-as-born-in-kenya-and-raised-in-indonesia-and-hawaii/.

Chapter 8: Where the Plot Was Hatched

1. Bruce Johnson, "The Cloward-Piven Way," American Thinker, September 18, 2012, http://www.americanthinker.com/blog/2012/09/the_cloward-piven_way.html.

2. Sam Rolley, "Duke Professor: White People Are Racist No Matter What," Personal Liberty Digest™, September 27, 2013, http://personalliberty.com/2013/09/27/duke-professor-white-people-are-racist-no-matter-what/.

3. Ed Morrissey, "Obama: We'll Bankrupt Any New Coal Plants" Hot Air, November 2, 2008, http://hotair.com/archives/2008/11/02/obama-well-bankrupt-any-new-coal-plants/.

4. Natalie Gewargis, "'Spread the Wealth'?" ABC News, October 14, 2008, http://abcnews.go.com/blogs/politics/2008/10/spread-the-weal/.

Chapter 9: The Murder Weapons

1. "Bum Rap for Rahm," FactCheck.org, January 13, 2011, http://www.factcheck.org/2011/01/bum-rap-for-rahm/.

2. Peter Ferrara, "President Obama: The Biggest Government Spender in World History," Forbes, June 14, 2012, http://www.forbes.com/sites/peterferrara/2012/06/14/president-obama-the-biggest-government-spender-in-world-history.

3. Amy Payne, "Morning Bell: $16,000,000,000,000," The Heritage Foundation, September 5, 2012, http://blog.heritage.org/2012/09/05/morning-bell-16000000000000/.

4. Terence P. Jeffrey, "+106%: Obama Has More than Doubled Marketable U.S. Debt," CNS News, February 18, 2014, http://cnsnews.com/news/article/terence-p-jeffrey/106-obama-has-more-doubled-marketable-us-debt; "Monthly Statement of the Public Debt of the United States," U.S. Treasury's Bureau of the Fiscal Service, January 31, 2014, http://www.treasurydirect.gov/govt/reports/pd/mspd/2014/opds012014.pdf.

5. Jeffrey, "+106%: Obama Has."

6. See http://usdebtclock.org.

7. Gregory Gwyn-Williams Jr., "National Debt Stacked in Dollar Bills Would Stretch from Earth to Moon Five Times," CNS News, July 26, 2013, http://cnsnews.com/mrctv-blog/gregory-gwyn-williams-jr/national-debt-stacked-dollar-bills-would-stretch-earth-moon-five.

8. "U.S. Debt Exceeds Annual Economic Output," CBC/Radio-Canada, January 9, 2012, http://www.cbc.ca/news/business/story/2012/01/09/us-gdp-debt.html.

9. "United States Government Debt to GDP," TRADINGECONOMICS.com," http://www.tradingeconomics.com/united-states/government-debt-to-gdp.

10. Martin Crutsinger, "U.S. Deficit Tops $1 Trillion for Fourth Year," KomoNews.com, October 13, 2012, http://www.komonews.com/news/business/US-deficit-tops-1-trillion-for-fourth-year-174041751.html.

11. Ed Morrissey, "Change: Obama's Addition to National Debt now Surpasses Bush," Hot Air, March 20, 2012, http://hotair.com/archives/2012/03/20/change-obamas-addition-to-national-debt-now-surpasses-bush/.

12. Stephen Dinan, "U.S. Debt Jumps a Record $328 Billion—Tops $17 Trillion for First Time," *Washington Times*, October 18, 2013, http://www.washingtontimes.com/news/2013/oct/18/us-debt-jumps-400-billion-tops-17-trillion-first-t/.

13. Tracy Withers, "U.S. to Get Downgraded amid Fiscal 'Theater,' Pimco Says," Bloomberg, October 17, 2012, http://www.bloomberg.com/news/2012-10-17/u-s-to-get-downgraded-amid-fiscal-theater-pimco-says.html.

14. Ambrose Evans-Pritchard, "BIS Veteran Says Global Credit Excess Worse than Pre-Lehman," *The Telegraph*, September 15, 2013, http://www.telegraph.co.uk/finance/10310598/BIS-veteran-says-global-credit-excess-worse-than-pre-Lehman.html.

15. Jeffrey, "+106%: Obama Has."

16. Andrew Miga, "Elizabeth Warren Got Nearly $430,000 Teaching at Harvard," MassLive.com, updated January 17, 2012, http://www.masslive.com/politics/index.ssf/2012/01/elizabeth_warren_got_nearly_43.html.

17. "Public Service Loan Forgiveness," Federal Student aid, http://studentaid.ed.gov/repay-loans/forgiveness-cancellation/charts/public-service.

18. "Student Debt Levels—Now Averaging More than $35,000—Surprise to Half of 2013 College Grads," Fidelity Investments®, May 16, 2013, http://www.fidelity.com/inside-fidelity/individual-investing/college-grads-surprised-by-student-debt-level-exceeds-35000.

19. Tami Luhby, "Fed: Student Loans Soar 275% over Past Decade," CNN Money, May 31, 2012, http://money.cnn.com/2012/05/31/news/economy/fed-student-loans/.

20. Federal Reserve Bank of New York, " Quarterly Report on Household Debt and Credit," February 2014, news.dethronethebanksters.com/student-loans-hit-record-1-08-trillion-delinquent-student-debt-rises-to-all-time-high;"Student Loans Hit Record $1.08 Trillion; Delinquent Student Debt Rises to All Time High," Bankster News, http://news.dethronethebanksters.com/student-loans-hit-record-1-08-trillion-delinquent-student-debt-rises-to-all-time-high/.

21. Carmel Lobello, "An Ominous Trend: Student Loan Delinquencies Hit a Record High," *The Week*, November 18, 2013, http://theweek.com/article/index/252937/an-ominous-trend-student-loan-delinquencies-hit-a-record-high.

22. Center for Responsive Politics, "Top Contributors," OpenSecrets.org, no date, http://www.opensecrets.org/pres12/contrib.php?id=N00009638.

23. Yasemin Akcaguner"Columbia Thank You Day celebrates$6.1 billion capital campaign funding," *Columbia Daily Spectator*, April 3, 2014, http://www.columbiaspectator.com/news/2014/04/03/columbia-thank-you-day-celebrates-61-billion-capital-campaign-funding.

24. July 19 edition of *Time*, "Wayne Allyn Root is Quoted in Time Magazine!" Root for America!, July 18, 2010, http://www.rootforamerica.com/webroot/oldblog/index.php?m=07&y=10&entry=entry100718-065628.

25. Dick M. Carpenter II, Lisa Knepper, Angela C. Erickson, and John K. Ross, "License to Work," Institute for Justice, May 2012, pp. 7, 5, http://www.ij.org/images/pdf_folder/economic_liberty/occupational_licensing/licensetowork.pdf.

26. James L. Gattuso and Diane Katz, "Red Tape Rising: Regulations in Obama's First Term," The Heritage Foundation, May 1, 2013, http://www.heritage.org/research/reports/2013/05/red-tape-rising-regulation-in-obamas-first-term; Daniel Halper, "Report: 2012 Regulatory Rules More Costly than All Rules in 'Entire First Terms of Presidents Bush and Clinton, Combined,'" *Weekly Standard*, April 23, 2013, http://www.weeklystandard.com/blogs/report-2012-regulatory-rules-more-costly-all-rules-entire-first-terms-presidents-bush-and-clinton-combined_719020.html.

27. Gattuso and Katz, "Red Tape Rising."

28. "The Impact of Regulatory Costs on Small Firms," U.S. Small Business Administration, http://www.sba.gov/advocacy/7540/49291.

29. Jared G., "Who Really Lobbies for Regulation?" Greenback Cafe, January 22, 2012, http://www.greenbackcafe.com/who-really-lobbies-for-regulation_349.

30. Timothy P. Carney, *The Big Ripoff: How Big Business and Big Government Steal Your Money* (Wiley, 2006), pp. 2–6, 111–54, 177–94.

31. "Frequently Asked Questions about Small Business," U.S. Small Business Administration, March 2014, http://www.sba.gov/sites/default/files/FAQ_March_2014_0.pdf.

32. Pete Winn, "U.S. Policies Put Most U.S. Oil Off-Limits to Drilling," CNS News, July 7, 2008, http://cnsnews.com/news/article/us-policies-put-most-us-oil-limits-drilling.

33. Timothy P. Carney, "Industry, Not Environmentalists, Killed Incandescent Bulbs," *Washington Examiner*, March 3, 2014, http://washingtonexaminer.com/industry-not-environmentalists-killed-incandescent-bulbs/article/2541430; Brian Clark Howard, "Energy-Efficient Light Bulbs: How Much Do You Really Save?" MSN Real Estate, no date, http://realestate.msn.com/energy-efficient-light-bulbs-how-much-do-you-really-save; "The Great LED Lightbulb Rip-off: One in Four Expensive 'Long-Life' Bulbs Doesn't Last Anything like as Long as the Makers Claim," *Daily Mail*, updated January 27, 2014, http://www.dailymail.co.uk/news/article-2546363/The-great-LED-lightbulb-rip-One-four-expensive-long-life-bulbs-doesnt-like-long-makers-claim.html.

34. Penny Starr, "Under Obama, 11,327 Pages of Federal Regulations Added," CNS News, September 10, 2012, http://cnsnews.com/news/article/under-obama-11327-pages-federal-regulations-added.

35. "ObamaCare Tax: Full List of ObamaCare Taxes," ObamaCareFacts, http://obamacarefacts.com/obamacare-taxes.php; Mike Patton, "Is Obamacare an Economic Disaster?" Forbes, February 25, 2014, http://www.forbes.com/sites/mikepatton/2014/02/25/is-obamacare-an-economic-disaster/.

36. Tom Gara, "Union Letter: Obamacare Will 'Destroy the Very Health and Wellbeing' of Workers," *Wall Street Journal*, July 12, 2013, http://blogs.wsj.com/corporate-

intelligence/2013/07/12/union-letter-obamacare-will-destroy-the-very-health-and-wellbeing-of-workers/.

37. Karen Campbell, Guinevere Nell, and Paul L. Winfree, "Obamacare: Impact on the Economy," The Heritage Foundation, September 22, 2010, http://www.heritage.org/research/reports/2010/09/obamacare-impact-on-the-economy.

38. Sarah Hurtubise, "Survey: US Sees Sharpest Health Insurance Premium Increases in Years," Daily Caller, April 7, 2014, http://dailycaller.com/2014/04/07/survey-u-s-sees-sharpest-health-insurance-premium-increases-in-years/.

39. Aimee Picchi, "For Some, Obamacare Deductibles Deliver Sticker Shock," CBS Money Watch, November 9, 2013, http://www.cbsnews.com/news/obamacare-deductibles-deliver-hefty-sticker-shock/.

40. Sally Pipes, "Thanks to Obamacare, a 20,000 Doctor Shortage Is Set to Quintuple," Forbes, June 10, 2013, http://www.forbes.com/sites/sallypipes/2013/06/10/thanks-to-obamacare-a-20000-doctor-shortage-is-set-to-quintuple/.

41. Lisa De Pasquale, "First Union to Endorse Obama Now Slams Obamacare," Breitbart, March 19, 2014, http://www.breitbart.com/InstaBlog/2014/03/19/First-Union-to-Endorse-Obama-Now-Slams-Obamacare; "The Irony of ObamaCare: Making Inequality Worse," UNITE HERE, no date, http://cdn.ralstonreports.com/sites/default/files/ObamaCaretoAFL_FINAL.pdf.

42. "ObamaCare Will Hasten Income Inequality, Union Report Says," Fox News, March 10, 2014, http://www.foxnews.com/politics/2014/03/10/obamacare-will-hasten-income-inequality-union-report-says/.

43. "The Irony of ObamaCare: Making Inequality Worse," UNITE HERE; "ObamaCare Will Hasten Income Inequality, Union Report Says."

44. Lisa Myers and Hannah Rappleye, "Obama Admin. Knew Millions Could Not Keep Their Health Insurance," NBC News, October 28, 2013, http://investigations.nbcnews.com/_news/2013/10/28/21213547-obama-admin-knew-millions-could-not-keep-their-health-insurance?lite.

45. "Cleveland Clinic CEO: Three-Quarters of Americans Who Signed up for Obamacare Now Have Higher Premiums," CBS Cleveland, March 31, 2014, http://cleveland.cbslocal.com/2014/03/31/cleveland-clinic-ceo-three-quarters-of-americans-who-signed-up-for-obamacare-now-have-higher-premiums/.

46. Gara, "Union Letter."

47. "CBO/JCT Confirm That Obamacare Is a $1 Trillion Tax Hike: Democrats' Health Law Contains 21 Tax Increases, Including 12 on the Middle Class," Committee on Ways and Means, July 25, 2012, http://waysandmeans.house.gov/news/documentsingle.aspx?DocumentID=304547.

48. Jeffrey H. Anderson, "Bailing Out Health Insurers and Helping Obamacare," *Weekly Standard*, January 13, 2014, http://www.weeklystandard.com/blogs/bailing-out-health-insurers-and-helping-obamacare_774167.html#.

49. Ryan Grim, "Internal Memo Confirms Big Giveaways in White House Deal with Big Pharma," Huffington Post, Septemer 13, 2009, http://www.huffingtonpost.com/2009/08/13/internal-memo-confirms-bi_n_258285.html.

50. Alex Wayne, "Target to Drop Health Insurance for Part-Time Workers," Bloomberg, January 22, 2014, http://www.bloomberg.com/news/2014-01-21/target-to-drop-health-insurance-for-part-time-workers.html.

51. Becket Adams, "How Many Businesses Are Exempt? The Final Number of 'Obamacare' Waivers Is in . . . " The Blaze, January 6, 2012, http://www.theblaze.com/stories/2012/01/06/how-many-businesses-are-exempt-the-final-number-of-obamacare-waivers-is-in/; "List of 729 Companies and Unions with Obamacare Exemptions," Daily Paul, August 25, 2013, http://www.dailypaul.com/296870/list-of-729-companies-and-unions-with-obamacare-exemptions.

52. Roberton Williams, "How Big Is the Penalty if You Don't Get Health Insurance?" Forbes, November 7, 2013, http://www.forbes.com/sites/beltway/2013/11/07/how-big-is-the-penalty-if-you-dont-get-health-insurance/.

53. See the American Center for Law and Justice (ACLJ) site for details about the HHS mandate, https://aclj.org/Tags/HHS%20mandate.

54. Elizabeth Harrington, "Report: 'Avalanche' of Regulations still to Come under Obamacare," Washington Free Beacon, February 10, 2014, http://freebeacon.com/report-avalanche-of-regulations-still-to-come-under-obamacare/.

55. Sam Batkins, "Health Care Exchanges Impose $5.3 Billion in Costs, 16 Million Hours," American Action Forum, September 25, 2013, http://americanactionforum.org/research/health-care-exchanges-impose-5.3-billion-in-costs-16-million-hours.

56. "ObamaCare Could Lead to Loss of Nearly 2.3 Million US Jobs, Report Says," Fox News, February 4, 2014, http://www.foxnews.com/politics/2014/02/04/obamacare-expected-to-lead-to-loss-nearly-25-million-american-jobs-report-says/.

57. Susan Jones, "CBO: Obamacare Will 'Reduce Incentives to Work;' WH Spins It as 'Choice,'" CNS News, February 4, 2014, http://cnsnews.com/news/article/susan-jones/cbo-obamacare-will-reduce-incentives-work-wh-spins-it-choice.

58. "Obama Rewrites ObamaCare," *Wall Street Journal*, February 10, 2014, http://online.wsj.com/news/articles/SB10001424052702303650204579375310934336066.

59. Warren Mass, "IRS Demands Businesses Show 'Bonafide Reasons' for Layoffs," *The New American*, February 12, 2014, http://www.thenewamerican.com/usnews/health-care/item/17608-irs-demands-businesses-show-bonafide-reasons-for-layoffs.

60. Sarah Hurtubise, "Report: Premiums Rising Faster than Eight Years before Obamacare Combined," Daily Caller, March 18, 2014, http://dailycaller.com/2014/03/18/report-premiums-rising-faster-than-eight-years-before-obamacare-combined/.

61. Elise Viebeck, "O-Care Premiums to Skyrocket," The Hill, March 19, 2014, http://thehill.com/blogs/healthwatch/health-reform-implementation/201136-obamacare-premiums-are-about-to-skyrocket.

Chapter 10: *Braveheart*: Forward to the Past

1. "Obama: 'If You Like Your Health Care Plan, You'll Be Able to Keep Your Health Care Plan,'" PolitiFact.com, http://www.politifact.com/obama-like-health-care-keep/.

2. "Obama Says He Didn't 'Know Anything' about Probe into IRS Targeting," Fox News, March 26, 2013, http://www.foxnews.com/politics/2013/05/16/obama-to-meet-with-treasury-officials-over-irs-scandal/.

3. Josh Rogin, "White House: Obama and Biden Were Never Aware of Requests for More Benghazi Security," The Cable, ForeignPolicy.com, October 12, 2012, http://thecable.foreignpolicy.com/posts/2012/10/12/white_house_obama_and_biden_were_never_aware_of_requests_for_more_benghazi_security.

4. Tom Bevan, "What the President Said about Benghazi," RealClearPolitics," November 30, 2012, http://www.realclearpolitics.com/articles/2012/11/30/what_the_president_said_about_benghazi_116299.html.

5. John Hawkins, "5 Things the Obama Administration Had No Idea the Obama Administration Was Doing," Townhall, November 2, 2013, http://townhall.com/columnists/johnhawkins/2013/11/02/5-things-the-obama-administration-had-no-idea-the-obama-administration-was-doing-n1734940/page/full.

6. Paul Lewis and Philip Oltermann, "NSA Denies Discussing Merkel Phone Surveillance with Obama," *The Guardian*, October 27, 2013, http://www.theguardian.com/world/2013/oct/27/barack-obama-nsa-angela-merkel-germany.

7. "Supporting Small Businesses," Jobs & the Economy: Putting America Back to Work, WhiteHouse.gov, http://www.whitehouse.gov/economy/business/small-business.

8. Jennifer Epstein, "Obama: Gas Prices 'Make Things Harder,'" Politico, March 17, 2012, http://www.politico.com/politico44/2012/03/obama-no-silver-bullet-on-gas-117754.html.

9. "Five More Scandals Obama Knew Nothing About," The Washington Free Beacon, October 28, 2013, http://freebeacon.com/issues/five-more-scandals-obama-knew-nothing-about/.

10. "Obama: 'I'm a Warrior for the Middle Class,'" RealClearPolitics, September 22, 2011, http://www.realclearpolitics.com/video/2011/09/22/obama_im_a_class_warrior.html.

11. "Obama: 'This Is the Most Transparent Administration in History,'" RealClear-Politics, February 14, 2013, http://www.realclearpolitics.com/video/2013/02/14/obama_this_is_the_most_transparent_administration_in_history.html.

12. Paula Bolyard, "The Hill Calls Obama's 'Clinging to Their Guns and Religion' Comment a 'Gaffe,'" RedState, August 21, 2012, http://www.redstate.com/paulkib/2012/08/21/the-hill-calls-obamas-clinging-to-their-guns-and-religion-comment-a-gaffe/.

Chapter 11: Your Elevator Pitch

1. The $127 trillion total national debt plus unfunded liabilities, divided by the total U.S. population of 313.9 million Vance Ginn, "You Think the Deficit Is Bad? Federal Unfunded Liabilities Exceed $127 Trillion," Forbes, January 17, 2014, http://www.forbes.com/sites/realspin/2014/01/17/you-think-the-deficit-is-bad-federal-unfunded-liabilities-exceed-127-trillion/.

2. Amy Payne, "Morning Bell: $16,000,000,000,000," The Heritage Foundation, September 5, 2012, http://blog.heritage.org/2012/09/05/morning-bell-16000000000000/.

3. "How the 'Single Mother Factor' Was Responsible for Obama's Win," Examiner. com, no date, http://www.examiner.com/article/how-the-single-mother-factor-was-responsible-for-obama-s-win-1.

Chapter 12: The Seinfeld Strategy

1. "The Opposite," Seinfeld Quotes, pkmeco, http://www.pkmeco.com/seinfeld/opposite.htm.

2. "Obama Signs Trillion-Dollar 'Farm Bill', 80% Goes to Food Stamps," TeaParty. org, February 9, 2014, http://www.teaparty.org/obama-signs-trillion-dollar-farm-bill-80-goes-food-stamps-34440/.

3. Daniel Halper, "Food Stamp Growth 75x Greater than Job Creation," *Weekly Standard*, November 2, 2012, http://www.weeklystandard.com/blogs/food-stamp-growth-75x-greater-job-creation_660073.html.

4. Ira Stoll, "Yes, Actually, Obamacare Is the Biggest Tax Increase in History," *Reason*, July 9, 2012, http://reason.com/archives/2012/07/09/yes-actually-obamacare-is-the-biggest-ta.

5.   Sarah Hurtubise, "Report: Premiums Rising Faster than Eight Years before Obamacare Combined," Daily Caller, March 18, 2014, http://dailycaller.com/2014/03/18/report-premiums-rising-faster-than-eight-years-before-obamacare-combined/.

6.   "AmericaDeathWatch—Why Can't We Be like Canada?" AMERICA DEATH-WATCH, http://www.americadeathwatch.com/why-cant-we-be-like-canada.php/.

7.   Susan Jones, "Senator to Obama: 'Stop Stalling' on Keystone XL Pipeline," CNS News, December 18, 2013, http://cnsnews.com/news/article/susan-jones/senator-obama-stop-stalling-keystone-xl-pipeline.

8.   Ben Shapiro, "Obama Shuts Down 1.6M Acres to Oil Shale Development," Breit-bart, November 9, 2012, http://dailycaller.com/2014/04/08/obama-admin-leases-the-lowest-amount-of-federal-land-in-25-years/; "Costing American Jobs, Increasing Energy Prices," in "American Energy Roadblocks by the Obama Admin-istration," Committee on Natural Resources, http://dailycaller.com/2014/04/08/obama-admin-leases-the-lowest-amount-of-federal-land-in-25-years/; Michael Bastasch, "Obama Admin. Leases the Lowest Amount of Federal Land in 25 Years," Daily Caller, April 8, 2014, http://dailycaller.com/2014/04/08/obama-admin-leases-the-lowest-amount-of-federal-land-in-25-years/.

9.   "Oversight: Obama Admin. Decision to Include Gulf Drilling Moratorium in DOI Report," Committee on Natural Resources, http://naturalresources.house.gov/oversight/moratorium/.

10.   Mark Drajem, "EPA Takes First Step Toward Regulating Fracking Chemicals," Bloomerg, May 9, 2014, http://www.bloomberg.com/news/2014-05-09/epa-considers-requiring-disclosure-of-fracking-chemicals.html.

11.   Chris Tomlinson, Associated Press, "Economists: Texas Economy Strong, Getting Stronger," Yahoo! News, March 28, 2014, http://news.yahoo.com/economists-texas-economy-strong-getting-225507331.html;_ylt=Ai9krN_byTt_oVnqBtj7S6n-QtDMD;_ylu=X3oDMTBsNGg1aHNnBGNvbG8DYmYxBHBvcwM0BHNlYwNzcg—.

12.   Avik Roy, "Two Obamacare Mandates That Dramatically Expand the Internal Revenue Service's Power," Forbes, May 17, 2013, http://www.forbes.com/sites/theapothecary/2013/05/17/two-obamacare-mandates-that-dramatically-expand-the-internal-revenue-services-power/; Sam Graves, "The Tax Burden for Small Business Is Getting Worse," Fiscal Times, April 9, 2014, http://www.thefiscaltimes.com/Columns/2014/04/09/Tax-Burden-Small-Business-Getting-Worse; Joy Tay-lor, "14 IRS Audit Red Flags" (slideshow including "Running a Small Business," Kiplinger, updated February 2014, http://www.kiplinger.com/slideshow/taxes/T056-S001-irs-audit-red-flags-the-dirty-dozen-slide-show/index.html.

Chapter 13: Saving the Republican Party from Itself

1.   Mark Memmott, "Seahawks Fans Cause Earthquake, Set Noise Record," NPR, December 3, 2013, http://www.npr.org/blogs/thetwo-way/2013/12/03/248566190/seahawks-fans-cause-earthquake-set-noise-record.

2.   Mike Janela, "Seattle Seahawks Break Record for Loudest Stadium Crowd Roar," Guinness World Records, September 17, 2013, http://www.guinnessworldrecords.es/news/2013/9/seattle-seahawks-break-record-for-loudest-stadium-crowd-roar-51331.

3.   "12 Flag Raisers," A Gameday Tradition, SeaHawks.com, http://www.seahawks.com/12th-Man/flag-raisers.html.

4.   Christy Karras, "Boeing Celebrates Seahawks with 12th Man 747," Yahoo! Travel, January 30, 2014, http://travel.yahoo.com/blogs/compass/boeing-celebrates-seahawks-with-12th-man-747-235234752.html.

5.   "Conservatives Question US Chamber's Plan to Spend Millions to Defeat Tea Party Style Candidates in 2014," Fox News, January 11, 2014, http://www.foxnews.com/politics/2014/01/11/conservatives-question-us-chamber-plan-to-spend-millions-to-defeat-tea-party/.

6.   Rosa Ramirez, "10 Amazing Demographic Percentages of the 2012 Election," November 9, 2012, http://www.nationaljournal.com/thenextamerica/politics/10-amazing-demographic-percentages-of-the-2012-election-20121109.

7.   "Full List of Obamacare Tax Hikes," U.S. Congressman Jeff Duncan's website, http://jeffduncan.house.gov/full-list-obamacare-tax-hikes.

8.   Wayne Allyn Root, "Explaining Why Obama's Poll Numbers Are Close to Zero among White Voters," Townhall, March 12, 2014, http://townhall.com/columnists/wayneallynroot/2014/03/12/explaining-why-obamas-poll-numbers-are-close-to-zero-among-white-voters-n1807364/page/full.

9.   Melanie Batley, "Christie Facing Multiple State, Federal Probes for Misuse of Funds, Bridge-Gate," Newsmax, January 13, 2014, http://www.newsmax.com/Newsfront/chris-christie-sandy-funds-federal/2014/01/13/id/546701/.

Chapter 14: Make the GOP the Party of the Middle Class

1.   Shaila Dewan and Robert Gebeloff, "Among the Wealthiest 1 Percent, Many Variations," *New York Times*, January 14, 2012, http://www.nytimes.com/2012/01/15/business/the-1-percent-paint-a-more-nuanced-portrait-of-the-rich.html?pagewanted=all.

2.   Derek Thompson, "How You, I, and Everyone Got the Top 1 Percent All Wrong," *The Atlantic*, March 30, 2014, http://www.theatlantic.com/business/archive/2014/03/how-you-i-and-everyone-got-the-top-1-percent-all-wrong/359862/.

3.   Roberto Frank, "Buffett's Wealth Soared $37 Million a Day in 2013," CNBC, December 18, 2013, http://www.cnbc.com/id/101282625.

4.   Steve Hargreaves, "15% of Americans Living in Poverty," CNN Money, September 17, 2013, http://money.cnn.com/2013/09/17/news/economy/poverty-income/.

5.   Alexander Eichler, "Warren Buffett Wins, Goldman Sachs Loses in Big Loan Sell-Off," Huffington Post, April 12, 2012, http://www.huffingtonpost.com/2012/04/12/warren-buffett-goldman-sachs_n_1420804.html/; Bethany McLean, "No, You Can't Invest like Warren Buffett," Slate, August 30, 2011, http://www.slate.com/articles/business/moneybox/2011/08/no_you_cant_invest_like_warren_buffett.html; Jim Efstathiou Jr., "Buffett's Burlington Northern among Pipeline Winners," Bloomberg, January 23, 2012, http://www.bloomberg.com/news/2012-01-23/buffett-s-burlington-northern-among-winners-in-obama-rejection-of-pipeline.html.

6.   Quotes and excerpts from Saul Alinsky, *Rules for Radicals*, available on Crossroads, http://www.crossroad.to/Quotes/communism/alinsky.htm.

7.   Danny Tirza, "Israeli Security Fence Architect: Why the Barrier Had to Be Built," Al-Monitor, July 1, 2012, http://www.al-monitor.com/pulse/originals/2012/al-monitor/israeli-security-fence-architect.html.

8.   Edwin S. Rubenstein, "Rubenstein: Collecting Billions in a Loophole," *Washington Times*, April 16, 2013, http://www.washingtontimes.com/news/2013/apr/16/collecting-billions-in-a-loophole-fraudulent-tax-r/.

9.   Melanie Hicken, "Moody's Downgrades Chicago amid Pension Crisis," CNN Money, March 4, 2014, http://money.cnn.com/2014/03/04/news/chicago-credit-rating/.

10. Pajamas Media, "Wisconsin Goes from $3 Billion Deficit to $300 Million Surplus," *The New Media Journal*, http://nation.foxnews.com/2014/01/26/turnaround-1-billion-surplus-wisconsingov-scott-walker-returning-it-taxpayers; Mary Spicuzza and Matthew DeFour, "Turnaround! $1 Billion Surplus in Wisconsin.... Gov. Scott Walker Returning It to Taxpayers," Fox News, no date, http://nation.foxnews.com/2014/01/26/turnaround-1-billion-surplus-wisconsingov-scott-walker-returning-it-taxpayers.

Chapter 15: Tea Party Infusion

1.   "Rand Paul: 'We've Come to Take Our Government Back,'" RealClearPolitics, May 18, 2010, http://www.realclearpolitics.com/video/2010/05/18/rand_paul_weve_come_to_take_our_government_back.html.

2.   "Republican David Jolly Beats Alex Sink in Florida Special Election," Fox News, March 12, 2014, http://www.foxnews.com/politics/2014/03/12/republican-david-

jolly-beats-alex-sink-in-florida-special-election/; Kate Bradshaw, "Sink Announces Candidacy in District 13 Congressional Race," *Tampa Tribune*, October 30, 2013, http://tbo.com/pinellas-county/alex-sink-announces-her-candidacy-in-district-13-congressional-race-20131030/.

3. Jason Howerton, "If Historic Pa. Senate Race Has Any National Implications, Democrats—and Some Republicans—Should Start Worrying," The Blaze, March 19, 2014, http://www.theblaze.com/stories/2014/03/19/if-historic-pa-senate-race-has-any-national-implications-democrats-and-some-republicans-should-start-worrying/.

4. "Conservative Political Action Conference 2014, Straw Poll Results," C-SPAN, March 8, 2014, http://www.c-span.org/video/?318148-15/cpac-2014-straw-poll-results.

5. Rick Sincere, "CPAC Straw Poll Suggests Libertarian ARC in Conservative Movement," Bearing Drift, no date, http://bearingdrift.com/2014/03/09/cpac-straw-poll-suggests-libertarian-arc-in-conservative-movement.

6. "In Senate Race in Colorado, Dems Move to Portray Strong GOP Challenger as Extremist," Fox News, March 29, 2014, http://www.foxnews.com/politics/2014/03/29/in-senate-race-in-colorado-dems-move-to-portray-strong-gop-challenger-as/.

Chapter 16: The First Plank in the Platform

1. Robert Greenstein, Chye-Ching Huang , and Chuck Marr, "Can Governor Romney's Tax Plan Meet Its Stated Revenue, Deficit, and Distributional Goals at the Same Time?" Center on Budget and Policy Priorities, March 2, 2012, http://www.cbpp.org/cms/?fa=view&id=3695.

2. Jonathan Cohn, "The Romney Budget Is Even More Radical than the Ryan Budget," *New Republic*, August 13, 2012, http://www.newrepublic.com/article/106063/mitt-romney-praised-ryan-budget-adopted-most-important-features-now-hes-trying-disown.

3. Michelle Malkin, "5 Years Later: How's That Wreckovery Working Out for Ya?" MichelleMalkin.com, February 14, 2014, http://michellemalkin.com/2014/02/14/5-years-later-hows-that-wreckovery-working-out-for-ya/.

4. "Obama Jokes at Jobs Council: 'Shovel-Ready Was Not as Shovel-Ready as We Expected,'" Fox News, http://nation.foxnews.com/president-obama/2011/06/13/obama-jokes-jobs-council-shovel-ready-was-not-shovel-ready-we-expected.

5. See the list of "State Sales Tax Holidays" at the Federation of Tax Administrators website, http://www.taxadmin.org/fta/rate/sales_holiday.html.

6. Alex Ben Block, "California Sees Huge Drop in Film Production, Ranks behind Louisiana and the U.K.," The Hollywood Reporter, March 6, 2014, http://www.hollywoodreporter.com/news/financial-incentives-helped-louisiana-attract-686402.

Chapter 17: A Middle Class Contract with America

1. "Cuba to Cut One Million Public Sector Jobs," BBC News, September 14, 2010, http://www.bbc.com/news/world-latin-america-11291267.
2. National Economic Council, "The Small Business Agenda," U.S. Small Business Administration, May 2011, http://www.sba.gov/sites/default/files/Small%20Business%20Agenda%20NEC.pdf.
3. Richard Rubin, "Cash Abroad Rises $206 Billion as Apple to IBM Avoid Tax," Bloomberg, May 12, 2014, http://www.bloomberg.com/news/2014-03-12/cash-abroad-rises-206-billion-as-apple-to-ibm-avoid-tax.html.
4. Susan E. Dudley, "Costs of New Regulations Issued in 2012 Dwarf Those of Previous Years, According to OMB Report," Regulatory Studies Center of George Washington University, April 22, 2013, http://research.columbian.gwu.edu/regulatorystudies/sites/default/files/u41/20130422_OMB_Report.pdf.
5. "Quick Facts," Small Businesses for Sensible Regulations, http://www.sensibleregulations.org/resources/facts-and-figures/.
6. "Small Businesses and Manufacturers: Government a Barrier, Not a Help, to Economic Growth," National Association of Manufacturers, September 25, 2012, http://www.nam.org/Communications/Articles/2012/09/Small-Businesses-and-Manufacturers-Government-a-Barrier-Not-a-Help-to-Economic-Growth.aspx; "Executive Summary" of NFIB and NAM Survey of Small Businesses and Manufacturers, conducted by Public Opinion Strategies, posted September 25, 2012, http://pos.org/documents/executive_summary.pdf.
7. "Quick Facts," Small Businesses for Sensible Regulations.
8. Daniel de Vise, "Student Loans Surpass Auto, Credit Card Debt," Washington Post, March 6, 2012, http://www.washingtonpost.com/blogs/college-inc/post/student-loans-surpass-auto-credit-card-debt/2012/03/06/gIQARFQnuR_blog.html; Shahien Nasiripour and Chris Kirkham, "Student Loan Defaults Surge to Highest Level in Nearly 2 Decades," Huffington Post, September 30, 2013, http://www.huffingtonpost.com/2013/09/30/student-loans-default_n_4019806.html.
9. Jeffrey H. Anderson, "The Cost of Obama," Weekly Standard, February 14, 2012, http://www.weeklystandard.com/blogs/painful-cost-obama_629745.html.
10. Romina Boccia, Alison Acosta Fraser, and Emily Goff, "Federal Spending by the Numbers, 2013: Government Spending Trends in Graphics, Tables, and Key

Points," The Heritage Foundation, August 20, 2013, http://www.heritage.org/research/reports/2013/08/federal-spending-by-the-numbers-2013; "Government Revenue in the US," "Federal 2013 Government Revenue," Government Revenue in the United States of America website, http://www.usgovernmentrevenue.com/fed_revenue_2013US.

11. Suzy Khimm, "The Sequester, Explained," *Washington Post*, September 14, 2012, http://www.washingtonpost.com/blogs/wonkblog/wp/2012/09/14/the-sequester-explained/.

12. Paul Roderick Gregory, "The $995 Billion Sequester Cut Is Actually a $110 Billion Spending Increase," Forbes, February 19, 2013, http://www.forbes.com/sites/paulroderickgregory/2013/02/19/the-995-billion-sequester-cut-is-actually-a-110-billion-spending-increase/.

13. "Time for a Yard Sale? Selling Excess Property Could Net Government Billions," Fox News, December 28, 2012, http://www.foxnews.com/politics/2012/12/28/time-for-yard-sale-selling-excess-property-could-net-billions-for-cash-strapped/.

14. Chris Rodell, "Sin City's dirty little secret: It's full of churches," MSN, March 29, 2011, http://www.nbcnews.com/id/42074829/ns/travel-destination_travel/t/sin-citys-dirty-little-secret-its-full-churches/#.U3Nk9l6HDHM.

15. Caroline Fairchild, "Legalizing Marijuana Would Generate Billions in Additional Tax Revenue Annually," Huffington Post, April 20, 2013, http://www.huffingtonpost.com/2013/04/20/legalizing-marijuana-tax-revenue_n_3102003.html.

16. Kelly Phillips Erb, "It's No Toke: Colorado Pulls in Millions in Marijuana Tax Revenue," Forbes, March 11, 2014, http://www.forbes.com/sites/kellyphillipserb/2014/03/11/its-no-toke-colorado-pulls-in-millions-in-marijuana-tax-revenue/.

17. Diane Francis, "The Keystone Pipeline Is Obama's Best Revenge on Putin," *New York Post*, March 29, 2014, http://nypost.com/2014/03/29/the-keystone-pipeline-is-obamas-best-revenge-on-putin/.

18. "API: Nearly Two Dozen LNG Export Applications Waiting for Approval, Would Spur Massive Investment," WePartyPatriots.com, October 17, 2013, http://wepartypatriots.com/wp/2013/10/17/api-nearly-two-dozen-lng-export-applications-waiting-for-approval-would-spur-massive-investment/.

19. Patrick DeHaan, "No New Oil Refineries since the 1970s, But Capacity Has Grown," *U.S. News & World Report*, July 29, 2011, http://www.usnews.com/opinion/blogs/on-energy/2011/07/29/no-new-oil-refineries-since-the-1970s-but-capacity-has-grown

Chapter 18: Three Necessary Fixes

1. Mike Adams, "Big Pharma Profiteering Gone Wild: $1,000-a-Pill Hepatitis Drug in USA Sells for Less than $10 in Egypt," Natural News, March 26, 2014, http://www.naturalnews.com/044463_big_pharma_profiteering_sovaldi_overpriced_drugs.html.

2. Alexis Simendinger, "White House Staff Salaries Released; 141 Earn $100,000 or More," RealClearPolitics, July 1, 2011, http://www.realclearpolitics.com/articles/2011/07/01/white_house_staff_salaries_released_141_earn_100000_or_more_110454.html.

3. Karl, "Meet the Obama Super-PAC Mega-Donors," Hot Air, July 5, 2012, http://hotair.com/archives/2012/07/05/meet-the-obama-super-pac-mega-donors/; David Frum, "Trial lawyers could win bonanza in health care reform," CNN, November 9, 2009, http://www.cnn.com/2009/OPINION/11/09/frum.trial.lawyers.victory/index.html?_s=PM:OPINION.

4. Debra Beaulieu-Volk, "Defensive Medicine Accounts for One-Third of Health Costs, Hospital Execs Say," FierceHealthcare, April 11, 2014, http://www.fiercehealthcare.com/story/defensive-medicine-accounts-one-third-health-costs-hospital-execs-say/2014-04-11.

5. Floyd Norris, "No Surprise Fed Was Biggest Buyer of Treasuries in 2013," *New York Times*, February 21, 2014, http://www.nytimes.com/2014/02/22/business/economy/no-surprise-fed-was-biggest-buyer-of-treasuries-in-2013.html?_r=0.

6. "Hundreds of Cases of Potential Voter Fraud Uncovered in North Carolina," Fox News, April 3, 2014, http://www.foxnews.com/politics/2014/04/03/hundreds-cases-potential-voter-fraud-uncovered-in-north-carolina/?intcmp=latestnews.

7. "Vote Totals for Obama Exceed Registered Voters in Some Districts," Intelligent US Politics, http://intelligentuspolitics.com/vote-totals-for-obama-exceed-registered-voters-in-some-districts/.

8. Lachlan Markay, "Report: GOP Election Officials Forcibly Removed in Philadelphia," The Heritage Foundation, November 6, 2012, http://blog.heritage.org/2012/11/06/report-philadelphia-poll-watchers-forcibly-removed-for-partisan-reasons/; Madeleine Morgenstern, "Penn. Judge Orders Reinstatement of GOP Election Monitors Allegedly Kicked Out By Dems," The Blaze, November 6, 2012, http://www.theblaze.com/stories/2012/11/06/penn-judge-orders-reinstatement-of-gop-election-monitors-allegedly-kicked-out-by-dems/.

9. Mackenzie Weinger, "Report: 1.8M Dead Registered to Vote," Politico, February 14, 2012, http://www.politico.com/news/stories/0212/72830.html.

10. Cheryl Carpenter Klimek, "NAACP Marchers Protesting Voter ID Laws Advised to Bring ... Photo ID," BizPac Review, February 8, 2014, http://www.bizpacreview.

com/2014/02/08/naacp-marchers-protesting-voter-id-laws-advised-to-bring-photo-id-99508.

11. Patrick Howley, "Six-Time Obama Voter's Group Received Obama Administration Grant," Daily Caller, March 24, 2014, http://dailycaller.com/2014/03/24/six-time-obama-voters-group-received-obama-administration-grant/.

Chapter 19: The Most Important Sales Job in History

1. H. Paul Lillebo, "U.S. Elections—Grin and Win," *Blue Ridge Journal*, September/November 2004, http://www.blueridgejournal.com/brj-elections.htm.

2. Sasha Issenberg, "Why Obama Is Better at Getting Out the Vote," Slate, November 5, 2012, http://www.slate.com/articles/news_and_politics/victory_lab/2012/11/obama_s_get_out_the_vote_effort_why_it_s_better_than_romney_s.html.

3. Maggie Haberman and Alexander Burns, "Romney's fail whale: ORCA the vote-tracker left team 'flying blind,'" Politico, November 8, 2012, http://www.politico.com/blogs/burns-haberman/2012/11/romneys-fail-whale-orca-the-votetracker-149098.html.

4. Billy House, "What Can Republicans Learn from Steve Pearce?" *National Journal*, April 14, 2013, http://www.nationaljournal.com/daily/what-can-republicans-learn-from-steve-pearce-20130814.

5. Ibid.

6. "Hochberg, Audrey G.," OurCampaigns.com, http://www.ourcampaigns.com/CandidateDetail.html?CandidateID=45328.

Chapter 20: The Magic of Branding

1. Eric Scheiner, "Cancer Patient and ObamaCare Critic Says He's Being Audited by IRS," CNS News, December 2, 2013, http://www.cnsnews.com/mrctv-blog/eric-scheiner/cancer-patient-and-obamacare-critic-says-hes-being-audited-irs.

2. David Martosko and Lydia Warren, "Bullyboy White House Aide Sparks Outrage by 'Smearing' Terminal Cancer Patient Who Dared Speak Out against Obamacare," *Daily Mail*, November 4, 2013, updated November 5, 2013, http://www.dailymail.co.uk/news/article-2487518/Stage-4-cancer-sufferer-unhappy-Obamacare-gets-White-House-pushback.html.

3. Guy Benson, "Family of Six-Year-Old Cancer Patient Loses Coverage, Now Faces Soaring Premiums," Townhall, December 3, 2013, http://townhall.com/tipsheet/guybenson/2013/12/03/family-of-sixyearold-cancer-patient-loses-coverage-now-faces-soaring-premiums-n1756782.

4.   Guy Benson, "Brutal: Nevada Man Stuck with $407,000 Obamacare Bill," Townhall, March 19, 2014, http://townhall.com/tipsheet/guybenson/2014/03/19/video-nevada-man-stuck-with-407000-obamacare-bill-n1810971.

5.   "Losing Health Insurance Due to Obamacare," The Heritage Foundation, November 15, 2013, http://www.heritage.org/research/factsheets/2013/11/losing-health-insurance-due-to-obamacare.

6.   Sarah Hurtubise, "Survey: US Sees Sharpest Health Insurance Premium Increases in Years," Daily Caller, April 7, 2014, http://dailycaller.com/2014/04/07/survey-us-sees-sharpest-health-insurance-premium-increases-in-years/.

7.   Chris Conover, "Obamacare Will Cost 2.9 Million or More Jobs a Year," Forbes, February 24, 2014, http://www.forbes.com/sites/chrisconover/2014/02/24/obamacare-will-cost-2-9-million-or-more-jobs-a-year/.

8.   Avik Roy, "Obamacare May Be Causing a Shift to Part-Time Workers in Illinois," Forbes, February 24, 2014, http://www.forbes.com/sites/theapothecary/2014/02/24/obamacare-may-be-causing-a-shift-to-part-time-workers-in-illinois/.

9.   "Moms Are Mad over ObamaCare," GOP Research, March 10, 2014, http://www.gop.com/news/research/moms-are-mad-over-obamacare/.

10. "NY Small Business Forced to Drop Employee Insurance under Obamacare," Washington Free Beacon, January 17, 2014, http://freebeacon.com/issues/ny-small-business-forced-to-drop-employee-insurance-under-obamacare/.

11. Noah Rothman, "Poll: 41% of Small Businesses Froze Hiring Due to Obamacare, 19% Have Laid off Employees," Mediaite, June 21, 2013, http://www.mediaite.com/online/poll-41-of-small-businesses-froze-hiring-due-to-obamacare-19-have-laid-off-employees/.

12. Amelia Hamilton, "Obamacare Forces Bonnie Doon Ice Cream to Close," FreedomWorks, October 16, 2013, http://www.freedomworks.org/content/obamacare-forces-bonnie-doon-ice-cream-close.

13. Richard Pollock, "Feds Reviewed Only One Bid for Obamacare Website Design," *Washington Examiner*, October 13, 2013, http://washingtonexaminer.com/feds-reviewed-only-one-bid-for-obamacare-website-design/article/2537194.

14. Courtney Coren, "Tech Experts: HealthCare.gov Should Cost Less Than $10 Million," NewsMax, December 5, 2013, http://www.newsmax.com/Newsfront/health-care-website-cost-Chung/2013/12/05/id/540176/; Peter Gosselin, "Late It Cash Surge Foreshadowed Health-Law Woes," Bloomberg, October 24, 2013, http://about.bgov.com/2013-10-24/late-it-cash-surge-foreshadowed-health-law-woes/.

15. Patrick Howley, "Michelle Obama's Princeton Classmate Is Executive at Company That Built Obamacare Website," Daily Caller, October 25, 2013, http://dailycaller.com/2013/10/25/michelle-obamas-princeton-classmate-is-executive-at-company-that-built-obamacare-website/.

16.   Robert Oak, "ObamaCare Gets Outsourced amid Unemployment Crisis," *New York Post*, January 18, 2014, http://nypost.com/2014/01/18/obamacare-gets-outsourced-amid-unemployment-crisis/.

17.   Eugene Kontorovitch, "The Constitutionality of the ObamaCare 'Fix,'" The Volokh Conspiracy, November 14, 2013, http://www.volokh.com/2013/11/14/constitutionality-obamacare-fix/.

18.   Avik Roy, "Obama Officials in 2010: 93 Million Americans Will Be Unable to Keep Their Health Plans under Obama," Forbes, October 31, 2013, http://www.forbes.com/sites/theapothecary/2013/10/31/obama-officials-in-2010-93-million-americans-will-be-unable-to-keep-their-health-plans-under-obamacare/.

19.   Ed Morrissey, "Gallup: Majority of Democrats Have Positive Image of Socialism," Hot Air, February 5, 2010, http://hotair.com/archives/2010/02/05/gallup-majority-of-democrats-have-positive-image-of-socialism/.

20.   "Your Safety," National Park Service, no date, http://www.nps.gov/wica/planyourvisit/yoursafety.htm.

21.   Daniel Halper, "Report: U.S. Spent $3.7 Trillion on Welfare over Past 5 Years," *Weekly Standard*, October 23, 2013, http://www.weeklystandard.com/blogs/report-us-spent-37-trillion-welfare-over-last-5-years_764582.html.

22.   The $127 trillion total national debt plus unfunded liabilities, divided by the total U.S. population of 313.9 million, see Vance Ginn, "You Think the Deficit Is Bad? Federal Unfunded Liabilities Exceed $127 Trillion," Forbes, January 17, 2014, http://www.forbes.com/sites/realspin/2014/01/17/you-think-the-deficit-is-bad-federal-unfunded-liabilities-exceed-127-trillion/.

23.   Daniel Halper, "Food Stamp Growth 75X Greater than Job Creation," *Weekly Standard*, November 2, 2012, http://www.weeklystandard.com/blogs/food-stamp-growth-75x-greater-job-creation_660073.html.

24.   Maxim Lott, "US Gives 4 More F-16 Fighter Jets to Egyptian Government Despite Outcry," Fox News, April 11, 2013, http://www.foxnews.com/politics/2013/04/11/us-gives-4-more-f-16-fighter-jets-to-egyptian-government/.

25.   "Now Is the Time: The President's Plan to Protect Our Children and Our Communities by Reducing Gun Violence," WhiteHouse.gov, January 16, 2013, http://www.whitehouse.gov/sites/default/files/docs/wh_now_is_the_time_full.pdf.

26.   Susan Cornwell, "Congress Votes to Repeal Military Pension Cuts," Reuters, February 12, 2014, http://www.reuters.com/article/2014/02/12/us-usa-military-cuts-idUSBREA1B26A20140212.

27.   Terence P. Jeffrey, "U.S. Gov't Funding $313M in Mortgages—for Palestinians on West Bank," CNS News, August 27, 2013, http://cnsnews.com/news/article/us-govt-funding-313m-mortgages-palestinians-west-bank.

28. Emily Miller, "Miller: Obama Calls Racism on Criminal Background Checks," *Washington Times*, July 2, 2013, http://www.washingtontimes.com/news/2013/jul/2/now-its-racist-to-pass-on-hiring-ex-cons/?page=all.

29. Todd Starnes, "Christians Outraged over Team Obama's Assault on German Homeschooled Family," Fox News, March 4, 2014, http://www.foxnews.com/opinion/2014/03/04/christians-outraged-over-team-obama-assault-on-german-homeschool-family/.

30. Neil Munro, "Obama Hints at Another Quasi-Amnesty for Illegal Immigrants," Daily Caller, March 14, 2014, http://dailycaller.com/2014/03/14/obama-hints-at-another-quasi-amnesty-for-illegals/.

31. Edwin S. Rubenstein, "Rubenstein: Collecting Billions in a Loophole," *Washington Times*, April 16, 2013, http://www.washingtontimes.com/news/2013/apr/16/collecting-billions-in-a-loophole-fraudulent-tax-r/.

32. Matt Smith, "Obama Signs Bill Warding Off Fiscal Cliff," CNN, January 3, 2013, http://www.cnn.com/2013/01/02/politics/fiscal-cliff/.

33. Cheryl K. Chumley, "TSA Humiliates Cancer Patient: 'He's Wearing a Diaper!'" *Washington Times*, February 11, 2014, http://www.washingtontimes.com/news/2014/feb/11/tsa-humiliates-cancer-patient-hes-wearing-diaper/.

34. "TSA Pats Down 3-Year-Old in Leg Cast and Wheelchair (Video)," Huffington Post, March 19, 2012, http://www.huffingtonpost.com/2012/03/19/tsa-pats-down-3-year-old-_n_1361843.html.

35. Katherine Connell, "Obama: Voter-ID Laws Probably 'Partisan,' but Also Have 'Racial Element,'" National Review Online, August 29, 2013, http://www.nationalreview.com/corner/357131/obama-voter-id-laws-probably-partisan-also-have-racial-element-katherine-connell.

36. "Steve Stockman: Will Eric Holder Sue over Obamacare Photo IDs?" Twitchy.com, October 4, 2013, http://twitchy.com/2013/10/04/steve-stockman-will-eric-holder-sue-over-obamacare-photo-ids/.

37. Josh Gerstein, "Obama Administration Again Backs University of Texas in Affirmative Action Case," Politico, November 1, 2013, http://www.politico.com/blogs/under-the-radar/2013/11/obama-administration-again-backs-university-of-texas-176537.html; Allie Bidwell, "Obama Administration Ok's 'Lawful' College Affirmative Action Programs," *U.S. News & World Report*, September 27, 2013, http://www.usnews.com/news/articles/2013/09/27/obama-administration-oks-lawful-college-affirmative-action-programs

38. Daniel Greenfield, "Obama Bows to Cuban Dictator Raul Castro," FrontPageMagazine, December 10, 2013, http://www.frontpagemag.com/2013/dgreenfield/obama-bows-shakes-hands-with-cuban-dictator-raul-castro/; Allahpundit, "Sigh: Obama Bows to Chinese Leader," Hot Air, April 12, 2010, http://hotair.com/

archives/2010/04/12/sigh-obama-bows-to-chinese-leader/; Jeffrey T. Kuhner, "Kuhner: Obama Bowing to the World," *Washington Times*, April 16, 2010, http://www.washingtontimes.com/news/2010/apr/16/obama-bowing-to-the-world/?page=all.

39. John Steel Gordon, "Obama, Johnson, and Congress," The American, September 24, 2013, http://www.american.com/archive/2013/september/obama-johnson-and-congress; Jackie Calmes and Jonathan Weisman, "Obama Sets Conditions for Talks: Pass Funding and Raise Debt Ceiling," *New York Times*, October 2, 2013, http://www.nytimes.com/2013/10/03/us/politics/congress-budget-battle.html?_r=0&gwh=43F797CCB26FFDA1D3F700914480D916&gwt=pay.

40. Carrie Dann contributed, "White House Cancels Tours, Citing Sequester," NBC News, March 5, 2013, http://firstread.nbcnews.com/_news/2013/03/05/17197602-white-house-cancels-tours-citing-sequester?lite.

41. Ashley Halsey III and Luz Lazo, "Flights Are Delayed at Major East Coast Airports as Sequester-Related Furloughs Begin," *Washington Post*, April 22, 2013, http://www.washingtonpost.com/local/trafficandcommuting/flights-delayed-at-major-east-coast-airports-furloughs-blamed/2013/04/22/229bac7c-ab3e-11e2-b6fd-ba6f5f26d70e_story.html.

42. "U.S. Acknowledges Thousands of Illegal Immigrants Released from Jails," CBS News, March 14, 2013, http://www.cbsnews.com/news/us-acknowledges-thousands-of-illegal-immigrants-released-from-jails/.

43. Nick Wing, "Obama Africa Trip to Cost Up to $100 Million: Report," Huffington Post, June 14, 2013, http://www.huffingtonpost.com/2013/06/14/obama-africa-trip_n_3441510.html.

44. Faith Karimi and Matt Smith, "Obama Pledges $7 Billion to Upgrade Power in Africa," CNN, June 30, 2013, http://www.cnn.com/2013/06/30/world/africa/south-africa-obama-pledge/.

45. Sam Stein, "Sandra Fluke Receives Call from Obama after Rush Limbaugh 'Slut' Comments," Huffington Post, March 2, 2012, http://www.huffingtonpost.com/2012/03/02/sandra-fluke-obama-rush-limbaugh_n_1316631.html; John McCormack, "Weekly Standard: Target Sells Pills for $9 a Month," *Weekly Standard*, available at NPR, March 2, 2012, http://www.npr.org/2012/03/02/147820584/weekly-standard-target-sells-pills-for-9-a-month.

46. "Tuition and Fees," 2013–2014 Georgetown Law Student Handbook of Academic Policies, http://www.law.georgetown.edu/campus-services/registrar/handbook/upload/Tuition_and_Fees.pdf.

47. "Excrement Floats to the Top: First Tier Georgetown University Law Center," Third Tier Reality blog, February 26, 2012, http://thirdtierreality.blogspot.com/2012/02/excrement-floats-to-top-first-tier.html.

48. Andrew Seidman, "Obama Administration Favored Union Worker Pensions in GM Bailout, House Republicans Say," *Los Angeles Times*, June 23, 2011, http://articles.latimes.com/2011/jun/23/business/la-fi-gm-bailout-review-20110623; Tom Krisher, "U.S. exits G.M. stake; taxpayers lose $10.5 billion," NBC News, December 9, 2013, http://www.nbcnews.com/business/autos/u-s-exits-gm-stake-taxpayers-lose-10-5-billion-f2D11716261.

49. Shane Wright, "The Lie of Obama's Fairness Doctrine," FreedomWorks, July 25, 2013, http://www.freedomworks.org/content/lie-obamas-fairness-doctrine; David Harsanyi, "Obama's 'Fairness' Fiction," RealClearPolitics, April 11, 2012, http://www.realclearpolitics.com/articles/2012/04/11/obamas_fairness_fiction_113810.html; Rebecca Kaplan, "Obama Challenges Republicans to Support Paycheck Fairness Bill," CBS News, April 8, 2014, http://www.cbsnews.com/news/obama-challenges-republicans-to-support-paycheck-fairness-bill/.

50. Mark Modica, "Were Republicans Targeted in GM and Chrysler Dealership Closures?" National Legal and Policy Center, May 28, 2013, http://nlpc.org/stories/2013/05/28/were-republicans-targeted-gm-and-chrysler-dealership-closures.

51. Kent Hoover, "5 Things Businesses Should Know about Obama's Budget—No. 1. More IRS Agents (Video)," The Business Journals, March 4, 2014, http://www.bizjournals.com/bizjournals/washingtonbureau/2014/03/04/5-things-businesses-should-know-about.html?page=all; Andrew Malcolm, "36 Obama Aides Owe $833,000 in Back Taxes," *Investor's Business Daily*, January 26, 2012, http://news.investors.com/politics-andrew-malcolm/012612-599002-obama-white-house-staff-back-taxes.htm; Alex Spillius, "Tim Geithner's Tax Evasion," *The Telegraph*, January 22, 2009, http://blogs.telegraph.co.uk/news/alexspillius/8174427/Tim_Geithners_tax_evasion_/.

52. "Obama Ad Says Romney Stashed Money in Cayman Islands," PolitiFact.com, July 14, 2012, http://www.politifact.com/truth-o-meter/statements/2012/jul/17/barack-obama/obama-ad-says-romney-stashed-money-cayman-islands/.

53. Wynton Hall, "Jack Lew Holds Cayman Islands Fund Obama Called 'Largest Tax Scam in the World,'" Breitbart, February 14, 2013, http://www.breitbart.com/Big-Government/2013/02/14/Jack-Lew-Holds-Cayman-Islands-Fund-Obama-Called-Largest-Tax-Scam-In-The-World.

54. Patricia Campion, "Stunning Hypocrisy Is behind Obama's 'Fair Share' Rhetoric," Yahoo! News, April 17, 2012, http://news.yahoo.com/stunning-hypocrisy-behind-obamas-fair-share-rhetoric-221500533.html.

55. Obamamania, "Obama—Spread the Wealth Around," YouTube, https://www.youtube.com/watch?v=OoqI5PSRcXM.

56. Nina Melendez, "Socialite, Songwriter Denise Rich Renounces U.S. Citizenship," CNN Politics, July 11, 2012, http://www.cnn.com/2012/07/10/politics/denise-rich-citizenship/.

57. Alan Joel, "He Was against It before He Was for It: Obama on the Debt Ceiling in 2006 vs 2013," BearingDrift, http://bearingdrift.com/2013/09/19/he-was-against-it-before-he-was-for-it-obama-on-the-debt-ceiling-in-2006-vs-2013/.

58. Ali Meyer, "Debt up $6.666 Trillion under Obama," CNS News, February 4, 2014, http://cnsnews.com/news/article/ali-meyer/debt-6666-trillion-under-obama.

59. Goprapidresponse, "Obama: if You've Got a Business, You Didn't Build That," YouTube, https://www.youtube.com/watch?v=YKjPI6no5ng.

60. "Supporting Small Businesses," Jobs & the Economy: Putting America Back to Work, WhiteHouse.gov, http://www.whitehouse.gov/economy/business/small-business.

61. Penny Starr, "6,125 Proposed Regulations and Notifications Posted in Last 90 Days—Average 68 per Day," CNS News, November 9, 2012, http://cnsnews.com/news/article/6125-proposed-regulations-and-notifications-posted-last-90-days-average-68-day.

62. Joel B. Pollak, "Thank You, Obamacare: Families Pay $3000 More for Insurance; Obama Promised $2500 Decrease," Breitbart, September 25, 2012, http://www.breitbart.com/Big-Government/2012/09/25/Thank-You-Obamacare-Families-Pay-3000-More-Obama-Promised-2500-Decrease.

63. Roy, "Obama Officials in 2010: 93 Million Americans."

64. J. B. Wogan, "Green-Job Creation off Target for Now," PolitiFact.com, updated September 13, 2012, http://www.politifact.com/truth-o-meter/promises/obameter/promise/439/create-5-million-green-jobs/.

65. Tyler Durden, "Spain Youth Unemployment Rises to Record 57.7%, Surpasses Greece," Zero Hedge, January 8, 2014, http://www.zerohedge.com/news/2014-01-08/spain-youth-unemployment-rises-record-577-surpasses-greece.

66. Christopher Goins, "Michelle Obama: 'We Are in the Midst of a Huge Recovery,'" CNS News, October 15, 2012, http://cnsnews.com/news/article/michelle-obama-we-are-midst-huge-recovery.

67. "Remarks by the President at the Consumer Financial Protection Bureau," WhiteHouse.gov, January 6, 2012, http://www.whitehouse.gov/the-press-office/2012/01/06/remarks-president-consumer-financial-protection-bureau.

68. Michael Snyder, "10 Facts about the Growing Unemployment Crisis in America That Will Blow Your Mind," The Economic Collapse, November 10, 2013, http://theeconomiccollapseblog.com/archives/10-facts-about-the-growing-unemployment-crisis-in-america-that-will-blow-your-mind.

69. "Employment Data Show Low Labor-Force Rate for Men," *Wall Street Journal*, September 7, 2012, http://live.wsj.com/video/employment-data-show-low-labor-force-rate-for-men/B47D73B9-EEA5-4217-B0BF-738A2414FFA6.html#!B47D73B9-EEA5-4217-B0BF-738A2414FFA6.

70. "Carney: Drilling Has 'Dramatically Increased' in Last Three Years under Obama," RealClearPolitics, March 13, 2012, http://www.realclearpolitics.com/video/2012/03/13/carney_drilling_has_dramatically_increased_in_last_three_years_under_obama.html.

71. "Graphic of the Day: Drilling Permits down 36% under Obama Administration," Fox News, March 22, 2012, http://foxnewsinsider.com/2012/03/22/graphic-of-the-day-drilling-permits-down-36-under-obama-administration.

72. Barack Obama, "Transparency and Open Government" memorandum, WhiteHouse.gov, http://www.whitehouse.gov/the_press_office/TransparencyandOpenGovernment.

73. "Obama's Green Cronies Made DNC Cameo: Bundlers and Big Donors Tied to Billions of Stimulus Funds," The Green Corruption Files, September 21, 2012, http://greencorruption.blogspot.com/2012/09/obamas-green-cronies-made-dnc-cameo.html; John R. Lott Jr., "Where did stimulus money really go?" Fox News, March 23, 2013, http://www.foxnews.com/opinion/2012/03/23/where-did-stimulus-money-really-go/#ixzz2UPkkjOod.

74. Gregory Korte, "$162 Million in Stimulus Funds Not Disclosed," *USA Today*, updated October 6, 2010, http://usatoday30.usatoday.com/news/washington/2010-10-06-stimulus06_ST_N.htm?csp=34.

75. Hope Yen, "Postal Service Loss of $15.9 Billion Sets Record," Huffington Post, November 15, 2012, http://www.huffingtonpost.com/2012/11/15/postal-service-loss-_n_2137033.html.

76. Avik Roy, "Obamacare Bends the Cost Curve—Upward," National Review Online, September 24, 2013, http://www.nationalreview.com/corner/359352/obamacare-bends-cost-curve-upward-avik-roy.

77. Mark McKinnon, "It's about Medicare, Stupid!" The Daily Beast, June 10, 2011, http://www.thedailybeast.com/articles/2011/06/10/medicare-malpractice-how-doing-nothing-will-bankrupt-america.html.

78. Elizabeth Harrington, "Feds Spend $1.5 Million to Study Why Lesbians Are Fat," CNS News, March 11, 2013, http://cnsnews.com/news/article/feds-spend-15-million-study-why-lesbians-are-fat.

79. "Now Is the Time: The President's Plan to Protect Our Children."

80. Ibid.

81.   Deroy Murdock, "Murdock: Mexican Victims of Fast and Furious," *Washington Times*, July 10, 2012, http://www.washingtontimes.com/news/2012/jul/10/mexican-victims-of-fast-and-furious/?page=all.

82.   Kevin Liptak, Jethro Mullen, and Tom Cohen, "Climate Change Is Here, Action Needed Now, Says New White House Report," CNN, May 6, 2014, http://www.cnn.com/2014/05/06/politics/white-house-climate-energy/; John Nolte, "Global Warming Researchers Rescued from Antarctic Ice," Breitbart, January 2, 2014, http://www.breitbart.com/Big-Journalism/2014/01/02/global-warming-researchers-rescued-from-arctic-ice.

83.   Tara McGuinness, "Photos: This Is What an #ACA Surge Looks Like," The White House Blog, WhiteHouse.gov, March 29, 2014, http://www.whitehouse.gov/blog/2014/03/29/photos-what-acasurge-looks.

84.   "EU Drops 2030 Member State Renewables Targets," Windpower Monthly, January 22, 2014, updated February 6, 2014, http://www.windpowermonthly.com/article/1228154/eu-drops-2030-member-state-renewables-targets.

85.   Ibid.

86.   HoundDog, "Climate Change Is 'Perhaps the World's Most Fearsome Weapon of Mass Destruction'—John Kerry," Daily Kos, February 16, 2014, http://www.dailykos.com/story/2014/02/16/1278116/-Climate-change-is-perhaps-the-worlds-most-fearsome-weapon-of-mass-destruction-John-Kerry.

87.   Coral Davenport, "Senate Democrats' All-Nighter Flags Climate Change," *New York Times*, March 11, 2014, http://www.nytimes.com/2014/03/11/us/politics/26-democrats-plan-a-senate-all-nighter-on-climate-change.html?_r=0.

88.   "Fallout Continues after Patrick Cannon Arrested, Resigns as Charlotte Mayor, Fox News, March 26, 2014, updated April 25, 2014, http://www.foxcarolina.com/story/25080192/charlotte-mayor-patrick-cannon-arrested-by-fbi-on-federal-corruption-charges.

89.   Dante Ramos, "Rhode Island's Recipe for Political Trouble," *Boston Globe*, March 26, 2014, http://www.bostonglobe.com/opinion/2014/03/26/speaker-gordon-fox-resigns-ocean-state-recipe-for-trouble/dsm7E2faj5qzLZB4H6poZK/story.html.

90.   Steve LeBlanc, "A Tale of 3 Speakers—Salvatore DiMasi, Thomas Finneran and Charles Flaherty: Is Lure of Power Too Tempting?" MassLive.com, July 4, 2011, http://www.masslive.com/news/index.ssf/2011/07/a_tale_of_3_speakers_—_salvat.html.

91.   Scott Gold, Joe Mozingo and Maura Dolan, "State Sen. Leland Yee Arrested on Corruption Charges in FBI Sting," *Los Angeles Times*, March 26, 2014, http://www.latimes.com/local/la-me-yee-arrest-20140327,0,3801978.story#axzz2xDSMSVz7; Richard Gonzales, "The Story of Calif. Senator's Arrest Reads like Pulp Fiction," NPR, March 29, 2014, http://www.npr.org/2014/03/29/296022715/the-story-of-calif-senators-arrest-reads-like-pulp-fiction.

92. Don Thompson, "Califorrnai Senate Suspends Three Democrats," Huffington Post, March 28, 2014, http://www.huffingtonpost.com/2014/03/28/california-suspend-three-democrats_n_5050601.html.

93. Angela Couloumbis and Craig R. McCoy, "Kane Shut Down Sting That Snared Phila. Officials," *Philadelphia Inquirer*, March 17, 2014, http://articles.philly.com/2014-03-17/news/48269239_1_investigation-kane-ali.

94. Marc Levy, "Pa. State Sen. Leanna Washington Ordered to Stand Trial," 6ABC News, March 26, 2014, http://abclocal.go.com/wpvi/story?section=news/local&id=9480500.

95. Steve Tetreault, "Disclosures Show More Gift Purchase Payments from Reid's Campaign Fund to Granddaughter," *Las Vegas Review-Journal*, March 26, 2014, http://www.reviewjournal.com/news/disclosures-show-more-gift-purchase-payments-reid-s-campaign-fund-granddaughter.

96. Mike McAndrew, "Poll Shows Hillary Clinton Leading Republican Contenders in 2016 Presidential Race," Syracuse.com, March 4, 2014, http://www.syracuse.com/news/index.ssf/2014/03/poll_shows_hillary_clinton_leading_republican_contenders_in_2016_presidential_ra.html.

97. Evan McMurry, "Hillary Clinton Has Biggest Democratic Poll Lead in History," Mediaite, January 30, 2014, http://www.mediaite.com/online/hillary-clinton-has-biggest-democratic-poll-lead-in-history/.

98. Natalie Villacorta, "Karl Rove Hits Rand Paul for Bill Clinton Bashing," Politico, February 11, 2014, http://www.politico.com/story/2014/02/karl-rove-rand-paul-bill-clinton-monica-lewinsky-103369.html.

99. Adam Kredo, "State Dept. Misplaced $6B under Hillary Clinton: IG Report," *Washington Times*, April 4, 2014, http://www.washingtontimes.com/news/2014/apr/4/state-dept-misplaced-6b-under-hillary-clinton-ig-r/.

100. Paul Bedard, "Book: Clinton's State Told Benghazi Was a 'Terrorist Attack' Minutes after It Began," *Washington Examiner*, September 3, 2013, http://washingtonexaminer.com/clintons-state-told-benghazi-was-a-terrorist-attack-minutes-after-it-began/article/2535081.

101. John McCormack, "Millions of Americans Are Losing Their Health Plans Because of Obamacare," *Weekly Standard*, October 23 2013, https://www.weeklystandard.com/blogs/millions-americans-are-losing-their-health-plans-because-obamacare_764602.html.

102. Brianna Ehley, "Health Insurance: 14.5 Million to Get Massive Increases," The Fiscal Times, April 8, 2014, http://www.thefiscaltimes.com/Articles/2014/04/08/Health-Insurance-145-Million-Get-Massive-Increases.

103. "ObamaCare Could Lead to Loss of Nearly 2.3 Million US Jobs, Report Says," Fox News, February 4, 2014, http://www.foxnews.com/politics/2014/02/04/obamacare-expected-to-lead-to-loss-nearly-25-million-american-jobs-report-says/.

Chapter 21: Constitutional Convention

1. Joseph Rago, "Tom Coburn: The Doctor Who Is Sick of Washington," *Wall Street Journal*, January 31, 2014, http://online.wsj.com/news/articles/SB1000142405270 23039737045793526902068666428.

Chapter 23: Saving *YOU* from the Murder of the Middle Class

1. Kyle Caldwell, "Gold turns £27,800 into £1m," *The Telegraph*, November 13, 2013, http://www.telegraph.co.uk/finance/personalfinance/investing/gold/10445952/Gold-turns-27800-into-1m.html.
2. Graham Summers, "Since Losing the Peg, Gold Has Outperformed Stocks Except for the Tech Bubble," Seeking Alpha, October 17, 2013, http://seekingalpha.com/article/1752332-since-losing-the-peg-gold-has-outperformed-stocks-except-for-the-tech-bubble?source=email_rt_mc_related_2.
3. "Gold Beat Stocks Except During the Tech Bubble," Zero Hedge, November 23, 2013, http://www.zerohedge.com/contributed/2013-11-23/gold-beat-stocks-except-during-tech-bubble.
4. Ibid.
5. "Key Asset Class Returns for 2000–2013," Evanson Asset Management, January 2014, http://www.evansonasset.com/index.cfm?Page=161.
6. Dan Caplinger, "Why Is Gold Crushing the Stock Market This Year?" DailyFinance, March 18, 2014, http://www.dailyfinance.com/2014/03/18/gold-crushing-stock-markets/.
7. "Global Gold Coin and Bar Demand Surged 28% to Record 1,654 Tonnes in 2013," Zero Hedge, February 18, 2014, http://www.zerohedge.com/contributed/2014-02-18/global-gold-coin-and-bar-demand-surged-28-record-1654-tonnes-2013.
8. Nat Rudarakanchana, "It's Official: China Consumed, Mined & Imported the Most Gold ever in 2013," International Business Times, February 18, 2014, http://www.ibtimes.com/its-official-china-consumed-mined-imported-most-gold-ever-2013-1556182.
9. Tyler Durden, "How China Imported a Record $70 Billion in Physical Gold without Sending the Price of Gold Soaring," Zero Hedge, March 23, 2014, http://www.

zerohedge.com/news/2014-03-22/how-china-imported-record-70-billion-physical-gold-without-sending-price-gold-soarin.

10. Agustino Fontevecchia, "Central Banks Bought More than $3B in Gold in 2013: UBS," Forbes, March 2i7, 2013, http://www.forbes.com/sites/afontevecchia/2013/03/27/central-banks-bought-more-than-3-trillion-in-gold-in-2013-ubs/.

11. Tyler Durden, "Guest Post: Whom to Believe on Gold: Central Banks or Bloomberg?" Zero Hedge, March 26, 2013, http://www.zerohedge.com/news/2013-03-26/guest-post-whom-believe-gold-central-banks-or-bloomberg.

12. Michelle Miller, "Food Prices Soar as Incomes Stand Still," CBS News, February 15, 2014, http://www.cbsnews.com/news/food-prices-soar-as-incomes-stand-still/.

13. "$1 in 1954 = $8.14," The Cos$t of Living, http://thecostofliving.com/index.php?id=116&a=1; "No. HS-25. Money Income of Families—Median Income in Current and Constant (2001) Dollars by Race and Type of Family: 1947 to 2001" in "Statistical Abstract of the United States," U.S. Census Bureau, 2003, http://www.census.gov/statab/hist/HS-25.pdf; "Average Price of a New Car?" Forbes, May 10, 2012, http://www.forbes.com/sites/moneybuilder/2012/05/10/average-price-of-a-new-car/; Steve Hargreaves, "15% of Americans Living in Poverty," CNN Money, September 17, 2013, http://money.cnn.com/2013/09/17/news/economy/poverty-income/; "Historical Gold Prices—1833 to Present," National Mining Association, http://www.nma.org/pdf/gold/his_gold_prices.pdf; Henry E. Hilliard, "Silver," U.S. Geological Survey, http://minerals.usgs.gov/minerals/pubs/commodity/silver/880798.pdf.

14. Alex Williams, "Bernanke Has Set the State for the Fed's Collapse—Jim Rogers," Mineweb, December 31, 2013, http://www.mineweb.com/mineweb/content/en/mineweb-political-economy?oid=222934&sn=Detail.

15. "Gold's Bigger Picture," Swiss America, February 2014, https://www.swissamerica.com/offer/bigpic.php.

16. Howard Portnoy, "U.S. Borrows $58,000 a Second: GOP Congressman Wants Debt Clock in House," Examiner.com, April 18, 2011, http://www.examiner.com/article/u-s-borrows-58-000-a-second-gop-congressman-wants-debt-clock-house.

17. Michael W. Chapman, "Postal Service Faces $100B in Debts and Unfunded Benefits," CNS News, March 14, 2014, http://cnsnews.com/news/article/michael-w-chapman/postal-service-faces-100b-debts-and-unfunded-benefits.

18. Tim Hume and Jen Christensen, "WHO: Imminent Global Cancer 'Disaster' Reflects Aging, Lifestyle Factors," CNN Health, February 4, 2014, http://www.cnn.com/2014/02/04/health/who-world-cancer-report.

19. Dr. Mercola, "Sugar Consumption Accounts for a Big Chunk of Healthcare Costs," Mercola.com, March 29, 2014, http://articles.mercola.com/sites/articles/

archive/2014/03/29/sugar-consumption-healthcare-costs.aspx?e_
cid=20140329Z1_nonbuy_DNL_art_1&utm_source=dnl&utm_
medium=email&utm_content=art1&utm_campaign=20140329Z1_nonbuy&et_
cid=DM43279&et_rid=470707728; Julie Corliss, "Eating too much added sugar
increases the risk of dying of heart disease," Harvard Health Publications, February 6, 2014,http://www.health.harvard.edu/blog/eating-too-much-added-sugar-
increases-the-risk-of-dying-with-heart-disease-201402067021; Conner
Middelmann Whitney, "Cancer cells love sugar, and they're not fussy: Fructose
and glucose found to fuel pancreatic cancer cell growth," *Psychology Today*, August
10, 2010, http://www.psychologytoday.com/blog/nourish/201008/cancer-cells-
love-sugar-and-theyre-not-fussy.

20. "Medical Errors, the FDA, and Problems with Prescription Drugs," The Cancer
Cure Foundation, http://www.cancure.org/medical_errors.htm; "Adverse Drug
Reactions May Cause over 100,000 Deaths among Hospitalized Patients Each Year,"
Whale, week of April 15, 1998, http://www.whale.to/drugs/iat.html; "Car Crash
Fatality Statistics," STATISTIC BRAIN, November 27, 2012, http://www.statistic-
brain.com/car-crash-fatality-statistics-2/; "Pharmaceutical Overdose Deaths,
United States, 2010," *Journal of the American Medical Association*, vol. 309, no. 7,
February 20, 2013, p. 658.

21. "Americans Do Not Get All the Nutrients They Need from Food," Council for
Responsible Nutrition, http://www.crnusa.org/pdfs/CRNFactSheetNutrientShort-
falls.pdf.

22. "Vitamin D and Cancer Prevention," Vitamin D3 World, http://www.vitamind-
3world.com/VitaminD_Cancer_Prevention_lung_breast_colon.html; Anthony
W. Norman, "A Vitamin D Nutritional Cornucopia: New Insights Concerning the
Serum 25-Hydroxyvitamin D Status of the US Population," *American Journal of
Clinical Nutrition*, vol. 88, no. 6, December 2008, pp. 1455–1456, http://ajcn.nutri-
tion.org/content/88/6/1455.full.

23. *J Clin Pharmacol.* 1993 Mar; 33(3):226-9; *Biofactors.* 1999; 9(2-4):291-9; *Lipids and
Aging.* 1989; 24(7):579-84; *Exp Gerontol.* 2006 Feb;41(2):130-40; *Int J Food Sci Nutr.*
2006 Nov-Dec;57(7-8):546-55.

24. "Magnesium," Linus Pauling Institute: Micronutrient Research for Optimum
Health, http://lpi.oregonstate.edu/infocenter/minerals/magnesium/.

25. Please see Magtein.com, http://www.magtein.com/thescience.html.

26. "Curcumin," Linus Pauling Institute: Micronutrient Research for Optimum
Health, http://lpi.oregonstate.edu/infocenter/phytochemicals/curcumin/.

27. "Essential Fatty Acids," Linus Pauling Institute: Micronutrient Research for Optimum Health, http://lpi.oregonstate.edu/infocenter/othernuts/omega3fa/.

28. "Resveratrol," Linus Pauling Institute: Micronutrient Research for Optimum Health, http://lpi.oregonstate.edu/infocenter/phytochemicals/resveratrol/; "Grape Seed," University of Maryland Medical Center, http://umm.edu/health/medical/altmed/herb/grape-seed.

29. Please see www.BioCellCollagen.com.

30. Please go to http://www.pdrhealth.com/drug_info/nmdrugprofiles/nutsupdrugs/alp_0159.shtml, accessed July 16, 2007; S. Sorbi, P. Forleo, C. Fani, and S. Piacentini, "Double-Blind, Crossover, Placebo-Controlled Clinical Trial with L-Acetylcarnitine in Patients with Degenerative Cerebellar Ataxia," *Clin Neuropharmacol*, Mar–Apr;23(2):114–18, http://www.ncbi.nlm.nih.gov/pubmed/10803803.

31. E. C. Verna and S. Lucak, "Use of Probiotics in Gastrointestinal Disorders: What to Recommend?" *Therapeutic Advances in Gastroenterology*, 2010 Sep;3(5):307–19.

32. D. S. Kalman, C. M. Colker, M. A. Swain, G. C. Torina, Q. Shi, "A Randomized, Double-Blind, Placebo-Controlled Study of 3-Acetyl-7-Oxo-Dehydroepiandrosterone in Healthy Overweight Adults," *Curr Therap Res*. 2000;61(7):435–42.

Chapter 24: Take Ownership of Your Future

1. wkorach, "Federal Spending on Education up 375% Learning Scores Down!" The Report Card, July 24, 2012, http://education-curriculum-reform-government-schools.org/w/2012/07/federal-spending-on-education-up-375-learning-scores-down/.

2. Instapundit.com, http://pjmedia.com/instapundit/?s=parental+malpractice.

3. "Costs and Financial Aid," Sidwell Friends School, http://classic.sidwell.edu/admissions/financial_aid.htm.

4. Ari Fleischer, "How to Fight Income Inequality: Get Married," *Wall Street Journal*, January 12, 2014, http://online.wsj.com/news/articles/SB10001424052702304325004579296752404877612?mod=trending_now_5; Courtney Coren, "Ari Fleischer: Marriage Can Solve Income Inequality," Newsmax, January 13, 2014, http://www.newsmax.com/Newsfront/marriage-income-inequality-children/2014/01/13/id/546815.

5. Robert Rector, "Marriage: America's Greatest Weapon against Child Poverty," The Heritage Foundation, September 5, 2012, http://www.heritage.org/research/reports/2012/09/marriage-americas-greatest-weapon-against-child-poverty.

Index

.01 percent, the, 172–75, 223
0.1 percent, the, 172
99.9 percent, the, 172
99.99 percent, the, 173

A

ABC, 58
abortion, 53, 97, 128
Adelson, Sheldon, 21
Affordable Care Act, 124. *See also*
  Obamacare
Afghanistan, xxi, 31, 189
alcohol, xx–xxi, 215, 227, 280, 291
alcoholism, xx–xxii
ALICE (All-purpose Lightweight
  Individual Carrying Equip-
  ment), 295
Alinsky, Saul, 41–43, 45, 109, 129,
  158, 177, 246, 255
  Lucifer dedication of, 43

America
  collapse of, 12–15, 42, 74, 107–
    12, 129–31, 164–66, 272,
    279, 292–99
  compared with *Braveheart*,
    133–38
  Founding Fathers of, 29, 68, 80,
    167, 175, 190, 222, 263
  government of, xx–xxii, 10–11,
    13–14, 21, 24, 29, 31–34, 39,
    47–50, 53–56, 57–76, 80, 84,
    87–89, 108, 110–11, 116–20,
    125–29, 131, 135, 151–53,
    164–66, 180–84, 190, 210–
    18, 223–25, 264–67, 292, 302
  middle class of, xix, xxii–xxiii,
    3–5, 9, 11–15, 17–21, 25,
    27–40, 42–43, 56, 57–59,
    64–68, 71–72, 75, 69, 83–85,
    91–92, 93, 97, 106, 111–13,
    118–120, 122–27, 133–38,
    140–41, 145–48, 151, 168,

mp Soaring Eagle provides the healing power of laughter to
ousands of seriously ill children by giving them the opportunity
go to a medically supervised camp at no cost to the campers and
milies.

ho We Help
zona families with Campers ages 6-15 living with serious illnesses.

ow We Help
Camp is provided FREE of charge
Year Round Programs
24 Hour Medical Care
Illness Specific Camper Weekends
Sibling Camper Weekends
Illness Specific Family Retreats
Summer Travel Programs
Camp Outreach

ow You Can Help
Volunteer
Attend an event
Be a Corporate Partner
Donate

elp Us Deliver the Healing Power of
aughter

www.CampSoaringEagle.org